Sociology of Law

Since the classic contributions of Weber and Durkheim, the sociology of law has raised key questions on the place of law in society. Drawing together both theoretical and empirical themes, Mathieu Deflem reviews the field's major accomplishments and reveals the value of the multiple ways in which sociologists study the social structures and processes of law. He discusses both historical and contemporary issues, from early theoretical foundations and the work of Weber and Durkheim, through the contribution of sociological jurisprudence, to the development of modern perspectives to clarify how sociologists study law. Chapters also look at the role of law in relation to the economy, politics, culture, and the legal profession; and aspects of law enforcement and the globalization of law. This book will appeal to scholars and students of the sociology of law, jurisprudence, social and political theory, and social and political philosophy.

MATHIEU DEFLEM is Associate Professor in the Department of Sociology at the University of South Carolina. He has published dozens of articles in journals and books, is the author of *Policing World Society* (2002) and the editor of *Sociologists in a Global Age* (2007), *Sociological Theory and Criminological Research* (2006), *Terrorism and Counter-Terrorism* (2004) and *Habermas, Modernity and Law* (1996). His website is www.mathieudeflem.net

Sociology of Law

Visions of a Scholarly Tradition

MATHIEU DEFLEM
University of South Carolina

CAMBRIDGE
UNIVERSITY PRESS

CAMBRIDGE UNIVERSITY PRESS
Cambridge, New York, Melbourne, Madrid, Cape Town, Singapore, São Paulo, Delhi

Cambridge University Press
The Edinburgh Building, Cambridge CB2 8RU, UK

Published in the United States of America by Cambridge University Press, New York

www.cambridge.org
Information on this title: www.cambridge.org/9780521673921

First published 2008

Printed in the United Kingdom at the University Press, Cambridge

A catalogue record for this publication is available from the British Library

Library of Congress Cataloging in Publication Data

Deflem, Mathieu.
  Sociology of law : visions of a scholarly tradition / Mathieu Deflem.
    p. cm.
  Includes bibliographical references and index.
  ISBN 978-0-521-85725-3 (hardback) – ISBN 978-0-521-67392-1 (pbk.)
  1. Sociological jurisprudence. 2. Law and the social sciences
  3. Law–Sociological aspects. 4. Jurisprudence–Sociological aspects. I. Title.
  K370.D44 2008
  340′.115–dc22

ISBN 978-0-521-85725-3 hardback
ISBN 978-0-521-67392-1 paperback

Contents

Preface and acknowledgements

This book presents a theoretically driven and research oriented vision of the sociology of law on the basis of a discussion of the major accomplishments in this sociological specialty since its initial formulation by the classics and its further development in the era of modern and contemporary sociology. A model of the sociology of law is offered that is driven by the central theoretical questions of the sociological discipline as they have been addressed since the classic contributions in the works of Max Weber and Emile Durkheim as well as their maturation throughout the history of sociology. This discussion thereby also addresses a variety of selected empirical themes that have been fruitfully addressed in sociological research on law and that have contributed to our understanding of the place and role of law in society.

Reviewing the history and systematics of the sociology of law from its beginnings to its present state, the scope of this book may be immodest. Yet, the objectives of this work are precise: it seeks to reveal the value of the manner in which sociologists study the structures and processes of law and law-related phenomena. The materials presented in this book present both theoretical and thematic discussions, including chapters on classical contributions in the sociology of law, modern and contemporary theoretical perspectives, the place and role of law in relation to other important social institutions, including economy, politics, culture, and social structure, and selected problems in relation to the enforcement of law and its globalization. In the hope of making this book sociologically relevant as well as intellectually exciting, each theoretical section includes relevant thematic aspects of law, while each thematic section is approached in a manner that is theoretically informed. The requirement for theory to be applied in the context of concrete socio-historical settings is as obvious as is the need for research findings and substantive issues to be framed on the basis of theoretically meaningful models. As such, this book aims to be both informative about the sociology of law and lay bare some of the sociologically relevant patterns and dynamics of law in society and its multiple components in a variety of socio-historical conditions.

I want to make clear from the outset what the purpose of this book is. First and foremost, this book is meant to appeal to students and scholars in the sociology of law and satisfy their need for a thoughtful review and discussion of the major achievements in their specialty area. The sociology of law is a growing and ever more popular field, typically taught at the advanced undergraduate (college) level and in (post)graduate seminars that prepare for masters and doctoral degrees. Although this book is not conceived as a textbook which directly seeks to teach students a particular area of sociological research, I am none-theless hopeful that it will be particularly useful for the teaching of the sociology of law in university settings. Specifically, this book can be used by instructors in the sociology of law who – teaching with this book, rather than trying to rely on a book to do the teaching for them – are actively engaged in stimulating students' learning experience. As time and interests permit, this educational goal can be realized by using this book in a comprehensive or more selective fashion.[1]

The sociology of law has in the present day matured to the point that it has accumulated a considerable amount of valuable contributions that cover a wide variety of theoretical perspectives and research efforts on a multitude of substantive themes. This book tries to capture the level of maturity that has been accomplished in the development of the sociology of law, but the discussions are inevitably also selective and influenced by the author's background in intellectual and other relevant respects. The scope of this book should in any case be sufficiently broad to introduce and situate important variations and manifestations of the sociology of law, selected components of which can subsequently be explored in more detail on the basis of an additional reading of the scholarly literature. The level of scholarship that I sought to attain in this work, also, should facilitate these objectives, for a tremendous disservice would be done to our students were we not to expose them to the best our discipline has to offer in a manner that is intellectually proficient. I must leave it to the readers, of course, to determine whether or not I have been able to achieve these goals in this work.

---

[1] Accompanying this book, a website has been set up that contains a variety of instructional and research materials on the sociology of law: www.socoflaw.net.

Over the three years since the original proposal for this book was written, I have incurred many intellectual and otherwise relevant debts. First of all, I wish to thank my graduate assistants at the University of South Carolina who have helped me in more than only instrumental ways during the completion of this work. Kyle Irwin was an able aide during the early development of this project when a convincing proposal for this book had to be crafted. Lisa Dilks subsequently worked with me throughout much of the writing of the book and was especially helpful in locating relevant literature and providing feedback and support. Shannon McDonough read various drafts of the book and endured my seemingly endless and, no doubt annoying, requests to track down additional literature or repeatedly review various sections of the manuscript. For their energy and dedication, I thank my assistants most kindly.

I thank the University of South Carolina for providing the means to be able to rely on research assistance as well as for the comfortable institutional setting and warmth that comes with Southern living. The beautiful weather I was fortunate to see, if mostly not otherwise experience, through the window of my spacious office has been a more than useful motivation in the progression of my work. I also thank my colleagues in the USC Sociology Department for leaving me alone to write this book and do my work in peace. Their most concrete feedback on my scholarship – anonymously provided during the annual ritual of a mandated faculty evaluation – I took as an important encouragement in the spirit of the most strongly motivating model of collegiality. I express special thanks to Patrick Nolan and Paul Higgins for their patience and listening skills during our many conversations in the Department.

I am grateful to Carrie Cheek, John Haslam, Timothy Ryder, and all the other good folks at Cambridge University Press for seeing this book through production. The idea to write this book, like most books, did not come from the author alone. The initial impetus for this work developed during conversations with Sarah Caro, then a Senior Commissioning Editor at Cambridge University Press. I am grateful to Sarah for introducing the idea of a book on the sociology of law to me and for letting me introduce the idea for another book on the sociology of law to her. I hope she likes what I eventually came up with.

I am grateful to Alan Hunt, Joachim Savelsberg, and Richard Schwartz for their often critical but always helpful comments on a draft manuscript. For commenting on selected chapters of this book and for other, likewise useful feedback that contributed to the development of this work, I thank Donald Black, Andrés Botero Bernal, Elizabeth Heger Boyle, Stacy Burns, Maureen Cain, David S. Clark, April Dove, Brian Gran, John Griffiths, Terence Halliday, Samantha Hauptman, Alexander Hirschfeld, Christine Horne, Fiona Kay, Pam Koch, Naomi Kolberg, John Lande, Ron Levi, Gary T. Marx, Marecus Matthews, Carmen Maye, Wayne McIntosh, Kwai Ng, Carlos Petit, Matthew Silberman, John Skrentny, Philip Smith, William Staples, Michele Taruffo, Edward Tiryakian, Michael Welch, and Justine Wise.

I have also learned much about the sociology of law through my involvement in the profession, where I have gotten to know many good people who are trying to make the sociology of law a better place to be. I am grateful for all of their support. A paper based on this work was presented at the annual meeting of the American Sociological Association in New York in 2007. Invitations to write short essays on aspects of law and its sociological study for *The Blackwell Encyclopedia of Sociology*, *Encyclopedia of Law and Society*, and *Encyclopedia of Globalization* also helped my thinking for this book (Deflem 2007a, 2007b, 2007c). A shorter version of Chapter 5 appeared in Spanish in the Columbian journal *Opinión Jurídica* thanks to the kind invitation and able translation skills of Andrés Botero (Deflem 2006b).

For constructive feedback on a draft version of this book, I thank the wonderful participants of the graduate and undergraduate courses in the sociology of law, which I taught at the University of South Carolina in the Fall of 2006 and Spring of 2007. More generally, I wish to express my sincere gratitude to the many students it was my pleasure to meet in the more than ten years since I have been engaged in the teaching of the sociology of law. It has been an extremely gratifying experience to have learned from my students so much, possibly even more than they will have learned from their teacher. Let us continue to place trust and hope in the dialogue of teaching and learning that is education. Lastly, I thank anyone else who has, intentionally or not, been supportive of me these past few years. May we live to see the dawn.

Introduction: sociology, society, law

When we speak of "law," "legal order," or "legal proposition," (*Rechtssatz*), close attention must be paid to the distinction between the legal and the sociological points of view.

— Max Weber (1922c: 1)

By speaking of law *and* society we may forget that law is itself a part of society.

— Lon L. Fuller (1968: 57)

Recovering the sociology of law

The development of the sociology of law cannot be told simply as it evolved since the sociological classics, for there is, in the case of this sociological specialty, no such history directly emanating from the discipline's earliest foundations. Although the classical scholars of sociology dealt with law elaborately on the basis of their respective theoretical perspectives, their works did not provide the initial onset for the sociology of law as we know it today. And even though there were scholars – especially in Europe – who sought to develop a distinctly sociological approach to law in the earlier half of the twentieth century, the so-called "sociological movement" in law that emerged in the years after World War II – especially in the United States – was primarily a product of the legal profession by way of some of the less practically inclined members in legal scholarship. These scholars sought to found a tradition of sociological jurisprudence and other perspectives of legal scholarship informed by social science in order to articulate an interest in the effects of law on society and, conversely, the influences of social events on substantive and procedural aspects of law. The contribution of such forms of legal thought was a scholarly attention for the societal context of law beyond the technical confines of legal training, but a systematic grounding in sociology or in other social sciences was not yet prominent. It was not until the advent of a later generation of sociologists who (re)turned to the sociological study of law, as it had been developed by the classics, that sociological jurisprudence and related strands of legal scholarship made way for the development of a specialty devoted to the study of law in the discipline of sociology. Especially during the 1960s, sociologists again took up and seriously developed the study of law from their unique disciplinary viewpoint. The modern sociology of law not only furthered the application of sociological knowledge to unravel the patterns and mechanisms of law in a variety of social settings, it also contributed to have other social sciences develop their respective approaches to the study of law and to bring these various social-science perspectives together under the banner of a law and society tradition, which has steadily gained in popularity in many parts of the world.

The relative success of the law and society movement in recent decades has, despite its scholarly and institutional achievements, also had some unanticipated consequences. Most noticeable is the lack of distinctness that is occasionally accorded to the sociological study of law, as other social scientists have begun to stake their respective claims in the study of law. This development not merely led the sociology of law to become one among other social-science perspectives of law that are presumably on equal footing, it remarkably also brought about an appropriation of the sociology of law in those fields that are not organizationally nor intellectually situated in the discipline of sociology. Additionally, the success of the law and society movement and its incorporation of the sociology of law also led to a marginalization and exclusion of the specialty area from its own disciplinary settings, indicating a Balkanization of the discipline that has been observed with respect to other specialties as well (Horowitz 1993). The resulting situation is such that the sociology of law has, some exceptions notwithstanding, lost its distinct place in socio-legal studies as well as in sociology. Yet, in bringing out the specific properties of the sociology of law in order to recapture its disciplinary and interdisciplinary standing, this book does not advocate the position that the sociology of law is superior to the other social sciences that form part of the broader domain of socio-legal studies, nor that the sociology of law is a superior specialty field in the discipline. The claim that I seek to defend in this book, instead, is that there is a unique contribution to the study of law that is sociological and that, for this reason, the specialty deserves its place among the other specialties in sociology as well as among the other disciplinary perspectives in socio-legal studies.[1]

Both in order to frame the sociology of law as a disciplinary specialty and to secure its place in the interdisciplinary law and society field, the sociology of law is to be judged first and foremost by the standards of its foundations in sociology. Sociology of law is always and necessarily sociology. It is from this basic insight that this book is written to explore the disciplinary focus of the sociology of law through a discussion of its theoretical orientations and substantive applications. Theoretical pluralism and substantive thematization are taken as a guide to bring out what is unique about the sociology of law as one specialty among several others in a discipline to which it must always relate, as well as with respect to other social-science approaches to the study of law. These objectives are far from trivial for at least two reasons.

First, within sociology, the sociology of law is in many ways still an underdeveloped specialty area, not in terms of the quality of its contributions, but in terms of its reception and status. The relative lack of attention to law in sociology can be seen, for instance, by the fairly recent institutionalization of the sociology of law in the American Sociological Association, where the specialty section Sociology of Law was founded only in 1993. Of course, internationally the cases vary. For example, the Polish Section of the Sociology of Law was founded in 1962, the same year when the Research Committee on Sociology of Law in the International Sociological Association was established.[2] But it is clear that sociologists of law still have to actively make the case towards their peers that their specialty too belongs to the discipline at large.

Second, the retreat of the sociology of law away from the discipline into the law and society field has been detrimental to a proper

---

[1] The understanding of the sociology of law as a specialty area is far from uncontested as the historical and intellectual unfolding of the sociology of law throughout this book will show. For rival statements on the real and desired relationship between the sociology of law and (socio-)legal scholarship, see Banakar and Travers 2002; Comack 2006; Cotterrell 1983, 1986, 1992; Dingwall 2007; Evan 1992; Ferrari 1989; Griffiths 2006; Guibentif 2002; Kazimirchuk 1980; MacDonald 2002b; Posner 1995; Rottleuthner 1994; Scheppele 1994; Schwartz 1978; Simon and Lynch 1989; Travers 1993.

[2] The developmental path of the sociology of law across national cultures is further discussed in the Conclusion.

understanding of what sociology can accomplish with regard to the analysis of law and what the relationship is and should be between (socio-) legal scholarship and sociological perspectives of law (see Savelsberg 2002). Misunderstandings concerning the proper place and role of the sociology of law have tragically also affected its perception by socio-logists in other areas of research. The reasons for this development are no doubt many and also relate to the relative inability or unwillingness on the part of (some) sociologists of law to resist the pull of the law and society movement, brought about, at least in part, not by any intellec-tual considerations, but by the relative attractiveness of employment in law schools. In light of these realities, the ambitions of this study are at its most immodest, for this book is driven towards the objective that the sociology of law must once and for all reclaim its position as a uniquely useful approach relative to other disciplinary perspectives on law. An analysis of the sociology of law's most important accomplish-ments in theoretical and empirical respects may serve this aim.

Sociology of law: a preliminary classification

Before an analysis can be made of the sociology of law's main theoretical and substantive accomplishments, the sociological spe-cialty needs to be framed within an intellectual and institutional context. A useful preliminary specification can be provided on the basis of the work of Max Weber, who, in the best tradition of German sociological thought, clarified the role of sociology among other disciplines and correspondingly specified the place of the sociology of law relative to other knowledge systems about law. Specifically, following a typology based on Weber's (1907) work as explicated by Anthony Kronman (1983: 8–14), three approaches to the study of law can be differentiated. First, internal perspectives of law study law in its own terms, as part of the workings of law itself, in order to contribute to the internal consistency of law by offering intellectual grounding to as well as practical training in the law. The development of legal scholarship or jurisprudence corresponds to this efficiency-oriented body of knowledge.[3] Second, transcending the legal perspective of law,

---

[3] The term jurisprudence refers to the internal study of law (or legal scholarship) as well as to the activity of legal decision-making in the courts and the body of law that is established on the basis of such decisions. Unless specified otherwise, the term is in this book used in the meaning of legal or law-internal scholarship.

moral or philosophical perspectives of law are engaged in a normatively oriented quest to search for an ultimate justification of law on the basis of a moral principle and to criticize existing conditions of law relative to the extent to which they meet this normative standard. The philosophy of law provides such evaluation-oriented models of thought about law. Third, external perspectives of law engage in the theoretically driven empirical study of law to examine the characteristics of existing systems of law, including the state and development, the causes and effects, and the functions and objectives of the institution and practices of law. In their ambition to examine the characteristics of law, external perspectives share an orientation to analysis. Such analysis needs to be framed within the contours of a disciplinary activity in order to specify the kind of questions that can be asked. One can thus distinguish the various social sciences that study law in terms of one of its relevant dimensions, be they historical, cultural, political, economic, or social.

The ideal-typical distinction between internal (efficiency-oriented), moral (evaluation-oriented), and external (analysis-oriented) perspectives in the study of law does not imply that there are no relations among them. Analysis-oriented perspectives of law, for instance, provide information that moral perspectives can and do use to develop their reflections on law, though perhaps not as often as social scientists would hope. Internal perspectives of the law, also, can be useful to provide information that can be subject to analysis, although it is also the case that technical knowledge of the law cannot be a substitute for analysis. Among the various disciplines that tackle law externally, also, relations can and have been developed to mutually enrich the various perspectives from the social and behavioral sciences and the humanities. Situated in the external dimension, the sociological approach must furthermore be clarified in view of the pluralist nature of sociological theorizing.

Turning to the subject matter of the sociology of law, what is it that we talk about when we talk about law? Although the definition of law provides a ground of debate among the various theoretical traditions in the sociology, a minimal strategy can be followed to sociologically conceive of law as a particular category of rules and the social practices associated therewith. Definitions of law within the sociological community will further vary and contract or expand as law is understood more precisely within the contours of a specific theoretical perspective, but the focus on rules and practices will always be present or at least implied. This dual conception of law incorporates Emile Durkheim's (1895) perspective of social facts as involving both material and non-material (ideal or cultural) conditions and circumstances, an analytical distinction that opens up rather than limits analysis and enables more precise propositions on how these variable components relate. Durkheim's work also leads to usefully specify the status of rules and practices of law on the basis of his theory of normative integration (Durkheim 1893a, 1893b). As rules, law refers to an institutionalized complex of norms that are intended to regulate social interactions and integrate society. The practices of law refer to the whole of roles, positions, interactions, and organizations that are involved with those norms in variable ways.

The inherently normative dimension of law must not be confused with its moral evaluation. As prescriptions on how social interactions should be regulated or how society should be ordered, norms always refer to an ideal state. But as institutionalized norms, legal rules have a factual existence that is beyond any ideal. Legal norms exist in the concrete settings of socio-historical societies and are never mere abstractions. Likewise, the practices of law will also contain normative elements, for instance by defining the legitimacy of law through rule-violating behavior or by justifying law through enforcement of its provisions. From the analytical viewpoint, a study of law as (ideal or cultural) rules and (material) practices is always oriented to an investigation of the factual dimensions of law. The duality of law implies that law, like any other aspect of society, is a normative issue with factual dimensions. It is because of this duality of law that its organization and function can be studied from the different perspectives specified by Weber. To Durkheim, the ability to approach law as a factually existing element of society (law as a social fact), irrespective of law's normative objectives and its self-understanding in moral terms, was synonymous with the sociology of law.

The sociological focus on norms needs an additional clarification to prevent misunderstanding. Critical legal scholar Richard Abel (1995: 1) once quipped that his (socio-legal) work on law dealt with "everything about law except the rules." Abel's comment may be provocative towards an internal understanding of law, but it is not helpful in articulating a concept of law that is useful for sociological analysis, for law also involves rules apart from practices. Yet, the status of rules or legal norms cannot be assumed to be wholly exhausted by reference to its internal aspirations. Legal norms are explicitly formulated in order to regulate behavior and integrate society, but this primary function of law will not necessarily coincide with law's actual consequences. The whole of legal norms, as of norms in general, cannot be defined in terms of their actual capacity to regulate action and integrate society, but only in terms of their explicit function of regulation or integration. Thus, a sociological concept of law does not omit the study of rules, but instead differentiates between the proclaimed objectives of legal norms, on the one hand, and the actual workings and consequences of law, on the other. This sociological orientation breaks both with a moral and internal understanding of law to enable sociological analyses of law in its manifold relevant dimensions.

What, then, is the formal subject matter of sociology? Regardless of their specialty areas, sociologists are always engaged in the study of society. Only the discipline of sociology retains a focus on society as a whole without restricting its knowledge to any one institutional dimension of society (Habermas 1981a, 1981b). Thus, sociologists of law will always place law within the context of society. In this respect, the very expression "law and society" is sociologically puzzling for it assumes that law is not part of society. Sociologists of law therefore side with legal theorist Lon Fuller (1968) that it would be more appropriate to speak of law-in-society and to approach law accordingly as a social issue that begs for sociological elucidation, just as do other social institutions and social practices.

Extending from the conception of the primary function of law (social integration), law can be situated relative to other social institutions such as economy, politics, and culture. To provide for an initial clarification of the sociology of law, it is not primarily relevant precisely which social institutions can be differentiated sociologically on the basis of which principle of differentiation. The differentiation of law as an institution of integration next to economy, politics, and culture is evidently indebted to Talcott Parsons' four-functional systems theory (see Chapter 5). Yet, the model is here used, not in a specific functionalist sense, but as a guiding orientation that can situate law within society and specify the relations of law with other social institutions. It is only for these analytical purposes, which enable a discussion of a variety of theoretical perspectives, that this model influences the division of chapters in the discussion of substantive themes of law in Part III of this book. Relatedly, this book also relies on a systems concept of law (and society) for strict analytical purposes of differentiating law from other social institutions and functions of society and, additionally, to differentiate various components of law. From this viewpoint, law can thus be analyzed in terms of its constituent parts and the interrelationships among them. Additionally, this perspective includes both static and dynamic components in order to differentiate between the structure and process of law and other social institutions. As structure, law can be analyzed in terms of its composition of constituent parts and how they are connected with one another. As process, law can be analyzed in terms of the processes of change and continuity that affect law both internally, among its constituent parts, and externally, between law and other institutions.

Themes and structure: an overview

Discussing the history and systematics of the sociology of law, this book contains twelve chapters divided over four parts. The first two parts are theoretical in orientation while the chapters in the latter two parts primarily offer thematic discussions. Theoretically, this book starts from the centrality in sociological thinking about law in the works of Max Weber and Emile Durkheim. Inasmuch as these classics relied on other social-science and pre-sociological perspectives of law that were current in the nineteenth century, the most important features of the theoretical developments on law before the institutionalization of sociology will be explored as well. It is also on the basis of the contributions of the sociological classics, their predecessors and heirs, that the most fundamental thematic aspects of the place of law in society will be elucidated.

In the first chapter, intellectual traditions of law will be discussed that, emanating from the Enlightenment, helped to pave the way for the development of the social sciences. Attention will be paid to pre-sociological thinkers who devoted their work to the study of law or who later became influential for the study of law, including Baron de Montesquieu, Cesare Beccaria, Jeremy Bentham, Alexis de

Tocqueville, Henry Maine, and Karl Marx. Also discussed in this chapter are early sociological authors such as Herbert Spencer, William Graham Sumner, Georg Simmel, and Ferdinand Tönnies, whose works in the area of law have not always been well remembered or lacked influence in later developments in sociology of law scholarship.

While some early sociological thinkers have not been unequivocally received as classics, the sociologies of Max Weber and Emile Durkheim are indisputably foundational to modern sociology, including the sociology of law. The next two chapters of this book are therefore devoted to the relevant works and influence of both masters of sociological thought. Given Weber's well-known and lengthy discussions on law and the generous reception of his work, the centrality of Weber in the sociology of law is obvious. Though perhaps less discussed by contemporary sociologists of law, Durkheim's work is as important as Weber's and will in this book be revisited to situate the sociological study of law around the key feature of social issues, including law, as involving both factual and normative dimensions. Recent discussions of the value and validity of Weber's and Durkheim's sociologies of law will be incorporated in these chapters.

Moving on to theoretical developments in modern sociology of law, Chapter 4 will focus on the intellectual move towards the sociology of law as it primarily took place in Europe among sociologically inclined legal thinkers and sociologists of law, specifically Leon Petrazycki and the scholars that emanated from his teachings, including Nicholas Timasheff, Georges Gurvitch, and Pitirim Sorokin, as well as other early European sociologists of law, such as Eugen Ehrlich and Theodor Geiger. It is to be noted that these scholars came from the European continent, although several of them would in the course of their careers move to other parts of Europe and even cross the Atlantic. Despite these scholars' migration, however, their impact on the development of the sociology of law was relatively small.

In the United States, as discussed in Chapter 5, another intellectual lineage developed towards the modern sociology of law, one that was more distinctly rooted in legal scholarship rather than in sociology. Especially the work of the noted American legal scholar Oliver Wendell Holmes led the way towards the development of sociologically oriented schools of jurisprudence by conceiving of law as a reflection of surrounding societal conditions. The work of Roscoe Pound emanated from this tradition into the new movement of sociological jurisprudence. Likewise, the legal realism of Karl Llewellyn can be understood in this move towards an increasingly scientific analysis of law. The decisive moment in the transition towards the sociology of law in the United States, however, did not come from within jurisprudence but was located squarely in sociology, specifically the structural functionalism of Talcott Parsons. The major theorist of the modern era of sociology, Parsons' efforts led to the canonization of the European classics and also involved an autonomous attention to the study of law. Emanating from Parsons was a bona fide school of legal sociology, which also partnered with jurisprudence, particularly the work of Lon Fuller.

In Chapter 6, the major theoretical schools of the modern sociology of law are explored on the basis of three central dividing lines. First, in opposition to the perceived consensual thinking of structural functionalism, there emerged a conflict-theoretical perspective in sociology that was also influential in the specialty area of the sociology of law. Second, modern theories in the sociology of law are divided, because of the peculiar relation between law and morality, over the possibility and desirability of a normative sociology of law or a resolutely scientific approach. This controversy is especially well reflected in the opposition between the jurisprudential sociology of Philip Selznick and Philippe Nonet and the pure sociology of law developed by Donald Black. And, third, opposing the macro-theoretical focus of structural functionalism are various perspectives whose analyses are located at the level of social interaction. Among these perspectives are both subjectivist sociologies oriented at the understanding of action, such as symbolic interactionism, as well as objectivist approaches that seek to explain behavior, including social exchange and rational choice theory. Crystallized around these three dividing lines are also many of the most recent developments in contemporary sociology of law, which will be discussed at various points in the remaining chapters.

Parts III and IV of this book revolve around substantive themes and are in this sense more empirical in orientation and also include discussions of research in the sociology of law. Each of these chapters, however, will discuss a selected substantive issue in a manner that is sociologically meaningful and will thus also incorporate theoretical materials. Aspects of the discussions in Parts I and II will reappear in terms of the theoretical orientations that have already been introduced, but also with respect to some of the more recent theoretical developments in contemporary sociology of law.

The chapters in Part III address how sociologists have studied law in relation to other institutions of society, specifically economy, polity, and culture, as well as law's function in terms of social integration (or law's relation to itself). In terms of the relation between law and economy, attention will go to sociological research on the mutual dependencies of legal and economic life, especially in the context of market societies. Among the novel theoretical perspectives that have addressed this interrelationship, neo-institutionalist perspectives of organizations will be discussed in the light of research conducted from this approach on organizational adaptations to legal regulations. Theoretically contrasting the new institutionalism is a model of juridification that will be applied to the evolution of the welfare state.

The connection between law and polity is an intimate one in modern societies because of the function of legislation. Chapter 8 will discuss this relationship specifically in terms of the diverging theoretical perspectives on law and democracy, including its implications for the possibilities of a scientific sociology of law, on the basis of a confrontation of the theories of Jürgen Habermas and Niklas Luhmann. The works of these contemporary giants of social thought will be compared in terms of their respective theories on law to guide an overview of empirical work on the relation between democracy and law, including work on voter disenfranchisement, democratic deficits brought about by legislated criminalization, and procedural justice in dispute resolution.

A separate chapter on the legal profession will serve to elucidate sociological work dealing with an important aspect of the integrative function of law. The sociology of the legal profession will be particularly discussed from the viewpoint of law's claim to autonomy. After providing a sociological perspective of professionalization, the most important transformations of the legal profession will be reviewed, including the diversification of the profession. The increasing diversity among the legal profession has also enabled the appearance of the so-called Critical Legal Studies movement in legal scholarship. Rather than a sociological or socio-legal approach, it will be shown, the Critical Legal Studies movement is a manifestation of the professionalization of law. In contrast, research in legal sociology on inequalities in law, specifically on gender inequalities

among legal professionals, will make the case for a distinctly sociological approach.

In the final chapter of Part III, the relation between law and culture
will function as a central vehicle for sociological discussions on the
relation between values and norms. After sketching the treatment of
norms and values in sociology from Durkheim onwards, separate
attention goes to the rise of postmodern perspectives and deconstruction theories as radically alternative perspectives. This theoretical
discussion will be used as a framework to review recent work in the
sociology of law on the relevance of class, gender, and race and
ethnicity. After an overview of research on the increasing diversity of
cultural values in modern society, the discussion will turn to the
individualism of modern culture that is at its roots. In this context,
attention will go to sociological research on law and medicine, the
regulation of same-sex marriages, and the legalization of abortion.

The final two chapters of this book pertain to certain special
problems associated with law, specifically the enforcement of law and
its globalization. While not driven by a specific theoretical model of
law, the choice to focus on these two matters of law is not arbitrary.
A review of work on social control will reveal that the study of the
enforcement of law adds a theoretically important element to the
analysis of law beyond legislation and the administration of law in
courts. Chapter 11 will extend the sociological attention to law in
order to center on the mechanisms of social control that accompany
legal systems. The focus on social control will theoretically allow for a
discussion of the thought of Michel Foucault and its relevance for
the sociology of law in the areas of policing, surveillance, sentencing,
and punishment.

Whereas the structures and processes of social control need to be
discussed by logical necessity within the framework of the sociology
of law, the globalization of law presents a challenge to the contemporary study of law because of its empirical relevance. Chapter 12
will discuss sociological scholarship on law and globalization in terms
of some of its most important present-day manifestations and the
repercussions thereof for the sociological understanding of law. A review
will be offered of theoretical perspectives on law and globalization,
especially in terms of their relevance for the notion of jurisdiction, and
relevant empirical work will be reviewed in various matters ranging from the making and administration to the enforcement of law.

In the Conclusion to this work, finally, the issues and themes addressed in the various chapters will be highlighted in terms of the central objective of this book to bring out the value of the sociology of law on the basis of a review of its accomplishments. The Conclusion will also situate the discussions in this book in the light of the sociology of law traditions that exist in various national cultures across the world.

Objectives

This book seeks to present a vision of the sociology of law on the basis of a review of the most important theoretical and empirical developments in this sociological specialty.[4] Most currently available books reviewing the sociology of law are textbooks, theoretical overviews, and compendiums.[5] Other works are not distinctly sociological but offer contributions to the interdisciplinary field of law and society studies.[6] Compared to many other specialty fields, the sociology of law has produced only a small number of books that offer a systematic overview of the specialty's theoretical developments and substantive research domains. Most of these books are either thematically structured or based exclusively on an outline of theoretical perspectives.[7] The present book seeks to accomplish more than that by offering a

---

[4] The notion of articulating a vision of and for the sociology of law is inspired by Donald Levine's comprehensive study of the development of sociological theory in his *Visions of the Sociological Tradition* (Levine 1995).

[5] See, for instance, the textbooks and theoretical overviews by Galligan 2007; Hunt 1978; Milovanovic 2003; Rich 1978; Roach Anleu 2000; Sutton 2001; Treviño 1996, Turkel 1996; and the edited volumes by Aubert 1969; Brantingham and Kress 1979; Brickey and Comack 1986; Carlen 1976; Evan 1962a, 1980; Freeman 2006; Johnson 1978; Larsen and Burtch 1999; MacDonald 2002a; Mertz 2008; Podgórecki and Whelan 1981; Reasons and Rich 1978; Sawer 1961; Schwartz and Skolnick 1970; Seron 2006; Silbey 2008; Simon 1968; Treviño 2007.

[6] See, e.g., Bankowski and Mungham 1980; Cotterrell 1994, 2006; Friedman 1976; Friedrichs 2001; Grana, Ollenburger, and Nicholas 2002; Kidder 1983; Lyman 2004; Rokumoto 1994; Sarat 2004; Vago 2005; Weinberg and Weinberg 1980.

[7] Among the more systematic discussions of the sociology of law are books by Aubert (1983), Banakar (2003), Cotterrell (1992), Grace and Wilkinson (1978), Henry (1983), Irwin (1986), McDonald (1976), McIntyre (1994), and Tomasic (1985). The non-English European literature is particularly well developed in providing systematic treaties of the evolution and status of the sociology of law as an academic specialty (e.g., Arnaud 1981; Gephart 1993; Lévy-Bruhl 1967; Rehbinder 2003; Röhl 1987; Schuyt 1971).

comprehensive discussion of important theoretical problems and substantive concerns and, thereby, contribute to demarcating the contours of the sociology of law as a distinct and distinctly sociological specialty area.

Uncovering the intellectual development and institutional history of the sociology of law, this book hopes to offer a meaningful analysis of this scholarly tradition as it has been practiced for more than a century now. The various chapters, therefore, do not merely offer listings of theories and themes in the sociology of law, but instead present an integrated discussion in order to reconstruct a model for the sociology of law that takes into account the more and less fruitful paths that sociologists have taken since the origins of the discipline. This book will not take sides in the theoretical conflicts that exist among sociologists of law and the thematic choices they have inspired, but will instead indicate how these issues and dilemmas have contributed to the march of the sociology of law as we know it today. For example, the point is not to argue for or against Weber's or Durkheim's theory of law on some particular point, but to show how these and other theoretical perspectives have contributed to the building and development of the sociology of law, which paths could have been taken from prior developments, which ones were, and which were not, bringing out how each discussed theoretical movement and empirical theme fits the broader framework of sociological scholarship on law. The most important conclusion that I hope readers will reach from this book is that the sociology of law offers something unique and valuable among the various specialty fields in the discipline and alongside of other social-science perspectives of law. The diversity of theoretical developments and substantive themes in the sociology of law ought not to be viewed unduly in terms of conflicting approaches. Although certain positions have to be taken on important debates and although this book surely represents a perspective, it must also be possible, on the basis of a guiding principle which Robert Merton (1976: 169) referred to as "disciplined eclecticism," to view the complementary nature of theoretical and other relevant developments in the sociology of law. Transcending any specific issue of theoretical dissent or substantive variation in research, this book hopes to make the case for a sociological specialty as such.

PART I

Theoretical foundations of the sociology of law

1 | *Law and the rise of the social sciences*

Thinking about law is as old as law itself, for legal discourse is always a part of law. But even beyond the boundaries of law, it is difficult to make a clear beginning on the discourse on law. Thinking about the social role of law is part of this discourse as well, but not all thought that relates to society is sociological. At the same time, sociology originated from the evolution of philosophy, the humanities, and the move towards the development of other social sciences. It is therefore more than merely a matter of intellectual curiosity to review the intellectual schools of law in the nineteenth century that emanated from the Enlightenment to gradually pave the way for the institutionalization of the various social sciences and the establishment of sociology.

Necessarily selective, this review will in the first instance discuss those pre-sociological thinkers who paid special attention to law in their thought and the not always overlapping category of those whose works have been influential to the development of the modern sociology of law. Among the latter category is most distinctly the social philosophy of Karl Marx, while the former category includes the works of such classical thinkers as Baron de Montesquieu, Cesare Beccaria, Jeremy Bentham, Alexis de Tocqueville, and Henry Maine. Also reviewed in this chapter are the works of early sociologists whose discussions on law have only moderately influenced later developments in the institutionalization of the specialty. Among these relatively neglected classic contributions are the works of Herbert Spencer, William Graham Sumner, Georg Simmel, and Ferdinand Tönnies.

The dawn of the social sciences

Too numerous are the scholars outside the contours of legal scholarship and education who have discussed the role of law in society. Even restricted to the precursors of the nineteenth-century origins of sociology, this review can merely sketch a few episodes in the pre-sociological days of social thought on law. A useful entry into the origins of early social thought on law emanates from the critique of the conception of natural law, the most extreme opposite of even the most rudimentary form of social and sociological thinking. Natural law is the notion that law bears no relation to the actual workings of society but is instead the reflection of universal concepts of truth and justice so profound and foundational to existence that law is held to emanate from nature itself. As such, natural law theories preclude the very essence of social thinking on the origins, conditions, and effects of law as a social reality. Going back to the Aristotelian conception of law in ancient Greece and transported into Western society via medieval thought, such as the philosophy of St. Thomas Aquinas, natural law theory dominated legal thought in Europe for a long time. Only on the basis of analysis and critique of the principles of justice and order purportedly embodied in natural law could any social thought on law develop.

The breakthrough of the Enlightenment from the eighteenth century onwards would open up the world of law to the reflection of critical-analytical thinking. The Enlightenment refers to the period and move-ment in (European) philosophy, including not only ethics but also art and knowledge, that placed the human ability to think and critique at the center of intellectual life. Best summed up in the words of the eighteenth-century German philosopher Immanuel Kant, the Enlight-enment is defined as the public use of reason based on the ability of thought (Kant 1784). Enlightenment thinking is critical in potentially laying bare the societal and historically contingent conditions of existing social institutions such as politics and law. Rather than merely assuming that laws reflect the unalterable conditions of nature, law can become an object to be studied in terms of its societal constitution in particular periods and societies. As such, Enlightenment thinking does not merely take away the assumed stability of law, but can instead also lead to suggestions on how law can be organized to better serve its purposes given the societal circumstances to which it pertains.

A first important break with natural law was provided in the writings of the French political philosopher Baron de Montesquieu (1689–1755).[1] De Montesquieu argued that law was related to a

---

[1] De Montesquieu's most important work on law is *Spirit of Laws* (Montesquieu 1748). For a discussion from the viewpoint of the sociology of law, see Ehrlich (1916).

society's culture and determined by various external circumstances, including social and natural conditions as well as historical antecedents. Laws were not good or bad in an absolute sense, but could be evaluated in terms of their relative degree of justice and morality. From this conception, de Montesquieu went a step further and, as a critic of the French absolutist monarchy, was among the first philosophers to argue for a democratic constitution of law. In order to ensure that laws would be reflective of the people's will, de Montesquieu specifically argued that two important principles needed to be guaranteed. First, on the basis of the principle of the division of power principle, the location of power could not be unduly centralized, but had to be spread across the center of power (the monarch) and intermediate bodies of representation, such as parliaments, voluntary groups, and churches. Second, on the basis of the separation of powers principle, the exercise of power would have to be functionally specialized into three branches of government: (1) the legislative branch to pass laws; (2) the executive branch to enforce and administer laws; and (3) the judicial branch to interpret and apply laws. De Montesquieu's philosophy has historically been influential for many forms of democratic government, and it has also been the basis of the principle of legal autonomy that guides much of the inner workings of the law and the status of legal professionals (see Chapter 9). In the context of this historical overview, however, it is more important to emphasize in de Montesquieu's thought that it broke open the possibilities of unfettered thinking on the social dimensions of law and would ultimately pave the way for a real analysis, with scientific means, of law as a social institution.

Similarly arguing against the excesses brought about by absolutist rule, the Classical School of law and, in particular, of criminal law is important to discuss in this context because its ideas indicate how the justification of rights and law shifted from the central powers of monarchy and aristocracy to the growing class of an increasingly powerful bourgeoisie.[2] Showing how the development of social thought itself was influenced by the very conditions of the society its attention is devoted to, the Classical School emerged in conjunction with the rise of capitalism. The influence of capitalism is best observed

---

[2] On the history of criminological thought and the relevance of the Classical School, see Pasquino 1991 and contributions in Becker and Wetzell 2006.

in the Classical School's fundamental notion that human conduct is guided by a principle of economic rationality in that it is conceived as the outcome of a weighing of the anticipated costs and benefits of action alternatives. Accompanying this conception is the notion that people are free and should therefore be held accountable for their actions. Under those conditions, the law should emphasize due process requirements to establish guilt or innocence, with minimal government intrusion and a primary deterrent function assigned to punishment.

Among the key proponents of the Classical School are Cesare Beccaria and Jeremy Bentham. Although today known mostly among criminological scholars for their theories of crime and criminal justice, both thinkers developed more comprehensive theories of law that form part of the progress towards the development of an authentic social science of law. The Italian political philosopher Cesare Beccaria (1738–1794) is best known for his 1764 pamphlet, *Dei Delitti e delle Pene*, in which he condemned the death penalty.[3] Beccaria opposed capital punishment on the grounds that the state cannot legitimately claim the right to take lives and because the death penalty is neither necessary nor useful. The reasoning behind this argument is Beccaria's contention that capital punishment does not have a deterrent effect towards other, potential and actual, wrongdoers for it is not the severity but the certainty of punishment that determines its deterrent impact.

Other proposals of legal reform suggested by Beccaria that hint at a more humane system – such as proportionality of the punishment relative to the crime committed and the public nature of legal proceedings – were likewise inspired, not by any humanistic ideals per se, but by a utilitarian orientation that contemplated the nature of human behavior as essentially rooted in the pursuit of self-interest. Therefore, to avoid a condition of all-out violence, citizens engage in a mutual contract whereby they agree to give up some of their freedoms in order to secure a peaceful co-existence. Influenced by the idea of social order as a contract, Beccaria thus defended the idea that the main function of the state is to enforce laws that limit a boundless pursuit of self-interest. For such laws to be effective, they need to be made public so they are widely known and involve swift and certain

---

[3] Beccaria's work is translated as *On Crimes and Punishments* (Beccaria 1764). See, also, Beirne 1991.

forms of punishment that increase the relative cost associated with a violation of law, conceived as a breach of the terms of the social contract.

Offering a more systematic formulation of the utilitarian framework, the British philosopher Jeremy Bentham (1748–1832) developed a political and legal philosophy on the basis of the principle of economic rationality that human conduct is guided by a search for pleasure and an avoidance of pain.[4] Bentham was originally trained as a lawyer and admitted to the bar, but he became a leading critic of the existing British legal system and sought to reform the law on the basis of his utilitarian philosophy. In his work, Bentham applied his utilitarian philosophy to law to argue that the legal system should be founded on the principle to provide the greatest possible happiness to the greatest possible number of people. Complementing the theory of human behavior as guided by the hedonic calculation to maximize utility from the individual's perspective is thus a theory of society on the basis of the social calculation to maximize utility from the aggregate point of view. To ensure an egalitarian society, Bentham argued, laws had to be applied fairly and equally to all, due process requirements had to be obeyed before a person could be found guilty or innocent, and evidence had to be investigated. Furthermore, judicial discretion had to be minimized by limiting judges' power only to a determination of guilt and innocence, while punishments were to be based on a calculation of the pleasure, pain, and mitigating circumstances associated with a legal violation and its penalties. In its concern for the effects of law, the role law actually played and could play in society, and the function of law as an aspect of policy and an instrument of social engineering, Bentham's work betrays a turn towards a social science of law, or towards what Bentham (1792) calls "law as it is."

The mounting criticisms of Europe's absolutist political systems would continue to be expressed by philosophers and thinkers throughout the nineteenth century. In most cases these works were marked by a distinct normative orientation, yet they also contained more empirical and theoretical directions. As such, these works paved the way for both the development of political philosophy and their

---

[4] Bentham's major works dealing with law include *Introduction to the Principles of Morals* (1789). See, also, the discussion by Lyons 1991.

applicability to the development of modern systems of government, on the one hand, as well as the elaboration of the social sciences, on the other. The works of Alexis de Tocqueville and Henry Maine are important to discuss in this context because they provide an important bridge between classical and modern thought and also devoted explicit attention to the role of law.

The French political historian Alexis de Tocqueville (1805–1859) had been a student of law and worked as a substitute judge before he became an elected representative and briefly served as France's minister of foreign affairs.[5] In 1831, he visited the United States on behalf of the French government to study the US prison system. From the copious notebooks de Tocqueville kept during his nine-month journey, he would write his now famous work, *Democracy in America* (Tocqueville 1835/1840). De Tocqueville's admiration for democracy was rooted in the idea that only a democracy could provide a balance between freedom and equality, a notion akin to the principle of the social contract. Some special attention was given by de Tocqueville to the role of law and, especially, the place of judges in the US democratic system. Scrutinizing judicial authority in the United States, de Tocqueville particularly noted the power of judges to refuse to apply laws they held to be unconstitutional. As such, judges had political power in influencing the effective implications of the legislative process. Through participation in the (relatively restricted system of the) electoral process and the jury system, also, some degree of popular participation in the legislative and judicial systems was ensured. De Tocqueville especially commended the qualities of the jury system to bring about an education into the law and create a sense of civic responsibility in contributing to society and its government.

De Tocqueville's work on the democratic system of the United States was primarily meant to formulate normative guidelines towards the reform of the French political regime. Yet, because of its comparative orientation, it also provided an important basis for the study of law in society. Even more distinguished in its scholarly merits for the study of law from a comparative-historical viewpoint is the work of Henry Maine (1822–1888).[6] Maine was originally trained as a lawyer and

---

[5] De Tocqueville's most relevant work on law and power is the two-volume work, *Democracy in America* (Tocqueville 1835/1840). See Goldberg 2001.

[6] Maine's central ideas on law are found in his ground-breaking book, *Ancient Law* (Maine 1861). See, also, Cocks 1988; Hunt 2002.

practiced and taught law in the British system. On the basis of his lectures, he wrote *Ancient Law* (1861) in which he traced the connections between Roman jurisprudence and the system of British law. To this historical study he added important comparative insights, aided by a stay of several years in India, that would enable him to eventually teach historical and comparative jurisprudence at Oxford University. Although the goal of Maine's historical and comparative works was to acquire insight into the British legal system, its implications offer the way towards a more systematic study of law. For in seeking to bring out the potentially reforming qualities of law as an instrument of social change, Maine studied law as it was actually practiced by professionals and experienced by lay people.

In his historical work, Maine argued that societies of different historical epochs will share characteristics in their legal systems if they also share other societal circumstances. Thus, for example, Roman feudalism and, many years later, British feudalism shared basic characteristics in their legal systems. According to Maine, a stable pattern could be observed in the evolution of law across societies, specifically in the form of three stages from the development of primitive over feudal to modern societies. In primitive society, law is not formalized but based entirely on the structures of kinship, which are typically patrilineal and justified on the basis of divine inspiration and right. In the second stage of development, the autocratic rights of the patriarchal leader become subject to the demands of other leaders to be based on the prevailing customs of society. The third stage of legal development is ushered in when, under the influence of the spread of literacy and writing, laws become embodied more permanently in written codes. The codification of laws allowed for legal decisions to be compared, relative to one another and relative to the applied legal code, and to be rationally structured into a coherent set of laws in view of constructing an efficient legal policy.

As the form of law changed, Maine suggested, so too did its substance. In the course of history, family dependency gradually diminishes in favor of individual responsibility, rights, and obligations, as manifested in the increasing relevance of the practice of contract and the decline of social regulation by status. Whereas status is ascribed and determined by connection with one's family and, therefore, stable from birth onwards, contract exemplifies the outcome of negotiation among free and independent individuals on the basis of their achieved positions and qualities. Contract, in the sense in which Maine uses the term, therefore, is not necessarily a particular document in writing that specifies certain obligations among parties, but a more generalized notion of agreement among free individuals who, in the context of a society, engage in social relations of various kinds.

What the utilitarians and the historical-comparative scholars of law shared was an attention to the study of law for mostly practical purposes of reform, which, however, was conducted in such a way that it also set off the origins and development of the systematic study of law from a more resolutely analytical and scientific point of view. As much, therefore, as utilitarianism and the historical school offer political and legal philosophies that have a strongly normative quality, they also contain empirical observations of the actual workings of law, in the comparative-historical context, moreover, of different societies and different epochs. These rudimentary seeds of anthropological and historical reflection would later mature more fully into specialized academic disciplines. Early sociology would likewise benefit from the roots of nineteenth-century social science and especially inherit from its predecessors an evolutionary perspective. These characteristics are perhaps best reflected in the writings of Karl Marx, whose work may count as the crowning moment of the merging of normative and systematic-analytical aspirations. Historically, also, the evolution of modern sociology has been such that separate attention must be devoted to the work of Marx, although the value of his work for sociology remains hotly disputed and, as will become clear in the next section, the actual contributions Marx made to the study of law were minimal. The comprehensive nature of Marx's work and its impact on contemporary social thought, however, deserve that it be treated separately.

The perspective of historical materialism

The German-born philosopher Karl Marx (1818–1883) left behind a very extensive and complex intellectual legacy. For the purposes of this book, it will be useful to introduce Marx's ideas on law within the framework of the perspective of historical materialism.[7] The

---

[7] Marx's essential works include *The Economic and Philosophical Manuscripts of 1844* (Marx 1844), *The German Ideology* (Marx 1846), and *Capital* (Marx 1867), all of which are available online via the Marx & Engels Internet Archive: www.marxists.org/archive/marx/index.htm.

evolution in the thinking of Marx, which itself is subject to considerable intellectual controversy, will not be dealt with in this exposition in favor of an explication of Marx's general theoretical perspective of society and law. At the most general level, historical materialism refers to the study of society from a viewpoint that conceives of history as the outcome of opposing forces. Marx thus broke with a more conventional linear notion of history as involving a steady progress on the basis of a cultural, economic, or otherwise social variable, in favor of a more conflictual notion of history in terms of societal forces that invoke one another precisely because they are in opposition. Marx borrowed this so-called dialectical conception of history from the German philosopher Georg Wilhelm Friedrich Hegel, yet, in contrast to Hegel's idealist perspective, Marx transplanted the method to apply to a materialist theory of society. Thus, the political, cultural, and socio-historical conditions of a society are explained as the outcome (synthesis) of opposing forces (thesis and antithesis) that are of an economic nature. Besides explaining the material conditions of society historically, Marx defended the viewpoint that, on the basis of a dialectical analysis, all things existing should be criticized in order to contribute to laying bare the injustices that exist in society and work towards the betterment of society. Philosophy should have a practical intent and be guided by explicitly political motives. Theory and praxis have to come together in order to explain as well as change the world.

Marx applied the perspective of historical materialism to investigate and critique the society of his days, that is, nineteenth-century industrial societies that were undergoing rapid transformations under influence of the expansion of capitalism. Marx argued that the essence of modern society lay in its economic transformation from feudalism to capitalism. Whereas feudal societies were predominantly agricultural and centered around the power of landowners over serfs, capitalism developed from a gradual concentration of the means of production in technologically advanced factories. The owners of these means were relatively few in number but extremely powerful in being able to control the labor of a relatively large number of workers and determine their wages. The owning class, Marx argued, can thus create enormous amounts of wealth, which do not have to be shared with the large class of workers who are powerless and alienated. Worker alienation under capitalism takes on at least four forms: (1) alienation from the product of one's labor because the product does not belong to the worker; (2) alienation from labor itself because labor, under conditions of a division of labor, constitutes but a fragment of the production process; (3) alienation from social relations because they are valued only in terms of market conditions; and (4) alienation from oneself because one's entire existence is dominated by the demands of capitalism.

Marx's theory is not to be understood merely as a theory of the economy, for his analysis of capitalism is meant to provide the basis for an analysis of society. The economic organization of society is its material core from which all other social developments in matters of politics, culture, and law can be explained. This is summarized in Marx's famous dictum that the infrastructure of a society determines it superstructure. Thus, the division between the economic classes of owners and non-owners appears at the societal level as a class antagonism between the relatively small but powerful bourgeoisie and the relatively large but powerless proletariat. The bourgeoisie can articulate its economic power also at the political, cultural, and legal level because of its control over all important institutions of society, such as government, the legal system, art, science, and education. The economic interests of the bourgeoisie, therefore, also become articulated at the societal level as the dominant interests that count for society as a whole. Because the basic conflicts of a society are always economic, according to Marx, only the destruction of capitalism in favor of a communist mode of production, whereby the workers collectively own and control the means of production, would ensure a successful revolution of society into a more just social order.

Marx did not develop a comprehensive perspective on law and his ideas on law are scattered throughout his writings, especially in some of his earlier works. Marx's theory of the state provides the most useful entry into his perspective on law.[8] Congruent with his materialist perspective, Marx asserts that the economic conditions of society determine what type of state will develop, which in a capitalist society

---

[8] Marx's theoretical ideas on law can be retrieved from some of his major works (see note 7) as well as in other writings (Marx 1842, 1869, 1846). Extracts from Marx's central writings on law are available in a collection edited by Cain and Hunt (1979). For discussions on Marx's legal theory, see Cain 1974; Easton 2008; Fine 2002; Hirst 1972; Kelsen 1955; Pashukanis 1924; Phillips 1980; Stone 1985; Young 1979.

implies that the state will be controlled by the bourgeoisie as an instrument to secure economic rights and to moderate class conflict. "The executive of the modern state," Marx (1848: 475) writes, "is but a committee for managing the common affairs of the whole bourgeoisie." Thus, the capitalist state represents and secures the power of the dominant economic class which now also becomes the politically dominant class. Interestingly, Marx argues that the democratic republic, rather than being a more egalitarian form of government relative to centralized autocratic regimes, is the most advanced form of the capitalist state, for it totally disregards the property distinctions that have arisen under capitalism.

Similar to Marx's notion of the state, his perspective on law is instrumentalist and views the legal system in function of its role as an instrument of control serving bourgeois interests. Rather than abiding by a principle of the rule of law that holds that it is just for the law to be applied equally and fairly to all, Marx maintains that capitalist law actually enhances the conditions of inequality that mark capitalist society. Specifically, Marx contends that the capitalist legal system contributes to, as well as legitimates, the inequalities that exist as a result of capitalist economic conditions. In the practice of law, it is revealed that the legal system contributes to inequality because capitalist law establishes and applies individualized rights of freedom, which benefit those who own while disfavoring those who are without property. The formal equality that is granted in law by treating the various parties that are in contract with one another or with the state as equal contributes to sustain and develop the economic inequalities that exist among legal subjects. Legal doctrine, moreover, justifies the practices of capitalist law on the basis of a notion of justice claimed to be universally valid but which in actuality serves the interests of only the dominant economic class. As such, the law takes on the form of a bourgeois ideology. In its ultimate triumph, moreover, the ideology of capitalist law becomes widely accepted, even among those members of society who are economically disadvantaged and thus additionally subject to the inequalities brought about by the legal system.

The very essence of the theory of historical materialism implies that Marx did not devote much separate attention to law as one element of the superstructure of capitalist society. "There is no history of politics, law, science, etc.," Marx writes in *The German Ideology* (Marx 1846). Yet, in a few instances Marx did write about aspects of law, albeit only briefly and clearly within a materialist framework that placed a premium on the economic conditions that underlay the constitution of law. For instance, in a series of essays published in the *Rheinische Zeitung*, a newspaper which Marx edited for a number of years, Marx (1842) critiqued the new law on the theft of wood that had been promulgated in Prussia in 1842. The law prohibited the gathering of wood in the Rhenish forests although it had been a customary practice for peasants to pick up and use for their own benefit whatever wood had fallen on the ground. The official grounds for the law were that it would protect the forest and allow for natural regeneration. Marx debunks this official story in favor of a materialist analysis that starts from the observation that wood had become an important commodity in the development of capitalism as wood was used for shipbuilding, for the development of railroads, and for the construction of machines. Thus developed the need to control the production of wood and make the gathering of wood in forests illegal. The law benefited the bourgeois class also in a direct way because the forest owners received the fines that were collected by a specialized forest police from those who violated the law.

In a short essay on the right of inheritance, Marx (1869) similarly turns to an analysis of economic conditions to critique the reforms that had been proposed on inheritance laws whereby property can be passed down from one generation to the next. Some socialist reformers had suggested to abolish this right because it concentrated wealth, but Marx argued that such a proposal was utopian because it could not possibly alter existing economic conditions. Instead, Marx argues, any truly revolutionary proposal in the context of a capitalist society would have to start with a change of the economic conditions. "What we have to grapple with," Marx writes, "is the cause and not the effect – the economical basis, not the juridical superstructure" (Marx 1869).

The early sociologists

The work of Marx was not immediately influential in the development of the sociology of law as no direct historical path led from his thought to subsequent sociological schools of thought. Marx's work, however, was later appropriated by critical sociologists who sought to break with the consensual thinking that they felt characterized much of mainstream sociology in the years after World War II (see Chapter 6). Even more ambivalence is shown in the history of sociology considering the fact that the selective appropriation of the early thinkers in sociology has occasionally also implied that some early social scientists who did develop explicitly sociological perspectives – and who did apply them to the study of law – have been all but forgotten in modern and contemporary sociology, including the sociology of law. A review of some of these forgotten classics of sociology is in order to at least highlight their contributions to sociology and the sociology of law for reasons of intellectual curiosity.

Historical thinking, often evolutionary in kind, was in vogue in much of sociology and social philosophy throughout the nineteenth century. This is perhaps nowhere better illustrated than in the work of the British sociologist Herbert Spencer (1820–1903).[9] Often described as social Darwinism, the evolutionary thought of Spencer was in fact written largely independent of and before that of his friend Charles Darwin. It was Spencer also who coined the phrase "survival of the fittest" and applied it to the evolution of society. Spencer argued that principles of natural selection and survival of the fittest could explain how human societies developed from relative simplicity and homogeneity to growing complexity and heterogeneity. Evolving from primitive or militant societies that are characterized by war and status as the main regulatory mechanisms, modern or industrial societies are primarily guided by peaceful negotiation and contractual obligations voluntarily agreed upon among free citizens. In the modern phase of human development, Spencer argued, the influence of governmental control declined in favor of individual liberty and the negotiated contractual obligations that are freely agreed upon among individual subjects.

As an evolutionary utilitarian, Spencer opposed government influences and public programs aimed to alleviate social concerns, such as hunger, poverty, and illness, in favor of minimal government regulation whereby policy and law would mainly serve to secure the freedom of the state's subjects and enforce the formal relations that

---

[9] Spencer's major works in sociology are *The Study of Sociology* (Spencer 1873) and the three-volume *The Principles of Sociology* (Spencer 1876/1882/1896), the second volume of which contains a section on "Laws" (pp. 513–537). See also Spencer's critical essays on legislation (Spencer 1853, 1884).

they engage in. The only natural limitation to individual freedom is the recognition of freedom in others. On the basis of this liberal individualist standpoint, Spencer maintained that government action and law in modern societies would primarily have to protect human liberty. Spencer formulated this perspective on the basis of an evolutionary theory of law from primitive to modern society. Most essentially, law transforms from the regulation of inequalities in status among people to the equal treatment of citizens in voluntary cooperation with one another. In modern society, therefore, Spencer advocated a policy of extreme *laissez faire* liberalism, whereby all law is to be condemned unless it is the expression of the consensus of individual interests and thus meant to promote and preserve individual liberty. Spencer was opposed to legislative efforts aimed at ameliorating the conditions of the poor and the weak and, correspondingly, also condemned any legal intrusions on free trade. The only rightful purpose of law was an administration of justice that sought to police and protect individual rights. In this sense, Spencer's thought goes against that of the eighteenth-century utilitarians who favored a conception of law as social engineering.

The liberal evolutionary thinking of Spencer influenced some early American sociologists, most notably William Graham Sumner (1840–1910).[10] Sumner was originally educated in history and theology and for some years was a priest in the Episcopal church. He was attracted to sociology after having read an essay by Spencer, upon which he began to develop his sociological thought on the basis of an evolutionary conception of human history. In 1872, Sumner became a professor of political and social science at Yale University and there began teaching courses in sociology from 1875 onwards. In his writings, Sumner advocated an evolutionary perspective of society that, like Spencer's, limited the proper function of the state to administering the contracts individuals mutually and freely agreed upon. A steadfast defender of capitalism, or what he called "free-trade liberalism," Sumner opposed any and all attempts through government action and legal policy to promote social equality because they are in contradiction with the societal conditions of evolution that favor survival of only the strongest elements of society. Importantly, Sumner's thought was, by

---

[10] Sumner's most important publication is *Folkways* (Sumner 1906). See, also, Ball, Simpson, and Ikeda 1962.

its own ambitions, not based on philosophical speculation but on a
scientific orientation to uncover the underlying basic patterns and
causes of human history and societal development. Sumner therefore
turned his efforts to comparative-historical investigations to uncover
the laws of society.

Sumner died before he finished a planned book on the systematics
of sociology, but his 1906 book *Folkways* contains significant insights
on his theory of law. With the term "folkways" Sumner refers to the
habits of individuals and the customs of the society, which arise
from efforts to satisfy certain needs. Folkways turn into mores when
customs that pertain to the more important functions and institutions
of society become of a more coercive nature and are endowed with
sanctions. Embedded within mores are rights, conceived as ethical
conceptions of justice. From mores also develop laws, although laws
will never fully express rights. Along with the transformation of
society, the nature of law changes as well. In pre-modern societies,
the regulation of social life is not guided by formally enacted laws.
Pre-modern law, therefore, is customary and typically not codified. In
modern societies, by contrast, law is formally enacted by governments
and written down. Regardless of the stage of societal development,
law must, according to Sumner, reflect the mores of society in order
to be an effective regulator of human behavior. As an instrument of
social change, law can fulfill its proper role only if it conforms to the
mores of a society or one of its sub-groups to which laws are applied.

Turning to some of the earliest practitioners of sociology in Germany
will reveal additional characteristics of the study of law during the
founding days of the discipline. The sociology of Georg Simmel (1858–
1918) is commonly known for its contributions to the formal study of
society and its observations on the development of modern culture.[11]
It is as part of his formal sociology that Simmel devoted attention to
the role of law. Specifically in his study of the quantitative aspects
of group life, focusing on the influence of the number of individuals

---

[11] Among Simmel's key sociological writings are his books *Soziologie* (1908a) and
Grundfragen der Soziologie (1917). Several of Simmel's article-length
contributions appeared in English during his lifetime in the *American Journal
of Sociology*. An edited volume by Kurt Wolff (1964) assembles many of
Simmel's central ideas, including his most important excursions on law from
Soziologie (Simmel 1908b).

associated with one another on the forms of social life, Simmel introduced a conceptualization of law in relation to custom and morality. Custom is conceived as an undifferentiated normative order that includes more specific rules, religious principles, and conventions. Both morality and law differentiate from custom. Morality refers to the capacity of individuals to confront themselves with normative principles. It is the private confrontation of one's behavior with the social codes of custom. Law is formally enacted at the level of the group or society through specialized organs that determine its contents and oversee its enforcement. Law is reserved for matters that are considered indispensable to the functioning of society as a whole, not mere private concerns. Law is coercive for the whole of the society to which it applies, while morality applies only to the individual. Custom stands in between morality and law as the two poles of a continuum ranging from free individuality to societal coercion. The movement among custom, law, and morality relates to quantitative aspects of the group, according to Simmel, inasmuch as small societies or smaller groups within a larger society are primarily guided by custom, while the enlargement of a united society favors the transition from custom into law.

Simmel did not investigate any concrete empirical dimensions of law in society, but besides his conceptualization of law, he did occasionally specify the role of law in some of his other theoretical excursions. In his work on the social forms of subordination and superordination, for example, he discusses various kinds of subordination, such as subordination under an individual, a plurality, and a principle. The latter form, Simmel maintains, is the most dominant kind of subordination in modern society, and it is particularly revealed in the subordination to law. Rather than subjecting to a leader or a plurality, in modern society people subject to an objective law as a form of depersonified subordination. The subjugation to law also translates in individual consciousness, but the power of obligation stems from the super-personal validity of the law, which now appears as an object.

The work of Simmel's compatriot Ferdinand Tönnies (1855–1936) deserves special mention in this overview of relatively neglected classics – and not only for historical reasons. For Tönnies's theoretical and empirical writings in sociology were not only extremely extensive and systematic as part of a comprehensive sociological vision; Tönnies also developed a distinct evolutionary theory in which law played a central role.[12]

Tönnies's perspective of society centrally revolves around the conceptualization of the two distinct societal types of *Gemeinschaft* (community) and *Gesellschaft* (society). Importantly, *Gemeinschaft* and *Gesellschaft* are concepts representing ideal-types of a strictly analytical character. All societies, according to Tönnies, spring forth from the human will, which can either be essential as based on temper and character, or arbitrary in being able to differentiate among means in view of specified objectives. Tönnies conceives of *Gemeinschaft* societies as expressions of the essential will, organically organized around family, village or town, whereas *Gesellschaft* societies are based on mechanically structured arbitrary-will orientations organized in metropolis and state. The shift from agriculture to industry and the rise of free trade, the modern state, and science Tönnies considers the essential features of the gradual transformation from *Gemeinschaft* to *Gesellschaft*. Tönnies does not conceive of the historical evolution of society in unilinear terms as involving a shift from *Gemeinschaft* to *Gesellschaft*, but instead posits that any social formation will always but in varying degrees reflect characteristics of both types.

Tönnies's sociology of law is a vital component of his theoretical perspective (also forming a bridge to his elaborate theoretical and empirical work on crime) and is developed on the basis of a more general theory of social norms. Tönnies defines social norms as commands and prohibitions that have validity for the individuals of a social entity and are differentiated among three classes: (1) order: the most general whole of norms providing unity to social life; (2) law: the totality of rules whose proclamation and enforcement are a function of a formal court; and (3) morality: the higher prohibitions and commands that spring from the idea of a beautiful and noble life. Order, law, and morality are differently expressed under conditions of *Gemeinschaft* and *Gesellschaft*. In *Gemeinschaft*, the social norms

---

[12] Tönnies's first work, *Gemeinschaft und Gesellschaft*, originally published in 1887, provided the basic framework upon which he continued to found his later works (Tönnies 1887, 1935a, 1935b), including his perspective of sociology and theory of norms and law (Tönnies 1922, 1931). For an overview of Tönnies's thought and research in the areas of law, criminal law, and criminology, see Deflem 1999.

are: (a) the common understanding of concord; (b) the commanding and compulsory norms of custom and (c) the supernatural order of religion. In the *Gesellschaft* type, the social norms are: (a) the conventional norms governing commerce, class, trade, and individualism; (b) the legislation that is proclaimed by the state; and (c) the public opinion that expresses the sentiments of the people. Given the ideal-typical nature of Tönnies's conceptual scheme, the categories of order, law, and morality are always but in varying degrees based on, respectively, concord and convention, custom and legislation, and religion and public opinion.

Tönnies devoted a substantial part of his work on *Gemeinschaft* and *Gesellschaft* to law and suggested a transformation of natural law from common or customary law to contract or statutory law. Tönnies argues that the evolution of law revealed that while all law is both natural and artificial, the artificial element in law had become dominant in the course of history, involving a gradual evolution from common to statutory law. The most critical element of common law is that it had unleashed the capacity to trade and to form relationships in freedom. Thereupon, law gradually formalized in being elaborated, universalized, systematized, and codified because of a rationalization of jurisprudence in terms of efficiency and liberalization and because of an accompanying decline of family organization and habits. Whereas the law of habits (*Gewohnheitsrecht*) was a function of custom, modern legislation-law (*Gesetzesrecht*) was sanctioned by its purpose outside and possibly even against tradition. The resulting state of legal evolution in modern *Gesellschaft*-type societies, according to Tönnies, is not that modern law would only take on the form of the whole of laws proclaimed and enforced by the state. Tönnies stresses the fact that legislation had been monopolized by the state, but also argues for the relative autonomy of law in relation to the remains of other types of (customary) law and the social institutions of politics and economy. The relative part of *Gesellschaft*-like state legislation in comparison to other types of *Gemeinschaft* law within the legal constellation of a society Tönnies argues to be an empirical matter.

Conclusion

Reviewing the history of pre-sociological legal thought, a development can be noted in the progression of thought from the Classical

School and the utilitarians over historical jurisprudence to the historical materialism of Karl Marx. Betraying a struggle over similar issues of societal and intellectual importance, normative aspirations and scholarly intentions mesh in variable ways. Whereas the utilitarians were oriented towards a social engineering perspective that sought to reform politics and legal policy on the basis of a theoretical assumption of utility rather than an analysis of the conditions of human conduct, the historical orientation was more distinctly analytical in its perspective, and social policy recommendations were more of a practical nature formulated on the basis of concrete investigations. In this light alone, it is an odd circumstance in the later development of modern sociology that the work of Karl Marx, which reintroduces a normative orientation in social thought, would be the most influential of the perspectives discussed here. The work of Marx is on theoretical grounds not evidently connected to the aspirations of sociology, but historically Marx's writings have informed a considerable body of sociological writings until this day.

It is peculiar to the history of sociology, including the sociology of law, that some of the more distinctly sociological authors of the nineteenth century – with the exception of Max Weber and Emile Durkheim, of course – only moderately influenced later developments in sociology and have been all but forgotten by sociologists today, even though they developed comprehensive perspectives and engaged in substantial analyses of societal conditions and institutions, including law. The curious situation of the development of sociology is therefore such that although the works of the likes of Spencer, Sumner, Simmel, and Tönnies are explicitly sociological – no less so than those of Weber and Durkheim, if perhaps not as masterful – as well as theoretically informed and empirically oriented, they are part of the past of sociology but not its history as one of the building blocks of modern developments. What most early sociological works on law share with one another as well as with the more historically inclined pre-sociological thinkers is a focus on the transformation from pre-modern to modern law (which is variably conceived but typically coined in an evolutionary scheme) and, relatedly, a conceptual concern over the relationship between law as the whole of formally enacted rules, on the one hand, and a more comprehensive view of law as the whole of social practices associated with such rules, on the other (Vandekerckhove 1996). These characteristics of thinking on law in one form or another – and for better or worse – are the essential foundations of modern sociology as we know it today.

The early development of the sociology of law nicely illustrates that the history and systematics of sociology can only be distinguished analytically (Alexander 1987). This pertains to both the pre-sociological movement towards the sociology of law as well as to its later development. The philosophical precursors to the sociology of law function as the necessary but insufficient conditions for a genuine sociology of law. For to ponder law in the reality of its societal existence or even to query law's social constitution is not to be equated with a systematic sociological study of law. Moreover, the review in this chapter showed that some of the authors who contributed in their work in more distinct sociological ways than others nonetheless have historically had less influence on the development of the sociology of law than some of those scholars who paid less attention to the sociological study of law or to the study of law from any viewpoint. In the latter case, the work of Marx is most exemplary. To be sure, Marx made a contribution to social science by suggesting the instrumentalist theory of law in contributing to and justifying social inequality. But Marx was not alone, and other scholars with a more pronounced sociological commitment studied law more intensely, although they do not fare well in our collective memory. The sociology of law of Ferdinand Tönnies, for example, is virtually unknown today even though it presents an elaborate and systematic scheme of thought consistent with his broader sociological orientation.

The next chapters will turn to the contributions of Max Weber and Emile Durkheim. Among the three classics now considered central to modern sociology, it is clear that Marx did not focus on law to any degree of intellectual satisfaction, while the sociological contributions of Weber and Durkheim are not only influential but foundational to the sociology of law. Given Weber's lengthy discussions on law and the generous reception of his work, the centrality of Weber in the development of the sociology of law needs little argument. Though somewhat less discussed among contemporary sociologists of law, Durkheim's work, it will be shown, is as important as Weber's, especially in terms of its orientation of the sociology of law around the key dimensions of social issues as involving both factual and normative dimensions.

2 | *Max Weber on the rationalization of law*

Among the sociological classics, Max Weber is widely considered the founding father *par excellence* of the modern sociology of law. When Weber observed that social life in the modern era had become more and more rationalized in a purposive-rational sense, he not only contemplated the central role of economy, state, and bureaucracy, but along with it also discussed the role of law as the basis of modern political authority. Weber specifically outlined the characteristics of a formally rationalized legal system that is primarily guided by the application of procedures. Yet Weber's work offers not merely a detailed presentation of the unique features of modern law. His analysis of law is an intrinsic part of his sociology, in terms of both its perspective to the study of society and its theoretical propositions on the conditions of modern society.

Weber developed his perspective on law as part of a more general sociology, the contours of which will have to be explained first in order to fully grasp his theory of law. In the systematic nature and comprehensive scope of its contribution, Weber's analysis is rivaled only by that of Emile Durkheim, whose sociology of law was likewise part and parcel of a more fundamental sociological perspective and theory of society. It will therefore be useful in this chapter to situate Weber's sociology of law in the context of his sociological approach and theory of society, not merely to fully understand Weber's contribution to the study of law, but also to be able to usefully contrast it in the next chapter with Durkheim's thought as the two most foundational contributions to the sociology of law.

Interpretive sociology

The son of an authoritarian father and a devoutly Calvinist mother, Max Weber (1864–1920) was a well-read student, who attended the University of Heidelberg and, upon fulfilling his military service, the

University of Berlin. After completing his studies in law, economics, and other social-science subjects, Weber for a short period became a lawyer and then began teaching. Having briefly taught law, in 1894 he went on to teach economics at the University of Freiburg and, three years later, at the University of Heidelberg. Suffering from nervous illness, Weber gradually reduced his teaching activities and, in 1899, stopped teaching altogether. Following a few years of rest and travel, he resumed an active life in writing and various involvements in political and social affairs. Weber again took up a formal teaching position in 1918, when he became a professor in Vienna and Munich. In 1920, he died at age 58.

Any sociological orientation that has a highly systematic character and is comprehensive in scope rests critically on a basic ontological understanding of the nature of society. The sociology of Max Weber most fundamentally rests on a perspective of society as being made up of social relations or human interactions.[1] Interactions take place between two or more actors and are guided by the motivations and intentions of the actors involved. In contrast with behavior, which is not meaningful but causally determined, human (inter-)action is essentially (inter-)subjective and meaningful. Given that social relations involve reciprocal interactions between two or more individuals, the meanings of all actors may not be identical or harmoniously linked to one another, but all interactions are guided by motives. The task of sociology, according to Weber, is to understand human conduct inasmuch as it is meaningful. The procedure associated with uncovering the motives of action is referred to as understanding (*Verstehen*).

Despite the emphasis on the understanding of human action, Weber is also interested in the formulation of general principles of social action. Subjective understanding does not preclude explanation, for Weber holds that by reaching an understanding of human action, sociology can also explain that action's course and consequences. The method of understanding is not subjective because it relates to the motivations and intentions of the various actors involved. While the understanding of motives and meanings must proceed from an emphatic attitude, the sociological techniques to grasp meaning are replicable

---

[1] Weber's most important theoretical writings are available in the posthumously published collection, *Wirtschaft und Gesellschaft* (Weber 1922a translated as 1922b).

and verifiable on the basis of established standards of methodology. These techniques include direct observation of an emotive action and understanding by means of identifying a motivational link between meaning and action. The sociological perspective oriented at uncovering the motives of human interactions is referred to as interpretive sociology.

Weber's insistence on the objective nature of interpretive sociology relates to his famous doctrine of value-freedom. The fact that there is a differentiation of subject (action) and object (behavior) and, correspondingly, a distinction between social and natural sciences does not mean that the social sciences, which deal with inter-subjective phenomena, cannot be objective in their analyses. The social sciences cannot seek to establish the ideals or normative principles of human conduct, but they can, on the basis of a differentiation of the means and ends of action, make scientific judgments on the rationality of means given certain ends. Sociologists can therefore also determine the principles on which certain attitudes and actions are based. Sociology, then, can be value-free. Of course, because sociology is a human activity that also relates to subjective interactions, sociology entertains a special connection with values (*Wertbeziehung*). Weber argues that all scientific activity rests on certain ideals or viewpoints that cannot be justified scientifically, such as the selection of relevant facts out of reality. The identification of events out of a stream of events and of their causes and effects necessarily rests on certain assumptions. However, while this identification is selective, it must also be verifiable by others and therefore be conducted on the basis of systematic methods. Exemplifying the ideal of value-freedom (*Wertfreiheit*), Weber maintained that sociologists cannot bring their own personal values to the findings and judgments they have arrived at in the conduct of their research, even though their initial choice of the subject matter may have been guided by personal values.

Ideal-type and elective affinity

In order to ensure that a sociology oriented at reaching understanding would not fall prey to psychological reductionism and amount to nothing but the disorder of a sheer endless amount of individual-level findings, Weber developed the perspective of the ideal-type. Interpretive sociology is distinct from sheer subjective interpretation by the identification of a particular motive of conduct in terms of a broader frame of normativity. What this means is that for any human action to be sociologically interpreted, it must be shown to have a motive that makes sense to the actor as a member of a society or a subsection thereof, within its own distinct culture, structure, norms, and expectations. For instance, it makes sense sociologically that a person prays on the occasion of a personal tragedy, not because of that person's psychology, but because of the ethics associated with praying in the context of a particular religious background. The act of praying can thus be sociologically elucidated as religious conduct and differentiated, moreover, from other human action based on different normative orders, such as science and law.

Ideal-types are constructed by abstracting and combining a limited number of elements from reality in order to open up the chaos of empirical events to description and understanding. The purpose of an ideal-type is entirely analytical, and it is only through application that an ideal-type can be found to be useful or not. In its most basic form, an ideal-type refers to the definition of an observable phenomenon, such as law, culture, and society. At a higher order of analysis, ideal-types are constructed out of the specific characteristics of phenomena in order to explain the historical and contemporary conditions that account for the state and development of society.

As an example of the methodology of ideal-types, Weber differentiated four types of human interaction: (1) traditional action is carried out under the influence of custom or habit; (2) affective action is guided by an emotion; (3) value-rational action is guided by a belief in the intrinsic value of a particular mode of conduct irrespective of its consequences; and (4) purposive-rational action is based on a conscious calculation of means towards a given end. In specifying this ideal-typical construction of human action, Weber sought to demonstrate the rationality of a variety of types of conduct, none of which stands above any other. More important for the development of Weber's theory of society, his ideal-typical construction of action also forms the foundation of an important observation on the course of modern society, by showing that modern societies are marked by an increasing influence of purposive-rational action and a relative loss of traditional action. Weber observed that more and more aspects of modern society, be they political, economic, or cultural, are marked by a predominant reliance on calculable considerations to employ the most efficient means given certain goals.

Weber argued that the progressive influence of purposive-rational thought across social institutions showed the theoretical necessity to break through both materialist and idealist models of explanation to indicate the elective affinity (*Wahlverwandtschaft*) that exists among societal conditions. Weber's theory of social stratification, hence, not only distinguishes between classes on the basis of economic ownership, but between class, status, and party. A class is defined by Weber in terms of shared (economic) interests on the basis of property and income, while status groups are (culturally) determined by a recognized estimation of honor and prestige, and parties are united in terms of (political) power and domination. Unlike Marx, therefore, Weber does not conceive of economic conditions as more basic than other societal forces, nor does he agree with the inverse theory of cultural idealism that values determine the material forces of society. Weber instead argues that various societal processes and conditions may share similar characteristics and developments and mutually influence and reinforce one another. Weber's theory can thus be described as multidimensional. An exposition of Weber's theory of society will further explain the meaning and value of Weber's perspective.

The rationalization of society: economy, politics, and bureaucracy

Weber argues that modern societies are most essentially marked by a high degree of purposive rationalization. The purposive type of rationalization is also referred to as formal rationalization because the mode or form of conduct at the level of means is more important than the substance or goal of action. In other words, it matters less what is done than how it is done. In more and more spheres of social life, efficient calculations are made to reach certain ends. Weber's theory applies to many important societal institutions, including science, politics, culture, and law, but it is useful to expand on his idea with reference to free market capitalism, which Weber developed in his famous study on the Protestant ethic (Weber 1920). According to Weber, an elective affinity exists between the ethic of Calvinism and the mode of capitalist conduct to use the most efficient means to accumulate wealth. In Calvinist belief, only a finite number of people are chosen or predestined to receive divine grace. In order to ensure oneself and others to be among the chosen ones, one must apply oneself to acquire as much wealth as possible while simultaneously avoiding pleasure. On the basis of Calvinist doctrine, work in the material world becomes the highest possible positive ethical attitude. Once capitalism was historically established, according to Weber, its religious core is no longer relevant and economic rational conduct of life becomes an independent power. The Calvinist idea of the calling is a support for capitalism that, in the end, is no longer needed. Having thus demonstrated a religious influence on capitalism, Weber argues that a more complete explanation of the course and outcome of capitalism should also "investigate how Protestant Asceticism was in turn influenced in its development and its character by the totality of social conditions, especially economic" (Weber 1920: 183).

In the context of modern societies in the West, Weber applied the rationalization model to many other dimensions of society. Weber's discussions on the rationalization of politics deserve special consideration in this book because they form a bridge into his sociology of law. At the most general level, Weber ideal-typically distinguishes three kinds of political power on the basis of the kind of legitimacy it enjoys: (1) traditional authority is based on the belief in a traditional source of power; (2) charismatic authority is based on the belief in the extraordinary qualities of a political leader; and (3) rational-legal domination is based on a system of laws and is the typical form of legitimacy in the context of the modern state. Weber defines a state as a political community which, within a particular territory, successfully claims a monopoly over the legitimate use of physical coercion. Weber's definition is thus an instrumental one, defining the state not in terms of any objectives, but solely with reference to its means. Besides the monopolization of the legitimate use of physical force as a means of domination, a state also exercises political authority within a particular territory through the organization of armed protection against outside attacks (by the military), the protection of vested rights (administration of justice), the cultivation of cultural interests (in the administration), the enactment of law (through legislation), and the protection of personal safety and public order (police).

Showing again the relevance of purposive rationalization, Weber argues that the administration of the various state functions is handed over to specialized institutions or bureaucracies that are purposely designed for the implementation of the state's relevant policies. Bureaucracies are for Weber one of the most important characteristics of modern rationalized societies as they indicate the extent to which the world has become calculable in terms of efficiency considerations and the extent to which the mysteries of the world that were embodied in traditionalistic ethical life have become demystified in favor of a rational calculus. Bureaucracies perform administrative tasks in order to secure an efficient functioning of state (and the market economy, which is likewise bureaucratically administered). The purposive-rational logic of the bureaucratic form of organization can be observed from its main characteristics: (1) bureaucracies are subject to a principle of fixed jurisdictional areas; (2) they are firmly ordered in a hierarchy of positions; (3) bureaucratic work is based on written documents or files; (4) the executive office is separated from the household; (5) bureaucratic positions require specialized training; (6) the bureaucratic activity is a full-time job; and (7) the management of offices is guided by general rules that can be learnt. It is only in the context of modern capitalist societies, Weber argues, that bureaucracies take on this specific form because, under influence of the division of labor in society, they are marked by a high degree of specialization and accompanying concentration on efficiency considerations.

In the further development of the bureaucratic form, Weber observes that bureaucracies are typically stable and operate exclusively on the basis of "formalistic impersonality" and the methodical discipline of a consistently rationalized execution of the received order (Weber 1922a: 128). Under circumstances of increasing bureaucratization, the bureaucratic experts can take control not only of the implementation but also the direction of political agendas. Then, Weber argues, the political master may find himself in the position of "a dilettante against the professional expert" (Weber 1922a: 572).

The rationality of modern law

Weber's theory of the state is intimately related to his sociology of law, most clearly because domination in the modern state is legitimated by legality. Politics and law are further related because the legality of rational domination finds its purest expression in the bureaucracy, which is governed by formal procedures and a system of law. Yet,

Weber's sociology of law also stands by itself and must be treated accordingly both because of its systematic character and because of its influence on later developments in modern sociology. Weber's special interest in law is not surprising given that he had been a student of legal science, wrote his doctoral dissertation and his *Habilitationsschrift* – a second dissertation written to receive a university teaching position – about aspects of medieval and Roman law, and had briefly worked as a lawyer. Necessarily selective given the range of Weber's writings on law, this review will highlight the basic contours of Weber's sociology of law, especially in light of its reception in contemporary sociology.[2]

As was the case with other classic German scholars, such as Simmel and Tönnies, Weber's perspective on law rests on a basic conceptual typology. Weber distinguishes law from custom and convention. Custom is defined as a practice that is valid because of practical convenience. The validity of convention is acquired through an external guarantee, but this guarantee is merely informal by means of public disapproval. The validity of law, finally, is externally guaranteed through a specialized staff that is expressly in charge of compliance with legal rules and enforcement of violations. "An order will be called law," Weber writes, "if it is externally guaranteed by the probability that coercion (physical or psychological), to bring about conformity or avenge violation, will be applied by a staff of people holding themselves specially ready for that purpose" (Weber 1922c: 5). Thus, Weber's definition of law is distinctly sociological in specifying the actual conditions of law in society, without normatively engaging in a juridical debate on the intrinsic validity of law. The only validity of law the sociologist is interested in, according to Weber, is that which derives from the subjective considerations of the members of a community. Yet, the belief in the validity of legal rules need not be shared among all or even many members of society. Instead, for there to be law, there must

---

[2] Weber's major ideas on law are expressed in the chapter on *Rechtssoziologie* (Sociology of Law) in *Wirtschaft und Gesellschaft* (Weber 1922a translated as 1922b). The chapter on law and other relevant sections of *Economy and Society* have also been published in English in a separate volume (Weber 1922c). Particularly helpful among the secondary sources is Anthony Kronman's (1983) book-length treatise on the philosophical underpinnings and implications of Weber's sociology of law. See also the overviews and discussions by Andreski 1981; Boucock 2000; Feldman 1991; Kettler 1984; Quensel 1997; Rehbinder 1963; Sahni 2006; Schluchter 1981: 82–138; Stangl 1992; Stoljar 1961; Swedberg 2006; Trubek 1972, 1985.

be an external guarantee of legal coercion by means of a specialized apparatus of enforcement.

In order to explain the form of rationalized law in modern society, Weber differentiates between various types of rationalization that can affect law. Specifically, he distinguishes substantive and formal rationalization. In general terms, substantive rationalization is based on certain values and conceptions of justice, whereas formal rationalization rests on general rules and procedures. In the political sphere, for instance, substantive rationalization distinguishes an autocracy from a democracy by being based on the divine will of a ruler rather than the popular will of the people. At the level of formal rationalization, autocracy and democracy are distinguished by being based on charisma and legality, respectively.

Weber specifies the ideal-types of formal and substantive rationality in terms of lawmaking (legislation) and lawfinding (adjudication) as the two central aspects of law. From the substantive viewpoint, Weber argues, lawmaking and lawfinding are rational when they reflect general norms that exist outside the contours of legal principles and the logical generalizations of law itself, such as ethical imperatives, ideological and religious beliefs, and political maxims (natural law). Law is substantively irrational when legal decisions are influenced by the concrete factors of a case on the basis of ethical, emotional, or political considerations rather than by general rules (traditional law). As an example, Weber mentions the case of traditional Chinese law, in which legal officials could decide freely from case to case, bound only by a general reliance on sacred tradition. Likewise, Weber considers so-called "khadi justice" (named after the judge in a Muslim court) an instance of substantively irrational law because its jurisprudence lacks any consideration of general rules and is exclusively based on the unique, legal as well as extra-legal, circumstances of each individual case. With respect to formal rationality, Weber argues that law is irrational when legal decisions are based on means which are not intellectually controllable, such as in the case of oracles and ordeals. Oracles involve proclamations of law that are judged to be divine or sacred because of the authority of their source, usually a high priest. In a trial by ordeal, the accused is subjected to a painful task, the completion of which determines guilt or innocence. Because in such cases there are no general standards of legal decision-making, formally irrational law is unpredictable (charismatic law). By contrast, law is formally rational when it is solely based on general characteristics that pertain to the facts of the case (positive law).

According to Weber, the rationalization of modern law in Western societies takes on the specific form of formal rationalization. Rationalized law is formal and abstract, exemplifying the disenchantment of the modern world. At the most general level, the quantity of law increases as societies grow and become more complex, because there is an increased need to have specified legal rules in a society that is more anonymous and diverse. The various members of large-scale societies do not readily know what is lawful and what is not, so that law has to increase in terms of the rules it incorporates and the degree of explication of those rules.

Accompanying the increase in the quantity of law, there is also an increase in the formal qualities of law. The formal rationalization of law implies that laws are codified, impartial, and impersonal. The codification of law refers to the fact that law is written down. The impartiality of modern law is revealed in its aspiration to be applied equally and fairly to all. Modern law is impersonal by being applied regardless of the personal characteristics of those involved. Only unambiguous general characteristics of the facts of the case are taken into account.

Exemplifying the formal rationalization of law, Weber discusses the historical move from status contracts to purposive contracts. Status contracts allow for a change in the position of the parties involved, for instance to become one's relative or acquire a slave, typically by invoking some magical or divine power. Purposive contracts do not affect the status of the parties involved but only aim to achieve some specific result or performance, such as the acquisition of a good in exchange for money. Formal rationalization in the case of purposive contracts, Weber maintains, increases freedom because it allows people to make calculations to predict the legal consequences of their conduct. The freedom granted by formal rational law, however, remains itself also a formal matter, as inequalities that exist, for instance in terms of economic position or political rights, are not taken into account. The formal freedom legally guaranteed to all thus impedes on the actual possibilities to satisfy the values and needs of many.

Weber observes that formally rational law is typical for capitalist societies, but he argues that the relation between modern law and capitalism is complex. Formally rational law and capitalism tend to go hand in hand, but the relation is not one-directional. Exemplifying his perspective of elective affinity, Weber suggests that the formal rationalization of law came about under influence of a mixture of economic, cultural, political, and legal conditions. Economically, the spread of capitalism contributed to the development of the formal rationalization of law. For instance, the increasing centrality of private contract law was a function of the maturation of capitalism. At the same time, Weber argues that modern law has developed such that it also influenced economic conduct. A rigorous system of adjudication, for instance, benefits economic market developments. Yet, modern capitalism can also flourish in less formally rationalized legal systems. At the cultural level, the secularization of law led to discarding the substantive irrationality and religious charisma and mystery from law, while, politically, the expansion of bureaucratic government, because of its interest in clarity and orderliness, also benefited the formal rationalization of law. Most importantly, Weber argues, the formal rationalization of law accelerated because professional laypeople began to play an increasingly important role in the courts. Weber argues for a centrality of professionalization in these developments because he considers the training of professional lawyers as the most important factor towards the formal rationalization of law. Formal rationalization is especially pushed forward by the development of legal education in the European-continental fashion of academic law, whereby law is treated as a science in order to build and study a logical and rational system of abstract norms. The primary movers of law, particularly in terms of the direction towards greater formalization of the law, are thus themselves legal (intrajuristic).

The drift towards formal rationalization of law is not steady over time nor evenly accomplished across modern societies. From a comparative viewpoint, Weber notes that formal rationalization of law is more fully accomplished in the European system, which is predominantly based on codified laws. By contrast, the Anglo-American legal system relies more on court decisions and precedents, whereby judges still retain an element of charisma (see Chapter 9). Historically, Weber observes that legal formalism has also been challenged by the occasional resurgence of social law, based on such emotionally colored ethical postulates as justice and human dignity. There is thus a tension between formal and substantive rationalization. The technically rational machine of modern law increases the substantive irrationality of modern law because formal justice infringes upon the ideals of substantive justice. However, such resurgences of value-irrationalism have equally been opposed, Weber observes, by attempts to reestablish objective legal standards and conceive of law as a technical tool.

The legacy of Weber

The relevance and influence of Weber's work in modern sociology cannot be neatly demarcated and measured, for there is simply no modern sociology that does not at least situate itself with respect to Weber's theories and, almost as often, is influenced by many of the key ideas in his work. In the sociology of law, more specifically, Weber's writings are likewise an omnipresent reality, as a theoretical foundation, an exemplary model of analysis, or, at the very least, a source of critique.[3] Among the components of Weber's thought to have had a lasting impact can be included: the notions of elective affinity and ideal-type and the related conceptualizations of authority, economy, culture, and law; the separation of sociological and juridical viewpoints in the study of law and the related stance on (and disagreement over) value-freedom in sociological inquiry; and the attention towards the form and consequences of modern rationalization. A sharper view of the nature and scope of the legacy of Weber's work in the sociology of law can be gained from a glance at the secondary literature that has explicitly addressed the virtues and shortcomings of Weber's approach to law in both theoretical and empirical respects.

From the viewpoint of empirical research, Weber's thesis on the formal rationalization of modern law in the West and the conception of the relation between formal and substantive (ir)rationality have received most attention. These interrelated questions strike at the heart of the empirical validity of the Weberian quest to uncover and explain what is unique about Western rationalization and modernity. Weber's theories in this respect contain at once comparative and historical components, situating Western law relative to other legal systems and tracing the historical development towards modern systems of law. With respect to the comparative dimension in Weber's

---

[3] On Weber's influence in the sociology of law in various nations, see the contributions in Lascoumes 1995. See also the exegitical works mentioned in Footnote 2 and the writings cited in this section.

sociology of law, attention has been devoted to Weber's interpretation of non-Western legal systems. Robert Marsh (2000), for example, has critically received Weber's categorization of the traditional Chinese legal system of the Ch'ing Dynasty, which was in place from 1644 until 1912, as being a substantively irrational system that involved legal decisions that varied freely from case to case. Marsh argues that the decision-making powers of Chinese legal officials were in fact much more limited, not because of any influence of traditional religion, but because of a legal obligation to adhere to written law, particularly to secularly inspired sub-statutes that had been promulgated in addition to the sacredly grounded statutes of Chinese law. Judicial decisions, such as in the case of the pronouncement of sentences, also had to be accompanied by a citation to the relevant (sub-)statute of the Ch'ing code. This code, furthermore, was based on extra-legal ideological systems, specifically the Confucianist values of social solidarity and hierarchy and a legalist conception to adhere to rules. Marsh concludes that the legal system of the Ch'ing Dynasty should be categorized as a substantive rational type of law, guided by an ideological system other than that of law itself.

Parallel to the observations on the proper interpretation of Chinese law are discussions on Weber's analysis of Muslim law or khadi justice. It has been argued that khadi justice should be interpreted as substantively rational inasmuch as it is based on the all-encompassing religious principles of Islam (Marsh 2000). Yet, it has also been argued that the Koran as such did not function as the basis for khadi law, but that legal specialists employed their own independent judgment and speculation to interpret the ethical teachings of Islam and the words and deeds of the Prophet (Turner 1974). The khadi legal system was unstable and fluid because of the patrimonial context in which the law was administered. In the administration of justice, Islamic law favored certain classes of the population more than others, especially those engaged in commerce, precisely by conceiving of all people, except slaves, as equal legal subjects. At the same time, Islamic law was bound by religious tradition. Patricia Crone (1999) therefore suggests that the key theoretical element might not be rationalization but differentiation of societal objectives and their corresponding institutions, including the separation of the political order (the state), the religious world (church), the order of production and consumption (economy), and the organization of knowledge (science). In

Europe, the legal system develops as the state progresses and takes control of the legislative function. Taking the state as the central motor of the peculiar form of legal development in Europe, Islamic law by contrast is withdrawn from the control of the state and instead embodies the religious values of Islam.

With respect to the historical trend towards the formal rationalization of law, discussions on the validity and value of Weber's work have particularly concerned the process of rationalization in the area of criminal law. Joachim Savelsberg (1992), for instance, has shown that the historical trend in modern criminal law reform during the twentieth century, especially in the United States, involved a process of substantivation that implied a commitment to values related to social reform, therapy, and rehabilitation. Non-legal principles related to justice thus brought about a trend towards social law in the area of criminal justice. More recently, however, this substantivation process has met with opposition, especially because of observed disparities in sentencing outcomes and the lack of due process, and attempts have been made to reintroduce principles of formal-rational law in the form of sentencing guidelines (see Chapter 11). While Weber realized that calls for social law opposed formal rationality in law, he also assumed that calls for law as technique would ultimately prevail. Savelsberg shows that the latter is not always possible because the socio-structural conditions that brought about legal substantivation continue to exist and hinder any return to the days of formal rationalization.

Other scholars have gone even further to modify Weber's views and suggested that the area of criminal law is essentially marked by irrationalization (Anspach and Monsen 1989; Stangl 1992). It is observed that modern criminal legal systems, such as in Germany and the US, allow for a great amount of discretion or, in Weber's terms, free decision-making from case to case. Although prosecutors and judges operate within an environment of laws, they have considerable leeway to choose which criminal charges to bring against a person and select among available sentences. Such discrepancies are brought about by the conflicting underlying principles that mark modern criminal-legal systems, such as the classical emphasis on deterrence, on the one hand, and interventionist notions of rehabilitation, on the other.

Similarly indicating problems with the empirical basis of Weber's theories is Ronen Shamir's (1993a) argument that Weber's conception of the evolution towards formal rationality is too restricted because of its reliance on the case of German law (at the dawn of the twentieth century). Shamir qualifies Weber's theory of the basis of formal rationalization in statutory law to suggest that precedents and legal decisions in the case of the United States were conceived as a basis for rationalization in opposition to codified law, which was seen as an embodiment of substantive-rational law. In the early 1800s, for instance, American judges and lawyers opposed attempts to rigidly codify the legal system because it was thought to undermine the autonomous capacity of law to methodically decide upon the appropriate forms of law. A shift came about during the New Deal era of the 1930s when social reforms guided new efforts of legislation at the federal level, setting in a process that would later lead to a substantivation of criminal law and, yet again later, renewed attempts at formal rationalization. What is suggested in this pattern, then, is the value of a cyclical perspective of formal and substantive rationalization.

Related to some of the discussed empirical themes, sociologists of law have also theoretically engaged with several of the key ideas in Weber's oeuvre. These theoretical excursions contain interpretations and commentary on the value of Weber's work for the sociological study of law and as such anticipate some of the theoretical fault lines that have emerged in the development of the sociology of law since the classics (see Part II). Among the most discussed themes has been the Weberian conception of the relationship between formally rationalized law and the development of capitalism. In general, Weber argued against a Marxist interpretation of law (as an instrument of capitalism), but rather than defending a straightforward idealist anti-Marxian theory, Weber suggested, in line with his multidimensional approach of elective affinity, that the formal rationalization of law, because of its reliance on calculability, was a contributing factor to the rise of capitalism. Complicating the matter further, Weber had to acknowledge on the basis of historical evidence that the relationship between formally rationalized law and capitalism is not always present. In particular, in the case of British legal and economic development, Weber observed that capitalist development had gone ahead without a high degree of formal rationalization of law.

The theoretical literature has in different ways answered to this so-called "England problem" in Weber's work. David Trubek (1972) has pointed out that Weber himself is inconsistent in making three conflicting arguments: first, that British law, despite its lack of formal rationality, nonetheless promoted the development of capitalism; second, that British law was marked by a degree of predictability despite its non-statutory nature; and, third, that the British case was an exception to the rule. Kronman (1983) similarly suggests a contradiction in Weber's thought to imply arguments for the development of capitalism in the United Kingdom both despite and because of the nature of British law.

Other scholars have sought to analyze the British case in more precise terms to allow for a better understanding rather than a dismissal of Weber's theory. Sally Ewing (1987), for instance, argues that Weber never drew a connection between economic rationalization and a formal-rational conception of legal thought (of what law is), but with a formal-rational mode of the administration of justice (of how law is applied). As such, formal rationality can apply to both the logical and gapless system of rules that characterizes civil law nations (such as Germany) and to the legally secured and enforceable guarantees of rights that mark common law countries (such as the UK). Assaf Likhovski (1999) defends a similar argument that no England problem exists because Protestant influences on British law during the seventeenth century included demands for legal rationalization and an increased measure of predictability in law. Crone (1999) interprets the relationship between capitalism and law again differently to suggest that British law favored the bourgeoisie and was thus formalistic for the rich, but substantively irrational for the poor, so that it encouraged the development of capitalism despite not being formally rational.

In Weber's work, most developments of law are argued to be caused by intra-legal conditions, whereas the influence of and on other conditions, especially economic and political ones, is typically maintained to be indirect or empirically variable. As such, Weber's approach exemplifies a "causal agnosticism" (Kronman 1983: 119) in terms of the "complex web of causal factors" (Feldman 1991: 222), "convergence of factors" (Walton 1976: 7), or "constant inter-relationships" (Brand 1982: 96) that exist among economic, political, cultural, and legal forces (see also Treiber 1985). The causally undetermined orientation in Weber's thinking exemplifies his notion of multidimensionality (elective affinity), yet it also leaves his work open to charges of theoretical indecisiveness and conceptual ambiguity (Sterling and Moore 1987). In any case, Weber's perspective confirms the tension between formal and substantive rationality in law and, relatedly, the potentially conflicting relationship between legal and economic rationality, which may be heightened as capitalism progresses (Turkel 1981), necessitating sociological inquiry to unravel in precise terms important dimensions of the complex relationship between law and economy (see Chapter 7).

Discussions on Weber's England problem are of more than mere historical significance, for they relate to important theoretical considerations concerning the explanatory power of and interrelationships among economy, politics, law, and other differentiated components of society. Weber's perspective of multidimensionality has been variably interpreted in the course of the development of sociological theory. Although scholars such as Kronman (1983) have argued that there is an underlying thematic unity to Weber's work despite its density and seeming lack of homogeneity (Andrini 2004), the disjointed nature of Weber's writings on law (which come from a posthumous collection) as well as the not always sharply formulated relationship between his sociology of law and his other works, especially his political sociology (Spencer 1970), have not benefited from an unambiguous interpretation. Anticipating some of the significance of these developments for the sociology of law (Chapter 6), Weber's work on causal relationships in matters of law and society has been received very differently, ranging from a conflict-theoretical appropriation of Weber's thought as complementary with Marx (Albrow 1975; Zeitlin 1985) to both Marxist critiques (Walton 1976) and anti-Marxist interpretations stressing the value of Weber's conceptions of the relative autonomy of law (Turner 1974).

In close relation to the reception of Weber's ideas on causality are discussions on the call for value-freedom in his work. The perspective of sociology advocated by Weber is oriented to being uncommitted, whereas jurisprudence is by definition guided by a legal dogma related to the practical concerns of the legal professional (Kronman 1983). The sociologist is not guided by values, beyond those intrinsic to academic inquiry, but at the same time takes values seriously to the extent that they are relevant to social action and social institutions. It has been argued that the tension in this perspective produces methodological difficulties (Andreski 1981; Trubek 1986). Specifically, while Weber explicitly advocated an interpretive perspective of understanding, much of his work involves other, especially historical and comparative, research strategies. Some scholars, moreover, have pointed out that there are in fact strong philosophical principles present in Weber's work (Beirne 1979; Brand 1982; Cain 1980; Campbell 1986; Vandenberghe 2005). Weber recognized the ambivalent implications of the rationalization of modern law, whereby increased calculability is also seen to imply increased disenchantment, but he also advocated strong leadership and clarity in the business of politics and law as technique.

Conclusion

The sociology of Max Weber counts among the great achievements in social thought and is foundational to modern sociology. Weber's methodological orientation led the way to the development of an array of orientations in interpretive sociology, and his multidimensional perspective of society has likewise inspired many generations of sociologists. In various specialty areas of sociological thought, particularly in political and economic sociology, Weber's influence is immeasurable. The somewhat less pronounced attention in modern sociology to Weber's work on law, relative to his other contributions to the study of modernity, is a function of the relative degree of general inattention paid by sociologists to law and, relatedly, the slow development of the sociology of law as an academic specialty field, but not of the place of law in Weber's oeuvre. For both in the intellectual unfolding of Weber's thought as in the construction of a comprehensive theory of modernity, law takes up a central role that is on equal footing with his studies of economy and politics.

To the sociology of law, Weber's work is indispensable. His theories of the rationalization of law and the function of law in terms of regulation through procedure have offered important thematic orientations to the sociology of law (of what is relevant to be studied). Of enduring significance has especially been the focus on the regulation of interaction in the form of rationalization through standardized procedures and decision-making in lawmaking and lawfinding on the basis of general principles. In terms of its approach (how to study law sociologically), what Weber's work exemplifies in striking fashion is the relevance of historical time in terms of a multidimensional conception of society. Weber also paid attention to the variable patterns of these developments in different societies, such as in his discussions on the differences between the US tradition of precedent law and the European-continental emphasis on written law. As such, Weber offers the foundations of a comparative-historical sociology of law that centers on the dualities of law in the modern era. And although it has been noted that Weber's sociology of law was conceptually indebted to legal scholarship (Turner and Factor 1994), it is a remarkable achievement that Weber's work exemplified a transition from legal to sociological thinking within the span of a lifetime, even though this transition took several decades to be completed at the institutional level (see Chapters 4 and 5).

The rise of modern rationalized law Weber relates to economic and political factors. Rationalized law is executed in the bureaucratic apparatus of the state but also serves the free-market economy. In the economic sphere, legally guaranteed contractual freedom ironically leads to the free use of resources without legal restraints. Laws that regulate the market as a free zone of trade and industry thus imply a relative reduction of the coercion that comes with prohibitory norms. It is this theme of the particular, not economic-deterministic, conditions of the relation between modern law and the capitalist economic order that receives a different, but likewise distinctly sociological treatment in Durkheim's work.

3 | Emile Durkheim on law and social solidarity

It is the singularly most notable achievement of Emile Durkheim that he worked consistently and successfully towards the institutionalization of sociology as an academic discipline. In the sharpness of his formulation of the material and formal subject matter of sociology, in the innovativeness of his methodology, and in the ability to build a sociological school of thought, Durkheim knows no equals. It is the good fortune of the sociology of law to be able to rely not only on Durkheim's sociological project in general, but also on his contributions to the sociological study of law in particular.

Durkheim's analysis of law in his sociological study of the moral foundations of the division of labor is well known among sociologists. To empirically examine the transformation of society from the mechanical to the organic type, Durkheim turned to the evolution of law as an indicator of the changing moral foundations of society. Durkheim's central concern, to show that modern society is characterized by a solidarity that preserves individualism, remains valuable today. The value of this approach is not exhausted with reference to the empirical adequacy of Durkheim's theses on law, such as concerning the evolution from repressive to restitutive law. For in addition to sketching an empirical model of law in society, Durkheim's sociology of law also encompasses an innovative approach to the study of law. This approach centrally revolves around the recognition that the normative dimension of society enables both evaluative as well as scholarly perspectives. It is the foundational task of sociology to think about society in resolutely analytical terms. As law is always intimately connected to social norms and a society's moral understanding, also, few insights are more central in the sociology of law than the connection of law with the function of social integration. Reviewing Durkheim's contributions to the sociology of law, this chapter will, similarly to the chapter on Weber, introduce the key elements of Durkheim's approach to sociology and his theories of society and additionally incorporate assessments of the value and validity of the Durkheimian perspective of law.

The science of society

The son of a rabbi, Emile Durkheim (1858–1917) was an exceptional student, who attended the prestigious Ecole Normale Supérieure before he began teaching philosophy in 1882. Five years later, he became a professor of pedagogy and social science at Bordeaux, where he stayed until 1902 when he took up a professorship in education and sociology at the Sorbonne in Paris. Durkheim was centrally involved in developing and institutionalizing sociology as an academic discipline, but he also reflected upon the political and social conditions of his society. In 1898, Durkheim founded the *Année Sociologique*, the first sociology journal in France. Suffering from poor health, overwork and, most tragically, the death of his son in World War I, Durkheim died at the age of 59.

Influenced by the work of Auguste Comte, who in the 1830s had first coined the term sociology to denote the positive science of society, and the German tradition of moral statistics, an early social science devoted to the descriptive study of the characteristics of states, Durkheim conceives of sociology as the scientific study of social facts.[1] Defined as ways of being in society that are coercive over and external to individuals, social facts include both ideal representations, such as culture and law, and material circumstances and actions, such as demographic and economic conditions. Social facts are coercive over individuals because their conditions cannot be violated without consequence. In the case of ideal representations, sanctions are indicative of the coercive force of social facts, such as when punishments are handed over to those who break laws or when public disapproval is expressed over violations of norms. In terms of material conditions, social facts have a relatively mechanistic coercive power because they

---

[1] Durkheim's sociological approach is clarified in *The Rules of Sociological Method* (Durkheim 1895) and applied in his works on the division of labor (Durkheim 1893a translated as 1893b), suicide (Durkheim 1897), and religion (Durkheim 1912). Many of Durkheim's books and most important articles are available in their original French prose via the website "Les Classiques des Sciences Sociales": http://classiques.uqac.ca/classiques/Durkheim_emile/ durkheim.html.

determine the chances individuals have to engage in certain activities. Poor economic conditions, for instance, will influence the probability of employment in individual cases.

The coercive force of social facts, according to Durkheim, allows for their identification and study, especially in the case of ideal representations such as social norms, because observable sanctions function as the indicators of social facts. Because social facts are external to individuals, they cannot be reduced to their individual manifestations, which are always partly social and partly unique to the individual. Social facts are also not shared by each and every member of a society in the same degree. Thus, Durkheim argues, social facts can have only society as such as its substratum, and it is society, as a reality *sui generis* (of its own kind), that is the object of sociology. Because society cannot be reduced to individual-level ways of acting, sociology cannot be reduced to psychology.

In terms of its methodology, Durkheim's sociology is based on the maxim that social facts must be considered as things. This basic principle implies that the sociologist must discard all preconceptions about society. Differentiated from the normative orientations of social philosophy, sociology must be conducted from a value-free framework in order to objectively study society as a moral order. Additionally, the sociologist should define the subject matter in terms of its common external characteristics and without exclusion of any relevant phenomena. This rule is important because many subject matters in sociology, such as family, religion, and law, also form part of other types of knowledge at the personal and social level, such as morality, religion, and politics, and relatedly have a terminological usage in everyday language that may not be sociologically appropriate. Sociological definitions of social facts are arrived at on the basis of the observable dimensions of the phenomenon under investigation. Crime, by example, is classified as behavior that receives punishment. Finally, the sociologist must isolate social facts from their individual manifestation so that they can be studied objectively without too much variation from one individual case to the next.

The empirical study of social facts in Durkheim's models proceeds from a description of types of societies in terms of degrees of complexity to their explanation in terms of cause and function. The function of a social fact refers to the purpose it fulfills, whereas the cause of a social fact must be located historically in an antecedent factor.

Sociological functions and causes are always social and cannot be retrieved in the individual psyche. Once cause and function are identified, a sociological method of proof by comparison can be conducted. In the comparative method, cases are compared whereby two social facts are simultaneously absent or present, so that the variations displayed in these combinations can be discovered to provide evidence that a fact (cause) led to another fact (effect). This method is guided by the basic rule that one cause leads to one effect. Durkheim realizes that such a method cannot actually prove causes and effects, but it can lead to falsifications. Also, a stability of findings from a large number of cases adds value to inferences on causal links and functional patterns.

The social division of labor

Durkheim applied his sociological methodology to the study of several important social facts, most famous among which are his studies on suicide, religion, and the social division of labor. Durkheim's work on the division of labor, first published in 1893 and originally written as his doctoral dissertation, contains his basic theory on the evolution and nature of society, including the transformation of law. The central purpose of Durkheim's work is to construct a science of society as a moral order and to discover empirically how social solidarity is maintained in modern society despite the growing autonomy of the individual that has resulted from the division of labor. To Durkheim, importantly, the division of labor is not only and not even primarily an economic reality but a much broader societal phenomenon. Durkheim therefore speaks of the social rather than the economic division of labor.

Durkheim argues that the division of labor is a result of a more encompassing evolution from mechanical to organic societies. Mechanical societies are composed of similar replicated parts, such as families, hordes, and clans. Within such societies, the *conscience collective* or collective consciousness,[2] defined as "the totality of beliefs and

---

[2] Durkheim's term *conscience collective* has been translated into English both as "collective consciousness" and "collective conscience." Both expressions can be misleading and should, in any case, not be understood to imply any psychologistic reading of a group mind. With this qualification in mind, I hold on in this book to the term "collective consciousness" because it is most commonly used.

sentiments common to the average members of a society" (Durkheim 1893b: 38–39), reflects a type of solidarity that is achieved through similarity, for the collective practices and beliefs of groups in mechanical societies are shared by all of their members. Because the common belief systems are strong and there is virtually no individual differentiation, any offense against the collective consciousness, even when it pertains only to one member of the group, is perceived as a threat to the entire social order.

Over the course of history, Durkheim argues that mechanical societies gradually evolved into organic societies made up of functionally different organs, each of which performs a specialized role. While the bonds of tradition and family are loosened, the individual acquires special status both in terms of rights and responsibilities. The nature of the collective consciousness in organic societies is such that its hold over individuals is based on their distinct roles and contributions. Social solidarity, in other words, is achieved through differentiation. Organic societies are marked by a plurality of different value and belief systems. Violations of the collective consciousness will therefore be treated as offenses by individuals against individuals. Durkheim thus shows that although solidarity today is different in modern society, it is no less social and forceful than the solidary bonds of old.

Durkheim's theory of the causes of the evolution from mechanical to organic societies, like his perspective of the essence of what constitutes the division of labor, presents a radical alternative to historical materialism. Durkheim argues that two sets of conditions have to be fulfilled to enable the transformation from a mechanical to an organic society. First, certain material developments have to take place at the demographic level. There has to be a drawing together of individuals and an increase in active exchanges among them. Durkheim calls this an increase in a society's dynamic or moral density. The social volume, i.e., the total population of a society, has to increase as well. More dense and more populous societies necessitate a division of labor because the struggle for existence becomes more strenuous. The level of competition among people who are drawn together increases, leading to migrations. But once certain boundaries are met, migration is no longer possible and society will begin to differentiate internally in such a way that its members become interdependent. These material developments are necessary but insufficient conditions for the transition towards organic societies. Second, certain ideal developments have to be met, including a weakening of the influence of traditions and an increase in individualism in the belief system. The relative loss of influence of tradition occurs because in modern societies people are no longer bound to their place of origin but can spread out over relatively wide areas. The greater independence of individuals in relation to the group is demonstrated by the fact that the collective consciousness becomes progressively indeterminate and abstract.

Along with the division of labor, there is a general trend for social life to become regulated in a way that secures individual variation and social solidarity. Durkheim argues that it is only under exceptional circumstances that the division of labor does not produce organic solidarity, either because it takes place under conditions of an absence of rules regulating social relations (anomie) or because it is forced under conditions of economic-material inequalities. Only under such exceptional circumstances, pathological consequences, such as an abnormally high degree of suicide, can be expected. Economic life as such is not normal or pathological, Durkheim contends, it is its regulation or the lack thereof that determines its consequences.

Law and the evolution of society

Sociologists of law are fortunate to be able to rely on explicit insights on law developed by Durkheim in his study of the division of labor as well as in several of his subsequent studies.[3] The reason for this peculiar interest is that Durkheim conceived of law as the most important observable manifestation of the collective consciousness and its transformation. Because the collective consciousness is "an

---

[3] Next to his work on the social division of labor (Durkheim 1893a translated as 1893b), Durkheim's other central writings on law include a collection of lectures on politics and rights (Durkheim 1900a translated as 1900b) and a study on the evolution of punishment (Durkheim 1901a translated as 1901b). Particularly helpful among the secondary sources is Roger Cotterrell's (1999) book-length study on Durkheim's sociology of law, morality, and politics. See also the overviews by Chazel 1991; Clarke 1976; Cotterrell 1977; Lukes and Scull 1983; Tiryakian 1964; Vogt 1993.

entirely moral phenomenon which by itself is not amenable to exact observation and especially not to measurement" (Durkheim 1893b: 24), Durkheim studies law as the visible symbol of social solidarity. He classifies law not on the basis of juridical conceptions (such as the distinction between private and public law), but sociologically on the basis of the types of sanctions that are applied to the violations of legal rules. The attention Durkheim paid to law was thus primarily methodological: law serves as an indicator of social solidarity and, specifically, the development of mechanical to organic solidarity, which Durkheim argues can be observed in the evolution of law from a repressive to a restitutive system.

The essential characteristic of repressive law in mechanical societies is that it represents the strong unity that exists in society among the members of a strongly cohesive and simple unit such as a clan or horde. Repressive law is typically religious in nature. The moral beliefs and justifications on which repressive law and punishment are based are often not explicitly specified because they are widely known among the members of society. Infractions against the rules of repressive legal systems are immediately and severely punished because they threaten the existence of the collectivity as a whole. Removal from society through banishment or death is the typical form of punishment in mechanical societies.

In organic societies, there is a differentiation of restitutive and repressive law. Because individuals are more and more differentiated from one another, legal regulations are more abstract and general so they can apply universally to all individuals while not leveling the differences that exist among them. The elaboration of contract law, for instance, allows for a specification of relations among individuals, whereby the state only acts to oversee mutual obligations. In organic societies, law is secularized and highly codified. The sanctions that are applied to violations of restitutive law are oriented at a restoration of social relations among individuals, as in the case of monetary compensation, or between individual and society, as in the case of prison sentences that allow for release back into society. In organic societies, criminal law still serves repressive functions, but the growth of civil law indicates most clearly the rise of restitutive law. The increasing relevance of restitutive forms of law that accompany the development of the division of labor, according to Durkheim, ensure that the division of labor in economic life and elsewhere does not, under normal conditions, lead to social problems or disorder. Against Marx, Durkheim contends that the essential function of the division of labor is precisely to integrate society. In order for social solidarity in organic societies to be successfully achieved, however, the division of labor has to be accompanied by certain rules that regulate cooperation among the various specialized functions and roles. Durkheim argues that intermediary institutions, especially professional groups, can aid in this function by virtue of their placement in between the state and the individual.

Law and rights

In a series of lectures on morality and law delivered in the last decade of the nineteenth century and several times thereafter, Durkheim (1900a, 1900b) devoted special attention to the role of the state in the creation of rights. Primarily a work in political sociology, this study includes discussions on professional ethics, especially the role of professional groups, the function and form of the state, particularly the democratic state, and various rules and rights guaranteed by the state. The latter section contains additional insights by Durkheim on law.

As in *De la Division du Travail Social* (1893a), Durkheim turns to the study of moral and juridical facts as the observable expressions of morals and rights. Durkheim starts from the viewpoint that homicide and theft are the supremely immoral acts, graver than violations of professional and civic morals, because the rules concerning crimes against the person and against property are so general that they extend beyond the boundaries of any particular society. Historically, this was not always the case, as crimes against the group as a whole, such as religious crimes, were traditionally punished more severely. However, in contemporary (organic) society, crimes against the person and against personal property arouse the greatest resentment and receive the harshest sanction because they violate a morality that places the qualities of the individual above all else.

In a brief discussion on homicide, Durkheim engages primarily in a criminological analysis of murder rates, but his discussion on the nature of property rights forms the basis of a sociological theory of contract and law. According to Durkheim, the nature of property has historically changed as have the rights that are attached to it. Legally, the rights over property have been divided among three kinds: *ius utendi, ius fruendi*, and *ius abutendi*. The *ius utendi* (right to use) refers to the right to make use of things, such as the right to live in a rented property and the right to walk in a public park, while the *ius fruendi* (right to enjoy) is the right to the products of property, such as the rights to the rent on a house and the interest on a loan. Neither right includes a right to transform the property to which the right is attached. In the *ius abutendi* (right to use up), however, the property that is owned may be transformed or even destroyed, albeit under specified conditions. This legal typology, Durkheim argues, cannot lead to a specification of the essence of property, for what is distinct about (private) property is that the powers that are attached to it, no matter how broad or limited, are always exclusive to the owner. Private property is a right to possession that is exclusive, at least towards other individuals, as in some circumstances the state may still claim certain rights.

What is the basis of the private property right, according to Durkheim? To exist, private property must be respected. Mirroring his theory on the evolution of religion, Durkheim argues that it is not the thing that is owned nor the sacred or divine blessing it has received, but society as such that endows property with an exclusive right. This can be observed from a study of the contract as the primary means (besides inheritance) through which property can be transferred. Innovations in law were required as contracts evolved from so-called real contracts, whereby the contract takes place only when something is actually transferred, to consensual contracts of agreement to which an oath or invocation of a divine being was attached. From the consensual contract by solemn ritual evolved the purely consensual contract whereby the declaration of the will alone is sufficient grounds for the binding nature of the agreement. The power of transfer is then completely mental: "by the very fact that it is consensual, the contract is covered by sanction" (Durkheim 1900b: 203). The only condition attached to consent is that it must be freely given. In a final stage of development, the contract also has to be just in terms of the objective consequences of the contract. To be just, the contract must be objectively equitable.

Law and punishment

Besides his central works on law in the division of labor and his lectures on law and morality, Durkheim contributed a plethora of smaller essays and review articles in the areas of law and crime to the *Année Sociologique* journal. Among these articles is a study concerning certain quantitative and qualitative changes in punishment, which Durkheim argued to have taken place in the course of the transition from primitive to modern society (Durkheim 1901a, 1901b). Corresponding to his ideas on the evolution from mechanical to organic societies, Durkheim specifically forwards two theses on the evolution of punishment. The first thesis holds that punishment is less intense in more developed societies in which the central power is not absolutist. The repressive laws in mechanical societies regulate social relations unilaterally in a manner that accords all power and rights to one party. Prototypical is the master–slave relation. The justification of such laws is typically religious in nature and regulations are sanctioned on a supernatural basis. Punishment is intense and includes corporal punishments, such as the flogging of slaves, and symbolic of the crime that was committed, such as the chopping off of hands in the case of theft. Capital punishment exists in the form of public torture practices whereby the death of the offender is a final but almost incidental outcome.

Turning to modern society, Durkheim introduces a qualification that he had not used in his work on the division of labor. Durkheim recognizes that modern societies can still be absolutist, as in the case of autocratic monarchies and dictatorships, while being modernized in other respects such as in the economic realm. In the case of contemporary absolutist societies, punishment can remain harsh and involve such methods as public executions. Durkheim considers the case of absolutist modern societies not paradoxical to his theory on the transition from mechanical to organic societies, because an absolutist regime in modern times is in Durkheim's viewpoint a pathological, not a normal development. The high degree of repressiveness of punishment in this type of society, then, is not fundamental to its nature but is instead a function of particular historical circumstances. Under normal conditions of socio-historical development, modern societies are democratic, and punishment is less intense. The reason is that laws in democratic organic societies regulate relationships in bilateral terms as a contract among two or more parties, all of whom are considered equal before the law. The rules of such legal systems are also secular and sanctioned in terms of inner-worldly relations. Any offense is an offense against another human and, because of its inner-worldly orientation, does not arouse the same indignation as a violation against religious laws.

For his second thesis on the evolution of punishment, Durkheim again relies on the distinction between mechanical and organic society to argue that punishment in modern society becomes typically a deprivation of liberty. In other words, in organic societies, the prison system becomes the dominant form of punishment. The reason is that the prison provides not only an individualized form of punishment but is also purposively oriented at reintegrating the individual back into society and restoring social relations. In mechanical societies, conversely, imprisonment could not fulfill any such need since violations of law were conceived as threatening to the collectivity as a whole and could therefore not tolerate any reintegration.

The legacy of Durkheim

As in the case of Max Weber, the influence of the writings of Durkheim in modern sociology is so profound that it is impossible to conceive of sociology without his contributions. Durkheim's insistence on the need for a systematic study of society as a reality irreducible to psychological states counts among his most significant methodological insights. In terms of a theory of society, Durkheim's work contributed to the development of a distinctly sociological perspective that focused on the societal constitution of social life in the non-materialist terms of a moral order centered around the integrative strength of the collective consciousness. Studying the integrative capacities of society in terms of a transition from mechanical to organic societies, Durkheim turned to the study of law as an observable indicator of morality. Durkheim's methodological choice is obviously fortuitous to the sociology of law in having provided both a novel approach to the sociological study of law and a theory on the evolution of law. In several later works, moreover, Durkheim also studied the historical transformation of the state, of rights, and of punishment.

Restricted to the secondary literature that has explicitly addressed the merits and limitations of Durkheim's sociology of law, both empirical and theoretical criticisms have been offered. In terms of the empirical elements in Durkheim's sociology of law, several studies have been conducted that have led to doubts about the unilinear development Durkheim sketched from repressive to restitutive law and the related changes in punishment (Lukes and Scull 1983). The empirical weakness in Durkheim's work on the division of labor was first brought up by Robert Merton (1934), who argues that Durkheim relied on deficient ethnographic data and offered no basis for the association he sketched between types of law and social solidarity. Merton suggests that research from numerous field studies has demonstrated that primitive societies, marked by a low degree of division of labor, possess restitutive law, which Durkheim reserved for organic societies. Likewise, advanced societies also reveal important elements of strong communal interests.

In line with Merton's criticisms, a systematic study on legal evolution has been undertaken by Richard Schwartz and James Miller (1964) that has implications for aspects of Durkheim's sociology of law. On the basis of information from fifty-one societies, Schwarz and Miller focus specifically on three aspects of legal development: counsel, defined as the use of non-kin advocates in the settlement of disputes; mediation, or the use of a non-kin third party intervening in dispute settlement; and police, conceived as the specialized armed force organized to enforce laws. The findings of the study indicate that the function of police is associated with social development, contrary to Durkheim's theory. The reason for the deficiency in Durkheim's thought, Schwartz and Miller suggest, may be that Durkheim employed different criteria in measuring penal and non-penal legal systems. For the existence of repressive law, Durkheim maintained that relatively little organization was needed, whereas restitutive law was said to exist only where an elaborate system of magistrates, lawyers, and tribunals has developed. Thus, Schwartz and Miller argue, Durkheim ensured proof of his theory, not on the basis of fact, but as a result of conceptual ambiguity. An evolution from repressive to restitutive law does not appear to be associated with the division of labor.

Although methodological concerns can be raised concerning the inference of historical conclusions on the basis of comparative data (Schwartz 1965; Turkel 1979; Udy 1965), the implications for Durkheim's theories of comparative studies similar to Schwartz and Miller's has been addressed by a number of scholars. Howard

Wimberley (1973), for instance, conducted a comparative study of legal development that showed the relevance of the influence of the strength of a society's authority system, a political variable which Durkheim did not consider in his original work on the division of labor. In the light of such findings, Uprenda Baxi (1974) suggests that Durkheim's work can be refined. For example, Baxi suggests that the absence of police, as it was defined and measured in the Schwartz and Miller study, might still imply that other systems of enforcement exist in the considered societies. The very creation, application, and authoritative nature of decision-making processes themselves may fulfill enforcement functions. As to the presence of restitutive law in simple societies, Baxi argues that Durkheim did not argue that restitutive law does not exist in societies with a low degree of division of labor, but that it there holds a lesser position.

In reply to Baxi's concerns, Schwartz (1974) argues that his study of legal evolution was not primarily intended to prove or disprove Durkheim. A true test of Durkheim would have to rely on an unambiguous formulation of Durkheim's theory into a testable hypothesis to compare the relative degree of repressive and restitutive sanctions over a range of societies differing in degree of division of labor. A re-analysis Schwartz conducted on the basis of Baxi's criticism over the conceptualization of police and enforcement yields findings that contradict Durkheim's theory. Other scholars have likewise argued that the actual development of law is the reverse of Durkheim's theory (Sheleff 1975). Anthropological studies show that primitive societies differentiate between religious and secular laws and also exhibit legal systems that contain reciprocal obligations. Likewise, comparative and historical analyses reveal that modern legal systems contain many repressive aspects, not only in the traditional areas of criminal law, but also in areas concerning private behavior and religious ethics where a repressive logic has infiltrated.

Durkheim's work on the evolution of punishment has likewise been scrutinized. In a systematic study of forty-eight societies, Steven Spitzer (1975) finds that, contrary to Durkheim's theory, punitive intensity is inversely related to societal complexity, although political absolutism is seen to vary with punishment in the direction Durkheim specified. Collective definitions of deviance do not disappear as societies become more complex, but, affirming Durkheim's view, offenses against collective objects are punished more severely. This association, however, holds for both mechanical and organic societies. Against Durkheim, also, simple societies are more likely to punish individual offenses more severely, while organic societies tend to reserve harsh punishments for crimes against the collectivity. Finally, while Durkheim rightly observed that the deprivation of liberty in the form of the prison has become the most applied form of punishment in modern societies, he neglected that other forms of exclusion besides the prison, such as banishment, are common to primitive societies.

In terms of their theoretical implications, empirical studies on legal and penal evolution have led to the criticism that Durkheim viewed law and punishment too exclusively as reflections of societal value systems and in terms of a functional need for normative integration, while disregarding the organizational dimensions of law as a system of rules imposed by political authorities as part of the instrumental apparatus of systems of domination (Cartwright and Schwartz 1973; Spitzer 1975). It then becomes important to study the power dynamics that exist in the creation and administration of legal systems (Calavita et al. 1991). Relatedly, the Durkheimian emphasis on the function of punishment to express and strengthen social solidarity might also benefit from a more careful analysis of the historically determined causes and objective consequences as well as functions of punishment in its multiple forms (see Chapter 11).

Theoretical models of law and punishment that are critical of some of Durkheim's argument can still value the Durkheimian approach for its ability to analyze law and punishment, not as abstract histories of ideas, but in close conjunction with the structural characteristics of society. More radical interpretations, of course, argue that the problems with Durkheim's evolutionary sketch must have a "domino effect on his work in general" (Sheleff 1975: 19), justifying a dismissal of Durkheimian sociology or at least leading to an extreme rein-terpretation of his work (Pearce 1989). In a critical reception of Durkheim's theories of punishment, David Garland (1983) makes the astute observation that criticisms of Durkheim that are based solely on an empirical examination of hypotheses derived from his work (which are not always clearly related to Durkheim; see e.g., Lanza-Kaduce et al. 1979) must remain modest on the theoretical implications thereof for an assessment of Durkheim's sociology. Not only can differences exist between the concepts used in Durkheim's work and the indicators that are employed in empirical studies (Baxi

1974; Cotterrell 1977), different theoretical models may underlie the propositional models that are constructed in order to meet empirical adequacy criteria (Gibbs 2003). Irrespective of criticisms on specific theses offered by Durkheim, therefore, it is possible to apply elements of Durkheim's sociological approach in contemporary research, for instance in the development of a cultural sociology of punishment (Garland 1991b, 2006; Smith 2003; see Chapter 11).

In line with the emphasis on theory as approach, a variety of diverging interpretations of Durkheim's sociology of law have been offered that, as in the case of the reception of Weber's writings, anticipate some of the theoretical differentiation that has emerged with the development of the modern sociology of law. Even more so than in the case of Weber, also, Durkheim's work has oftentimes been selectively reviewed, typically concentrating on his book on the division of labor, but not incorporating his later works on law, rights, and punishment (which were not widely available, especially not in English translation, until more recently). Also overlooked have been the contributions by some of the legal specialists and law professors associated with the *Année Sociologique* and their influence on and from Durkheim (Chazel 1991; Cochez 2004; Cotterrell 2005; Vogt 1983). With these qualifications in mind, several theoretical puzzles have been identified in Durkheim's work on law.

Among the most discussed theoretical elements in Durkheim's legal sociology is the conceptualization of law and state as reflective (indices) of the collective consciousness, as measurable manifestations of a society's value system. Durkheim recognized that the state (through its legislative functions) and the legal system (in the administration of justice) also contributed to form the collective consciousness. Yet, these conceptions of state and law—in their dual, reflective and creative, roles *vis-à-vis* social values—remain in an unclarified tension in Durkheim's work (Clarke 1976; Clifford-Vaughan and Scotford-Morton 1967). Roger Cotterrell (1977) has in this respect remarked that the reflective nature of law only applies to the repressive legal type, which can express the strong collective nature of mechanical society, but not to the restitutive type that is typical for organic societies because in these societies there are no collectively held values to express. This interpretation, however, overlooks that Durkheim's conception of the reflective nature of law applies to the structure, not the content of the collective consciousness. In mechanical societies, law expresses unity, and in organic societies, law expresses diversity. Under conditions of an organic society, also, law becomes not only more organized, it is then also in more need of justification to maintain legitimacy (Gould 1993).

The conceptual tensions in Durkheim's work exhibit two problematic qualities, the relevance of which will become more prominent as the sociology of law unfolds. One, Durkheim did not draw a sufficient distinction between values and norms and for the better part assumes that value systems produce distinct normative patterns in rather unproblematic ways. In relation to this undifferentiated concept of morality, Durkheim conceives of law only on the basis of its higher degree of organization, particularly through the administration of justice in courts. Two, conceiving of both state and law as reflective of a society's value system or collective consciousness, Durkheim does not always sufficiently differentiate and outline the connections between the state and the legal system. It is mainly in relation to this critique that some scholars have argued that Durkheim overlooked power dimensions in the creation of legal systems, especially in societies that are characterized by the development of a strong state (Lukes and Scull 1983; Spitzer 1985). Others, however, have challenged this negative assessment as being based on a theory that is not Durkheim's, but one derived from a conflict-theoretical tradition that, as will be discussed in Chapter 6, stretches back to Marx. A re-evaluation of Durkheim's legal sociology is therefore in order, specifically on the basis of his views on the regulatory functions of the professional group (Cotterrell 1999; Didry 2000). The basic intent of Durkheim's work on the division of labor was not the construction of a sociology of law but of a more encompassing theory of integration, which implied, contrary to Marx, that it is not the economic order as such but the collective consciousness accompanying economic development which determines the degree of cohesion of society. In the case of organic societies, Durkheim argued, integration is not always accomplished because of anomic conditions of weak or insufficient regulation. Therefore, intermediary institutions, particularly professional groups, had to be placed between the state and the individual to secure adequate regulation. Durkheim was well aware that the state could be a less than efficient regulator and that the law legislated by the state did not always serve to maintain social solidarity, for which reason precisely he suggested to shift the necessary regulatory powers to the professional group.

The question of whether the law must be viewed in close connection with the political system is not primarily an empirical, but a theoretical question, one which has occupied the sociology of law throughout its development in the proliferation of diverging schools of thought. Taking a closer look at Durkheim's work in its own terms, it is important to note that the primary intention of Durkheim's legal sociology was to show that the structure of society has an influence on the form and substance of law. Durkheim's studies of law were not primarily meant to construct an evolutionary perspective on the changes in law over time, but to organize the empirical characteristics of law in terms of a theoretical perspective of society (Cotterrell 1977, 1991). The theoretical objective of Durkheim's work serves to order the empirical manifestations of law. In this respect, it can also be suggested that Durkheim's theoretical objectives primarily relate to the social conditions and changes that were taking place in the (organic) society of his days. His theory can therefore not be understood as a theory of legal development across all societies (Turkel 1979). Consequently, it might be more appropriate to conceive of Durkheim's concepts of mechanical and organic society and the companion notions of repressive and restitutive law, not as categories of a typology of society and law, but as ideal-types that can function as heuristic devices to frame historical developments and comparative analyses (Merton 1934).

Finally, it is to be noted that even those scholars who are very critical of some of Durkheim's contributions to the sociology of law recognize that his work is of seminal value in its analytical potential to link the law as a social fact with the extra-legal dimensions of the organization of society. The analytical positioning of law in society is the most fundamental component of any sociology of law. Adopting such an analytical perspective, Durkheim's work also produced many findings that were and remain counter-intuitive in the light of the law's self-understanding and common-sense wisdoms about the nature of law. And although it is clear that Durkheim views law as an expression of the structure of morality and by and large neglected the potential politicization as an instrument of power (Cotterrell 1999), it would be an all too one-sided reading of Durkheim to conclude that he paid no attention to power and conflict. Particularly note-worthy is Durkheim's conception of anomie and his perspective on the role of professional groups, which relate intimately to his study of social integration and law.

Conclusion

The sociology of Emile Durkheim is foundational to sociology in a manner that is on equal footing only with the work of Max Weber. Durkheim's methodological orientation opened the way to the deve-lopment of a structural sociology engaged in causal and functional analysis and led to demarcate the sociological study of society as a unique activity irreducible to other academic enterprises. Likewise, his perspective of society as a moral social order with integrative functions has served as an important source of inspiration (and critique) among modern sociologists. Although the study of law was in Durkheim's work as central as in Weber's (Schluchter 2003), Durkheim's work is generally given somewhat less prominence in the modern sociology of law than Weber's. This differential reception relates to the fact that Weber was more consistently and expertly involved in the study of law, not least because of his technical background in law, than was Durkheim to whom the proper contours of the sociological study of society were more important. Also, the Durkheimian emphasis on the integrative capacities of law has not been as favorably received in modern sociology – especially not during the decades when the sociology of law became more fully institu-tionalized – as has Weber's multidimensional perspective of ration-alization (see Chapter 6). However, it is striking that Durkheim's theoretical program appears to have influenced and stimulated more empirical studies than Weber's work.

As the coming chapters will show, Durkheim and Weber are the two major foundational influences on a wide range of diverging schools of thought. To anticipate these theoretical puzzles and their substantive implications, it will be useful to conclude this section with a brief comparative glance at the contributions of Weber and Durkheim. On a methodological level, Weber advocated an interpre-tive sociology engaged in the unraveling of the motivations driving social actions, whereas Durkheim advocated a structural-level analysis of social facts in terms of a causal and functional analysis. Analyzing the basic structures and processes of society, Weber developed a multidimensional theory focused on the interplay between a mixture of political, economic, cultural, and other societal forces, whereas Durkheim defended a distinctly sociological theory that gave primacy to cultural influences and conceived of material conditions as necessary but insufficient factors. These diverging sociological models led Weber to emphasize rationalization processes based on efficiency standards, while Durkheim placed a premium on the increasingly individualist nature of the collective consciousness. Consequently, Weber conceived of law in terms of its rationalization processes, specifically the increasing reliance in modern law on procedure, whereas Durkheim primarily focused on the integrative capacities of law in the light of changes in the societal value system. As will be revealed in the coming chapters, in having specified the objectives and methods of sociological inquiry, Weber and Durkheim have provided the most foundational theoretical, methodological, and substantive insights on society that remain of concern in sociology, including the sociology of law, until today. Remarkably, however, the intellectual line of progression from the classics to the modern sociology of law is not a direct one, but runs through developments that took place from within the law.

PART II

Development and variations of the sociology of law

4 | *The theoretical move towards the sociological study of law*

The classics of sociology have provided our discipline with a variety of analytical tools that remain useful to this day. Yet, the role of the founders of sociology in the development of an independent sociology of law is ambivalent. Ironically, this qualification applies least of all to the writings of Marx, whose work would become distinctly influential in the sociology of law even though he all but ignored the study of law. The case of Weber is more complicated. Weber's excursions on law were so detailed and rich from a technical viewpoint that they may have inadvertently hindered a proper sociological understanding and adequate reception by a later generation of sociologists. In the case of Durkheim, law was early on in his work a central but primarily methodological interest that reappeared only intermittently in his later work. Central sociological problems of law, such as the form of law under conditions of increasing rationalization and the integrative capacities of law in the light of increasing individualism, are always present in the works of Weber and Durkheim, so much so that they are not always treated separately in the form of a clearly defined specialty field. Besides, the specialization of subfields within sociology is a development that is distinct to modern sociology.

It may have been in part because of the not always clearly demarcated treatment of law in classical thought that modern sociology has only gradually been able to claim a distinct interest in the study of law. More importantly, however, the development of the sociology of law as a disciplinary specialty was slowed down by the monopolization of the study of law in legal scholarship and the development, independent from sociology, of legal thought as it evolved in the profession. To this very day, it remains somewhat of a struggle to have the sociology of law accepted as a distinct and valid enterprise by legal scholars and other legal professionals. Emblematic of this misunderstanding is the curtailment of law as the whole of legal norms and the systematic study thereof for purposes of consistency and, correspondingly, an inability to acknowledge law as a social issue that must be sociologically explored. It is an ironic but consequential reality of the sociological study of law that it has been hampered in its development by the stubborn resistance of forces coming from within its subject matter.

The development of sociological thought, on the one hand, and the monopolization of legal thought by the legal profession, on the other, form the essential forces that can analytically be used to frame the maturation of the sociology of law as an institutionalized specialty. In light of some of the difficulties the institutionalization of the sociology of law faced during the second half of the twentieth century, it is remarkable that in the years prior to and shortly after World War II the prospects of the sociology of law were not unfavorable. The first half of the twentieth century was, in fact, a productive period in the development of the sociology of law. Specifically noteworthy are the writings of several sociologically minded legal scholars and sociologists of law, specifically Leon Petrazycki and the scholars that emanated from his teachings, Nicholas Timasheff, Georges Gurvitch, and Pitirim Sorokin, as well as other European scholars, such as Eugen Ehrlich and Theodor Geiger. The scholarly and sociological orientation to law in the works of these scholars, it will be shown, provides an important intellectual bridge between classical and modern sociology of law.

From scientific jurisprudence to legal sociology: the Eastern-European tradition

Among the European precursors to the modern sociology of law, the legal scholar Leon Petrazycki (1867–1931) stands out for the scientific ambitions and systematic nature of his thought as well as the foundational influence of his work on a number of later scholars in the sociology of law.[1] Born in a wealthy family of Polish ancestry,

---

[1] Petrazycki published his writings in German, Russian, and Polish. His most important work available in English translation is *Law and Morality* (Petrazycki 1905–1907), originally published in 1955, which contains selections and summaries of two Russian volumes that originally appeared in 1905 and 1907 (see also Petrazycki 1933). Of two early German-language books, written while Petrazycki studied in Berlin, the two-volume *Die Lehre vom Einkommen* (Petrazycki 1893/1895) contains an Appendix that already includes some of his

Petrazycki grew up in a part of Russia that had been annexed from Poland. He graduated from the law school in Kiev, Russia, and spent a few years on a scholarship in Berlin, Germany, where he already wrote much of his later more elaborately developed theory of law. In 1898, Petrazycki became a professor of philosophy of law in St. Petersburg, Russia, and also served as a member of the legislature and the Supreme Court when Russia went through brief democratic periods. After the Bolshevik Revolution, he fled Russia and went to Warsaw, where he took up the first chair of sociology.

Petrazycki was like no other European scholar of the time engaged in the systematization of a scientific, more specifically a psychological-realistic, theory of law. Petrazycki would thereby also contribute, especially via the works of some of his students, to the development of a more distinctly sociological tradition. Petrazycki's theory starts from the basic premise that theories of law need to be grounded on either a normative or a realistic perspective. According to Petrazycki ([1905–1907] 1955: 9), a normative theory of norms is always a theory of ideals, of "phantasms" or "phantoms," and it can therefore not be scientific. Adopting a realistic perspective, Petrazycki considers the reality of law to be found in the factual experiences of law on the part of human beings. Legal phenomena, thus considered, are "psychic processes" (1955: 8). Psychic or mental processes include the categories of the active will, passive cognition, passive emotions, and bilateral impulsions. Impulsions are bilateral because they refer to a passive experience of something to which an urge actively responds. Impulsions induce behavior, especially when they are strong. Most impulsions in everyday life are relatively weak and unconscious, but conditions such as the counteracting of an impulsion and its provocation will strengthen them.

Some impulsions, such as hunger and fear, lead to a specific type of behavior, whereas other impulsions, such as a command, may produce different kinds of behavior depending on the contents. Among the latter kind, the impulsion of duty is particularly relevant for

basic theoretical ideas. Much of Petrazycki's later work remains unpublished and is available only on the basis of drafts and some of his students' lecture notes (Lande 1975). For expositions of Petrazycki's work, see Banakar 2002; Baum 1967; Clifford-Vaughan and Scotford-Morton 1967; Denzin 1975; Gorecki 1975a, 1975b; Kojder 2006; Lande 1975; Motyka 2006; Skapska 1987; Sorokin 1956; Timasheff 1947, 1955.

Petrazycki's legal theory. The impulsion of duty occurs in response to an idea of conduct that is evaluated in normative terms. The idea may refer to something judged to be wrong and thus lead to an experience of duty to not do something, or it may refer to something right, creating the duty to act accordingly. The latter category, consisting of so-called ethical impulsions, forms the essence of the reality of law. Ethical impulsions can be of two kinds, depending on whether or not the duty that is experienced corresponds to another person's right. Morality refers to ethical impulsions to which no rights of another correspond, while law is defined as the whole of ethical impulsions whereby someone's duty corresponds to another's right. Because the rights of others are involved, legal impulsions are stronger than moral ones. In order to be effective, legal impulsions need to be clearly defined and uniformly interpreted. The former function is reserved for the legislative bodies in a society, be they the legislature (at the level of the state), legal customs, precedents, or small-group rule-making decisions such as they are reached by parents, teachers, and friends. Legal interpretation is a major function of legal scholars and of the judiciary.

The making explicit of a legal impulsion can be very sharply formulated by an act of lawmaking, such as an enactment of law by statute or a decision in a court. Petrazycki refers to the whole of such legal impulsions that are based on images of a fact of lawmaking, at the level of the state or any other subsection of society, as positive law. By contrast, intuitive law refers to impulsions that are perceived as binding even without an image of any fact of lawmaking. Within the category of positive law, Petrazycki pays special attention to those impulsions encompassing images of lawmaking that are officially protected and enforced by state officials. Referred to as official positive law, this category of legal impulsions is more uniform across society, while the intuitive laws of individuals and social sub-groups may differ widely among one another and, furthermore, differ from official positive law. The discrepancies between intuitive law and officially positive law is one of the core problems associated with law in society. As people experience intuitive law to be very different from the positive law that is officially sanctioned, they experience the legal and social order as unjust. Groups within society may try to change positive law to be brought into accord with their sense of intuitive law. As other powerful groups resist any changes to positive law, the strength of intuitive law on the part of deprived groups may grow to the point where a revolution can ensue.

According to Petrazycki, legal impulsions have important consequences and perform important functions in society. Legal impulsions bring about an organization of power and a distribution of wealth in society as well as a corresponding coordination of action. Especially when impulsions become uniform, coordinated systems of political and economic behavior are brought about. This process accounts for the rise of the state as the dominant political structure on the basis of a concentration of impulsions of supreme power, on the one hand, and the market as the dominant economic form on the basis of binding contracts, on the other. The psychological basis of the organization of power and the distribution of wealth brought about by positive law are central in Petrazycki's theory.

Legal impulsions are also an important source of social change. In general, Petrazycki adopts an evolutionary framework of increasing complexity. Intuitive law first develops in simple societies as a psychological response to behavior that is either harmful or useful for the group. Due to a need for increasing uniformity among these impulsions, intuitive law becomes based more and more on lawmaking facts, thereby creating positive law. The establishment of positive law, in turn, produces new legal impulsions, which can be transformed at the intuitive level. Lawmakers have a specially significant role in seeking to bring about social change by purposely directing impulsions. This function of social engineering or legal policy, to be understood in the psychological sense of bringing about a change in attitudes, Petrazycki considers essential in law. The ultimate goal of legal policy is the peaceful co-existence of people, or what Petrazycki calls "active rational love," while other goals, such as crime prevention and economic growth, are secondary goals. In order to achieve these goals, lawmakers should have scientific evidence of the impacts their lawmaking activities will have on the human mind. Lawmakers would have to rely on the insights from scientists to determine this impact. Should the experts disagree, experimental tests can be conducted. Changing people's attitudes through law, legal policy ultimately has an important educational objective.

The work of Petrazycki had an immediate influence on the theoretical development towards the sociological study of law, especially as a result of his early teaching at the University of St. Petersburg, where a so-called "Petrazycki school" was formed, that consisted of, most notably, Nicholas Timasheff, Georges Gurvitch, and Pitirim Sorokin. What is peculiar about this movement towards the sociology of law is both the explicit attention Petrazycki's students paid to law and, at the same time, the manner in which they moved toward a more distinctly sociological treatment, away from Petrazycki's psychological theory. This movement to sociology, however, came at a price, as it also entailed, particularly in the work of Sorokin, a move away from the study of law or, at least, from a systematic effort to develop a sociology of law. Additionally, the Petrazycki school dissipated in both a geographical and an institutional sense and lacked the cohesion necessary to build a lasting tradition. A review of the main ideas from the Petrazycki school will bring out some essential aspects of their contributions to the sociology of law.

Nicholas Timasheff (1886–1970) followed the path of his teacher Petrazycki by leaving his native Russia in 1921, a few years after the Bolshevik Revolution.[2] Timasheff subsequently worked in Germany, Czechoslovakia, and France, before settling in the United States in 1936, where he taught at Harvard for a few years and then moved to Fordham University in New York. Like his mentor at the University of St. Petersburg, Timasheff was primarily interested in developing a realistic theory of law, one, however, that would be distinctly concerned with the social dimensions of law. Timasheff defined the sociology of law, in relation to jurisprudence as the study of legal norms, as the study of human behavior in society inasmuch as it is influenced by legal norms and, in turn, influences those legal norms. Sociology of law is nomographically oriented at discovering the laws of causality concerning the dual relation between norms and normative behavior, while jurisprudence is an ideographic science oriented at the logical interdependence of legal norms. Sociology and jurisprudence are thus complementary but separate disciplines. Philosophy of law, conceived as the evaluative study of the ultimate ends of law, is not a third scholarly discipline next to jurisprudence and sociology, however, for it cannot be scientific, according to Timasheff.

---

[2] Timasheff's most important work is *Introduction to the Sociology of Law* (Timasheff 1939; see also Timasheff 1938, 1957). On the person and work of Timasheff, see Hunt 1979; Schiff 1981.

Timasheff conceives of law as a social phenomenon on the basis of a theory of social coordination as the result of the recognition by members of society, or the imposition on them, of stable patterns of conduct. Timasheff differentiates four forms of coordination. Ethical and non-ethical types of coordination are based on the norms that are, respectively, approved and disapproved by the members of a society. Imperative and non-imperative forms of coordination refer to coordination based on, respectively, norms that are imposed by a centralized authority and norms that are not so imposed but stem from the mutual influence among members of a society. On the basis of this classification, Timasheff constructs a typology of coordination types: non-ethical non-imperative coordination, ethical non-imperative coordination, non-ethical imperative coordination, and ethical imperative coordination. The first type is purely theoretical and cannot be found in any existing society. The second, purely ethical type is created by custom and morals. The third, purely imperative type of coordination is created by despotic governments, whereby regulations and decrees are promulgated that lack any sanctioning by group conviction. The fourth type is most important, because ethico-imperative coordination is created by law to combine group conviction and centralized power activity. Law to Timasheff is thus a cultural phenomenon formed at the overlapping section of ethics and power.

Timasheff's theoretical perspective of the sociology of law proceeds to discuss ethics and power as two central types of action coordination before analyzing law at the intersection of both. Timasheff conceives of ethics and power as social forces that contribute to the social order as does law. All three institutional spheres are considered in terms of the manner in which they contribute to the creation of social uniformities in behavior at a societal level. Parting from Petrazycki's psychological theory, Timasheff focuses on the social level of standardized behavioral tendencies or habits that correspond to ethics, power, and law. In the case of law, Timasheff argues that legal rules contribute to the equilibrium of the social order by being both recognized and obeyed by the members of society while simultaneously also being recognized and supported by the rulers of a centralized authority. Behavior that does not conform to legal expectations falls outside the social order: by definition, coordinated behavior is normal behavior. Norms that are not recognized by the state are not law but form part of custom and morality. Through law, therefore, both the convictions of the group and the activities of the power center combine to secure the realization of stable patterns of conduct.

The primary function and observable consequence of law, according to Timasheff, is to secure equilibrium by the production of uniform and conforming social behavior in order to achieve peace, security, and organization in society. To Timasheff, the function and the actual consequences of law in principle overlap: "the triumph of law is the rule" (Timasheff 1937: 226). "What is the force of law?" thus becomes the central question in Timasheff's sociology of law, and the answer lies in the simultaneous enforcement of the law by central power and its validity among the members of society (1937: 226). The coalescence of ethics and power in law, according to Timasheff, is not a matter of premise or assumption but is an observable fact of life. Primitive societies, therefore, had no law for they were exclusively guided by social norms of ethics. The gradual transformation from primitive to modern forms of coordination, i.e., the development of law, was primarily influenced by changes in the activities of the forces of power as a factor of differentiation. Active power centers began to intervene in the settlement of disputes surrounding social norms and gradually this role of enforcement became a permanent function of power. At this stage, law is first created, from which further types of law differentiate as new legal rules are explicitly proclaimed through lawmaking. If there is a mere recognition among the members of a society concerning ethical rules, the state can sanction them to form customary law. If the state sanctions laws that are explicitly created by power structures other than the state itself, there is autonomous law. And, finally, if the state also creates law through legislation on top of enforcing it and other types of law, there is state law. Although there is a historical trend observable, according to Timasheff, from customary to autonomous and state law, all three types continue to co-exist in modern society. Across modern societies, moreover, legal orders tend to be very similar to one another because of a similarity of influencing conditions and as a result of a process of imitation whereby one legal system is used as the model for other systems of law.

Georges Gurvitch (1894–1965) was a Russian-born scholar educated at the University of St. Petersburg who, like his spiritual mentor Petrazycki, fled his native land after the communist takeover by the

Bolsheviks.[3] In 1920, Gurvitch moved to Prague, where he stayed for five years, after which he permanently settled in France, interrupted only by World War II when he taught at the New School for Social Research in the United States. Like Timasheff, Gurvitch adopted principles of Petrazycki's basic notion of law transposed from the level of individual psychology to the level of a sociology of society.

Most essentially, Gurvitch develops a dialectical perspective on law that leads to a complex classification of various types of law depending on various levels of social reality and corresponding types of sociological analysis. Gurvitch defines law in objectivist terms as the whole of legal norms that are factually embodied in a particular social context. More specifically, legal norms are normative facts that attempt to realize a particular idea of justice "through multilateral imperative-attributive regulation based on a determined link between claims and duties" (Gurvitch 1942: 59). Sociology of law is defined as the study of the full social reality of law, including the symbols of law as they are embodied in rules, the values associated with law, and the collective beliefs and intuitions that relate to these values.

Gurvitch's perspective on the social dimensions of law relates to his conception of social reality as consisting of various planes or depth-levels of analysis. The highest level of social organization is the morphological level of the physical characteristics of objects and institutions. The deepest level of social reality, to which Gurvitch pays most attention, consists of a society's collective mentality or human spirit. As a final analytical consideration in Gurvitch's perspective, a typology is constructed of three problems in the sociology of law. First, as a matter of systematic sociology or micro-sociology, law is studied as a function of forms of sociality and levels of reality. Second, differential or typological sociology includes the study of the legal typologies of particular groups and societies. And, third and finally, from the viewpoint of genetic sociology or macro-sociology, law is studied in terms of its patterns of change and development in a society.

---

[3] Gurvitch's most systematic work in the sociology of law was first published in French in 1940 and, two years later, translated into English (Gurvitch 1940, 1942; see also Gurvitch 1941a, 1941b). For supplementary information on Gurvitch's life and work, see Banakar 2001; Belley 1986; Hunt 1979, 2001; McDonald 1979.

After offering a lengthy overview of historical precursors to the sociology of law, Gurvitch proceeds in his *Sociology of Law* to offer an ever-increasingly complex classification and differentiation of law from the three viewpoints of systematic, typological, and genetic sociology. Sketching only the most basic elements of this perspective, the micro-sociological analysis studies various kinds of law as a function of different forms of sociality and as a function of the various layers of depth within each sociality form. Forms of sociality can be spontaneous or organized. Within the spontaneous type, sociality can occur by simple interdependence (among I and Others) or by interpenetration or fusion (into We). The fusion in the latter form can be weak, strong, or complete. Correspondingly, the forms of sociality are differentiated as mass, community, and communion, respectively. The sociality types based on simple interdependence are further subdivided according to the intensity of the degree of rapprochement, separation, or a combination of both.

Gurvitch arrives at a first classification of types of law on the basis of the contrast between sociality by interdependence and sociality by interpenetration. In the We-type of sociality, social law is based on confidence. Ranging from mass over community to communion, social law increases in validity and decreases in level of violence in enforcement. In the I-Other form of sociality, individual or inter-individual law is based on distrust, revealing itself most typically in a combined form of separation and rapprochement, such as in con-tractual law. Gurvitch's classifying does not stop here for he also considers each kind of law at various depth-levels depending on the degree of organization, ultimately involving an ideal construction of 162 kinds of law.

The systematic-sociological viewpoint is constructed similarly as the micro-sociological perspective. Gurvitch first differentiates between types of groups or collective units on the basis of various classification criteria, such as the scope or inclusive nature of groups, their duration, functions, degree of divisiveness and organization, form of constraints, and degree of unity. Again various kinds of law at multiple depth-levels are distinguished, introducing, among others, typological contrasts between unitary, federal, and confederate legal systems, national and international law, and various types of social law ranging from the spontaneous kind to social law that is represented in democratic state law. Finally, in terms of a genetic sociology of law, Gurvitch breaks with a simple evolutionist perspective and argues that legal changes are often marked by contradictory tendencies.

Pitirim Sorokin (1889–1970) is the third important member of the Petrazycki group whose work deserves discussion in this chapter.[4] Politically active at a young age (Sorokin was imprisoned for political defiance both during the czarist and communist regimes), Sorokin graduated under Petrazycki in the area of criminal law. He would become most influential as a central player in the institutionalization of modern sociology in the United States. In 1919, Sorokin founded the first sociology department at the University of St. Petersburg, and after he had fled Russia in 1923 because of his criticisms of the Soviet regime and spent a year in Prague, he went to the United States. There, he spent six years at the University of Minnesota before moving to Harvard, where he founded the Department of Sociology. Sorokin's sociological perspective on law stands out less than that of his fellow Petrazycki students, not for lack of interest, but because Sorokin's work covered a multitude of specialty areas, including rural sociology, the sociology of knowledge, social mobility, war and revolutions, altruism, social and cultural change, and sociological theory.

It is fortunate from the viewpoint of the sociology of law that Sorokin's magnum opus, the four-volume *Social and Cultural Dynamics*, also includes a discussion on law as one important component of culture (Sorokin 1937–1941, 1957). Sorokin's study is massive in scope, covering some 2,500 years of cultural history in the areas of art, science, ethics, law, and social relations. In general terms, Sorokin's theory suggests that history goes through a pattern of recurrent fluctuations between so-called ideational and sensate cultural systems. Ideational periods are marked by a spiritual orientation, whereas sensate periods are driven by materialist, hedonistic, and cynical values. Neither form has ever existed in purity, but cultural systems approximate one or the other type more or have characteristics of both in a mixed form (the idealistic type). Transformations from one system to the other over long periods of time lead to periods of crisis and transition, marked by high degrees of violence and war. These transformations are driven by an immanent determinism, whereby

---

[4] Sorokin's major work is the four-volume, *Social and Cultural Dynamics*, which is also available in abridged form (Sorokin 1937–1941, 1957; see also Sorokin 1928: 700–706, 1947, 1963). On Sorokin's life and work, see Johnston 1989; Timasheff 1963.

systems change according to their own inherent potentialities and on the basis of a principle of limits, which implies that growth in one direction alone cannot last.

Turning to the ethico-juridical aspect of culture, Sorokin distinguishes between various types of ethics on the basis of his general fluctuation model of cultural change. The ideational ethical system is an absolutist system oriented at bringing about unity on the basis of principles that emanate from a supreme being. By contrast, the ethics of a sensate system are oriented at increasing happiness and are relativistic in terms of changing social conditions on the basis of rules made by the members of society. Law functions as the best source or "social mirror" of ethics (Sorokin 1957: 430). Sorokin defines law as the whole of imperative-attributive convictions of the members of a society and is one element of ethics next to morality, which refers to the whole of imperative convictions that are not attributive. The attributive qualities of law imply that legal norms (or law-norms) are two-sided by attributing a right to one party and a duty to another party. Among the law's functions, it most essentially regulates organized interaction by distributing rights and duties among interacting individuals and by organizing a system of enforcement.

Sorokin notes that there may be a discrepancy between official law, i.e., those law-norms which are obligatory for all members of society and protected and enforced by the authoritative power of government, and unofficial law, i.e., law-norms which are not politically overseen but may be restricted to other groups. When this discrepancy grows, official law is modified or replaced by a new official code. Taking the area of criminal law as an example of the historical fluctuations between ideational and sensate cultures, Sorokin finds that ideational cultural systems tend to have criminal laws that incorporate religious values. Accordingly, crimes include violations against religious and absolute moral principles. Punishments for these crimes tend to be severe. Conversely, in sensate cultures, crimes against religion are eliminated from criminal statutes in favor of utilitarian considerations concerning crimes against the social and political order. Codes concerning crimes against property and bodily comfort are prevalent in this type. Punishment in sensate cultures tends to be somewhat less severe, although severity of punishment does not depend as much on the type of culture as on the degree to which any type has crystallized. During moments of transition, punishments are more severe than when either the sensate or ideational type have engrained themselves more firmly. The scope and severity of punishable acts thus follows a cyclical wave fluctuation.

The sociological movement in law: European perspectives

Petrazycki and the members of the school named after him were not the only scholars of European descent to aid in the establishment of the sociology of law in the years before World War II. Other European scholars in the areas of legal philosophy, legal science, and legal sociology were likewise engaged in intellectual efforts that were historically and/or theoretically helpful towards the development of a sociological study of law.[5] Without attempting to provide a more comprehensive overview, it makes sense to discuss the work of two German-language scholars, Eugen Ehrlich and Theodor Geiger, because the themes in their respective writings show striking similarities with some of the insights from the Eastern-European precursors.

Eugen Ehrlich (1862–1922) was an Austro-Hungarian legal scholar who received legal training at the University of Vienna.[6] In Vienna, Ehrlich also taught for a few years before spending the rest of his professional career at the University of Czernowitz in a region of Europe that belonged to Romania and the Soviet Union and that is now part of the Ukraine. Ehrlich lived in a society that was comprised of many different ethnic groups, marked by a high degree of linguistic and cultural diversity. The Austro-Hungarian legal system at the time of Ehrlich's life could not be expected, in its uniformity, to adequately regulate these various cultures, who in their daily lives relied on their own cultural and legal codes. Political instability was also characteristic

---

[5] For overviews of some sociological and sociologically oriented theories of law that are not discussed here, see, for instance, Timasheff 1957: 433–445 and Passmore 1961 on the so-called Uppsala School surrounding the Swedish legal realist Axel Hägerström; Kelsen 1912 on Ignatz Kornfeld; Benney 1983 on Antonio Gramsci; Cefaï and Mahe 1998 on Marcel Mauss; Heidegren 1997 on Helmut Schelsky; and Pound 1945 on Hans Kelsen, Franz Jerusalem, and Barna Horváth.

[6] Ehrlich's major work in the sociology of law is his 1913 book, *Grundlegung der Soziologie des Rechts*, translated in 1936 as *Fundamental Principles of the Sociology of Law* (Ehrlich 1913a, 1913b; see also Ehrlich 1922). For useful secondary analyses, see Banakar 2002; Kelsen 1915; Partridge 1961; Timasheff 1957: 437–439; Treviño 1998.

of the town of Czernowitz where Ehrlich spent most of his career. Czernowitz belonged to the Austro-Hungarian monarchy from 1867 until 1918 when it became part of Romania, after which it became part of the Soviet Union. These experiences of cultural diversity and political instability greatly influenced Ehrlich in the development of his work, specifically his notion of living law.

Ehrlich develops his theory in contrast to the prevailing legal-theoretical viewpoints of his time. He contrasts the practical science of law (*Rechtslehre*) with the theoretical science of law (*Rechtswissenschaft*). Whereas a practical science seeks to accomplish certain ends, such as providing greater logic to its subject matter, a theoretical science is concerned with studying the reality of law for its own sake. According to Ehrlich, almost all existing legal science is practical in orientation. In order to establish an independent body of thought on law, Ehrlich seeks to develop a theoretical science that is based on a study of the reality of law, more specifically a sociology of law that focuses on the social reality of law.

Ehrlich's perspective of legal sociology is based on a theory of social associations, defined as social relations in which people recognize certain rules as binding and regulate their conduct according to those rules. These relations may be simple, such as in the case of face-to-face groups, or complex, as in the case of the state. Associations are, according to Ehrlich, ordered on the basis of four major so-called facts of the law. The facts of the law are pre-legal in the sense that they shape norms of conduct, in turn leading to the development of norms of decision to regulate disputes. These facts include usage, domination, possession, and disposition. First, usage is the mere fact that a particular practice has remained in existence for a particular length of time. Usage is relevant to the ordering of social relations inasmuch as the customs of the past become the norms of the future. Second, existing relations of domination and subjection are the basis for the regulation of relations between superiors and subordinates, such as in the family (between children and parents) or in society at large (between serfs and masters). Third, the distribution of possessions forms the basis of order so that benefits can be derived from property. And, fourth, dispositions or declarations of the will are expressed in contracts and testaments. The facts of the law always precede any legal propositions that may be based upon them. For instance, the legal propositions concerning marriage and family presuppose the existence

of marriage and family as associations. Likewise, there must be possession before there can be laws regulating property.

Ehrlich conceives of social life as being essentially guided by norms
of conduct, not by legal norms or statutes alone. Stated in Ehrlich's
specific terminology, the legal relations and legal institutions that exist
in society are to be considered primary to the norms of decision or
legal propositions as they are applied in the courts. Ehrlich refers to
the whole of law dominating social life, even though it may not have
been posited in legal propositions, as living law. The whole of legal
propositions he refers to as juristic law. The significance of living law
can be observed in various aspects of everyday life, whether they
are legally recognized as such or not. Ascertaining the relevance of
living law, the sociology of law proposed by Ehrlich is concrete in its
methodological focus.

Because living law is primary in social life, Ehrlich considers it
central to the development of juristic law. However, while a society's
social relations and cultural conditions influence the development of
juristic law, the latter has much less of an influence on living law. Many
relations in society fall outside the purview of juristic law and many
disputes are settled without resource to legal propositions. Living law
may be very different from the norms of decision as they are used in
courts and relied upon by legal professionals. The goal of living law,
also, is not primarily dispute and litigation, but peace and cooperation.

Manifesting the practical consequences of his theoretical orientation, Ehrlich argues that legal propositions have to be consistent with
the codes of living law to be effective. Ehrlich therefore favors British
common law over European-continental civil law, because in the
former system judges and lawyers can bring in elements of living law,
while the latter system is highly codified and rigid. According to
Ehrlich, judicial decision-making should be liberated from any
constraints to derive the best judgments in light of the customs of
the people that laws are to be applied to. To accomplish such free
decision-making or a free finding of law appropriately, judges have
to be creative and gifted with great minds to adequately grasp the
relevant aspects of living law. By considering the general norms of
conduct as an essential part of the law, Ehrlich transcends a narrow
juridical conception. As such, Ehrlich opposes the prevailing view of
his days that law would primarily stem from the authority of the state
and be bound to statutory specifications.

Theodor Geiger (1891–1952) was born in Munich, Germany, and studied law before starting a professional career in a government department concerned with trade statistics.[7] In 1924, he began an academic career, first as lecturer and then as professor of sociology. Upon the Nazi seizure of power, Geiger fled to Denmark, where he took up that country's first professorship in sociology. Geiger was not only a sociologist of law but was also involved in many other specialty areas such as urban sociology, the sociology of knowledge, and the methodology of social research.

Inspired by a resolute commitment to scientific, especially quantitative, methods of research, Geiger's sociology rests on a multidimensional perspective of society as involving a multitude of social levels, differentiated on the basis of a variety of attributes, such as profession, education, upbringing, living standard, power, religion and culture, race, and political opinion. Geiger's interests focus on the variable sources of the constitution of social order as the coordination of the behavior of members of a group. Law is one such specific source of social order, formed around certain norms, which the sociology of law studies at a social level. The social reality of a norm can be inferred from its binding force to bring about a certain kind of behavior under specified conditions. The force of norms can be brought about by the group collectively, by certain segments of the group, by individual members, or by a specialized institution.

Geiger initially conceived of his approach as a formal sociology of law that was aimed at studying law in relation to social order and social structure. Yet, he later also developed a substantive sociology of law that focuses on the content of legal norms and the internal structure of law. According to Geiger, norms are to be defined in terms of their binding nature, which rests on the chance that deviations will be sanctioned. Norms are legal norms only when a society is structured as a state with a central power. Although never the only source of social order, law in a state emanates as one central outcome of power.

---

[7] Most of Geiger's work is published in German and Danish. His most important writings in the sociology of law include an early book of comparative law on children born out of wedlock (Geiger 1920) and two later writings, including a theoretical work on law and morality (Geiger 1946) and a study on law and social structure (Geiger 1947). Parts of the latter book are available in English translation in a collection of Geiger's work (Geiger 1969: 39–122). See also Mayntz 1969.

As a result of the conversion of power into law, the enforcement of legal norms becomes organized and regulated and is handed over to and monopolized by specialized agencies. Under these conditions, the probability of obedience to legal norms increases, and legal norms enacted by specialized agencies are likely to effectively mold the conduct of members of society, while norm-deviating conduct is more likely to be sanctioned.

From the psychology to the sociology of law

In the European cultures of social thought, the early days of socio-logical thinking on law outside the classics were essentially marked by a theoretical move towards the development of the sociology of law as a specialty area from within scientifically inclined currents in jurispru-dence. In some European traditions, particularly in the work of Geiger, the sociology of law was still primarily understood as an effort to meet the practical ambitions of jurisprudence to provide for better law. Geiger's main contributions are methodological, rather than theore-tical, in urging for systematic studies of law that abide by rigorous standards of data collection and analysis. A theoretically more infor-med understanding of the sociology of law was offered by Ehrlich, who differentiates between a legal science with practical ambitions and a body of thought on law, such as the sociology of law, that has purely academic aspirations. Nonetheless, Ehrlich posits a relationship between these two conceptions of legal thought by suggesting that the "juristic science of the future" would consist of a sociologically informed study of law that does not engage in mere abstract thinking on the basis of the principles of legal statutes, but that relies on a free finding of all law in society, whether it is recognized by statute or not (Ehrlich 1913b: 340). As such, Ehrlich hoped that the sociology of law would ultimately inform existing legal science to build a new order of "sociological legal science," as Kelsen (1915: 839) calls it.

In terms of the development towards an independent sociology of law in Europe, the work of Petrazycki takes center stage, not because of its psychological orientation, but because it presented a resolutely scientific treatment of law as a necessary step towards the sociological study of law as an activity with academic rather than practical ambitions. Though psychologistic, Petrazycki's theory turns attention away from an abstract understanding of legal norms and, additionally, brings out the relevance of the active motivation and orientation towards the law that must exist on the part of legal subjects for law to be valid. As such, Petrazycki's work points to the problem of the legitimacy of legality that is of critical concern to the sociology of law, albeit in a non-psychological understanding. Rejecting abstract norms as a topic of investigation and instead focusing on the concrete human experiences thereof, Petrazycki engages in a strategy that is formally similar to Durkheim's sociological approach (of studying law as an observable indicator of social solidarity), yet, unlike Durkheim, Petrazycki was unable to locate the reality of norms at the social level.

The three members of the Petrazycki school, Timasheff, Gurvitch, and Sorokin, most essentially advanced the development of the sociology of law by breaking with their teacher's psychological understanding of law in favor of a more resolutely sociological conception of law as a social institution. Timasheff stresses the functional role of law in providing a coordination of action. Gurvitch's dialectical analysis is likewise distinctly sociological in moving away from the level of individual consciousness to the level of the group as a reality *sui generis*. Sorokin adopts Petrazycki's perspective of the function of law but analyzes law historically in the fluctuation of society. As such, the work of Petrazycki was institutionally significant for the development of the sociology of law, although it theoretically served as a negative model.[8]

Irrespective of its intellectual gains (and shortcomings), what the Petrazycki school also brought about was an institutional development of the sociology of law by virtue of the migration of the school's members outside the boundaries of Eastern Europe. However, the consequences of this migration were essentially ambivalent. In the United States, Timasheff's work could not rely on a well-developed tradition of the study of law in sociology, so that his work was largely received and discussed in jurisprudence. Moreover, Timasheff's failure to put to scrutiny the causes of the suggested overlap between the functions and consequences of law, not to mention the discrepancies that can exist between them, does not make his work useful for

---

[8] The one exception to Petrazycki's lack of theoretical influence in the modern sociology of law is the work of the Polish sociologist Adam Podgórecki, who developed an empiricist micro-sociology of law with humanistic ambitions on the basis of Petrazycki's work (Podgórecki 1974, 1982, 1999; see also Ziegert 1977).

sociology where the functions and consequences of law are distinguished precisely to enable analysis. Behavior that is conforming to legal norms cannot, from the sociological viewpoint, merely be assumed to be conforming because of those legal norms. Gurvitch was during his career more distinctly located within the sociological enterprise, but his work too had relatively little influence in the sociology of law. Gurvitch addressed many of the theoretical problems that are predominant in the sociology of law, yet his work is extremely dense and lacking in clarity, which did not help its reception. Sorokin's work on law adopts a perspective of law that is conceptually identical to Petrazycki's yet that gains in originality by its empirical treatment in the study of the dynamics of society. Within this empirical framework, however, the study of law is but one small element in a much more complex study of the dynamics of society. Ironically, it was precisely because of its distinctly sociological stature that Sorokin's work on law had virtually no impact on the development of the sociology of law as a specialty area.

Conclusion

Besides the works of the sociological classics, early European social thought also produced other significant developments that paved the way towards the sociology of law. Among them are particularly the works of Leon Petrazycki, his students Nicholas Timasheff, Georges Gurvitch, and Pitirim Sorokin, as well as other scholars such as Eugen Ehrlich and Theodor Geiger. The fact that the writings of Petrazycki and his students have had no lasting theoretical influence does not deny their historical role in the theoretical development towards a more mature sociology of law. Arguably the most distinct and sociologically useful central common theme in the works of the early European sociologists of law is the focus on the differentiation of and interplay between living law and positive law (Treviño 1998). A central advance of the works of these scholars was their sociological orientation to the study of law, which was enabled by turning away from the formalism of legal theory to instead center attention on the social relationships associated with law, the functional control of law in society, and the extra-legal dimensions of law. With respect to the appropriate level of analysis in the sociology of law, an indispensable transformation was accomplished in the move from the psychological to the social dimensions of law.

The development of the sociology of law in Europe primarily entailed a transformation of the appropriate analysis of law from the psychological to the social level and a specification of law as a social institution and practice. But several of the early European scholars still held on to the notion that sociological analyses could and should play a role in bringing about a greater sense of morality and justice in law. In order for there to be an institutionalized sociology of law as a field of academic inquiry, however, the sociological study of law would have to escape from the bounds of legal thought. Because of the stubborn resistance from the more developed tradition of jurisprudential thought, however, it would take considerable time before the maturation of an independent sociology of law would be realized. In fact, as the discussion in the next chapter will clarify, the development of a sociology of law in the United States faced even more complications than in Europe. The differential development of the sociology of law on both sides of the Atlantic relates intimately to the structure and objectives of legal education and the implications thereof for the study of law from legal as well as sociological viewpoints.

5 | *From sociological jurisprudence to sociology of law*

The development of the sociology of law cannot be restricted to the history of sociology but must also consider elements in the history of legal thought, especially those emanations from legal scholarship claiming to be sociologically informed. This condition particularly applies to the United States, for when the first attempts were made in European sociology to carve out a niche for the sociology of law, there was at the time no such similar development in American sociology, where studies of law were conducted only very rarely in sociological scholarship (e.g., Gillin 1929; Thomas 1931).[1] Instead, as an early precursor to the sociology of law there developed a perspective known as sociological jurisprudence. Established by Harvard law professor Roscoe Pound, sociological jurisprudence was an extension of the legal thought of the famous US jurist Oliver Wendell Holmes, Jr., who had formulated a conception of law as reflecting a nation's development. Inspired by Holmes and the turn towards a scientifically informed jurisprudence, sociological jurisprudence additionally paved the way for the school of legal realism, which benefited most from its systematization in the work of Karl Llewellyn.

The American traditions of sociological jurisprudence and legal realism take the place of the work of Petrazycki in Europe as being among the precursors towards the sociology of law. However, because

---

[1] In rather sharp contrast with the relative neglect of the study of law in early American sociology stands the attention paid to crime and deviant behavior by such prominent sociologists as Edwin Sutherland, Thorsten Sellin, and Robert K. Merton. However, early developments in criminological sociology were not primarily centered on law and also did not typically feature prominently in the development of an institutionalized sociology of law, some exceptions not withstanding (see Chapter 6). Until this day, the relation between criminology and the sociology of law as institutionalized specialties, if not as scholarly contributions, remains difficult (Savelsberg 2002; Savelsberg and Sampson 2002; Silbey 2002; see Chapters 6 and 11).

these early schools in the United States were part of legal rather than sociological scholarship, an additional effort was needed from within sociology to establish the subfield of the sociology of law. In this respect, American sociology was fortunate in being able to count on the work of the Harvard sociologist Talcott Parsons as the crowning moment of the modern sociology of law. Parsons developed a perspective on law that was sociological both by being informed by his systems-theoretical perspective and by being in line with the great traditions of classical sociology, which Parsons, more than anyone else, helped to make a central aspect of the theoretical discourse of modern sociology. This chapter will analyze the development towards the modern sociology of law from the American school of sociological jurisprudence to its successor of legal realism and on to the sociology of Parsons and the relevant works of some of his followers.

The sociological movement in law: the American tradition

The grand moment in the transition towards a scientific and sociological approach in legal scholarship in the United States is found in the thought of Oliver Wendell Holmes, Jr. (1841–1935).[2] After having fought in the Civil War, Holmes received a law degree from the Harvard Law School. He entered legal practice and subsequently became a professor of law at Harvard and a member of the Massachusetts Supreme Court. From 1902 onwards, he served on the US Supreme Court, in which function he would draft many famous and influential opinions, often written in dissent from the majority of the Court.

Holmes's central ideas on law are based on a rejection of the doctrine of legal formalism that dominated American legal thought. The theory of legal formalism holds that the law is an internally consistent and logical body of rules that is independent from the variable forms of its surrounding social institutions. In interpretation and application,

---

[2] Among Holmes's most important works are his book *The Common Law* (Holmes 1881) and several important papers in the *Harvard Law Review* (Holmes 1897, 1899, 1918). Holmes's work has generated a very extensive secondary literature, including discussions on its relation to sociological jurisprudence and legal realism (see, e.g., Alschuler 2000; Burton 2000; Gordon 1992; Treviño 1994).

judges would accordingly be guided exclusively by a deductive system of abstract principles. Reacting against this perspective, Holmes argues that the law cannot be discussed in its own terms alone, for then the law is confused with morality and the moral values which law, by its own understanding, is purported to advance, regardless if or to what extent this is actually the case. Advocating a business-like understanding of the law, Holmes aims to unmask the view that the development of law is subject only to logic, when legal judgments are actually influenced by assumptions and preconceptions on the part of judges. "The life of the law has not been logic; it has been experience," Holmes (1881: 5) writes. Against legal formalism, Holmes argues that the law is a reflection of a nation's development. To determine what law actually does, it has to be studied in terms of the prediction that court decisions will or will not produce certain outcomes.

Reflecting his professional preoccupation with law, Holmes emphasizes the judicial aspects of law and argues that judges do not merely find the law in legal codes, which they apply in specific cases, but that in so doing, they also contribute to formulating law by selecting the relevant principles of law and precedents to decide the outcomes of cases. Precedents are not just given, for they are selected by judges on the basis of their conceptions of right and wrong. These normative conceptions often remain unspecified and unconsciously influence judges' opinions. Legal judgments purporting to be logical are often mere dogmatic principles, the specific origins of which are overlooked. To counteract subjective-ideological bias in law, Holmes argues that legal theory with a practical intent must be based on a historical study of the law and an enlightened skepticism on the meaning and impact of law on people's behavior. What the law needs is a jurisprudence, that is, a systematic theory of law, which must be formulated, not on the basis of abstract principle, but on the basis of accurately measured social desires. The ends that the law seeks to bring about should be well articulated by those who make legal judgments. Holmes therefore argues against formalism in law to suggest that judges look at the relevant facts in a changing society, including the sentiments and feelings of the members of society and the insights that are derived from scientific research.

Holmes's judicial theories played a major role in shaping the American traditions of sociological jurisprudence and legal realism. The perspective of sociological jurisprudence was systematically developed by Roscoe Pound (1870–1964).[3] Pound had graduated in the field of botany and had only minimal formal education in law, yet he would eventually come to enjoy a long academic career as a professor of law and Dean at the law schools of the University of Nebraska and Harvard. Pound coined the term sociological jurisprudence to refer to a new stage in the development of jurisprudential perspectives. Pound considered this new school of jurisprudence still formative at the time he introduced it in the early twentieth century, because the sociology upon which it relied was still a relatively young science.

In general, sociological jurisprudence refers to the study of law that takes into account the social facts upon which law proceeds and to which it is implied, in other words, the actual working, including the causes and effects, of law. Sociological jurisprudence, according to Pound, more specifically consists of six programmatic guidelines: (1) it studies the actual social effects of law; (2) it focuses on the effects of law to prepare for adequate legislation; (3) it seeks to make the rules of law more effective in view of the law's enforcement function; (4) it studies the social effects of law historically; (5) it seeks to contribute to an equitable application of law in all cases; and (6) it aims to advance the ultimate purpose of law in terms of social control.

The emphasis in sociological jurisprudence is thus on the actual workings of the law, not merely on legal doctrine and law-internal theory. Pound phrases this difference in perspective in the now famous distinction between law in action and law in the books. Pound argues the differentiation between law in action and law in the books to have been brought about by a general lag of law relative to social conditions, the failure of legal thought to take into account advances in the social sciences, the rigidity of legislation, and defects in the administration of law. From the viewpoint of sociological jurisprudence, legal

---

[3] Among Pound's most important books are *Law and Morals* (Pound 1926), *Social Control Through Law* (Pound 1942), and the five-volume work, *Jurisprudence* (Pound 1959). Several of his article-length discussions specifically deal with the perspective of sociological jurisprudence (Pound 1907, 1910, 1912, 1923, 1927, 1928, 1932), including its relation to legal realism (Pound 1931) and the sociology of law (Pound 1943, 1945). For useful discussions on Pound's perspective of sociological jurisprudence and its relation to sociology, see Braybooke 1961; Cossio 1952; Cowan 1968; Hoogvelt 1984; N. E. H. Hull 1997; McLean 1992; Stone 1965; White 1972; Wigdor 1974.

decisions must be investigated for the effects they bring about and the conditions under which they do so in terms of the social, economic, and political development of society. Rather than setting up a closed self-sufficient jurisprudence on the basis of legal principles, sociological jurisprudence seeks to study how the law ought to be adapted to adequately respond to changing societal conditions. Law is thereby conceived as a means towards an end.

With respect to the end of law, Pound argues that law is a form of social control, defined as the ordering of human relations in politically organized societies in terms of the fulfillment of the claims, demands, and desires, which people individually or collectively seek to satisfy. Law is not the only means of social control – Pound also mentions religion and morality – but in the modern context (of the early twentieth century) all other means of social control are subordinate to law. "Today," writes Pound (1923: 356), "the legal order is the most conspicuous and most effective form of social control." Pound conceives of the objectives of law more specifically in terms of a theory of social interests, of which he differentiates six categories: (1) general security, such as physical safety and the health of the population; (2) the security of institutions, such as those in the realm of politics, economy, and religion; (3) moral standards of behavior; (4) the conservation of social resources; (5) economic and political progress; and (6) individual life and rights. As a means of social control, law must give concrete expression to social interests and offer reconciliation when conflicting interests arise. Judicial decisions in this sense contribute to the maintenance of the social order as a form of social engineering. It is to be noted that individual rights, in Pound's understanding, form only one element among the social interests which law must fulfill, thus transcending the individualist conception of rights and duties that dominated American law and jurisprudence.

Pound's conception of law as social control betrays his leanings on currents of the American sociology of his day. With regard to the historical development towards the formation of sociological jurisprudence, Pound considers the positivist social philosophy of Auguste Comte most essential. Other early sociologists Pound occasionally refers to in his work include Spencer, Durkheim, and Weber. Yet, in terms of the systematics of the perspective of sociological jurisprudence, he relies on sociologists that were working in a distinctly American tradition, most notably Lester Ward, whose work was influential for

Pound because of its focus on social problems and sociological questions of justice, and Edward Alsworth Ross, who developed a systematic sociological theory of social control. It is worthwhile to devote some attention to Ross's perspective of social control, for it is among the most distinctly sociological insights that influenced the work of Pound.

Edward A. Ross, who for a few years in the early twentieth century was a colleague of Pound at the University of Nebraska, is most famous for his theory of social control, which he developed in a series of journal of articles that were later published in book form (Ross 1901). Broadly conceived to refer to a society's capacity to regulate itself without resource to force, social control is defined in opposition to coercive control as a form of social ascendancy or dominance of society over individuals meant to harmonize the different interests and activities that exist among them. A constant function in society, social control is secured through the operation of various social institutions, such as education, art, beliefs, public opinion, religion, custom, and law. With respect to the social control functions of law, Ross (1896) mainly discusses the enforcement capacity of law on the basis of a system of punishment. Legal sanctions have a function towards society as a whole by publicly and ceremonially showing disapproval of certain forms of behavior in such a way that all members of the community accept the law as the will of the community. Legality alone, however, is insufficient for the control of society and must be supplemented by public opinion as the whole of social sanctions towards unacceptable behavior. Harmonizing with Ross's conception, the perspective of social control employed by Pound implies a view of the function of law as securing social integration or, in Pound's words, "the whole scheme of the social order" (Pound 1927: 326). This notion of social control is thus broader than, and not to be confused with, the presently more common usage of the term in relation to crime and deviance (see Chapter 11).

In the context of sociological jurisprudence, the perspective of American legal realism deserves separate discussion, not only because it is another important manifestation of the reaction against legal formalism, but particularly because it set off an important intellectual debate on the study of law, many elements of which have remained influential in legal thought and the sociology of law until this day. The most central and, in terms of the history of sociological jurisprudence, most interesting representative of the school of legal realism is Karl Llewellyn (1893–1962).[4] Llewellyn graduated from law at Yale and taught as a professor of law at Columbia and Chicago. Influenced by the sociology of Sumner, Llewellyn's work was engaged in a critique of legal formalism on the basis of the postulate that law must be analyzed as a social institution. More specifically, Llewellyn was interested in studying how law operated in everyday situations and concrete cases. This ethnographic orientation, according to Llewellyn, would once and for all break with all forms of legal formalism and abstract discussions about law in terms of rules, legal precepts, and rights.

Llewellyn rejects the notion of interests as the object of law and the assumption that law, in terms of judicial decisions, governs human conduct. To Llewellyn, the question must always be if, when, and to what extent law as proscribed rule and law as actual practice actually converge or not. Llewellyn's general attitude in this respect is one of skepticism as he holds that there is less predictability in the conduct of law than a traditional view based on rules (as regulators of human conduct) would lead to conclude. In any case, without empirical investigations, Llewellyn argues, no generalizations can be made about the effects of law.

Llewellyn proposes a factual descriptive approach that focuses on the behavioral dimensions of law. He therefore distinguishes between the so-called "paper rules and rights" of ought that are used in legal doctrine, and the "real rules and rights" that are conceived in terms of behavior. Real rules are the actual practices of the courts, and real rights refer to the likelihood that in a given situation a particular kind of court action will be applied. The focus is not only on the behavior of judges but on that of any state official as well as all the laypeople involved in the law. On the basis of narrowly confined concrete case studies, realist analyses of law would eventually also be useful to contribute to legal reform.

---

[4] Llewellyn wrote several important theoretical articles about legal realism (Llewellyn 1930, 1931, 1949), many of which are included in the posthumously published collection, *Jurisprudence* (Llewellyn 1962). See also the overviews by N. E. H. Hull 1997; Twining 1985; White 1972. Llewellyn's most famous empirical study is *The Cheyenne Way* (Llewellyn and Hoebel 1941), a work about dispute resolution among the Cheyenne which contributed to the development of the anthropology of law (see Mehrotra 2001).

The legal origins of the sociology of law

Although sociological jurisprudence and legal realism are both intellectually indebted to the work of Holmes and the rise of the social
sciences, the ambitions and theoretical orientations of the two perspectives were the subject of an intense debate between its two respective leaders, Pound and Llewellyn.[5] Pound (1931) initiated this
debate by criticizing the legal-realist approach for engaging in a merely
descriptive study of law that cannot form the basis of science of law.
The goal of legal realism, to study the law accurately as it is rather
than what it is imagined to be, Pound finds useful but insufficient.
"Faithful portrayal of what courts and law makers and jurists do is
not the whole task of a science of law," Pound (1931: 700) argues, for
what the law does cannot be divorced from what it ought to do as a
tool of social control. Lacking such a broader understanding of law
and, consequently, unduly restricting its study, the realists are obsessed
with the numbers provided by descriptive studies. Legal realism would
also be reductionist in terms of its exclusive reliance on a psychology of
judicial behavior and its preoccupation with analyzing single cases of
law rather than uniformities at a social level.

   In response to Pound, Llewellyn (1931) clarifies the tenets of the
realist movement. He argues that legal realism conceived of law as
being in flux and having to be examined in terms of the ends it fulfills
(in concrete cases). Further, legal realism engages in a constant examination of the workings of the law and does not assume that discussions
on rules can substitute concrete analyses describing what law actually
does. Besides distrusting all theories of law that focus on rules and
instead developing a program for the study of law based on narrowly
confined sets of cases, legal-realist studies temporarily divorce factual
issues (of is) from normative issues (of ought). Legal realism focuses
exclusively on law as it is in terms of the conduct of the participants
of law and suspends any judgment on what the law ought to do.
Likewise, the researcher's stance on normative matters of law is kept
out of analysis.

   The debate between Pound and Llewellyn reveals an important point
of contention that has marked legal science as well as the sociology of

---

[5] See the critique on legal realism by Pound 1931 and the response by Llewellyn
   1931. See also the discussions in N. E. H. Hull 1997; Ingersoll 1981; White
   1972.

law until this day. It concerns the role of values and morality relative to law and its study. The legal realism of Llewellyn completely breaks with a conception of law as justice and instead primarily turns attention towards developing a methodology for the accurate study of law. In this approach, moreover, legal realism is resolutely objectivist, studying the actual conduct of the participants in law without preconceptions about law's functionality and moral implications. Adopting a behaviorist approach, moreover, legal realism is oriented at analyzing the interactive context of law, involving the conduct of legal actors. By contrast, the sociological jurisprudence tradition is a perspective of legal scholarship that relies on social-science insights in order to advance problems of policy in terms of justice. The sociological jurisprudence of Pound is primarily informed by a quest to improve the regulatory system of law. Pound's emphasis on the functions of law in terms of social control is, as such, not the expression of a mere academic interest but emanates from a pragmatist philosophy of law that seeks to develop an informed perspective of how law should be conceived given specified societal conditions. The difference between law in the books and law in action, that Pound argues to be very deep at times during his day, could thus be overcome through implementation in law of the insights derived from sociological jurisprudence.

The problem of the normativity of law has been part of the sociology of law since Durkheim, and it has remained part of the sociological study of law ever since, most sharply surfacing in the debate on the possibilities of a scientific sociology of law that would be instigated as soon as the sociology of law had been institutionalized as a more widely accepted subspecialty (see Chapter 6). The problem also translates more immediately in terms of the functionality of law and the conception of law as social control, a perspective that is crucial to the structural-functionalist view of law. In this respect, it is useful to recall the specific origins of this problem in the American schools of sociological jurisprudence and legal realism and the context in which they emerged. Intellectually, an influence of American pragmatist philosophy as it had been popularized by the likes of William James and John Dewey can be noted. Countering deductivism and formalism in thought, pragmatism rejects the notion that terms can have stable meanings or be true, instead attributing meaning and truth on the basis of the actual consequences in action of the acceptance of terms in particular contexts. Pragmatism influenced both sociological

jurisprudence as well as legal realism in their respective turns away
from legal formalism towards the reality of the workings of law.
However, whereas legal realism adopts a perspective of skepticism
towards generalizable pronouncements on the objectives of law,
sociological jurisprudence takes on a moralistic turn to contemplate
how the study of law can contribute to enhance the effectiveness of
law. The latter orientation is intellectually also indebted to the dominant form of American sociology at the time. Early American sociology emanated from a practical orientation towards the amelioration
of social ills and was not primarily a strictly intellectual activity that
had developed in the halls of academia (as was the case in Europe,
where sociological interests formed a basis for social reform activities, rather than the other way around). The concept of social control
introduced by Ross, for example, operates explicitly within the background of social problems, such as urbanization, poverty, alcoholism,
and prostitution, that had been brought about by the modernization
of society.

The moral commitment rooted in the American conception of law
as social control harmonizes with the Durkheimian conception of
social integration and the Petrazyckian attention to law as a means to
bring about social order. Nonetheless, European sociology and legal
scholarship were much more theoretical and academic in their foundations than their American counterparts, which had grown primarily
out of practical and professional aspirations. Whereas in the case
of sociology, these differences stemmed from diverging disciplinary
origins, in the European academe and the American movement
towards liberal reform, the differences in legal scholarship are to be
situated in the context of the differences between the European and
American legal systems themselves, more specifically the European
tradition of academic legal education and the American practice of
professional legal training (see Chapter 9). Therefore, the theoretical
development towards a sociology of law, rather than a sociological
jurisprudence, took place much quicker in Europe than it did in the
United States. Of course, the institutionalization of the sociology of
law would in Europe be hampered by the turmoil brought about by
the Bolshevik Revolution (and the dispersal of the Petrazycki school)
and World War II and the shifting international balance that followed
from it.

In the United States, the obstacles towards the development of the sociology of law were largely scholarly as the tradition of sociological jurisprudence took on such a strong hold in legal scholarship that it initially prevented the development of an independent sociology of law. The sociology of law that had by then emerged in Europe, moreover, was largely usurped by scholars of sociological jurisprudence rather than being discussed by other sociologists. Yet, the success of sociological jurisprudence cannot deny the fact that jurisprudence is not sociology, although the distinction is not always carefully maintained or recognized in the secondary literature (Cossio 1952; Cotterrell 1975; Zeigert 1999). However counter-intuitive the ideas of sociological jurisprudence and legal realism may have been (and continue to be) from the viewpoint of the legal professional, they remained ideas of legal theory and were not developed sociologically.

It is interesting to note that the scholarly differences between sociological jurisprudence and sociology of law were clearly recognized and respected by Pound. In an interesting article on "Sociology of Law and Sociological Jurisprudence," Pound (1943) observes that sociology of law proceeds from within sociology to law, whereas sociological jurisprudence operates in the reverse direction as a form of jurisprudence which, from within law, especially on the basis of the work of Holmes, utilizes insights from sociology. Pound notes that these differences in perspective are rooted in a fundamental difference between the respective objectives of sociology and jurisprudence. Whereas sociology is primarily theoretical or research-oriented, jurisprudence is practically oriented at contributing to the resolution of legal problems. Pound argues that sociological jurisprudence faces difficulties of acceptance from jurisprudence and sociology alike, from the former for deviating from the formal system of law and legal doctrine and from the latter for having a practical orientation and engaging in the formulation of value judgments.

In order to enable a development towards the sociology of law in the United States, what was needed would be one or both of two conditions: an acceptance of the European schools of the sociology of law by the discipline of sociology at large and/or a turn towards a sociological study of law from within sociology. As will be shown in the next section and in Chapter 6, it was mostly the second condition that propelled the development of the sociology of law and its institutionalization as a disciplinary subspecialty.

The modernization of classical sociology: Talcott Parsons

It would be a denial of the historical reality of modern sociology to neglect the contributions by the American sociologist Talcott Parsons. The influence of Parsons' work is sufficiently important to be considered in any history of sociology, theoretically and institutionally, first of all because it propelled the development of the structural-functionalist school, which acquired dominance during the decades following World War II. Additionally, it is equally if not even more important to argue for the centrality of Parsons' work in the establishment of modern sociology because it was mostly due to his efforts that the contemporary sociological enterprise now situates itself in relation to the classic scholars, most particularly Weber and Durkheim. It was also because of the work of Parsons and other representatives of structural functionalism that new generations of sociologists could begin to formulate alternative ideas that would deviate, sometimes sharply, from the premises and directions of the dominant functionalist perspective. For these reasons, the decisive break in the development of modern sociology, including the sociology of law, is found in the work of Parsons. The significance of these developments for the sociology of law is not only indirect, through the reception of the classics and the emergence of theoretical pluralism in sociology, but can also rely directly on the contributions to the sociology of law formulated by Parsons and some of his followers.

Talcott Parsons (1902–1979) obtained his college degree from Amherst College and initially contemplated a career in medicine.[6] During his college studies, his attention turned to the social and economic sciences and, in 1924, he commenced graduate studies at the London School of Economics and, a year later, at the University of Heidelberg in Germany. Parsons obtained a doctoral degree in economics from Heidelberg in 1927 during an apprentice year of teaching at Amherst. Thereupon, Parsons became a lecturer in economics at

---

[6] This exposition of Parsons' major theoretical ideas relies upon some of his major books, *The Structure of Social Action* (Parsons 1937) and *The Social System* (Parsons 1951), as well as two useful collections (Parsons 1967, 1977a). See Alexander 1983 for a helpful exposition of Parsons' thought.

Harvard, where, in 1931, he moved to the Sociology department that had just been set up by Sorokin. Parsons would initially only slowly move up in rank, but once his name was secured through the publication of major theoretical works, he would become the single most dominant sociologist of his time.

There are at least three lines of development in Parsons' sociology: the formulation of an action-theoretical perspective; the elaboration of a systems theory of society; and a more empirically oriented final phase with a strong evolutionist bent. It is particularly the middle period in Parsons' thought which produced his most important contributions to the sociology of law. Briefly turning to the first phase in Parsons' work, it was during his studies in Europe that Parsons was exposed to a great number of distinguished European writers, such as the anthropologist Bronislaw Malinowski, the functionalist anthropologist who taught at the London School of Economics, Max Weber, who had died only a few years before Parsons was at Heidelberg, Emile Durkheim, the founder of the French school of sociology, Alfred Marshall, the influential British economist, and Vilfredo Pareto, the Italian economist whose theories also inspired developments in sociology. While several of these scholars were not completely unknown to sociologists in the United States, none of them had attained the status of a classic in contemporary sociology, mostly because their works were not always available in translation and, as argued before, because US sociology positioned itself relative to research areas of social problems rather than theory.

In 1937, Parsons changed the face of sociology forever with the publication of *The Structure of Social Action* (Parsons 1937). On a theoretical level, the book presents a voluntaristic theory of action based on the (Weberian) premise that human action consists of meaningful connection between means and goals. Parsons also argues that the development of such a voluntaristic theory can be observed in the works of major social theorists, such as Weber, Durkheim, Marshall, and Pareto. Forgoing an overview of this so-called convergence thesis, what is important about Parsons' work in the present context is that it relied upon the works of various classic scholars with the express purpose of developing a theoretical perspective. Such an approach is today practiced widely and, in more and less appropriate forms, virtually identical to the enterprise of sociological theorizing. Substantively, Parsons' voluntaristic theory maintains that human conduct is meaningful and must be approached from a non-positivist perspective in terms of the motivations on the part of the actors. However, moving beyond a mere social psychology, Parsons argues that at a societal level there are limits to the variability of ends because human actions are organized around common systems of (ultimate) ends or values. Avoiding a Hobesian state of a war of all against all, human conduct is organized at the level of a common values system by means of socialization. To secure adherence to such a values system, social norms operate to regulate or control action. In the further development of Parsons' thought, the focus on action moves resolutely to the system's frame of reference of how normative integration is secured.

Parsons' systems theory offers an analytical perspective of society that is used to clarify how society can secure integration, particularly in the light of growing individualism. In general terms, Parsons applies the notion of system to refer to a whole consisting of related parts which perform specific functions in relation to one another and the maintenance of the whole. Specifying the functions of systems as adaptation, goal attainment, integration, and latency, Parsons contends that in modern societies four relatively autonomous subsystems have differentiated to perform one designated function: the economy, the political system, the societal community, and the fiduciary (or values) system. The social system and its various subsystems are conceived as open systems that engage in dual processes of interchange via various symbolic media. In the case of the social system, these media are: money in the economic subsystem, power in the polity, normative influence in the societal community, and value commitment in the fiduciary subsystem.

In the context of this book, many of the theoretical complexities (and problems) of Parsons' thinking need not be discussed and can be substituted by a less abstract explanation of Parsons' theory in terms of his analysis of the legal system. Indeed, besides his analyses of such social institutions as the family, religion, health care, the professions, and the polity, Parsons also devoted considerable explicit attention to the role of the legal system in modern society.[7] Most essentially,

---

[7] Parsons' ideas on the legal system are clarified in four articles (Parsons 1954, 1962a, 1968, 1978) and two related book reviews (Parsons 1962b, 1977b). Parsons also worked on a book with Winston White and Leon Mayhew that would include "a fairly extensive treatment of the place of the legal system in American society" (Parsons 1962a: 56). This book was never published,

Parsons views the legal system in terms of its integrative function as a central element of a modern society's societal community. Parsons (1959: 184) defines law as "any relatively formalized and integrated body of rules which imposes obligations on persons playing particular roles in particular collectivities." Demonstrating the analytical value of the functionalist systems approach, Parsons analyzes the role of law in relation to the other differentiated subsystems of society in the four-functional scheme and in terms of law's primary integrative function.

With respect to law's differentiation from the economic system, Parsons contends that the legal system cannot be adequately conceptualized with reference to the private interests that accompany the expansion of capitalism. Against a Marxist interpretation, Parsons argues that the profit motive cannot be assumed to govern all spheres of society and, additionally, that legal processes can not be analyzed in the utilitarian terms of profit maximization. Rather, the legal system remains relatively autonomous from the economic system inasmuch as the law is meant to negotiate between different interests that need to be brought into balance.

Parsons also maintains the relative autonomy of law with respect to the political system. The function of lawmaking is delegated to the polity in the form of the legislative function of government, but other legal functions are exclusively adjudicated by the legal system. In particular, the interpretation and sanctioning of legal norms are handled by courts and enforcement agencies. The polity also observes a functional separation of powers as well as the legally guaranteed preservation of individual rights of self-determination. The politicization of law, i.e., the instrumentalization of law by government for political purposes, is an empirical possibility, especially in societies that are not democratically organized, but not a theoretical necessity.

Parsons considers law, most importantly, as a mechanism of social control within the context of the social system's societal community. The legal system specifically fulfills the following functions: legal interpretation in courts of law; application of laws through administrative and juridical decision-making; sanctioning of laws by enforcement

however, and it bears little resemblance to the book on the American societal community that Parsons was eventually working on throughout the 1970s and which has recently been published on the basis of drafts (Parsons 2007). See also the discussions by Damm 1976; De Espinosa 1980; Deflem 1998a; Cotterrell 1992: 81–91; Rocher 1989; Wilkinson 1981.

agencies; and specification of jurisdiction to determine when and where legal rules apply. The integrative function of law has two dimensions, for law not only regulates interaction among the members of society (social integration) but also regulates the institutional structure of society and the exchange among subsystems (societal integration). With respect to law's integrative function, Parsons devotes special attention to the legal profession. The legal profession derives its special significance from the fact that legal professionals coordinate actions within the legal system under conditions set in the legislative process by means of the interpretation of legal norms in specific cases.

Finally, Parsons positions law in relation to the fiduciary system in the sense that he considers a society's values to provide the "sub-constitutional stratum of the legal system" (Parsons 1978: 48). In modern societies it is especially relevant to Parsons that religious laws have become secularized into procedural legal requirements that are formulated in terms of general principles legitimizing equality of participation through the institutionalization of rights and duties. In the United States, in particular, a Protestant ethic and an accompanying emphasis on free inquiry have largely shaped the American common law tradition, stressing the particularities of each court case and accounting for the individualistic nature of many laws. "The Puritan influence," Parsons (1978: 49) writes, "was sufficiently important to justify putting the development of law together with that of the devotion to callings in economic enterprise and science."

The legacy of structural functionalism

Harmonizing with the widespread influence of Parsons' work during his days, his sociological approach to law was able to bring about an actual school of sociologists of law working in the Parsonian tradition, including Harry Bredemeier, Leon Mayhew, and William Evan. The works of these scholars theoretically aimed at conceptualizing the role of law as a mechanism of social control and the functional processes of interchange between law and the other subsystems of society, often with more explicit regard for the problems and tensions associated with law than can be found in Parsons' work (Bredemeier 1962; Davis 1962; Davis et al. 1962; Evan 1960, 1961, 1965; Mayhew 1968b, 1968c, 1971). Moreover, these sociologists conducted empirical tests of various propositions derived from within the structural-functional framework in specific cases of law, such as issues surrounding the implementation and legitimacy of specific laws (Evan 1959, 1962b; Evan and Levin 1966; Mayhew 1968a).

While there were a number of Parsonian scholars engaged in socio-logical studies of law, their influence on the further development of law has been relatively minimal, not only because of the decline of Parsons' dominance from the 1960s onwards, but mostly because the Parsonian scholars were not sufficiently involved as specialists in the sociology of law to have a lasting impact in the specialty area. Most ambitious in its scope and most consistent in the area of the sociology of law was the work of William Evan. Yet, Evan's work suffers from not being more systematically presented until 1990, at a time when the sociology of law had evolved well beyond the functionalist paradigm (Evan 1990).

The relevance of Parsons to the sociology of law, however, goes beyond the contributions of his direct followers. Beyond the works of the functionalist sociologists of law, the relevance of Parsons' socio-logy of law is felt in a more enduring fashion through the reception and influence of his work in the development of the discipline of sociology. In this respect, it is important to observe the lasting, if largely indirect, positive impact of Parsons' thought on many strands of contemporary sociological theorizing as are the many theoretical schools that have been formulated, often in direct reaction to Parsons, as alternatives to the functionalist approach. These aspects of Parsons' legacy have inevitably affected the sociology of law as well. In this respect, the development of interactionist and conflict-theoretical pers-pectives in legal sociology can be seen in response to Parsons (see Chapter 6), while the lasting discussions in the sociology of law of the likes of Weber and Durkheim likewise owe a debt to Parsons.

Parsons developed his sociology of law largely on the basis of his sociology and the central ideas of the sociological classics he had there incorporated. Most noticeable are the Durkheimian attention to integration and the Weberian preoccupation with the specific form of modern law and its role in a rationalized society. But Parsons was also influenced in the development of his sociological perspective on law by insights from legal scholarship. Parsons knew some of the work of Roscoe Pound and had met the legal scholar at Harvard, auditing one of his seminars in legal philosophy in the 1930s. While generally appreciative of Pound's work, Parsons (1968: 48) found his conception of sociological jurisprudence "a little premature." While Parsons recognized that Pound was influenced by the sociologist Ross, the more distinctly sociological orientations in the study of law Parsons argued at that time to be "almost wholly continental European," including the works of Ehrlich, Petrazycki, Sorokin, Gurvitch, and Weber (Parsons 1968: 50). Parsons attributed the relative lack of influence of these European scholars in the United States to the differences between the European and American legal systems.

A more important source of inspiration for Parsons' thinking on law from within legal scholarship was the work of Lon Fuller, who was a colleague of Parsons at Harvard where Fuller was a professor in the law school. Without dwelling on Fuller's theory more systematically, it will suffice here to note that Fuller (1964) defended a view of law as a reflection of a society's moral values, which he conceived procedurally in terms of law's function to guide behavior. As a legal scholar, Fuller devoted most attention to proscribing how law should be structured to be more effective, but Fuller's basic conception of the objectives of law were closely akin to a functionalist notion of law as social control.

Parsons' interest in law and his reliance on Fuller's work led the two Harvard scholars to organize a series of graduate seminars on "Law and Sociology" in the late 1960s (Parsons 1968: 51). Interestingly, Parsons did not so much view this collaboration in terms of a necessity of sociology to learn from law as in terms of the role sociology could play in the development of an academic legal education. Fuller agreed with this view of bringing sociology into law rather than the reverse. Fuller (1968) observes that the sociology of law by the late 1960s had done much to bring out the social dimensions of law and had thus transcended the perspective, dominating the growing law and society movement, of looking at law in relation to society. The law and society movement was (and today still is) an interdisciplinary research domain that houses sociologists, anthropologists, economists and other social and behavioral scientists interested in the study of law. Fuller (1968) notes that the construction of such a comprehensive field and its successful institutionalization – in the formation of the Law and Society Association in 1964 and the founding of the *Law and Society Review* in 1966 – might lead scholars to overlook that law is always part of society and thus that law contains "within its own internal workings social dimensions worthy of the best attentions of the sociologist" (p. 57). The legal scholarship of Fuller, then, allows for a role of sociology, not merely as a partner of law understood as legal scholarship, but also as the privileged social science for the study of law as an institution.

Conclusion

The historical and intellectual development of the sociology of law in the United States is a peculiar and still little known story that should be of interest to legal scholars and sociologists of law alike. Historically, the scholarly study of the social dimensions of law in the United States grew out of the professional law schools, not directly out of classical sociology. The scholarship of Holmes, in particular, instigated a revolutionary turn in legal scholarship towards socio-logical jurisprudence. Systematized by Roscoe Pound, sociological jurisprudence relied on advances in the social sciences to develop a perspective of law as social control that remained committed to a normative orientation of legal policy to develop insights that could contribute to build a just system of law. In this respect it is note-worthy to observe that Pound clearly realized that jurisprudence and sociology have different origins and goals. The perspective of legal realism abandoned almost all of sociological jurisprudence's inherent normative orientations, yet its psychologistic understanding of law prevented any major influence on the sociology of law. Legal realism was instead more influential to the anthropology of law because of its emphasis on ethnographic methods. Because of its strongly empiricist orientation, legal realism also influenced the early law and society movement (Garth and Sterling 1998; Ingersoll 1981) and has more recently affected the launch of a movement of so-called Empirical Legal Studies (Suchman 2006). The attitude of skepticism in legal realism concerning the objectives of law also resonates with certain currents in Critical Legal Studies (Treviño 1994; Milovanovic 2003; see Chapter 9).

The development of sociological jurisprudence and legal realism was not primarily a function of the intellectual history of sociology and social science but of a development of the professionalization of law that also affected the sociology of law and socio-legal studies. In terms of their respective objectives, sociological jurisprudence and sociology of law differ in terms of their divergent attitudes towards the relation between law and morality. Historically, however, the modern sociology of law found in sociological jurisprudence – unlike legal realism – a precursor that helped shape its direction. In this sense, part of the development of the sociology of law related more closely to the social reality of law rather than the intellectual power of the sociological vision. In fact, legal scholarship in the United States was so involved with the social study of law that it had even managed to appropriate some of the early European sociology of law. The writings of Petrazycki, Timasheff, and Gurvitch, and even the sociology of law of Max Weber were during the years before the ascent of structural functionalism discussed much more by legal scholars than by sociologists.

The radical break towards the subfield of the sociology of law was offered by Talcott Parsons. By means of its application and extension by fellow functionalists as well as its critical reception by theoretical opponents of Parsonian thinking, Parsons' sociology of law had beneficial repercussions on an institutional level, stimulating the development of the sociology of law in a manner that is rivaled only by the institutionalization of the law and society movement. Whereas the latter, however, can claim success in terms of having built an enduring tradition with a large following, the former is superior in having set the intellectual foundations of an authentically sociological study of law. This discussion is not meant to deny that the Parsonian approach in the sociology of law was historically eclipsed in popularity by the law and society movement. The reconstructive analysis in this chapter has sought to recapture the stature that must be accorded to those that facilitated the sociology of law in an intellectual sense. For not only did Parsons develop a systematic sociological theory on the basis of the founding works of the likes of Weber and Durkheim, who thereby became classics, he also laid the groundwork for a distinctly sociological study of law that is independent from sociological jurisprudence. From then on, the subfield of the sociology of law within the broader sociological discipline need no longer place itself in a position of "defensive insularity" relative to sociological jurisprudence and other forms of legal scholarship (Cotterrell 1975: 388). It can instead cooperate with other approaches to the study of law in the social sciences and in jurisprudence, and it can, additionally, relate itself to other sociological subfields and to sociology as a whole. As the next chapter will show, this maturation of the sociology of law also involved a proliferation of a wide range of theoretical perspectives used to study law sociologically.

6 | Sociology of law and the antinomies of modern thought

The evolution of modern sociology has been marked by an increasing diversity of theoretical perspectives. Theoretical pluralism in sociology has developed to such an extent that it is today often unclear where theoretical lines are drawn, what they mean, and what the value of such diversity might be. Some scholars have condemned theoretical pluralism as a key weakness in sociology, showing a lack of unity in sociological thought, while others have seen in sociology's theoretical diversity a richness that reflects the complexity of social life.[1] Theoretical diversity also marks the specialty field of the sociology of law. This chapter will provide an overview of the main strands of theoretical perspectives in the modern sociology of law on the basis of a review of the theoretical ideas that emerged out of earlier orientations. This discussion should also be able to bridge the various theoretical perspectives with the substantively guided chapters in the next two parts of this book. As such, this chapter will look at once backwards and forward to theoretical developments in the sociology of law.

The analyses in this chapter are developed around the theoretical revolutions and evolutions that emerged in sociology since the gradual decline of the functionalist dominance. Historically, these developments took place roughly from the 1960s onwards and have continued to characterize the discipline at large and the sociology of law, in particular, until this day. The present-day situation is such that theoretical diversity has increased in ways more complex than the modern era of sociology that lasted roughly until the 1980s. But this presentation can be ideal-typically understood as a heuristic device to

---

[1] Discussions on the meaning of theoretical pluralism in sociology have been addressed, as early as the 1970s, in terms of a crisis of sociology (Gouldner 1970). More recent discussions have focused on the lack of cumulative knowledge, systematic theorizing, and other components of "what's wrong with sociology" (Cole 2001).

offer a systematic overview of the main theoretical schools and the underlying problems in the sociology of law. As stated before, this book does not seek to take sides in these theoretical battles but is meant to reveal the contributions that each theoretical movement in sociology has made to the study of law and to bring out how each movement fits the broader framework of sociological scholarship. This chapter will specifically revolve around three crystallizing theoretical moments in the sociology of law.[2]

First, the emergence of the so-called conflict-theoretical perspective in sociology challenged the structural-functionalist emphasis on equilibrium and order. The subfield of the sociology of law was well represented in this movement towards the development of critical perspectives by means of several seminal contributions, such as the works of William Chambliss and Austin Turk. The most important characteristics and representatives of this movement, including Marxist and non-Marxist conflict perspectives, will be reviewed.

Second, a theoretical controversy that is not exclusive but nonetheless very distinct to the specialty area of the sociology of law concerns the relationship between law and morality and the possibilities and desirability of a scientific sociology of law. Some sociological perspectives seek to retain law in an intimate relation with morality and justice in such a way that normative questions cannot be avoided. Among these normatively oriented perspectives of law is most famously the theory of jurisprudential sociology that was developed by Philip Selznick and Philippe Nonet. On the opposing side of this debate, the work of Donald Black occupies a central place. Black's pure sociology of law presents, in terms stronger and clearer than any other perspective in the discipline, a strictly scientific and resolutely sociological approach to law as part of a theory of social control as a dependent variable.

Third, interactionist and behavioral theories have responded to the functionalist preoccupation with structure and society at the macro-level. There are at least two noteworthy variations in these micro-theoretical perspectives. On the one hand, interpretive schools of thought have developed around a quest to understand human

---

[2] For alternative views of the intellectual history of the modern sociology of law, see the overview articles and books cited in the Introduction, especially notes 1 and 7.

interactions. Most famously, symbolic interactionism has contributed to this approach. On the other hand, other micro-oriented sociologists have sought to develop systematic theories of behavior in terms of a rationalist approach. Among the relevant theoretical perspectives from this viewpoint are exchange and rational choice theory.

Sociological conflict theory

A useful way to bridge the approaches in the sociology of law that were developed in the period before World War II and the more recent currents that lasted until the latter decades of the twentieth century is to consider the centrality of the work of Parsons and the theoretical debates that were ignited by the functionalist approach. To be sure, this discussion cannot be limited to the direct influence of Parsons' theories in the sociology of law, for, as explained in Chapter 5, that influence was relatively unpronounced. But it is important to stress the relevance of Parsonian theorizing in sociological theory as it affected many specialty fields, not least of all in terms of the critical reception of functionalist thought. The theories of modern sociology, in other words, must be seen in light of the theoretical schools which they represent and react against in the course of their respective developments in order to uncover both the historical and systematic aspects of theoretical movement.

The conflict-theoretical tradition in modern sociology revolves around the notion that conflict must be studied as an essential component of society. Conflict theory, therefore, is not to be equated with the sociology of conflict. All sociologists agree that there is conflict and that it can and should be studied. However, whereas an order-oriented perspective conceives of society as essentially involving processes of stability and integration, conflict-theoretical perspectives conceive of conflict as essential to the unraveling of the conditions of society. By implication, whereas an order-oriented sociology engages in a systematic and detached study of society, conflict theory involves a practical or critical attitude that is oriented towards change and the betterment of social conditions. Both with respect to its notion of conflict and its conception of knowledge and praxis, conflict theory can theoretically rely on the work of Karl Marx. Although the work of Marx was traditionally not considered of much relevance to sociology, this situation changed radically once critical or conflict-theoretical sociology gained in popularity. The modern manifestations of critical sociology, however, are also more autonomous and diverse than a mere recapturing of Marx's social philosophy, especially in the sociology of law, an area to which Marx after all contributed very little.

Historically, the roots of Marxist and critical thought in sociology go far back in time.[3] Early efforts in sociology relying upon conflict-theoretical and/or Marxist insights can especially be found among certain European writers, such as Antonio Gramsci, Georg Lukács, Theodor Adorno, Max Horkheimer, Herbert Marcuse, and other representatives of the Critical Theory perspective of the so-called Frankfurt School. However, many of these critically oriented works were not part of the mainstream enterprise of academic sociology, especially not in the United States, until they were later introduced in modern variations of sociology, typically as part of criticisms against structural functionalism. Thus, for instance, Lewis Coser (1956) developed a theory of conflict, in response to the functionalist understanding thereof, on the basis of a reception of the treatment of conflict in the writings of Georg Simmel. Other sociologists, such as C. Wright Mills, Ralf Dahrendorf, and Tom Bottomore, made more concerted attempts to introduce the thought of Marx into the sociological enterprise. Until the 1950s and 1960s, there was talk only of Marx or Marxism, but from then on there was also talk of a Marxist sociology, leading to a proliferation of works in this new theoretical approach. To explain the relevance of the conflict-theoretical development in the sociology of law, a closer look at the work of C. Wright Mills is useful because it responded directly against the dominance of structural functionalism in sociology.

The sociology of Mills is theoretically based on a reconstruction of Marx's thought infused with Weberian notions of power. In a biting critique directly targeted at Parsons, Mills (1959) argues for sociologists to adopt a sociological imagination with which intimate connections between larger structural issues (public issues) and the daily problems that confront individuals (personal troubles) can be established. It is the central shortcoming of Parsonian and other forms of mainstream sociology, according to Mills, that they are unable and

---

[3] On the origins and evolutions of critical sociology, including the development of Marxist sociology, see Collins 1975, 1994; Swingewood 1975.

unwilling to cultivate such as sociological imagination. The "grand theory" of Parsons, as Mills labeled the functionalist approach, is not only overly abstract, it also assumes, rather than demonstrates, and advocates, rather than merely observes, social harmony and stability.

Substantively, Mills critiques functionalism for not paying attention to the power structures of society. In an important study of the so-called power elite in American society, Mills (1956) argues that a key feature of twentieth-century American social life has been the concentration and centralization of power among a few elite groups. Power in American society has gradually been centralized around corporate, military, and political interests. The economic elite is dominant and controls the military and political elites, while the political elite is controlled by both the economic and military elites. Although the elites are relatively independent of one another, their respective memberships overlap. Members of the elites also possess similar social characteristics and backgrounds, for instance in terms of family, education, and cultural interests. Because of the elites' power to make consequential decisions and their capacity to shield from criticisms, Mills considered the power elite structure a major threat to American democracy.

Mills's multidimensional concept of power is clearly influenced by Weber, but he rejects Weber's notion of value-freedom. Instead, Mills argues, with Marx, for an activist scholarship on the basis of a role of the sociologist as an intellectual "craftsman" who can unite public issues with private troubles. Yet, rather than being driven by concerns over the appropriate sociological role or puzzles of a theoretical nature, Mills was in the development of his work driven by the conditions of American society and a quest to use knowledge to advance social change. In this connection, it is not insignificant to note the historical times when conflict theory emerged in sociology. From the late 1950s onwards, the optimism of the immediate post-World War II era in much of the Western world had begun to wane in view of the escalation of the Cold War and the nuclear arms race, the continuance of warfare and international violence, such as with the Korean and Vietnam wars, the growing sense of global injustices surrounding the uneven spread of capitalism and the disintegration of colonial powers, and the social ills that persist in many Western nations despite their relative wealth.

Towards a critical sociology of law

Several sociologists of law have applied insights from conflict-theoretical sociology, including Marxist thought, to analyses of their specialty area. Yet, as compared to the influence of conflict and Marxian thinking in sociology at large, these developments were in the sociology of law somewhat slower in coming.[4] Among the historical origins of a conflict-theoretical sociology of law, the contributions by William Chambliss, Austin Turk, and Alan Hunt stand out because of their foundational status and lasting influence.

In one of the most influential papers in the modern sociology of law, William Chambliss (1964) offers a study of vagrancy laws in terms of a historical study of the socio-economic contexts in which such laws had emerged and were applied. Chambliss differentiates four phases in the development of vagrancy laws as they were adopted in the United Kingdom and the United States. The first vagrancy law was passed in England in 1349. It made it a crime to give alms to anybody who was unemployed while being of sound body and mind. Under threat of prison, vagrants were forced to engage in labor. The passing of this law resulted from a need to secure cheap labor after the Black Death of 1348 had killed half the population and decimated the labor force. In a subsequent phase, the vagrancy law remained on the books but was not applied, because, Chambliss argues, feudal society was transforming into an industrial one. In a next phase, from 1530 onwards, attention again shifted to criminality, and the severity of punishment for violations against the vagrancy law increased because industry had expanded. The newly targeted crimes consequently concerned stealing and the robbing of merchants transporting goods. In 1743, finally, the categories of vagrancy further expanded to include all persons wandering, such as vagabonds. Thus, the function of the vagrancy law was extended beyond the control of labor to the preservation of order and the prevention of crime.

The focus of Chambliss's analysis of vagrancy laws is resolutely empirical, but its general theoretical indebtedness to a Marxist-structural perspective is clear as well. Chambliss's study was theoretically situated in response to programmatic statements that had called for a new

---

[4] For overviews of critical sociology of law, including Marxist perspectives, see Beirne and Quinney 1982; Chambliss and Seidman 1971; Collins 1982; Fine 2002; Milovanovic 1983; Spitzer 1983.

direction in the sociology of law. Among these early formulations, Chambliss mentions papers by Arnold Rose (1962) and Gilbert Geis (1959). Geis urged for the use of insights on law for criminology that could come from a greater collaboration between sociology and legal scholarship, while Rose formulated the objectives of the sociology of law, beyond a juridical understanding of law, in terms of questions about the social, political, and cultural dimensions of law. Yet, while such programmatic statements had distinct theoretical significance, they remained somewhat isolated and did not directly inspire many further developments in the sociology of law, at least not until Chambliss and others began to push the sociology of law in a conflict-theoretical direction.

Chambliss took on a more elaborate study of law as an instrument of power, first in a book-length treatise on law and power in the American context (Chambliss and Seidman 1971) and subsequently in many of his later writings (Chambliss 1973, 1999). Chambliss primarily developed a conflict-theoretical perspective on law in light of a practical need, in the turbulent times of the late 1960s and early 1970s, to develop a theory capable of asking questions pertaining to social processes of change and disintegration. Countering the notion of the legal order as reflecting principles of justice and right, Chambliss conceives of the law as a self-serving instrument to maintain power and privilege in the perpetual conflict of society. The legal order operates in such a way that it systematically discriminates against the poor and underprivileged while favoring the wealthy and powerful.

As late as 1971, sociologist Elliott Currie (1971) could observe the neglect of the influence of Marx's thought in the sociology of law and the underdevelopment of conflict-theoretical perspectives that resulted in a failure to view law as an instrument of power and class rule. Throughout the 1970s, however, attempts to inject Marxian thought in the sociology of law escalated in number. To complete such a program, it was necessary to distill from Marx's writings those elements that might be useful for a sociology of law, an endeavor that was not insignificant given Marx's relative silence on law. The clarification and introduction of Marx's ideas on law in sociology was particularly discussed by several Anglo-Saxon sociologists (Cain 1974; Cain and Hunt 1979; Hirst 1972). In order to accommodate a more distinct focus on law, these discussions were sometimes conducted with the aid of a recapturing of earlier interpretations of

Marx's theory, such as the writings of the Russian legal scholar Evgenii Pashukanis (1924), and the reinterpretation of Marx's thought by contemporary writers such as Louis Althusser, Antonio Gramsci, and Nicos Poulantzas (Hunt 1981a, 1981b).

Although introductions to and interpretations of Marx's thought on law were conducted until well into the 1980s and 1990s (Melossi 1986; Spitzer 1983; Vincent 1993), sociologists had by the 1970s also begun to use Marx's theories in the sociology of law, in both empirical and theoretical efforts, with sometimes sharply different results. While some scholars began to rely on Marx to develop a new direction in sociology of law and conduct empirical research accordingly (Beirne 1979; Hagan and Leon 1977; Lauderdale and Larson 1978), other interpreters took on the view that a sociology of law on the basis of Marx, given the basic ideas of historical materialism and Marx's reluctance to discuss law independently, was not possible unless such an enterprise was rooted in and remained part of a more general critique of capitalist society (Beirne 1975; Hirst 1972). The latter perspective was also defended by some Marxist sociologists working in the areas of crime and deviance (Quinney 1973, 1978).

Criminological sociology proved a fertile soil for a reception of Marxian ideas because of the shift in this specialty area, especially during the 1960s and 1970s, to turn away from the study of crime and criminals towards the analysis of social control and criminal law as important aspects of criminalization (Hopkins 1975). Additionally, it is noteworthy that the Marxist orientation in the sociology of law was more readily accomplished in the United Kingdom and countries of the European continent where scholarly traditions until this day tend to be more theoretical and more readily cross the boundaries of disciplines, such as from social philosophy to sociology and from Marxian thought to sociological theory. Excursions on the sociology of law programs developed by Austin Turk and Alan Hunt will show both the basic strategies of and the variability within the conflict-theoretical direction in the sociology of law.

The American sociologist Austin Turk (1969, 1976a, 1976b) developed a theoretical program for a non-Marxist conflict-theoretical sociology of law. Against the widespread notion in mainstream socio-logy to conceive of law in terms of conflict resolution, Turk outlines a perspective on law as a form of social power and a partisan weapon in social conflict. Law is a set of resources for which people contend in order to promote their ideas and interests or exercise power over and against one another. Turk specifies five kinds of resource control in law: (1) police power over the means of physical violence and the agents of control; (2) economic power over the material rewards and costs associated with law; (3) political power in the legal decision-making process; (4) ideological power of law as culture to control what is conceived as legal and just; and (5) diversionary power over the amount of attention and time invested in law. Turk encourages sociologists of law to investigate how the legal order operates in any given situation alongside of these dimensions in order to study whether and how law regulates or, on the contrary, generates social conflict.

A more distinctly Marxist version of a critical sociology of law can be found in the work of sociologist Alan Hunt, who since the late 1970s has consistently worked to develop a comprehensive vision of a Marxist perspective on law.[5] Hunt's approach is rooted in a critique of the evolution of the sociological movement in law from socio-logical jurisprudence to the (functionalist) theory of law as social control. Downplaying the significance of this transition, Hunt des-cribes both theoretical movements as bourgeois perspectives that fail to question the extent to which major legal ideals have not been realized in capitalist societies. Hunt also questions the dichotomy between consensus and conflict perspectives as it has traditionally been phrased. Both perspectives typically hold on to the notion of theories as models that are used to account for empirical variation. This requirement, however, Hunt argues to be incongruent with a radical theory based on Marx. Rather than attempting to be empi-rically correct, a Marxist theory asks questions and uses concepts on matters that are judged to be significant. A Marxist theory of law, in particular, should be developed on the basis of a concept of law that does not take as its starting-point the immediate form in which law appears, but rather has to conceptualize law in the context of a Marxian theory of society.

Hunt argues that law is to be viewed in terms of the reproduction of the social order, involving a continuous process whereby the domi-nant structures of society are shaped and reshaped within specific

---

[5] See Hunt 1976, 1980, 1981a, 1981b, 1985, 1995, 1997 and the essays collected in *Explorations in Law and Society* (Hunt 1993).

socio-historical circumstances. Among the social institutions and practices involved in this process, law functions as a means of domination. Seeking to overcome the dichotomy between consensus and conflict perspectives, Hunt argues that domination through law takes on the form of repressive and ideological domination. Repressive (or coercive) domination refers to the dimensions of law that function to advance and protect the interests of the ruling classes. In this repressive orientation, law stands in a special relation with state power as the state has control over the legitimate means of coercion. Legal violence is applied through the specialized agencies of the law-state complex, including the police and the courts. Repressive domination is a necessary condition for the development of ideological domination. Linking the coercive and consensual aspects of law, ideological domination refers to the activities and processes of law whereby the assent of a society's members is mobilized. Assent does not merely refer to the legitimacy of law, but conveys the notion that the ideas people hold about the law are constituted in the context of their social existence and, in turn, will affect the reproduction of society. Thus, the ideology of law contributes to legitimize the legal as well as broader social order to establish a condition of hegemony.

Normativity in the sociology of law: jurisprudential sociology

The relationship between law and morality has given the sociology of law a peculiar place among the specialties in the discipline. The earliest efforts to think about law socially were motivated strongly by normative aspirations. Durkheim was arguably the first sociologist who deliberately sought to separate this normative orientation from a sociological analysis of society as a moral order. Precisely in order to study morality sociologically, Durkheim turned to the analysis of law. How far Durkheim was hoping to ultimately infuse in society a morality that was sociologically grounded remains a point of some contention and need not concern us here. Suffice it to note, however, that sociologists of law have continued to struggle with the question of whether the normativity of law has special implications for the sociological study of law, specifically whether it implies that the sociology of law will always contain a normative or humanistic quality or whether it can and should be exclusively scientific in its approach.

Some of the earliest representatives of the sociology of law (most notably Gurvitch) conceived of the sociology of law as a companion to legal theory and treated both as subordinate to the philosophy of law which offers the most foundational viewpoint. In the functionalist school of the sociology of law, the normativity of law was bracketed in favor of a concept of law as social control. Normative questions were not judged unimportant but were relegated to the field of legal scholarship and sociological jurisprudence as well as philosophy of law. Yet, some representatives of the modern sociology of law in the second half of the twentieth century conceived of the intimate relation between law and morality such that normative questions could and should not be avoided. Among these scholars, Philip Selznick and Philippe Nonet have done most to develop a legal-sociological perspective that retains an intimate connection with normative and, relatedly, jurisprudential orientations.[6]

The development of jurisprudential sociology is based on a specific conception of the changing objectives of the sociology of law. In a first stage of development, the sociology of law mainly consists of efforts to determine its proper program and articulate theoretical discussions accordingly. In a subsequent stage, sociologists of law practice the program of the first stage by means of in-depth researches.[7] In the third and final stage, the sociology of law reaches full maturity and autonomy to address larger objectives and return to the moral impulse that initially set off the development of the sociology of law but that can now be tackled with confidence on a level of sophistication on the basis of insights derived during the second phase. The second and third stages are most critical from the viewpoint of jurisprudential sociology and mark the present era of the sociology of law. As a matter of sociological craftsmanship, sociologists of law study the law as an agency of social control in terms of the science of society

---

[6] See Nonet 1969, 1976; Nonet and Selznick 1978; Selznick 1959, 1961, 1968, 1969, 1992, 1999, 2004. See also Krygier 2002 and other contributions in Kagan, Krygier, and Winston 2002.

[7] In the American context, these early stages of development are mainly represented by the formative period of an institutionalized sociology of law during the 1950s and 1960s, when programmatic statements and overviews of the sociology of law first appeared in the mainstream journals. See, e.g., Aubert 1963; Auerbach 1966; Davis 1957; Gibbs 1966, 1968; Riesman 1957; Rose 1968; Skolnick 1965.

they know best. Yet, extending the level of sociological technique, sociologists of law ought to also take the next step and re-engage in the classic problems of legal philosophy and assess the normative components that are embedded in law in order to engage in an intellectual effort aimed at the creation of a society based on justice. Thus reasserting which values ought to be expressed in law, the sociology of law is ultimately in a position to formulate a new theory of natural law that avoids the pitfalls traditionally attributed to that perspective in favor of a pragmatist understanding that argues against a dichotomy between facts and values in favor of an approach that recognizes that values are embedded in social life and therefore remain a fundamental concern of sociology.

While the final stage of the sociology of law has not yet been fully achieved, Selznick and Nonet argue that some efforts have been undertaken to accomplish some of the stated objectives of working towards the larger project of the sociology of law in view of the betterment of the legal order. Actively engaged towards building a fully realized sociology of law, Selznick and Nonet applied their theoretical aspirations in various empirical studies. Contributing to the study of access to law, for instance, Nonet (1969) has analyzed the conditions that facilitate an effective use of law. Among other conditions, an appeal to law to be authoritative relies on how effectively legal authorities are sensitized and made responsive to popular demands. Legal competence is also a factor of the capacity of people to appeal to legal authorities, which they may derive from their politically and socially advantageous position or capacity to organize in groups. Other conditions that affect the appeal to law include the development of a positive attitude to law, whereby law is seen as a means of support in a particular cause.

In line with his interests in organizational sociology, Selznick (1969) has studied legality in the context of private organizations. As in public life, organizations in the private world are guided by efforts of social control that rely on specialized mechanisms to proclaim and enforce authoritative systems of rules. Law is not merely a functional necessity of social control, however, but must also be normatively understood to take seriously the values that are present in law. Rather than infusing principles of justice from the outside, a normative sociology of law uses the values that are latent in law as a source of evaluation conducted in the light of law and its participants.

From the viewpoint of jurisprudential sociology, the principle of the rule of law stands out among the ideals that are embedded in law. The key component of the rule of law is the restraint that is placed on the making and application of laws in favor of a specified set of standards that has to be met for law to be fair and just. Avoiding arbitrariness in law and increasing due process, the rule of law is never fully achieved but there is nonetheless a general trend towards an increasing realization of the ideal of the rule of law. Nonet and Selznick (1978) have articulated this interest most systematically in a study on the transition towards responsive law. The study takes up the basic questions of jurisprudence but treats them in a social-scientific way to examine the empirical variations that exist in the development of law in terms of such variables as the relation between law and coercion, law and politics, and law and morality. Three types of law are accordingly distinguished. Repressive law is primarily marked by an emphasis on order that is to be accomplished through an extensive and intensive system of coercion and subordinated to a strong political power. Autonomous law is a differentiated institution that requires legitimation and a restrained system of coercion and is relatively independent of politics. Responsive law is a facilitator of societal responses to social needs and ambitions on the basis of legal competence and a blending of political and legal powers. Nonet and Selznick suggest a developmental model from repressive over autonomous to responsive law, yet they do not conceive this transition as a description of actual historical events but rather as a model for the identification of potential for change, specifically in terms of the realization of certain values as they emerge in legal orders. Law is argued to drift towards responsive law and a growing quest for more justice because and when the legal order includes not only rules but also principles related to the satisfaction of human needs.

The theoretical perspective of jurisprudential sociology merges a moral evaluation and a historical description of the evolution of law and, additionally, situates this development within and beyond the confines of Western models of law as a universal development with cross-cultural variations. Underlying this approach is a dialectical conception of the relationship between (sociological knowledge of) law and (normative conceptions of) justice. On the one hand, justice depends on knowledge in that value judgments in the area of law and morality can be improved on the basis of relevant sociological knowledge. On the other hand, sociological analysis requires a selection of relevant facts that is grounded in both theoretical and practical questions. Selznick and Nonet thus argue that there should be a close connection between sociology of law and those branches of jurisprudence that are open to and fruitful for sociological inquiry. Sociology of law must take the ideas embedded in law seriously and therefore also be jurisprudentially informed so its efforts can be beneficial in determining policy.

The expulsion of normativity: pure sociology

On the opposing side of the debate over the normativity of law and its repercussions for sociological analyses of law, the work of Donald Black is of central importance. Since the early 1970s, Black has consistently contributed to advance a perspective in the sociology of law that is resolutely scientific in its methods and objectives and sociological in its approach.[8] Black formulates his perspective of a pure sociology of law both in response to the continued infusion of jurisprudence and matters of policy in legal sociology as well as the debate over the political and normative implications of certain strands in the sociology of law. Black is interested in formulating a general theory of law that can account for empirical variation irrespective of any value judgments or policy claims. Conceiving of law as governmental social control, Black's pure sociology is ultimately oriented at a general theory of all forms of social control, defined as the handling of right and wrong by defining and responding to deviant behavior. Exorcizing normative and legal questions from the sociology of law, Black does not imply that such questions are not relevant, only that they cannot be part of science and can therefore also not be legitimately addressed on the basis of science. The perspective of pure sociology does not deny the possibility of applied sociology, but argues that applied sociology must rely on pure sociology.

---

[8] Among Donald Black's central works are his seminal article on the boundaries of legal sociology (Black 1972a) and the elaboration of that program in *The Behavior of Law* (Black 1976). Also noteworthy are Black's application of his theory to the practice of law (Black 1989) and several more recent writings that clarify the epistemology and objectives of his theoretical approach (Black 1995, 1997, 2000, 2002, 2007). Black has also engaged in a debate with Selznick and Nonet, although their respective perspectives were developed independently of each other (Black 1972b; Nonet 1976; Selznick 1973).

The epistemological orientation that underlies Black's pure sociology is both scientific in its ambition to formulate a general theory and
sociological in terms of its paradigmatic orientation. Black conceives
of ordering variation in empirical reality as the goal of theory, defined
as a logical system of ideas that ties together a large number of observations in a coherent pattern. The criteria of scientific theory include:
testability to make the theory amenable to falsification as statement
about reality; generality in covering a wide variety of events; parsi-
mony in developing orderly statements; validity or empirical adequacy
in conforming to conditions in reality; and originality or novelty in
establishing creative or surprising systems of knowledge. The paradigmatic framework in which Black's theory is situated is distinctly
sociological. Rejecting teleological and anthropocentric premises that
take into account, respectively, normative and subjective dimensions,
Black's approach of social life is radically anti-psychological in developing a multidimensional perspective of social life, including law, as a
function of structural characteristics of social space. At the same time,
Black argues his theory to apply to variation in the handling of cases
and thus to apply to the behavior of the individuals who are involved
in cases as well.

Applying his perspective to the study of law, Black has developed a
number of propositions on the behavior of law (and other forms of
social control) across social space. Law is conceived of as a reality that
appears in variable forms of quantity and style. The quantity of law
refers to the amount of law that is available, for instance whether or
not a particular kind of human conduct is regulated by law and
whether or not a legal sanction is applied. The styles of law can be
penal, compensatory, therapeutic, or conciliatory, depending on the
methods and objectives of law and the standards upon which they are
based. Black subsequently proceeds to study the geometry of law on
the basis of variations in social space in terms of stratification, differentiation, integration, culture, organization, and social control. Stratification refers to the vertical structure of society in terms of the
inequality of wealth. Vertical space can be high or low in terms of
position or downward or upward in direction. Morphology refers to
the horizontal aspect of society, including the division of labor (differentiation) and the relative degrees of intimacy and distance (integration). Culture is the symbolic dimension of social life, including
expressed ideas about truth, beauty, and ethics, such as in science, art,

and religion. Culturally, societies and social groups can vary from being closely related to extremely distant. Organization refers to the degree to which a society is formally organized. Social control, finally, refers to the normative aspect of social life, including law as well as other mechanisms and institutions, such as custom, family, gossip, warfare, and religion.

Among the many specific propositions on the behavior of law proposed by Black, a few can be mentioned to illustrate the approach of pure sociology. Law varies directly with stratification: societies with higher degrees of stratification have more law. Law also varies directly with vertical space: status and wealth increase the amount of law. In terms of morphology, law is a curvilinear function of relational distance: law increases as people are less related until a point is reached where they are entirely isolated from one another. Law varies directly with culture: simpler societies have less law than more differentiated societies. With respect to social control, finally, law is argued to vary inversely with other forms of social control as other institutions performing functions of social control alleviate the need for law. On the basis of such propositions, pure sociology seeks to explain and predict the behavior of social life in terms of social space in value-neutral terms. Black argues pure sociology to involve a radical break from prior forms of legal sociology (and jurisprudence) that are subjectivist and concerned with practical and normative questions. Irrespective of the intrinsic merits of Black's approach, it is striking that the sharpness of his formulations has enabled much theoretical debate and empirical research.[9]

Micro-theoretical perspectives in the sociology of law

The third and final theoretical demarcation line, next to the debate over order and conflict and the dispute over normativity and objectivity, revolves around the appropriate level of sociological analysis. While structural functionalism as well as most versions of

---

[9] For more and less critical discussions on the theoretical merits of Black's sociology of law, see, for instance, Black 1979; Greenberg 1983; Horwitz 1983, 2002; Hunt 1983; Wong 1995. Empirical work developed on the basis of Black's theory is presented and discussed by Dawson and Welsh 2005; Doyle and Luckenbill 1991; Hembroff 1987; Gottfredson and Hindelang 1979a, 1979b; Lessan and Sheley 1992; Myers 1980; Mooney 1986.

sociological conflict theory share an attention for the broader social structures and processes that operate in society at the macro-level, alternative perspectives have been developed to focus on the micro-dimensions of social life at the level of social interactions. Among the central schools of these micro-oriented perspectives is symbolic interactionism, a theoretical approach that finds its origins in the work of the social philosopher George Herbert Mead.[10] Mead developed a theoretical perspective concerning the interplay among mind, self, and society on the basis of a psychological approach to human conduct. According to Mead, the human mind is uniquely gifted in using meaningful symbols in communication. Through interaction among individuals, the meanings of symbols are shared and the social order is constituted as the organized set of interactions among individuals.

Mead's theoretical ideas were little known and of no influence in sociology until they were appropriately framed and elaborated by the Chicago sociologist Herbert Blumer. Reacting explicitly against the structural orientation in functionalism, Blumer argues that social phenomena can only derive their reality from the concrete situations in which that reality is negotiated. The focus of sociology should thus be on the interpretive behavior of people in interaction and how processes of interaction shape the social order. The basic postulate of symbolic interactionism is that human beings act on the basis of the variable meanings that people, things, and ideas have for them. These meanings are socially constructed in the course of interactions. Because meanings are formed out of a continual process of interpretation in interaction, society is essentially fluid and dynamic.

Symbolic interactionism is a resolutely subjectivist sociological approach that is interested in interpretive studies of human inter-action. Congruent with the basic theoretical premises of the perspec-tive, the methodological preference is to abandon structured research projects geared at testing hypotheses in favor of ethnographic studies that seek to unravel the motives and meanings people attribute to their actions from an empathic viewpoint. Relying on qualitative techniques of investigation, such as participant-observation and in-depth inter-viewing, the goal of interactionist research is to construct so-called

---

[10] Mead's central theoretical ideas were collected on the basis of his lectures and published posthumously (Mead 1934). The theory of symbolic interactionism is best represented in the influential work of Herbert Blumer (1969).

grounded theories on the basis of the application of sensitizing concepts in natural research settings.

As with the development of certain strands in conflict theory, the sociology of law has benefited mostly from symbolic interactionism in the areas of criminological sociology, where symbolic-interactionist insights led to the development of labeling theory. Best represented in the classic work of Howard S. Becker (1963), the basic premise of labeling theory is that crime is not a type of behavior but rather a label that is attached to certain kinds of behavior. The sociological attention should thus turn away from a study of the causes of criminal behavior towards an analysis of the motives of action on the part of the persons who engage in deviant or rule-violating conduct and the persons and institutions who apply rules. Labeling theorists therefore study the processes of social control that define something as criminal (primary criminalization) and that apply laws and sanctions in certain contexts (secondary criminalization).

With its sociological attention shifting to the societal reactions to deviance, including the definition of crime in criminal law, labeling theory has been extremely influential in sociology (Schur 1968; Matsueda 2000). Symbolic interactionism has also been independently influential in the sociology of law irrespective of concerns for crime and criminal law.[11] By and large, however, the major influences of symbolic interactionism in the sociology of law have been methodological in popularizing an orientation towards qualitative research methods, without a major rethinking in sociological theorizing on law. Major efforts in line with this interpretive orientation, therefore, have advanced sociological knowledge on the actual workings of law in an interactionist framework (Carlin 1962; Lyman 2002; Meisenhelder 1981). Yet, novel theoretical programs in the sociology of law on the basis of interactionist perspectives are scant.

Among the more intellectually exciting efforts in legal sociology that is congruent with an interactionist framework, at least in methodological respects, is some of the recent work on legal consciousness. Research on legal consciousness centers on people's experiences and attitudes about the law, typically in order to address how the workings

---

[11] On the influence of symbolic interactionism in the sociology of law, useful overviews are provided by Brittan (1981); Travers (2002).

of law are sustained or challenged by such everyday perceptions.[12] From this perspective, Patricia Ewick and Susan Silbey (1995, 1998, 2003) defend a cultural perspective on law on the basis of narrative analysis. The authors suggest that narratives must not be seen in a narrow setting of their immediate narrator and audience, but should be situated within the wider structural contexts that determine whether narratives can bring about certain political effects. Differentiating between hegemonic tales that reproduce existing power relations and subversive stories that challenge the existing hegemony, it is argued that narratives of resistance to legal authority may not lead to institutional change, but can nonetheless have consequences beyond the immediate context if and when such stories become instructions about the sources and limitations of power.

In empirical research on the basis of in-depth interviews, Ewick and Silbey have applied their narrative framework to develop a grounded theory of legality, defined as people's perceptions of law. The study shows that people construct three categories of legality. In the schema "before the law," law appears as a neutral, objective, coherent, timeless, but also rigidly confining, realm that is largely separate from and stands above everyday life. In the "with the law" schema, law becomes a strategic game that is played with available resources, skills, knowledge, and experience. And, finally, in the schema "against the law," law is seen as a tool of the powerful that cannot be opposed openly but can nonetheless be resisted indirectly and in subtle ways. Ewick and Silbey's approach to the study of legal consciousness thus offers a structurally framed narrative analysis, which is exemplary of a recent wave of theorizing and research that offers a grounded perspective of legal inequality (see Chapter 10).

In the context of interactionist theory, mention should also be made of ethnomethodological analyses, which, like symbolic interactionism, have contributed to advance a micro-theoretical orientation in sociology. Ethnomethodology, however, is grounded differently in philosophical theory and sometimes differs sharply from symbolic interactionism. Developed by sociologist Harold Garfinkel, ethnomethodology is intellectually rooted in the philosophy of Alfred

---

[12] For examples of sociological work on legal consciousness, see Hoffmann 2003; Larson 2004; Marshall 2006; Nielsen 2000; Richman 2001. For conceptual overviews, see Ewick 2004; Silbey 2005.

Schutz.[13] The phenomenological philosophy of Schutz rests on the central idea that everyday life is guided by people's knowledge about what is typical about the situations they experience. Schutz argues that everyday life has a certain banal quality to it and that people have a sense of confidence about the situations they encounter and what they mean.

Extending from phenomenology, ethnomethodology refers to the study of the manner in which people deal with knowledge about the world in which they live. Garfinkel developed the perspective in social research that measured what happened when people's sense of confidence was shattered under conditions of unexpected happenings in otherwise well-known situations. In such so-called "breaching experiments," Garfinkel would request the study participants to ask for clarifications of anything which was said to them that might not be entirely clear. The research subjects would typically become agitated and angry and eventually terminate the conversation altogether. Garfinkel thus wants to show the taken-for-granted nature of people's social surroundings.

As language is the primary medium by which people express their knowledge of situations, there is in ethnomethodology a central concern for conversation analysis, a methodology that has become a research tradition in its own right. Unlike the qualitative research methods of symbolic interactionism, ethnomethodological investigations and conversation analyses are often very structured and systematic. The theoretical framework is microscopic in orientation but critical of the symbolic-interactionist preoccupation with interpretive understanding and instead focuses on formal aspects of conversations, such as processes of negotiation to start and end a dialogue and take turns in speaking.

Ethnomethodology and conversation analysis have been applied in various settings of law, such as court proceedings, police interrogations, judges and lawyers, and jury deliberation.[14] Garfinkel's ideas

---

[13] Alfred Schutz's most central sociological ideas are available in a volume of selected writings (Schutz 1970). Harold Garfinkel's most important book is *Studies in Ethnomethodology* (Garfinkel 1967). For an overview, see Maynard and Clayman 2003.

[14] On the influence of ethnomethodology in sociology of law, see Atkinson 1981; Dingwall 2002; Los 1981; Manzo 1997; Morlok and Kölbel 1998, 2000; Travers 1997: 19–36. Examples of ethnomethodological research in the area of legal sociology can be found in Burns (2005) and Travers and Manzo (1997).

actually originated in research on law, specifically on jury deliberations, and several groundbreaking studies in ethnomethodology were conducted in legal settings as well (e.g., Cicourel 1968). The special attractiveness of legal proceedings for ethnomethodologists stems from the fact that legal cases tend to be highly structured because of procedural requirements and, relatedly, that decisions in law have to be made in favor of one or another party on the basis of presented evidence, testimony, and other presentations of fact. Such decisions are oftentimes also the result of explicit verbal discussions, such as in the case of jury deliberation.

There exists a considerable literature of ethnomethodological studies in the sociology of law.[15] What these studies share is an attention for the study of communication in legal settings. Human communication in courtrooms and other legal settings is a particularly interesting type of institutional talk because it sharply reveals how notions of power and justice are at work in interactional exchanges. Yet, work from the standpoint of ethnomethodology and conversation analysis is oftentimes conducted by sociologists who do not primarily identify as sociologists of law, but rather as scholars of communication and interaction who apply their insights in the legal arena as one among many institutional fields. Thus, rather than developing sociological theories of law, these efforts are oriented at developing insights and research about human communication within a specific theoretical paradigm. As such, ethnomethodological and conversation-analytical studies of law do not so much offer sociologies of law as sociological studies of interaction in legal settings.

Behavioral perspectives in the sociology of law

A final theoretical perspective that has to be discussed in this overview of the contours of modern theoretical approaches in the sociology of

---

[15] Among the more important contemporary representatives of ethnomethodology in legal sociology are Robert Dingwall (Dingwall 1998, 2000; Greatbatch and Dingwall 1994, 1997), Paul Drew (Atkinson and Drew 1979; Drew 1992) and Max Travers (1997) in the United Kingdom; Martin Morlok and Ralf Kölbel (Morlok and Kölbel 1998, 2000) in Germany; and Michael Lynch (1982, 1998, Lynch and Cole 2005) and Douglas Maynard (1982, 1984a, 1984b, 1988; Maynard and Manzo 1993) in the United States.

law consists of micro-theoretical perspectives that are premised on behavioral assumptions. Like interactionism, behaviorist sociology captures a considerable variety of perspectives which are not always in complete agreement with one another, yet which do share various basic characteristics. In this overview, special attention will go to social exchange theory and rational choice perspectives.[16]

One of the earliest expressions of behavioral sociology is found in the work of George C. Homans (1910–1989), who was a colleague at Harvard of Talcott Parsons and became one of his major theoretical opponents. Homans's attack on Parsons was not only based on the critique that functionalism was too much concerned with the macro-level of society but also that Parsons' theory is a mere conceptual scheme that contained no clearly identifiable propositions that could be tested through research. Based on the behavioral psychology of B. F. Skinner, Homans developed a theory of human conduct based on the assumption that people will continue to behave in a manner that was rewarding for them in the past. From this basic premise, more detailed propositions are formulated to explain human conduct at the social level. Homans posits, for instance, that frequent interactions among people will lead them to develop positive attitudes towards one another and to increasingly share sentiments and actions, which in turn increases the likelihood of further interaction. This process continues within certain limits posed by practical constraints and considerations related to the diminishing impact of rewards that are repeated over time. Because society is assumed to be built up out of the behavior of individuals, psychological propositions can also explain emergent social phenomena.

Underlying Homans' perspective is the notion that humans are profit seekers who want to maximize rewards in their conduct with others. The basic theory adopts a notion of economic rationality, holding that human behavior is the outcome of a weighing of the anticipated costs and benefits of behavioral alternatives. In this sense, Homans's exchange theory is congruent with the premises of classical economics from which developed rational choice theory. Such an economic-rational model suggests that the basic elements of the

---

[16] On exchange theory, see the seminal work of George C. Homans 1958, 1961, 1964. On rational choice theory, see Gary S. Becker 1974, 1976, James S. Coleman 1990. See also the overviews by Cook and Whitmeyer 1992; Emerson 1976; Hechter and Kanazawa 1997; Hedström and Swedberg 1996.

(capitalist) economic order, such as the price of goods, can be explained as the result of rational strategies of conduct by the participants in the market who are oriented to a maximization of profits and a minimization of costs. Rational choice theory in sociology is an elaboration of these premises to explain all human conduct. In modern sociology, rational choice theory found its major expression in the work of Chicago sociologist James Coleman. A major strength of Coleman's work is that he also addresses macro-theoretical questions from a rationalist viewpoint. For instance, Coleman (1990) theorizes collective behavior, such as riots and fashions, on the basis of the postulate that it involves a rational transfer of control from one actor to another. Likewise, social norms are theorized to have emerged out of the relinquishing of partial rights of control over one's own actions in return for receiving partial rights of control over the actions of others.

Behaviorism has garnered increasing interest and debate in the sociology of law in recent years. Arguably most significant in this respect has been the work of the Chicago economist Gary Becker, who extended the domain of micro-economic analysis to a wide range of non-economic types of behavior, including human conduct in the realm of crime, education, and the family (Becker 1974, 1976; Becker and Landes 1974). In matters of crime, for instance, Becker argues that criminal conduct is the result of a rational decision based on a calculation of the benefits of the criminal act outweighing the costs thereof. Related to the influence of Becker (who won the Nobel Prize in economics), behaviorist theories have primarily been influential in the area of crime and criminal justice.[17] Criminological scholarship benefited from the economic insights on crime as a rational decision to develop neo-classical perspectives of criminal behavior that revive the basic tenets of the Classical School of criminology in a social-scientific direction. As a corollary to the view of crime as a rational decision, a theory of punishment and criminal law is suggested that is oriented at efficiently increasing the costs of crime. Such cost-enhancing strategies focus on the certainty, severity, and certainty of punishment as key variables contributing to the deterrent qualities of criminal justice.

---

[17] On the influence of behaviorism, especially rational choice theory, in the area of criminology, see Wilson and Herrnstein 1985. For discussions and overviews, see Paternoster and Simpson 1996; Nagin and Paternoster 1993.

Rational choice theories have been extremely influential in economics, where an entire law and economics movement has emerged that has also branched out into contemporary jurisprudence.[18] The law and economics approach has especially benefited from the writings of the Chicago legal scholar and federal judge Richard Posner, arguably today's most discussed legal theorist (Posner 1974, 1986, 1998). Theoretically closely akin to Becker (with whom he maintains a joint weblog[19]), Posner's legal theory is most essentially based on the application of economic models of utility-maximization to the study of law. Basically the theory holds that legal rules are to be examined in terms of their utility and efficiency to reach certain goals. Posner attributes both explanatory and instrumental value to the economic theory of law in explaining the form and substance of existing legal rules and seeking to find ways to increase the efficiency of the legal system. Posner's work is very influential in contemporary legal theory, where behaviorist approaches have generally experienced a rise in popularity. Relying on game theory, for example, Robert Ellickson (1991, 2001) has elaborated a perspective on law to suggest that formal law is not as essential to the maintenance of order as are informal means of conflict resolution. Ellickson theorizes that such informal norms develop among the members of close-knit groups because they serve to maximize their aggregate welfare.

In the sociology of law, behaviorist and rationalist theories have not been very influential, although there are some exceptions, especially in experimentally oriented studies (e.g., Horne 2000, 2004; Horne and Lovaglia 2008). Among the critics of rationalist theories, Lauren Edelman (2004a) argues that the contributions of the law and economics perspective should be amended by integration within the broader law and society tradition. The law and economics approach in particular needs to be complemented and rectified with sociological insights that can bring out a socially grounded theory of the relationship between law and the economy. Rationality then becomes an object of study, not a mere assumption, to be investigated at the social

---

[18] On law and economics, see the foundational work of Posner, 1974, 1986, 1998 and the discussions by Donohue 1988 and Ulen 1994. On the influence of the law and economics movement in sociology of law and socio-legal studies, see Rostain 2000.

[19] See www.becker-posner-blog.com.

rather than the individual level. In the sociology of law, institution-alist perspectives of law and organizations respond to these concerns (see Chapter 7).

Conclusion

It is a testimony to the maturation of the sociology of law that it harbors the major theoretical perspectives of sociology at large. Sociologists of law vary in their respective theoretical positions along the familiar lines of conflict versus order, structure versus agency, explanation versus interpretation, objectivism versus constructionism and contextualism versus behaviorism. Very distinct, but by no means unique to the sociology of law is the problem of norms, such as it surfaces most strongly in the opposition between jurisprudential sociology and pure sociology. Discussions on normativity are central in the sociology of law. In that sense, the sociology of law can serve as a reminder of the centrality of norms to sociological analysis and that every sociology must always deal with these questions. The sociology of law can rightly claim a unique accomplishment in not evading but, on the contrary, explicitly taking up critical problems for sociological theory and research that are posed by the normativity of society.

In comparison with the classic sociological contributions, the modern sociology of law has not been as convincing towards socio-logists outside the specialty area in reaffirming the centrality of law to sociology as a whole. In that respect, however, not only theoretical arguments are in order, for there are also institutional reasons why the sociology of law has remained somewhat on the sidelines in sociological discourse. The peculiar problem is that the sociology of law has remained confronted throughout its development with the proliferation of legal scholarship (in law) and the emergence and progress of socio-legal studies (in the social and behavioral sciences). Especially in view of the successful development of the law and society tradition as a multidisciplinary field, the reality is that many sociologists of law sought shelter outside of the disciplinary boundaries of sociology. Within the sociology of law, however, the contributions to the study of law have been manifold, both in theo-retical and substantive respects, and it is to these accomplishments that the remaining parts of this book will be devoted.

The chapters in Parts III and IV revolve around substantive themes and are in this sense more empirically oriented, involving reviews of various research efforts in the sociology of law. However, each of the coming chapters will discuss work in the sociology of law in relation to a substantive issue of society in a manner that is sociologically meaningful and will thus also incorporate theoretical queries and recent advances in the formulation of theoretical and conceptual frameworks. Aspects of the theoretical discussions introduced in the previous chapters will regularly reappear in the coming parts, both in terms of revealing the fruitfulness of the theoretical orientations that have already been introduced as well as with respect to introducing some of the more recent theoretical developments that emerged from or in response to the previously discussed perspectives. As explained in the Introduction, this review is necessarily selective, but it should capture the most important theoretical innovations and exemplary cases of empirical research in the sociology of law to function as a doorway to other contributions.

PART III

Sociological dimensions of law

7 | Law and economy: the regulation of the market

Relying on the analytical approach that was introduced in the Introduction, the following four chapters of this book focus on the interdependent relations that exist between law and other societal institutions and functions, specifically between law and economy, law and politics, law and normative integration, and law and culture. As mentioned before, this perspective is indebted to the systems theory of Talcott Parsons, yet the model is here used in a strict analytical manner to open up multiple research questions that can be approached from a variety of theoretical positions.

In the specification of the employed analytical model in this book, important theoretical positions can be differentiated that have moved sociology on at least three different levels. First, the suggested analytical model of society corresponds to the social sciences of economics, political science, sociology, and (cultural) anthropology. Among these disciplines, the role of sociology has historically been unique because of its focus on integration as an important function for society as a whole without restricting attention to any one of society's constituent parts alone (see Habermas 1981b: 4–5). Second, the model can also be read in terms of the sociological specialty areas of economic sociology, political sociology, sociology of law, and cultural sociology. What separates these specialty fields from the social sciences that specialize in their corresponding institutional areas is that they share and hold on to a sociological attention to society as a whole. In fact, the connection that is made theoretically and that is researched empirically between a specific institutional field of attention and society's other institutional components is equivalent to sociological specialization. And, third, the sociology of law must therefore also retain, in view of its focus on an important integrative component of society, an interest in law's relation to other social institutions. This interest, moreover, cannot be curtailed to the questions that mark the respective realms of other sociological specialty areas. As much as, for example, a political sociologist differs from a political scientist, so does the sociologist of law who studies law in relation to the economy differ from an economic sociologist.

Turning to the attention the sociology of law has paid to the relation between law and economy, this chapter will discuss work that has focused on the regulation of a variety of issues of economic life, including laws concerning labor and labor relations, property, and the regulation of aspects of business enterprise such as laws concerning unionization and trust formation. The theoretical entry into these discussions is provided by sociological perspectives of law concerning the interconnections that exist between law and organizations. As in the case of business enterprises, modern organizations of various kinds appear as private actors whose behavior is legally regulated. Among the more important theoretical developments, so-called institutionalist perspectives have been proposed to examine the variations that exist in the mechanisms and effects of the regulatory strategies that have been developed within organizations as a result of external legal pressures. Broadening the theoretical and thematic scope beyond the institutional level of organizational life, additional attention will be devoted to an analysis of the welfare state as it has evolved, in stronger and weaker forms, across Western societies. A model of juridification will be relied upon to chart these developments from the viewpoint of the sociology of law.

Variations of institutionalism

An appreciation of contemporary sociological analyses of the dynamics between law and economy can start from theoretical perspectives in the sociology of organizations, specifically the emergence and transformation of so-called institutionalist perspectives.[1] The origins of this development are less of a detour than might be expected, not only because the sociological classics viewed law as an institution that was in specific ways linked to the economy, but especially because some of the earliest practitioners of the modern sociology of law related their

---

[1] This discussion relies on the overviews on institutionalism provided by DiMaggio and Powell (1991); Edelman (1996); Nee (1998); Selznick (1996); and Suchman and Edelman (1996). On the influence of institutionalism in sociology and applications of the perspective, see Brinton and Nee 1998; Powell and DiMaggio 1991.

work intimately to economy and organizations. The pioneering work of Philip Selznick is critical in this respect because it ventured into the areas of sociology of law and the sociology of organizations.

Important for present purposes is that Selznick (1957, 1969) advanced a perspective on the manner in which authoritative systems of rules, analogous to formal laws proclaimed by the state, developed within private organizations. Private organizations, Selznick showed, develop their own normative structures to which the participants of the organization are expected to conform and for which sanctions can be applied in case of rule violations. The crystallization of normative structures surrounding certain societally recognized functions, such as education, childrearing, and the production and distribution of goods and services, is referred to as institutionalization. An institutionalist perspective of organizations, in general terms, thus focuses on the manner in which certain ways of conduct within an organization acquire the nature of a normative structure, which in many ways is equivalent to a formal legal system and which creates both opportunities and constraints on what can be done within the organization.

The sociology of organizations has adopted institutionalist perspectives, not primarily in view of its relevance for the sociology of law, but in response to economic analysis of organizations. On the basis of the classical liberal model, organizations are viewed as rational actors who adopt rules and procedures because they are efficient given certain ends. The central contribution of institutionalist theory in sociology is not so much to question this form of rationality, but to contextualize it within a socio-historical framework that constitutes the content, form, and meaning of rationality. The economic rationality that operates in the free market, in other words, is not treated as a mere given. Institutionalist perspectives are skeptical towards rational-actor models of organization and tend to be more macroscopic in orientation. Emphasizing the relationship between organizations and their environments, institutionalists also explain the normative structures in organizations in terms that may be quite different from the organization's own formal accounts of its operations. For example, an organization may formally enact safety rules to protect its members from physical mishaps, but such rules might actually serve to shield the organization from being held accountable if an accident occurs. Likewise, certain rules may be in place that do not contribute to, and may even conflict with, the organization's efficiency. The process of institutionalization that accounts for the development of such normative structures falls outside the purview of a traditional economic model and has to be analyzed sociologically.

The so-called new institutionalism that evolved from a critique of the work of Selznick retains the central view of organizations as being socially embedded, but differs on the mechanisms and sources of institutionalization in organizations. The traditional or old institutionalism is a cultural theory that centers on values and norms (of what ought to be done), whereas the new institutionalism is a cognitive theory concerned with classifications and scripts (of what can be done). The normative orientation in Selznick's work is theoretically supported by a Parsonian view of institutionalization that focuses on conformity to norms on the basis of processes of internalization. The cognitive orientation of the new institutionalists, by contrast, theoretically relies on the perspective of the construction of reality developed by Peter Berger and Thomas Luckman (1967). The social-constructionist perspective suggests that society is a human construct as well as an objective reality, more specifically involving a process that includes: the construction of society as a particular human social order (institutionalization); the human experience thereof as a reality on its own (objectification); and the potential problem that the human element in the social order is no longer recognized (reification). What is important for neo-institutionalists is that the process of institutionalization is a cognitive, not a normative matter, whereby institutions are conceived as cognitive constructions that control human conduct even prior to any internalization of sanctioning norms. Organizational compliance occurs because certain routines are taken for granted as the way things are done, without any conception of alternatives. The taken-for-granted nature of organizational behavior is particularly well revealed in the fact that contradictory normative structures may co-exist within the same organization.

Furthermore, whereas rational market theories conceive of the conduct of individuals within organizations on the basis of principles of profit maximization, a traditional institutionalist perspective attributes organizational compliance to a normative duty, infusing value to an institutionalized response beyond its technical requirements. The new institutionalism, by contrast, argues that organizations are influenced by their broader environment through institutional isomorphism, that is, on the basis of the similarities that exist among organizational structures and practices under comparable environmental conditions. Organizational isomorphism is the result of the pressures organizations experience to establish legitimacy within the world of institutions and therefore adopt a certain form and content in order to survive and be accepted as a legitimate organization.

Law and organizations: beyond law and economics

The central focus of institutionalist research in the sociology of law centers on the interrelationships between law and organizations, specifically the manner in which organizations adapt to relevant changes in the legal arena.[2] Organizations comprise not only economic corporations or business groups but also public organizations of various kinds, such as government agencies and voluntary associations. However, with Weber in mind, organizations can more generally be viewed as purposely constructed institutions, which are subject to a more general process of rationalization affecting various spheres of social life. It was for this reason that Weber was able to focus on the form of bureaucratization irrespective of whether state or market organizations were involved.

A useful entry into the area of law and organizations in the sociology of law is to bring to mind the rationalist perspective of law and economics. Rationalist economic theories explain the behavior of organizations in terms of efficient adaptations to external market conditions. The principles of efficiency and rationality are adopted within organizations because they are rewarded on the market. Understood as the whole of formally enacted rules, law is one of the many coercive exogenous forces that influence organizational behavior. Contrary to rationalist market approaches, institutionalist perspectives in the sociology of law argue that rationality is socially constituted,

---

[2] The merging of the sociology of law and the sociology of organizations, specifically in the form of the application of new-institutionalist principles in theory and research on the dynamics between law and organizations, has been most centrally advanced by Lauren Edelman and her associates (Edelman 1990, 1992, 2002, 2004a, 2004b; Edelman and Stryker 2005; Edelman and Suchman 1997; Suchman and Edelman 1996). See also Heimer 2001; Stryker 2003. For a reverse approach, to develop an approach to law from the viewpoint of economic sociology, see Swedberg 2003.

not an objectively given reality. Organizations rely on rational myths that may not be inherently accurate but that are effective because they are widely shared.

Applied to the field of the sociology of law, institutionalist perspectives also change focus and even correct some of the underlying themes in the institutionalism of organizations. Institutionalist sociology of law complements the cognitive perspective of the new institutionalism in explaining how institutionalization occurs (the mechanisms of institutionalization) by focusing on the behavioral responses to institutionalization once it has taken place (the effects of institutionalization). Also, by taking law more seriously, institutionalism in the sociology of law does not just conceive of law as formally enacted rules ("law in the books") but adopts a broader conception of law as also involving variability in application, differentiality in enforcement, pluralism in authority, and ambiguity in meaning ("law in action"). In this sense, the basic lesson of the sociology of law for the sociology of organizations is to consider that law is also culturally constituted. Yet, conversely, sociologists of law can learn from institutionalist organizational theory that organizations, including market corporations and bureaucratic administrative agencies, are not to be conceived solely in terms of technical efficiency and/or profit maximization, but as culturally constituted entities. As such, institutionalism provides a corrective to an overly rationalist interpretation of organizations that might result from a Weberian preoccupation with purposive rationalization and efficiency.

The fact that organizations are viewed as culturally constituted leads to the primary insight in the sociology of law and organizations that organizational behavior in response to the legal environment includes both symbolism as well as substance. Isomorphism reveals the non-rational nature of the similarities that exist among organizations. Important from a sociology of law viewpoint is the fact that isomorphism has different sources: it is mimetic when organizations copy successful practices from one another; normative when it results from professionals moving across organizations; and coercive when organizations react to external regulatory structures such as law. From this perspective, legal compliance in organizations is not merely seen as a rational cost-saving strategy but may take on a variety of forms. The nature of the adaptations to regulatory mechanisms can be symbolic or substantive (Edelman 1992). Symbolic adaptations include certain ritualistic and ceremonial activities, whereas substantive or instrumental responses go to the heart of the matter. For instance, in response to legal rules concerning discrimination on the basis of race, a private company may (symbolically) appoint an affirmative action officer or (substantively) ensure equal pay across racial lines. Importantly, symbolic and substantive types of action can be related as symbolic responses may have substantive impacts. For example, an appointed affirmative action officer may have a deep-rooted commitment to racial fairness and feel loyalty towards minorities, thus bringing about real changes in racial equality. The difference between symbolic and substantive organizational responses to law shows that organizations are an important site where laws are implemented with various levels of efficacy.

A final important lesson from institutionalist theory applied in the sociology of law is the notion that the legal environment is not primarily seen as a constraint on organizational freedom but as constituting organizational activity. Reviewing research on law and economy can reveal the complex dynamics that exist among these institutional spheres. Based on a minimal specification of the possible effects of law on the economy, law can be facilitative, regulatory, or constitutive (Edelman and Stryker 2005). As a facilitator, law appears rather passive as providing a set of tools, such as lawsuits, which organizations can use in the conduct of their business. As a regulator, law more actively intervenes in organizational conduct, even contrary to market principles, by promulgating rules that impose certain restrictions on economic activity, for instance concerning antidiscrimination, environmental protection, antimonopolization, and antitrust. Constitutive of reality, finally, law specifies what organizations are and how they are to relate with one another. In this sense, legal rules define and classify organizations, specify how they can be formed and how they can end (bankruptcy laws), and in which shape they can conduct certain activities (e.g., as a Limited, an Incorporated).

Especially because of law's constitutive role, law cannot simply be viewed as exogenous to the realm of organizations. Instead, law is endogenous to the social realm it seeks to regulate. An endogenous perspective on law views the relationship between law and economy within a societal context in which both institutional spheres are formed. Thus, law and economy are institutional spheres that are differentiated but not completely distinct. Economic or organizational

activity centers around the societal dimensions of management, efficiency, and productivity, while law revolves around legal actors and
principles of rights, justice, and governance. Such a conceptualization
also shows the value of looking at the interrelations among law and
economy in terms of a mutual interplay or, in Parsonian terminology,
a process of double interchange.

The regulation of business

Reviewing research on the interplay between law and economy
presents a formidable challenge given the extent of relevant research.
Additionally complicating the picture (of this and all other thematic
research areas addressed in this book) is not only the fact that relevant
empirical research exists within a multitude of disciplinary perspectives, but also that there has been considerable cross-fertilization
across these research traditions. Given the objectives of this work to
reveal the disciplinary contours and value of the sociology of law, the
reviews of research in this chapter will focus on sociological efforts.
Particularly discussed will be research that is outstanding by virtue
of its relevance within the specified area of investigation, impact on
the field, and exemplary status relative to the discussed theoretical
frameworks.

Research on law and economy in the context of industrialized
nations has generally shown a trend towards greater intervention in the
market. The theoretical line extending from the critique on classical
liberalism to the sociological theories of Weber and Durkheim can be
recalled to broadly chart the relevant aspects of this development.
Whereas liberal and Marxist models of the regulation of economic life
contemplate, in respectively a condoning and a criticizing manner, the
legalization of the free market in terms of *laissez faire* politics, Weber
and Durkheim no longer held on to such simple models. Weber argued
for the relevance of a relatively autonomous state in relation to the
market, while Durkheim contemplated the relevance of systems of
normative regulation accompanying the division of labor. The course
and outcome of the development towards the legalization of business
is undeniable, but it has taken on different forms and has variably
affected economic life in a variety of socio-historical conditions.
A closer look at sociological research on aspects of American labor law
will reveal some of these complexities.

American labor law regulates important dimensions of employees' and employers' rights and obligations, including the rights of workers to organize unions, engage with their employers in deliberations over wages, and hold strikes.[3] The very notion of unionizing labor is antithetical to the philosophy of free-market liberalism as it is incompatible with the notion of formal equality among individual participants in the market. Historically, indeed, unions were initially conceived as criminal conspiracies against employers and their property as their conduct was thought to interfere with the freedom of trade. Legally, both the organization of labor, such as in unions, as well as collective action among workers, particularly strikes, were outlawed.

By the mid-nineteenth century, changes took place in labor conditions that benefited the organization of workers. The formation of unions was no longer considered illegal, but their activities were legally restricted. What followed was a period during which legal injunctions against unions became commonplace and the courts blocked any effective union activity. Statutes that were passed at the legislative level favoring workers' rights, moreover, were overturned by the higher judicial courts. In the 1908 decision of *Adair v. United States*, for example, the Supreme Court overturned a federal law of 1898 that made it illegal for employers to fire employees on the basis of union membership. The Court found that the statute was unconstitutional because it was in violation of the equality of rights between a worker and an employer to engage in a contract. In another 1908 decision, the Supreme Court argued that legal action could be taken against unions on the basis of antitrust statutes, which, ironically, had been passed against the organization of capital rather than labor.

A sharp turn in US labor law came about in the years following the Great Depression of 1929–1930, when a profound crisis in capitalist development led to massive unemployment and poverty. New legislative efforts were taken to secure and expand workers' rights. In 1932, for example, the Norris-La Guardia Act was passed that recognized workers' rights to participate in labor unions in order to better their working conditions and negotiate wages. The Act also limited the power of courts to issue injunctions against unions in case of nonviolent labor disputes. Such legislative efforts protecting union

---

[3] For sociological analyses of US labor law, see McCammon 1990, 1993, 1994; Wallace, Rubin, and Smith 1988; Woodiwiss 1990.

formation and activity increased after 1933 as part of the New Deal policies of the Roosevelt administration. In 1935, the National Labor Relations Act or Wagner Act was passed and became one of the most important and enduring pieces of New Deal federal legislation. The Act was designed to promote collective bargaining agreements between unions and their employers in order to redress the inequality in bargaining power that exists between employers who are organized in corporate forms of ownership and employees who do not possess full freedom of association or actual liberty of contract. The Act was explicitly designed to encourage collective bargaining and protect workers' rights of unionization for the purpose of negotiating the terms and conditions of their employment. The Act also established a new federal agency, the National Labor Relations Board, that has arbitration power in disputes between labor and management over unfair labor practices.

Sociologically it is important to observe that the periods in US labor law before and after the 1930s are distinguished not on the basis of varying degrees but of varying kinds of legal and government intervention. The period before the 1930s is one of repressive intervention aimed at suppressing workers' rights in favor of a resolute commitment to liberal capitalism, whereas the period thereafter is marked by an integrative interventionism oriented at pacifying the opposition between labor and capital in order to protect the free market. Repressive intervention is primarily conducted at the level of the courts, whereas integrative intervention is largely a function of federal legislation.

The very fact that labor relations take place between employees and employers inevitably implies a delicate balance between rights that may shift to one side or the other. Indicating the variability in the effects the legal environment can have on economic life is the manner in which labor law evolved since the 1930s. At first, many employers refused to recognize the terms of the Wagner Act, backed up by appellate courts which ruled the Act to be unconstitutional. In 1937, the Supreme Court upheld the constitutionality of the Act, but a year later decided that employers could permanently replace employees who were out on strike. Employers were also constitutionally protected to express their opposition to unionization. In 1947, after a year of an unprecedented number of strikes that had been instigated by heightened demands for higher wages following World War II, the so-called Taft-Hartley amendments severely restricted several provisions of the Wagner Act by requiring unions to give sixty days' notice before organizing a strike and allowing employees to petition to oust their union or invalidate any existing collective bargaining agreement. The restrictive impact of the Taft-Hartley Act on strikes, however, was mediated at the level of union organization and was only felt when more militant factions were removed from the labor movement.

Corporate legality

At the organizational level, a wealth of institutionalist research on law and economy has demonstrated the variable impact of law on economic life.[4] Recent research in this area has focused on the effects of laws directed at increasing diversity, providing safety, and protecting employees from discrimination in the workplace to show that many of these regulatory mechanisms have had variable and ambiguous influences on organizational policies. For example, the Civil Rights Movement of the 1960s and the new laws that were passed in its wake produced a normative environment in which employers were pressured to create formal protections to guarantee due process rights. As such, organizations responded to threats posed by the legal environment. But organizations also vary considerably in how they respond to the pressures of the legal environment.

Neo-institutionalist research has shown that organizational policies regarding discrimination complaint cases are often subsumed under managerial goals concerning smooth employment relations. While such a redefinition typically does not prevent the resolution of a complaint, it does prevent the condemnation and labeling of organizational discrimination in cases where it is present. Similarly, the adoption of due-process governance practices in organizations has been found to be influenced by changes in the legal environment, with public agencies and non-profit associations at the forefront of

---

[4] This section relies on research by Dobbin, Sutton, Meyer, and Scott 1993; Edelman 1990, 1992; Edelman, Erlanger, and Lande 1993; Edelman and Suchman 1999; Edelman, Uggen, and Erlanger 1999; Sutton and Dobbin 1996; Sutton, Dobbin, Meyer, and Scott 1994. For additional applications of institutionalism in the sociology of law, see Burstein 1990; Burstein and Monaghan 1986; Dobbin and Kelly 2007; Kelly and Dobbin 1999; Larson 2004; Pedriana 2006; Pedriana and Stryker 1997; Skrentny 1994; Stryker 1989, 2001.

instituting such reforms. Yet, organizational adoption of due-process policies, such as disciplinary hearings and grievance procedures for non-union employees, is mostly symbolic in nature. Organizations show a commitment to equity and justice, irrespective of the actual functioning and effects of instituted practices of due process. Likewise, research on the impact of civil rights laws concerning equal employment opportunity has shown that affirmative action programs instituted in organizations are often merely symbolic and bring about little direct change in the employment conditions of minorities and women. Organizations mostly adopt equal employment grievance procedures because they have an aura of fairness and efficacy. Yet, congruent with the institutionalist perspective on the connection between symbolic and substantive organizational responses to the legal environment, the institutionalization of values congruent with equal employment may lead to increases in minority and female representation.

A particularly noteworthy effort in organizational theories of law is the groundbreaking study on gender inequality in American organizational life by sociologists Robert Nelson and William Bridges (1999) in their book, *Legalizing Gender Inequality*. On the basis of institutionalist theory, Nelson and Bridges argue that male–female pay differentials are significantly shaped by organizational wage-setting decisions. Gender differences in pay are not a mere product of the workings of the market, principles of efficiency, or a tradition of culturally pervasive sexism. Nelson and Bridges argue against the dominant economic theories of between-job wage differences, which holds that female jobs pay less than male jobs because of market forces that set the price of a job, in favor of an organizational inequality model that suggests that organizations tend to discriminate against workers in predominantly female jobs in at least two ways: (a) by denying them power in organizational politics; and (b) by reproducing male cultural advantages. Complicating the picture is that the courts, on the basis of an adherence to the principle of non-interference in the market, do not recognize the organizational dynamics that foster the sex gap in pay. As courts do not feel obligated to redress gender inequality in the workforce, they in fact contribute to legalize gender inequality.

Nelson and Bridges test their organizational theory of gender inequality on the basis of an analysis of litigated cases of four organizations that were sued for pay discrimination: a large American state university, a state employment system, a Fortune 500 retailing company, and a bank. Results of the analysis show that the specific contexts of the four organizations only partly account for sex differences in pay and that there remains a substantial gender gap even after control for determinants of wage differences and market influences. Persistent wage differences between the sexes are therefore due to organization-level practices. Information about the labor market, such as information about the supply and demand for particular types of work and the wages paid by competing employers, is ignored at the organizational level or selectively interpreted in the wage-setting process. In pay equity lawsuits, moreover, courts have largely adopted claims that labor markets determine wages. The widespread acceptance of this market perspective accounts for the ironic fact that women have had little success in legally challenging pay disparities despite the US Supreme Court ruling in *County of Washington v. Gunther* (1981) that employers can be held liable for pay disparities resulting from gender discrimination.

The political economy of welfare law

Institutionalist perspectives of the interplay between law and economy have mostly been applied in the United States. Many of the insights on the workings of law in economic life, however, can also be inferred to apply to other societies with market economies. Yet, at the same time, regional differences can be expected because of the variable cultural, historical, and political conditions in which market economies have developed. Broadening the scope of the institutionalist analysis of law and organizations, sociological work on the development of welfare law can be brought into play. Mirroring the difficult and shifting balance between the free-market economy and liberal and social democratic systems is the relative degree and impact of welfare law relative to capitalist development. Welfare laws aimed at alleviating a variety of social ills that in strict liberal-economic terms should be left to market forces, in fact, have become the subject of legislation and legal protection.

The creation of welfare law aimed at alleviating problems associated with the market, such as unemployment and workers' safety, has affected societies across the world, but in different ways. Generally, welfare law is more extensive in Europe than in the United States.

This differentiality is also shown in the contrasting sociological perspectives that have developed. In American sociology, welfare is typically treated as an aspect of social control, whereas the European literature posits welfare more distinctly in opposition to capitalism.[5] Linked with variations in cultural traditions are also variable/political conditions. But what is of importance in the context of this chapter is the manner in which the development of welfare legislation has evolved and impacted economic life, especially in European societies.

The development of welfare law can be usefully analyzed on the basis of a model of juridification in the context of the history of European welfare.[6] Juridification refers to an increase in formal law by means of an expansion of law through the legal regulation of previously informally regulated spheres of social life or by means of a densification of law to regulate social actions in a more detailed manner. Juridification processes take place under political conditions of modern state development (to be discussed in Chapter 8), but of interest here are the economic functions and consequences of this development. Specifically, four waves of juridification can be described to explain the development of European welfare law.

First, in the traditional bourgeois states of the absolutist regimes in Europe, the expansion of the capitalist economy was accompanied by the development of civil laws that grant liberal rights and obligations to private persons engaged in contractual relations. These regulations of civil law guarantee freedom in the market. In matters of public law, however, all political powers remain solidly in the hands of the sovereign ruler. Second, with the development of constitutional states, the private rights of citizens to life, liberty, and property are constitutionally guaranteed over and against the political sovereign, who is bound by law to not interfere with these liberal rights. Citizens are not, however, allowed to participate in the formation of government. The right to participate in government is granted during a third juridification wave when, under the influence of the French Revolution, democratic constitutional states develop and political participation rights are granted in the form of an expansion of the electoral

---

[5] See, for instance, Chilton 1970; Dwyer 2004; Lindsay 1930. For a contemporary perspective influenced by institutionalist theory, see Rogers-Dillon and Skrentny 1999.

[6] This exposition is based on the analysis by Jürgen Habermas (1981a: 522–534; 1981c: 356–364). See also Voigt 1980.

process. Finally, during the twentieth century, the democratic welfare state develops and welfare regulations bridle the workings of the free-market system in order to ensure a modicum of economic equality.

The juridification process of modern welfare law shows how modern legal development progresses towards a curtailment of some of the negative influences of market forces. As such, welfare regulations can lay claim to a degree of legitimacy as reflections of popular demands for justice and equality over and against the free market. However, the development of welfare law has ambivalent implications. On the one hand, welfare has granted effective rights to those whom the market has left behind. Yet, on the other hand, welfare laws have come about under a specific form that inherently favors the market (and the state). Specifically, welfare law entails a restructuring of legal interventions on the basis of an individualization of legal claims, while the conditions under which social laws apply are formally specified. Legal entitlements to welfare are also bureaucratically implemented via centralized and computerized means in impersonal organizations. And, finally, welfare claims are often settled in the form of monetary compensations, entailing a consumerist redefinition of social needs. As such, the specific form of the legal regulation of welfare claims is itself framed in the language and logic of the economy.

As a review of the historical path of welfare regulation shows, it is important to contemplate, besides the organizational filtering of law, the market logic of law itself. No doubt, not all law in advanced capitalist societies can be explained in terms of an economic logic, but it is important nonetheless to observe the marketization of law precisely then when laws are meant to alleviate social problems brought about by capitalism. In an even stronger sense the market influences on law are demonstrated by a dismantling of welfare law. In research on welfare regimes as diverse as those that existed in early nineteenth-century Britain and late twentieth-century America, for instance, sociologists Margaret Somers and Fred Block (2005) have shown that welfare is dismantled when the economic roots of poverty are substituted by the corrosive effects of welfare incentives on poor people in terms of a lack of personal responsibility, an addiction to dependency, and a moral perversity. Through this process of a conversion from poverty to perversity, market fundamentalism can delegitimate ideational and legal regimes of welfare. In view of such market dynamics, sociological analyses of law need to be able to uncover, not only the effects of law on economic life, but also when and how the form and content of law is shaped by market forces.

Conclusion

In view of the main theoretical perspectives in sociology, the relationship between the economy and other social institutions, including law, needs little justification. The theoretical contours of the centrality of the economy were already set by the sociological classics. What has generally been the most discussed aspect in the development towards an increasing interpenetration between law and various aspects of economic life in the context of modern market societies is the fundamental ambivalence that exists in the regulation of a sphere of social life that essentially claims freedom and autonomy. The path of regulation of the economy in industrialized societies has gone in the direction of an intervention by law that is meant to prevent any additional interventions.

In light of the widely recognized centrality of the economy in sociological scholarship, it is surprising that sociological work explicitly connecting law and economy is of relatively recent origins. In fact, the institutionalization of a specialized field of economic sociology itself is a rather recent phenomenon as well. In that sense, one of the central lessons of Weber and Durkheim has been adopted only slowly in the sociological mainstream. In recent decades, however, this situation has changed and sociological scholarship on the interplay between economy and law has moved center stage. Particularly advantageous for the sociology of law have been various strands of institutionalism that focus on the relationship between law and economy at the level of organizations. Whether through the normative focus of the old institutionalism or the cognitive orientation of neo-institutionalism, a distinctly sociological understanding is advanced about the workings of law in organizations, especially corporate organizations in free-market societies. Most striking is the general finding that the effects of law in terms of the primary function of integration and action coordination are observed to be mediated at the organizational level where law is confronted with other, non-legal institutional orders of modern market economies. Institutionalist research in such areas as civil rights and equal opportunity law has uncovered important limitations to legal policy.

Complementing the insights from institutionalist research in the sociology of law, a juridification perspective of the history of welfare regulation brings out an important degree of variability that exists across Western nations in terms of the extent and direction of legal intervention in economic life. As welfare policies are seen to be shaped by economic market imperatives, even and particularly in those societies where the welfare state is well developed, it is important to consider the market logic of law itself. Without resorting to a dogmatic orthodox Marxism, it would not be wise sociologically to forgo analysis of the ways in which the market shapes the course and outcome of law. Theoretically, therefore, it makes sense to contemplate when and how the endogeneity of law in economic and organizational life must be complemented with an endogeneity of the economy in law.

The perspective of juridification that was applied to the analysis of welfare law also brings out the relevance of legitimacy in the socio-logical discourse on law by showing the ambivalent nature of welfare policies in terms of popular appeals for justice and equality, on the one hand, and the persistence of the influence of market dynamics, on the other. Advocates of the old institutionalism (Selznick 1996; Stinchcombe 1997) have similarly argued that the neo-institutionalist theory of ritualistic compliance falls short in accounting for the fact that organizational adaptations to legal pressure lose legitimacy as soon as it is revealed that they are merely ceremonial in nature. Legitimacy can exist only when the normative dimension of law is recognized. In democratic societies, the connection between legality and legitimacy requires investigations on the foundations and effects of the legal system in terms of its relation with politics.

8 | Law and politics: the role of democratic law

Even more than is the case with the interplay between law and economy, the interrelationship between law and politics is of special significance to the sociology of law. The reason for the special attention that must go to the interrelation between law and the polity is that the function of lawmaking is assigned to the legislative branch of government, particularly in societies that are organized as nation-states and that have highly codified and formalized legal systems. In the context of democratic societies, furthermore, law appears as one of the most central mechanisms to ensure that the participation of the populace in a state's governance, as well as the outcome of government in the form of legislative decisions, abide by standards of democracy. In autocratic states and in societies where there is little differentiation between political and legal functions, in contrast, law operates as an instrument of political domination that has no popular basis of legitimation. With the democratization of political systems, the politicization of law is no longer a constant factor, but, on the contrary, law becomes a guarantee against the abuse of political power. In this sense, law serves as a critical link between citizens and their government.

A useful theoretical entry into sociological discussions relating to democracy and law is provided by the discourse-theoretical analysis of the conditions of democratic law. Discourse theory has been advanced by Jürgen Habermas in his theory of communicative action. Based on this theory, Habermas developed a conception of law that places democracy central to its analysis of society. In stark contrast with Habermas's theory stands the sociological perspective of Niklas Luhmann, who has formulated an autopoietic theory of law. Although both perspectives have developed mostly independently of one another, Luhmann's theory of law will in this chapter be situated in opposition to Habermas's to show the continued relevance of some of the theoretical dividing lines of the modern sociology of law, discussed in Chapter 6, in its most recent manifestations.

This chapter will first clarify theoretical perspectives on democracy and law that focus on law in one of three ways: (1) as a basis of democracy in terms of popular representation; (2) as an instrument of democracy with respect to the political decision-making process; or (3) as a deliberative sphere that must abide by procedural standards. The empirical relevance of democracy in law will subsequently be examined through a discussion of sociological work on the democratic deficits that exist in law despite the designated role of law in seeking to secure democracy in modern societies. Work on law and democracy in the sociology of law can serve as a strikingly counterintuitive as well as a distinctly sociological contribution to a debate that, inevitably, also has strong normative repercussions.

Law between legality and legitimacy: discourse theory

The German philosopher and sociologist Jürgen Habermas (born 1929) counts among the most influential thinkers of the second half of the twentieth century. Habermas's great influence is attributable not only to the strength of his work but also to its broad thematic scope and its inspiration from and relevance to a multitude of disciplinary perspectives in the social sciences and humanities. Habermas studied philosophy, history, psychology, literature, and economics at universities in Göttingen, Zürich, and Bonn. Following a few years as a freelance journalist, he became an assistant to Theodor Adorno, one of the intellectual leaders of the Frankfurt School, who along with Max Horkheimer had joined the University of Frankfurt after a period of exile during World War II. Habermas stayed at Frankfurt throughout the preparation of his *Habilitationsschrift*, which he eventually defended at the University of Marburg after Horkheimer had rejected the work. Habermas then became a professor of philosophy, first for a few years at Heidelberg and subsequently, at Frankfurt, where he stayed most of his career. Since his retirement in 1994, Habermas has continued to write extensively and participate in important public debates. Initially recognized as the leading representative of the so-called second generation of the Frankfurt School, Habermas has come to enjoy a reputation that makes his work stand by itself. Habermas's theory contains both sociological and philosophical aspirations. In what follows, attention goes to those aspects of Habermas's thought that are of a sociological nature and that are helpful to explain his theory of law and democracy and its relevance for the sociology of law.[1]

Habermas's perspective of the role of law in modern society builds on his broader theoretical perspective of the nature and transformation of society. Habermas's theory of society most fundamentally rests on a distinction between two types of rationality and two corresponding dimensions of society that have differentiated over the course of history. First, on the basis of communicative rationality aimed at mutual understanding, society is conceived of as a lifeworld. According to Habermas, mutual understanding among actors, which does not exclude the possibility of dissent as the result of an unresolved communication, occurs along three dimensions: communicative actions contain an objective claim to truth, a normative claim to rightness, and expressive and evaluative claims to authenticity and sincerity. The lifeworld of rationalized societies differentiates alongside these claims to provide certain cultural values, normative standards of integration, and the formation of personalities that can function in their social environment.

Second, on the basis of cognitive-instrumental rationality aimed at the successful realization of certain goals, society can be analyzed as a system. Beyond lifeworld rationalization, Habermas argues, modern societies have undergone a further differentiation in that certain systems have split off, or "uncoupled", from the lifeworld to function no longer on the basis of communicative action but on the basis of money and power. Actions coordinated on the basis of money and power in systems differ from communicative action in the lifeworld in that they aim at the cognitive-instrumental organization of the production and exchange of goods on the basis of monetary profit (economy) and the formation of government on the basis of power (politics). The formation of systems is as such not problematic, but it

---

[1] The major outline of Habermas's theory of society is found in the two-volume *The Theory of Communicative Action* (1981a translated as 1981b, 1981c). The initial formulation of Habermas's theory of law can be found in the second volume of that work (1981b: 522–547 translated as 1981c: 356–373) and in related writings (Habermas 1988, 1990). The mature version of Habermas's theory of law and democracy can be found in his book, *Faktizität und Geltung*, translated as *Between Facts and Norms* (Habermas 1992a translated as 1992b). Reviews and applications of Habermas's theory are provided by Deflem (1995, 1998a); Grodnick (2005); Raes (1986); and contributions in Deflem (1996); Rosenfeld and Arato (1998).

has problematic consequences when systems intrude on the lifeworld, that is, when communicative actions become instrumentalized on the basis of monetary or administrative needs. Habermas refers to this process as the colonization of the lifeworld.

In *The Theory of Communicative Action*, Habermas attributes to law the central role of institutionalizing or "normatively anchoring" the independent functioning of the steering media of money and power. The legal institutionalization of money and power is central in bringing about the uncoupling of the economic and political systems from the lifeworld. Habermas posits a special connection between law and politics by arguing that political authority historically originated from judicial positions. In the framework of societies organized around the state, also, markets have arisen that are steered by the medium of money. Law plays a special role in this differentiation because the independence of state and market are legally institutionalized. The economic and political systems thus operate independently because they are "recoupled" to the lifeworld through the legalization of the media of money and power in, respectively, private and public law.

The underlying viewpoint of Habermas's discussion is that law can formally be conceived as the institutionalization of a practical discourse on norms. Habermas acknowledges with Weber the formal characteristics of modern law, but he also maintains that the technocratic rationalization of law does not exhaust the normative dimension of law. In other words, Habermas resolves the tension in Weber's work between legality and legitimacy by arguing that modern law, even when it is formally enacted by political authority and enforced accordingly, also requires popular legitimation in order to be recognized as valid among the subjects of law.

Habermas applies his concept of law to the development of welfare law in terms of a process of juridification. As discussed in Chapter 7, this process of juridification came about in four stages: first, the development of capitalism gave way to civil law, granting individual rights and obligations to private persons engaged in contractual relations; second, individual rights of non-interference are claimed against the sovereign; third, social rights are claimed in the political order through democratic participation; and, fourth, with the development of welfare law, social rights are claimed against the economic system. The last three juridification trends Habermas theorizes as lifeworld demands against the influences of state and market. More specifically, these stages of juridification represent attempts to secure political freedom, political equality, and, finally, economic equality. However, given the ambivalent impact of welfare law, Habermas argues, the demands of the lifeworld are also transformed into imperatives of bureaucratic and monetary organizations (individualization of legal claims, formalization of the conditions of application, bureaucratic implementation, and monetarization of compensation). In this sense, Habermas argues, law intervenes as a medium in a systemic way into the social relations of everyday life.

Thus, in its original formulation in *The Theory of Communicative Action*, Habermas attributes an ambivalent role to law, because, on the one hand, law as an institution is part of the lifeworld, while law as a medium operates on the basis of a systematic or instrumental logic. This conceptualization can only be maintained if a rigid separation is drawn between two types of law: laws that contain a claim to normative rightness, on the one hand, and laws that are subject only to a technical analysis on the basis of standards of efficiency, on the other. This separation neglects the possibility that law as a component of the lifeworld can be restructured by systems to bring about a colonization of law, rather than that law is itself a colonizing medium. In his later work *Between Facts and Norms*, Habermas has corrected this view to argue that modern law is always part of the lifeworld and thus that law can always be normatively grounded, but also that law can be colonized by systems' imperatives. As such, Habermas not only posits a special relation between law and politics through the legislative process and the democratic character of modern political power, he also maintains a special relation between law and morality. Both moral and legal norms are oriented at ordering social interactions and solving conflicts that may arise in interaction. Yet, whereas moral norms may have great legitimacy and appeal to principles of justice, they miss the coercive force and certainty that comes with legal norms. For the important functions of administration and enforcement, law resorts to the political system, the exercise of which is in turn legally regulated. The character of politics as a legitimate order based on democratic principles functions as a minimum condition to the democratic nature of law as well. As discussed later in this chapter, Habermas conceives of the relation between law and democracy in procedural terms.

Law beyond politics and morality: autopoiesis

Most radically in opposition to the perspective of discourse theory is the autopoietic theory of law developed by Habermas's compatriot Niklas Luhmann (1927–1998). Luhmann studied law at the University of Freiburg shortly after World War II and initially began a professional career in public administration. After spending an academic year on a scholarship at Harvard University, where he was exposed to the work of Talcott Parsons, Luhmann undertook further studies in sociology and thereafter became a university professor, first for a few years at the University of Münster and then for more than two decades at the University of Bielefeld. Upon his retirement in 1993, Luhmann remained a prolific writer until his death in 1998. Possibly because of the combined effects of the complexity of Luhmann's thinking and his writings not being widely translated, Luhmann's work has not been discussed as much in sociology and the sociology of law as has been the work of Habermas, with the important qualification that Luhmann has a substantial following in Germany and continental Europe.

Luhmann conceives of law and society in terms of a systems theory that is very different from Parsons'.[2] Luhmann's theory does not use the concept of system analytically but instead refers to systems as concrete existing entities that, in the case of society, have been brought about by the disintegration of unified worldviews that once secured the cohesion of social life in traditional societies. The weakening of a strong common worldview brought about an increasing complexity of action-alternatives and, in response, specialized systems of society were formed to reduce this complexity. According to Luhmann, these systems are self-referential or autopoietic. A term originally introduced in biology, autopoiesis is the characteristic of systems to operate independently of one another in terms only of their own respective codes. Applying this notion to society, Luhmann argues that the systems that make up society take up information from one another as elements of one another's environment. Interrelations among and intra-relations within systems take place on the basis of communications

---

[2] Among Luhmann's numerous writings are two book-length studies in the sociology of law (Luhmann 1972a, 1972b, 1993a, 1993b; see also Luhmann 1986, 1992, 1997). Helpful introductions and discussions are offered by King and Schutz 1994; Rottleuthner 1989; Ziegert 2002; and contributions in King and Thornhill 2006.

with certain codes. Communication, in Luhmann's theory, is purely an observable act that consists in the synthesis of information, utterance, and understanding or misunderstanding. Communication has no subject; it merely happens. Also, each system's specific code of communication determines the dynamics of inter-systemic relations. Systems are therefore cognitively open but operationally closed.

Luhmann conceives of law as the autopoietic system that forms and reproduces generalized behavioral expectations in view of conflict situations that need to be resolved. When a breach of the institutionalized expectations of law occurs, the legal system counter-factually reaffirms those expectations presented in the binary code lawful/unlawful. The program of law is a purely cognitive matter that can be phrased in terms of an "if-then" structure: if specific legal conditions are fulfilled, then a certain legal decision will be reached. The operational closure of the legal system is confirmed from the fact that a violation of legal norms does not invalidate those norms. On the contrary, rule violations lead to confirmations of the rule through prosecution and punishment.

The autopoietic characteristics of systems have special significance for Luhmann's theory of democracy and law. Because systems are operationally closed, Luhmann regards the systems of politics and economy as operationally differentiated from law. The legal system is related in specific ways to these systems, but it cannot interfere with nor be interfered with by them in their respective operations. For instance, while morality reduces complexity in terms of the binary code good/bad, the two-value code of the legal system (lawful/unlawful) does not harmonize with the code of morality. Moreover, while the political system puts pressure on the legal system by means of legislation, the legal system responds to this pressure by relegating legislation to the periphery of its system and centering the distinctly legal decision-making process in the courts. The political and legal systems maintain a relation of functional cooperation, but they cannot be placed in any hierarchical relationship to one another. The mutual cooperation (or structural coupling) between law and politics can be observed from the fact that the legal system relies on the political system to back up its decisions with coercive power, while the political system relies on the legal system to administer its decisions, albeit always in terms of the legal system itself. Legal communication thus always takes place on the basis of the code of law, to the exclusion of political and moral concerns.

Democracy and law: theoretical variations

Among the most important implications of the differences that exist between the theories of law developed by Habermas and Luhmann are their strongly divergent outlooks on the relationship between law and democracy. In order to explain these differences in a way useful to the sociology of law, a brief clarification is in order on the conceptualization of democracy in sociological and philosophical theory.[3] Politics always concerns a relationship between government and citizens, between those who govern and those who are governed. As indicated by the etymological origin of the word democracy from the Greek for people (*demos*) and power (*kratos*), a political system is democratic when government is organized with explicit reference to those who are governed. In a democratic system, there is always an interdependence between government and people in the form of electoral processes (representing the democratic input from the people to the government) and legislative decision-making (the democratic output from the government to the people). Various sociological theories and their philosophical counterparts can be distinguished on the basis of the specific manner in which this interrelationship between government and people is conceived.

First, input theories of democracy stress the participation of the citizenry in the formation of government via the electoral process. This sociological conception is derived from the republican philosophical perspective that postulates that government should reflect the common good of all members of the community (the republic). The central value associated with this theory is the equality of all citizens, as the rightful contributors in the making of their government, to participate in the electoral process and determine their political representation. Sociologically speaking, a governing system is thus more democratic the more it represents the will of the people through regularly held elections, competition between political parties, and the principle of majority rule. The sociological theory of the democratic political system proposed by Niklas Luhmann (1990, 1994) fits in this framework. On the basis of the autopoietic perspective, Luhmann maintains that democracy cannot mean a political system whereby

---

[3] This overview is based on my (Deflem 1998b) exposition and discussion of Habermas's theory of democracy in *Between Facts and Norms* (Habermas 1992a: 349–398; 1992b: 287–328, 1995).

people rule over people or whereby power is annulled, because all politics by definition differentiates between those who rule and those who are ruled. Luhmann also discards democracy as the principle according to which decisions must be made in a participatory manner, because this would lead to endless decision-making about decision-making. Instead, Luhmann proposes that democracy is the institutionalization of the difference between government and opposition. Government and opposition direct themselves in everything they do towards one another and, in their respective ways, towards the public. The ruling political parties orient themselves towards public opinion in order to retain government, while the parties who are at any one point in the opposition do the same to acquire government. Luhmann argues that the democratic code government/opposition is instructive because neither side can govern at the same time and there is always the possibility that the participating political parties will change their roles following an election.

Second, output perspectives of democracy emphasize the outcome of government in the form of legislative decisions that regulate social interactions. Corresponding to a liberal (in the meaning of liberty-granting) philosophical conception, the legislative function of political systems should be non-interventionist and thus guarantee the freedom of each individual citizen. Sociologically, democracies are argued to be rooted in effective political systems and productive economies. The theory of Seymour Lipset (1994) on the conditions of democracy is an example of this approach. Lipset argues that democracies should safeguard an independent and effective functioning of the market and the state in the form of constitutionally guaranteed rights. More specifically focused on the role of law, market perspectives, such as those articulated in the law and economics movement (see Chapter 6), fit well into this framework by emphasizing the rational decision-making powers of autonomously acting individuals driven towards the fulfillment of private needs.

Third, a procedural theory of democracy focuses attention on the procedures that are in place to establish democratic achievements and to have them remain open to debate and discussion. This notion is an extension of the pragmatist perspective formulated by John Dewey that the essence of democracy lies in the means by which a majority rule comes to be a majority, involving antecedent debate, and allowing for the potential to modify views to meet the needs of minorities.

Corresponding to the procedural perspective is the philosophical conception of deliberative politics that holds that democracies should guarantee that decisions will be reached under conditions that allow for open debate. The procedural understanding of democracy and law is advanced by Jürgen Habermas (1992a, 1992b), who argues that law can play a central role in democratic societies when it relies on a procedurally conceived notion of rationality realized by democratic principles in legislation, jurisprudence in the courts, and legal administration. In defending this procedural concept, Habermas devotes special attention to the constitutional foundations of democracy. In this respect, he finds most essential the embodiment within constitutions, not of specific values, but of norms that enable the peaceful co-existence of a plurality of ethical traditions.

Democratic deficits of law

The analysis of sociological perspectives of politics and law introduced through a comparative examination of the theories of law by Habermas and Luhmann yields three visions of law: (1) law as a basis of democracy; (2) law as an instrument of democracy; and (3) law as a deliberative sphere. As a basis of democracy, law is considered critical in securing equality in representation and participation of the electorate in the political process. As an instrument of a democratic political system, law can be evaluated in terms of the effects it brings about towards the community, especially in terms of the extent to which legal decisions preserve freedom and rights of self-expression for each and all. And, as a deliberative sphere, the legal (and political) arena ought to function by procedural standards that allow for open-ended discussions.

The suggested typology of democratic theories is useful to review sociological research on relevant aspects of law and democracy, including the constitutional basis of law, the role of the judiciary, the legislative process, the courts, and law enforcement. It is to be noted that there is a relative scarcity of sociological research that explicitly addresses law in terms of a theoretically founded concept of democracy. The relative lack of a well-developed tradition on law and democracy in the sociological community stands in stark contrast with the centrality of democracy in the fields of legal theory and legal philosophy. The normative nature of democracy may account for this differentiality as well as for the fact that sociological analyses of democracy and law sometimes have strong normative orientations that interfere with their analytical potential (e.g., Hirst 1986; Lukes 2006; O'Malley 1983). Be that as it may, it remains problematic for sociological research to not sufficiently contemplate the empirical dimensions of democratic regimes and their relationship to law.[4] Sociological analyses of law and democracy, however, are particularly instructive, as this review of selected relevant works will show, because they can reveal the shortcomings of the realization of democratic ideals in law on the basis of research on cases where legal realities are shown to clash with democratic principles despite the law's self-proclaimed function of providing justice and equality for all.

At once exemplary of the relevance of law as a basis of democracy (as the input of government) and insightful of the strength of systematic sociological research are the studies by sociologists Jeff Manza and Christopher Uggen on felon disenfranchisement in the United States.[5] Unraveling the origins and impact of US state laws prohibiting convicted felons and some categories of ex-felons from participating in the electoral process, Manza and Uggen's research shows that these laws greatly affect the democratic rights of a substantial part of the population. The impact of felon voting laws is currently very pronounced because of the presently unprecedented high rate of incarceration, especially among America's ethnic minority groups. Even more consequential than the high rate of incarceration is the fact that the majority of the people affected by felon disenfranchisement laws are ex-felons who reside in the community without full citizenship rights. In November 2004, an estimated 5.3 million felons and ex-felons, 2 million of whom were African Americans, were affected by these laws. The racial bias in felon disenfranchisement is not entirely incidental as relevant state laws are found to date back to periods of

---

[4] It is telling, for instance, that two recent volumes on the transformations of law and democracy at the turn of the century consist, with few exceptions, of contributions written by scholars in law and public policy, not sociology (Syracuse Journal of International Law and Commerce 2005; Schwartz 2006).

[5] Manza and Uggen's work on felon disenfranchisement is available in a book-length study, *Locked Out: Felon Disenfranchisement and American Democracy* (Manza and Uggen 2006), and a series of related articles (Manza and Uggen 2004; Manza, Brooks, and Uggen 2004; Uggen and Manza 2002; Uggen, Behrens, and Manza 2005; Uggen, Manza, and Thompson 2006; Behrens, Uggen, and Manza 2003).

racial conflict during and following the Civil War years. Although the 15th Amendment to the US Constitution prohibits curtailment of voting rights on the basis of race, felon disenfranchisement effectively accomplishes a racially biased restriction of the voting public.

The negative effects of felon disenfranchisement are revealed in a number of ways. In terms of democratic participation in the electoral process, felon disenfranchisement laws have significant political outcomes. Because of the overrepresentation of ethnic minorities, felon disenfranchisement laws can affect election outcomes in the case of close races in states with very strict disenfranchisement laws. Laws banning felons and ex-felons from voting thus likely affected the US presidential election of 2000, when George W. Bush narrowly defeated Democratic candidate Al Gore in the state of Florida. Furthermore, not only do felon voting laws directly exclude a substantial part of the population, they also indirectly restrict popular representation as research findings indicate that a large majority of Americans believe that convicted persons should have their voting rights restored upon release in the community. From a broader viewpoint, felon voting bans also affect the reintegration of ex-offenders as a strong correlation is found between the restoration of voting rights and ex-felons' readjustment into the community. Because criminal offending is subject to an intergenerational transmission process, moreover, the children of convicted felons, many of whom are unmarried fathers, are more likely to become offenders.

In its role as an instrument of democracy (as the output of government), law appears primarily in the form of legislation, which can be investigated in terms of the effects of lawmaking on the integration of society in view of the preservation of liberty-granting rights. Sociologically relevant research in this area extends from the regulation of social movement organization (Jenness 1999; Pedriana 2006) to religious freedom (Richardson 2006). Evaluating the impact of the lawmaking process on citizen rights, sociological work on moral panics serves as an especially useful entry into related aspects of democratic government.[6] Applied to a wide variety of research areas, such as the criminalization of drug abuse, street crime, abortion, and

---

[6] The theoretical foundations of the moral panic perspective come from Stanley Cohen's (1972) groundbreaking work on the youth gangs of the "Mods" and "Rockers" in the UK in the 1960s (see also Goode and Ben-Yehuda 1994). For an overview, see Thompson 1998.

freedom of expression, moral panic perspectives explore the societal conditions under which a person or a group of persons come to be defined as a threat to fundamental societal values and norms. Showing that sociological models and normative theories on issues of democracy do not necessarily harmonize, the notion of a moral panic has mostly been applied from the viewpoint of conflict-theoretical perspectives that rely, often implicitly, on a more collectivist rather than liberal understanding of democracy. However, in terms of its research on the effects of legislative activities surrounding certain forms of behavior, the moral panic tradition lays bare in very clear fashion how laws can affect members of communities in matters of their basic rights and capacities of self-expression. Given current concerns surrounding global terrorism and security in the post-9/11 world, sociological work on terrorism and immigration from the moral panic viewpoint is particularly insightful.

Research by Michael Welch is based on the moral panic perspective to show that the use and expansion of US immigration laws in the wake of terrorist events that hit the United States in the 1990s, particularly the World Trade Center bombing in 1993 and the Oklahoma City bombing in 1995, and even more so following the attacks on September 11, 2001, have effectively brought about a criminalization of immigration.[7] Since the passage of new immigration and antiterrorism laws in 1996, immigrants have been increasingly subject to detention and deportation, often for only minor offenses. Immigration inspectors thereby gained more power relative to the judicial review authority of immigration judges. Making important decisions regarding the status of immigrants and asylum-seekers, immigration officials lack accountability and democratic oversight. The list of deportable crimes has also been broadened and the removal process of immigrants has been expedited. Sometimes on the basis of secret evidence, immigrants have also increasingly been kept in detention centers where they have been housed alongside ordinary criminals.

---

[7] Welch's research on the criminalization of immigration is reported in his book, *Detained: Immigration Laws and the Expanding I.N.S. Jail Complex* (Welch 2002), and a series of related articles (Welch 2000, 2003, 2004; Welch and Schuster 2005). An expanded analysis of post-9/11 criminal policies is offered in Welch's (2006) work, *Scapegoats of September 11th: Hate Crimes and State Crimes in the War on Terror*.

Since the events of 9/11, Welch argues, the harshness of immigration policies has qualitatively shifted from a moral panic on the immigrant criminal to a moral panic on the terrorist immigrant. This new view of the immigrant has particularly affected the treatment of asylum-seekers in the United States. While moral panics often rely on publicity via the media, some of the relevant policies can take place in hidden ways. In the United States, in particular, asylum-seekers have been subjected to relatively quiet policies and practices of confinement that have not generated much public attention. Unlike the situation in the United Kingdom where there have been loud and noisy construction claims over cases involving so-called bogus asylum-seekers, asylum-seekers in the United States have been subjected to relatively lengthy periods of detention and other forms of harsh treatment without having been charged with a crime. Asylum-seekers are increasingly subject to a claims-making process by which they come to be treated as terrorist suspects and threats to national security. Immigration officials handle these issues without public scrutiny. For instance, just prior to the US-led invasion of Iraq in March 2003, asylum-seekers coming from a list of thirty-three nations were subject to immediate detention on the basis of a formal policy called Operation Liberty Shield. Although the program was abandoned after a month, other similar detention orders, such as those promulgated by the US Attorney General and those instituted in some states, have negatively impacted asylum-seekers.

Finally, focusing on the procedural qualities of law as a deliberative sphere, relevant research has been particularly conducted on matters that pertain to the workings of the courts, such as jury deliberation, discursive practices between judges and lawyers and between lawyers and their clients, and other procedural aspects of judicial processing. Of special interest to the sociological and socio-legal research community have been the practices of alternative dispute resolution that have developed as part of a broader theoretical and legal movement towards informal justice.[8] Challenging the formal, adversarial, and objectifying nature of adjudication or litigation in courts, alternative dispute resolution practices emerged in the United States particularly

---

[8] For overviews and discussions of alternative dispute resolution and the extensive literature thereon, see Barrett 2004; Brooker 1999; Langer 1998; Rebach 2001.

during the 1960s, although informal methods of conflict resolution date back many years and can be found in many societies. The main forms of alternative dispute resolution presently include arbitration, mediation, and negotiation. Arbitration is a type of conflict resolution whereby the parties in a dispute make their case to a third party or arbitrator who reaches a decision that may or may not be binding. Mediation is a more informal resolution strategy whereby a neutral third party or mediator facilitates communication between the conflicting parties in order to help them reach a mutually acceptable agreement. The most informal form of alternative dispute resolution, negotiation takes place only among the parties in a dispute without the involvement of a third party.

As a matter of procedural justice, alternative dispute resolution is meant to have the advantage over formal litigation of establishing ways to handle conflicts in a manner that is agreed upon by and thus acceptable to the parties involved, rather than forced down upon them through the formal and adversarial mechanisms of a court. Based on principles of reciprocity and consensus, alternative dispute resolution practices are also argued to be less time-consuming and less expensive than formal court trials. On the downside, alternative dispute resolution may lack a specified threat of obedience and remain unenforceable without clearly specified sanctions. The manner in which alternative dispute resolution practices are instituted, moreover, may actually make them less alternative than they were meant to be as inequalities may exist among the disputing parties depending on their capacity to engage in alternative dispute settlement and rely on adequate representation. Alternative dispute resolution may also lack the protections of an open court. Additionally, concerns have been raised that the increasing involvement of formally trained lawyers has ironically led to an infiltration of adversarial principles in, and a formalization of, alternative dispute resolution.

The emphasis on procedural aspects of deliberation and fairness in alternative dispute resolution practices, which harmonizes with the deliberative concept of democratic law, is confirmed by the interesting research on mediation that sociologist John Lande has conducted.[9]

---

[9] See Lande 2002, 2005a, 2005b, 2006. Related research in the sociology of law has focused on conflict resolution practices in the workplace (Hoffman 2005,

Lande situates the rise of alternative dispute resolution, particularly mediation, in the context of the general decrease of formal court trials in the United States over the past decades. In a sympathetic critique of Marc Galanter (2004), Lande argues that court trials are by no means vanishing, but that they have decreased considerably although the number of cases filed in the courts has increased. Among the reasons for the reduction in the trial rate are that alternative forms of dispute settlement have spread more widely and the courts have adopted a more managerial judicial role that is not only oriented at organizing trials. Also, considerable costs are associated with holding trials because of the personnel that is required, the jurors in the case of jury trials, the increasingly sophisticated high-tech equipment used in the courtrooms, and the expensive courtroom space that is needed.

Although the decrease in the trial rate allows courts to spend time on other activities, such as the training of new staff, assisting litigants, conducting pre-trial hearings, promulgating rules and procedures, and conducting a range of administrative duties related to the workings of the court, it can also create the impression that courts do not respond to citizens' needs to have their cases handled in an open and fair manner. In the light of such procedural problems, Lande suggests a number of strategies that might make the decision to go to trial more democratically accountable. Litigants should be afforded the option of going to trial or not in an informed and voluntary manner. The courts could also rely on and publicize information about cases that were settled without a trial. The organization of the courts and the training of legal professionals, furthermore, could be redesigned to meet the new realities of court activities, while alternative dispute resolution practices could be promoted to meet citizens' demands for adequate conflict settlement.

The rise of alternative dispute resolution practices and the decrease of the formal trial rate indicate the emergence of a legal environment that is more and more pluralist in nature. Besides the fact that the courts engage in many non-trial activities, they also do not provide the only or primary system for dispute handling. Among the increasingly common practices of alternative dispute resolution, mediation is one

2006). Also noteworthy in the context of deliberative models of democracy is the work of Margaret Somers (1993, 1995), who develops a political sociology of law, citizenship, and democracy. For a related psychological perspective on procedural justice, see the work of Tom Tyler 1990.

of the most common and popular forms. In mediation, as in dispute settling in general, procedural criteria are most often used to judge satisfaction. For instance, research shows that the parties involved in mediation are more likely to feel satisfied when they feel they have had sufficient opportunity for self-expression and participation in the proceedings. Likewise determinate of satisfaction is the perception that mediation was conducted fairly in a comprehensible, impartial, and uncoerced manner. Conceptions of legal justice in the handling of conflicts are not only relevant to the parties involved in a dispute. Sociologically as meaningful as the functions of dispute handling in terms of the immediate interests of the disputing parties are the functions of trials and other forms of dispute settlement on a broader societal level. Since Durkheim, it makes sociological sense to understand dispute handling practices as rituals that affirm the morality of society. Especially in democratically organized societies, therefore, procedural conceptions of justice are significant indicators of the power of law to provide a sense of social cohesion.

Conclusion

In the context of democratically organized political communities, the legal system takes up a very prominent place. Because the legislative function of law is assigned to a polity that is organized explicitly in relation to the people who are subject to government, the relation between law and democracy is an intimate one, both conceptually as well as empirically. From a theoretical viewpoint, variations in the relation between law and democracy can be usefully approached from the viewpoint of the contrasting theoretical perspectives of Jürgen Habermas and Niklas Luhmann. Presenting a contemporary variation on the division between normative and scientific perspectives in the sociology of law, the question on the normative underpinnings of law and politics is the most decisive issue that divides the thinking of Habermas and Luhmann. According to Luhmann, societal evolution has reached such a high level of differentiation that law is an autopoietic system, which no longer needs any justification in terms of normative points of view. In sharp contrast, Habermas not only argues that law in modern societies is still normatively grounded and enjoys a special relation to the political system, he also justifies sociologically (and advocates philosophically) a perspective of just law on the basis of a deliberative model of democracy.

Habermas's discourse theory and Luhmann's autopoietic theory offer distinct sociological perspectives of democracy. Among sociological perspectives of democracy and their related philosophical counterparts, a distinction can be made between perspectives that view democracy primarily in terms of its input by means of the will of the people being reflected in government, its output in terms of the repercussions of government conduct, especially legislation, and the manner in which a political community allows for a deliberative sphere of relevant opinions. Luhmann's autopoietic theory places a premium on the input of democratic government in emphasizing the role of the electorate in contributing to the distinction between government and opposition. In contrast, Habermas argues that law is legitimate when it is congruent with a procedurally conceived notion of democratic principles at various levels of lawmaking and government action.

Although the sociology of law has made little explicit use of the theoretical work that has been done on democracy and its role in modern societies, a substantial body of sociological research exists that addresses relevant issues of democracy and law in a number of contexts. Exemplary of this work are investigations on the impact of felon disenfranchisement laws in terms of principles of democratic participation, the effects of moral panics in view of the fulfillment of basic rights, and the manner in which various forms of conflict resolution handle disputes in more and less formal ways. What is revealed as a peculiar characteristic of the sociology of law in these various strands of research is that the most valuable contributions sometimes come from empirical investigations based on rigorous research even though the broader theoretical potential thereof is not always explicitly realized. As such, contemporary sociology of law still provides a primary service in offering empirical evidence and counter-evidence in the light of theoretical perspectives that were developed outside the boundaries of sociological scholarship and which within sociology are not always recognized as being related to ongoing research activities. To be sure, empirical research always fulfills a critical function and can be no more significant than when it provides the hard facts that theorizing must make sense of. Nonetheless, working towards the development of relevant theoretical foundations from within the sociology of law could strengthen the specialty area and lead it to be accepted on more equal footing with other fields of inquiry that can rely on traditions where theoretical advances and empirical progress have more readily gone hand in hand.

9 | Law and integration: the legal profession

In terms of law's function to secure social integration or regulate behavior, a central role is played by the legal profession as the experts of law. The legal profession is arguably the single most researched aspect of law in legal scholarship and socio-legal studies. Among the many topics studied are the history and transformation of the legal profession, the regulation of the profession, the structures and practices of legal education and admission to the bar, the relationship between attorney and client, and the organization of legal work. Indicating that this abundance of work is itself a function of the professionalization of legal work, most scholarly research on the legal profession comes from within legal scholarship and from perspectives of the law and society tradition that are part of or closely associated with legal education. The professionalization of scholarship dealing with the legal profession is also reflected in the most common questions that this research addresses, typically focusing on technical aspects that relate to the competitive business of the profession rather than the sociologically relevant dimensions of its societal dynamics.

The successful monopolization of the study of the legal profession by legal scholarship and its relative insularity from independent scholarly reflection testify to the profession's centrality as a matter of legal autonomy, which conceptually goes back to de Montesquieu's separation of powers principle. Sociologically relevant work on the legal profession has therefore not surprisingly been developed on the basis of theoretical frameworks that question, rather than merely assume the accomplishment of, law's aspiration of legal autonomy. The ideal of legal autonomy as a critical dimension of modern legal systems indeed forms one of law's most critical and sociologically challenging characteristics. Theoretically, strong differences exist on how the professionalization of the lawyer's role is accordingly to be conceived from a sociological viewpoint.

This chapter will begin by reviewing the most important sociological perspectives of the legal profession and subsequently discuss
the major empirical elements in the transformation of the legal profession. Of special interest is the so-called Critical Legal Studies
movement, which seeks to cast doubt on the idea of legal autonomy in
favor of a theory of the practice of law that intimately revolves around
power and differential access to justice. As the perspective of Critical
Legal Studies has taken place from within the legal profession, it is to
be situated in terms of the development of the legal profession itself,
particularly its diversification. This transformation towards increasing diversity, however, has also been addressed in sociology of law,
especially through research on inequality in the profession of law.

Law as a profession

The legal profession refers to the whole of occupational roles purposely oriented towards the administration and maintenance of the
legal system, including judges, lawyers, counselors, as well as experts
of legal education and scholarship. The designation of legal professional is important to be described narrowly in terms of its purposeful
involvement in law, for all members of society are involved in the law
as legal subjects. Only legal professionals are participants of the law
by virtue of their occupation.

Sociological work on the legal profession is only one approach next
to many others in various strands of socio-legal studies and, especially, legal scholarship. The fact that the legal profession is among
the most researched aspects of law is not an indication of a wider
interest among social and behavioral scientists in the professions, but
is a direct function of the professionalization of the legal occupation
itself. For, to the extent that the professionalization of the legal
occupation has been successfully accomplished, it brings about a
monopolization of all legal activity, including legal scholarship.

The aspiration to maintain occupational autonomy is one of the
legal profession's most critical and sociologically challenging characteristics. The autonomy of the legal profession is reflected in legal
education and various aspects of legal practice inasmuch as, over
time, the legal profession has been successful in controlling admission
to and the organization of law schools as well as the regulation and
execution of legal work by means of systems of supervision and

control. The independence of the legal profession is a concrete expression of the autonomy of law, with an independent judiciary as its main manifestation.

Although most scholarly research on the legal profession comes from within legal scholarship and from other law-and-society perspectives besides sociology, there also exists a distinctly sociological tradition that examines the societal aspects of the legal profession.[1] The sociology of the professions is historically most indebted to the work on the professionalization of legal work in modern societies that was first systematically explored by Max Weber and that was subsequently elaborated by Talcott Parsons in terms of the role of the professions in the legal system's integrative function. Weber's interest in the legal profession is already clear from his definition of law as a normative order that is guaranteed by a specialized staff. As discussed in Chapter 2, Weber also held the professionalization of the legal occupation to be the most important factor in the rationalization of law. Furthermore, in a formally rationalized system of law, legal professionals play a role that is rivaled in significance only by that of the experts of bureaucracies, because they are involved in the administration of law on the basis of acquired legal expertise in relevant rules and appropriate procedures. Legal professionals are experts of knowledge of, and know-how in, the law.

In the modern sociology of law, perspectives of the legal profession have been advanced on the basis of Talcott Parsons' work (see Chapter 5). Parsons' special interest in the legal profession was not only informed by his broader interest in the professions, but also makes sense in terms of the functionalist conception of the legal system as a mechanism of social control. Based on a Parsonian perspective, the successful acquisition of expertise in a particular occupational role is the most outstanding characteristic of professionalization. The legal professional is thus primarily someone who is knowledgeable about the law and who can provide specialized services to the general public

---

[1] Foundational contributions in the sociology of the professions include Abbott (1988); Freidson (1984, 1986, 2001); Larson (1977). Influential works in the sociology of the legal professions include Carlin (1962); Halliday (1987); Rueschemeyer (1973). See also the helpful discussions and overviews by Berends 1992; Davies 1983; Dingwall and Lewis 1983; Halliday 1983, 1985; Macdonald 1995; Murray, Dingwall, and Eekelaar 1983; Riesman 1951; Rueschemeyer 1983. This section partly relies on Deflem (2007a).

on the basis of this expertise. As such, the legal professional mediates between the polity as legislator, on the one hand, and the public as clients of the law, on the other. In the functionality of their activities towards the public, the legal professionals (as all professionals) can rely on their occupational tasks being valued as responding to a publicly recognized concern or serving a public good.

Parsons also argued, in line with Durkheim's vision of the occupational group, that professional organization was such an important force in modern society that it could successfully rival bureaucratic organization in state and market. Professionalization and bureaucratization are indeed not necessarily congruent forces as professionals can become independent to create their own culture and structure separate from the institutional settings in which they practice their work, such as is most clearly the case with the free professions of law and medicine. A separation between professionalization and bureaucratization is not accomplished when professionalization takes place within the boundaries of state bureaucratic organization, such as in the case of the police function (see Chapter 11).

Transcending the Parsonian framework, recent sociological perspectives have offered a variety of alternative viewpoints on the role of the legal profession. These approaches have focused on the role of expertise in professionalization and, relatedly, the function of professions in their orientation towards the public. At a general level, alternative theoretical perspectives question the functionalist notion of integration and instead analyze the legal system, including the legal profession, in terms of power and inequality. The Parsonian perspective is argued to be limited in this respect because it only questions the integrative functions of the legal profession inasmuch as the legitimacy of professional work is jeopardized in terms of certain strains towards deviant behavior, which lawyers may experience in the execution of their duties. Parsons (1954) argued that lawyers may experience pressure to yield to expediency in view of financial temptation or pressure from clients, excessive formalism to focus on the technicalities of the law, and sentimentality by exaggerating the substantive claims of clients. But the Parsonian perspective otherwise does not question that professions have garnered expertise in certain occupational tasks and that professionalization has functional benefits in serving the public good.

Recent sociological perspectives have suggested that expertise is not so much a good as it is a claim that is made, not only towards the public, but also towards the official authorities of a society, which can provide legitimacy to such a claim by granting a legally binding license to establish exclusive professional autonomy over a specified jurisdiction of activities. In this sense, the system of professions appears primarily as a struggle over control of certain jurisdictional areas of work over which control is sought and expertise claimed in matters of diagnosis, analysis, and treatment. It is the institutionalization of expertise in matters of law, for instance, that secures the special status of the legal professional on the basis of the state's formally granting such monopoly. Sociologists have also contemplated the more complex behavior of the legal profession once it has been successfully monopolized, when the profession seeks to influence the state and its legislative potential. Professions can therefore also be incorporated into bureaucracies, rather than be independent from them.

The notion that the legal profession serves a public interest has also been questioned as the profession has considerable power in framing issues, not in terms of clients' interests and concerns, but on the basis of the profession's conceptions of legal relevance and competence. The fact that lawyers are interested in serving their own needs to build prestige and acquire income may be more instructive of their activities than are the rationalizations of their work in terms of formal legal ideology. A formal code of ethics in professional conduct, likewise, may serve the public less than the profession itself by seeking to safeguard the status of the members of the profession and, simultaneously, prevent competition and establish social closure. One element of this closure is the mystification and glorification of legal work as involving activities closely following the preparations in legal doctrine and procedure provided in law school, when in actuality much of the lawyer's work can be routine and mundane.

Two recent developments in the study of the legal profession deserve special consideration and will be discussed in the following sections of this chapter. First, studies conducted over the past few decades have shown a greater diversity in the legal profession than the model of professionalization can account for. Second, and relatedly, the rise of the Critical Legal Studies movement that has critiqued the behavior of legal professionals irrespective of, and often contrary to, law's self-proclaimed ideals of justice and equity has evolved as another exponent of the transformation of the systems of the legal profession, especially of legal education. Critical Legal Studies must therefore also be seen in the context of the empirical transformation of the legal profession.

The transformation of the legal profession

Modern industrialized societies with varying legal traditions have a system of legal professions.[2] The profession of law, however, is not stable across time and space in terms of the degree of professionalization, the structure of the profession, and the organization of legal work. Historically, societies that have no legal system separated from custom and convention have no legal professionals, as multifunctional roles crystallize around powerful and wealthy leaders who speak truth in matters of religion, morality, and law. A specialized profession of law first developed in the Roman Empire, where men who were learned in the law initially worked on an amateur basis but gradually took on legal work as a profession on the basis of specialized training.

With Weber, the modern role of the lawyer can be seen as a product of the increasing complexity of society in economic, political, and cultural respects. The development of capitalist business increased the formalization of economic life and the need for legal experts qualified in the rational administration of business affairs. The secularization of law benefited the involvement of legal experts as well. And the expansion of bureaucratic government also increased the need for experts in regulatory clarity and order.

The professionalization of legal work, as mentioned, involves a public recognition of expertise and knowledge, an independent

[2] For the empirical information reported in this section, I have especially relied on the writings of Richard Abel on the history and structure of the American legal profession (Abel 1986, 1988, 1989) and the studies on Chicago lawyers conducted by John Heinz, Edward Laumann, and associates (Heinz and Laumann 1982; Heinz, Laumann, Nelson, and Michelson 1998; Heinz, Nelson, and Laumann 2001; Heinz, Nelson, Sandefur, and Laumann 2005; Nelson 1994). For additional analyses and overviews, see Boon 2005; Galanter and Palay 1991; Gorman 1999; Halliday 1986; Kritzer 1999; Sandefur 2001, 2007; Seron 1996; Shamir 1993b, 1995; Van Hoy 1995, 1997. For comparative perspectives of legal professionals in several nations, see the contributions in Abel and Lewis 1988–1989.

organization of the profession, and a monopoly over occupational jurisdiction. The development of professionalization has historically been uneven from one society to the next and has also produced different results in organization and legal practice. The evolution of legal education towards the specialized system of today first developed in the United Kingdom, where law became a recognized field of study as part of university education during the eighteenth century. The United States patterned much of its legal system on the English model, but early American local courts admitted lawyers to practice law on the basis of an apprenticeship, not a college or law degree. Gradually, in the United States, formal legal education developed to become a necessary basis for the practice of law. The requirements of legal education expanded from the organization of entrance exams, the addition of written tests, the lengthening of legal education to several years of study, and, eventually, the requirement of a college degree before admission to law school. The American system of professional law schools offering a JD (Juris Doctor) degree is relatively rare. In many other countries, law can be studied as an academic discipline at the college level, although instruction will be typically geared at legal practice, and supplementary requirements may be in place, such as a prior college degree and a post-degree apprenticeship.

Differences exist in the legal profession in common law and civil law nations, first of all with respect to legal education. Common law systems, typically derived from the British legal system, rely heavily on non-statutory or case law based on precedent of earlier court decisions. Civil law systems date back to Roman times and found expression in the codified legal systems of France, where a national code was originally introduced under Napoleon in 1804, and Germany, which introduced a unified code in 1900. With the increasing codification of law in common law countries and the growing significance of jurisprudence in civil law countries, the divisions between the two systems have been blurred. Nonetheless, differences persist in terms of legal education and the legal profession. Legal education in the civil law systems, such as they exist in continental Europe, for instance, primarily involve a study of codes and statutes, whereas the law schools of common law traditions rely on analyses of court cases in order to practice law.

The legal profession also appears differently in common and civil law nations in functional terms. In the United Kingdom and many other common law countries, a distinction exists between solicitors and barristers. Solicitors act as legal advisors to clients and select an advocate or barrister appropriate to the case at hand who will act in court as a trial lawyer. Some common law countries, most notably the United States and Canada, do not make the distinction between solicitor and barrister. In the United States, all lawyers who pass the bar exam can argue before the courts of the state in which the exam is organized (federal court appearance relies on an additional admission procedure). The relation between judges and advocates in nations with common and civil law traditions differs as well. The function of the judge in the adversarial system that is typical for common law systems is more passive relative to the lawyers who represent their respective party's position. In the inquisitorial system of civil law nations, the judge or a group of judges are more actively involved in investigating the case that is before them. With respect to control over the profession, the activities of the legal profession in civil law countries tend to be overseen by the government through a ministry of justice. Legal professionals in common law nations, by contrast, have typically instituted systems of self-regulation through professional groups in which membership may be mandatory to exercise legal practice. In the United States, for instance, the American Bar Association is a voluntary association formed in 1878, which certifies legal education programs and develops programs to assist legal professionals in their work.

Turning to sociological analyses on the transformation of the legal profession in the United States, research has shown important changes and structural differences in the legal profession. The number of lawyers in the United States has risen over time in response to changing demands for legal service and relative to the varying degrees of success with which professionalization was achieved. Until the formation of the American Bar Association and the state bar associations in the late 1800s to early 1900s, the legal profession was not well organized. Requirements for entry into the profession gradually became more stringent in an attempt to control the ethnic and class make-up of the profession and the number of available lawyers, with strong regional variations across states. Societal factors, including economic conditions, demographic changes, and immigration patterns, were also influential.

The increase in the number of lawyers accelerated during the 1970s at a rate much sharper than the general population increase. Presently, the total number of lawyers in the United States is almost one million. Most of them, about three-fourths, work in private practice, in small offices, or in larger law firms. Some 17 percent work either for a government agency or a private business, and only 1 percent are working in legal aid associations and law schools. Most law firms are relatively small, with only a handful of lawyers, but some have grown to employ one hundred lawyers or more.

Research on law firms has revealed that lawyers working in large law firms enjoy considerably more prestige (and income) than those working alone or in small firms. The factors contributing to the differentiation of two so-called "hemispheres" of occupational prestige among lawyers include the specialty of law that is practiced and the type of clientele that is served. For instance, prestige ranks high for copyright law, international law, and corporate law, and low for lawyers involved with civil rights law, criminal prosecution, criminal defense, and immigration law. In the top hemisphere of the profession are the lawyers who are employed in large national firms and who work in specialty areas that serve big and powerful corporations and institutions. These lawyers also tend to be involved less in court appearances and more in counseling of their relatively wealthy clients. Lawyers who work with high-status clients are bestowed more prestige and receive more financial and other rewards. The work they do is more professionally pure in being more distinctly legal, such as reviewing a lower-ranked lawyer's work and appearing in appellate courts.

In recent years, the number of lawyers serving corporate clients has risen. This increase is due to an increase in demand for legal work from corporate clients, especially in large metropolitan areas where the large law firms are typically located. In the urban areas, the number of lawyers has increased most sharply, and the scale of law firms has expanded greatly as well. Greater competition among the large law firms has led to their further increase in size and a move to larger geographical markets, including the international arena (see Chapter 12).

Lawyers in the bottom hemisphere are self-employed as solo practitioners or they work in small firms. They represent individuals rather than institutions and engage more in court work for personal legal services. Lawyers who work for private companies that can afford to institute their own legal division are much better compensated financially than are those who work for government agencies or in public office. Besides income, the hemispheres are also divided along the lines of ethnicity and race, legal education, and professional and social networks. Catholic and Jewish lawyers, for instance, tend to be excluded from the more prestigious large law firms.

Most lawyers in the United States are situated in the lower hemisphere. In the smaller firms, moreover, legal work has changed drastically in qualitative respects to become involved in very routinized deliveries of personal legal services, such as the writing of a will and the handling of a divorce. In these so-called franchise law firms, lawyers rely heavily on secretaries who become as essential to the legal production system as the legal professional. Marketing strategies for such firms are devised with advertising campaigns in the popular media in order to reach a wide clientele.

An important conclusion of research on the organization of the legal profession in the United States is that the profession is not monolithic but harbors a diverse group of more and less prestigious members engaged in a variety of more and less rewarding activities. Legal work that may be particularly valued among the public, either because it serves a distinct need as in the case of personal injury or divorce, or because it is morally valued, as in the case of civil rights, does not enjoy high professional esteem and is not highly rewarded financially. Although the top of the legal profession still primarily consists of white male lawyers of relatively affluent backgrounds who are educated in the top law programs, legal professionals today none-theless comprise a variety of practitioners more broadly representative of American society with respect to gender, educational background, race, and ethnicity. The stratification and diversity that presently exists in the legal profession may lead to a lack of professional unity that might also affect the standing of the profession as a whole. One remarkable consequence of the increasing differentiation of the legal profession has been the emergence of perspectives in jurisprudence that explicitly discuss matters of differential access to justice and diversity in the law as a matter of a jurisprudential critique in the Critical Legal Studies movement.

The diversification of jurisprudence: Critical Legal Studies

The activities of the legal professional comprise adjudication, advocacy, counsel, as well as legal scholarship. It is important to specify legal scholarship or jurisprudence as a legal activity because it demonstrates that the legal profession has an interest in studying itself in order to facilitate management on the basis of internal control and to prevent analysis on the basis of external observation. The Critical Legal Studies movement that developed in the halls of the law schools should therefore be seen as an outgrowth of the transformation of the legal profession and the changing conditions of the profession's claim to autonomy and monopoly.

In general terms, the Critical Legal Studies movement refers to a loosely connected group of legal scholars – mostly concentrated in the United States and to a somewhat lesser extent in the United Kingdom and other Western nations – who from the late 1970s onwards began to criticize the legal system on the grounds of the unfulfillment and betrayal of law's self-proclaimed ideas and ideals of justice, equality, and fairness.[3] Besides this general description, a central characteristic of the Critical Legal Studies movement is its theoretical, methodological, and political diversity and indeterminacy, making it hard to describe the perspective succinctly. In terms of its theoretical ideas, Critical Legal Studies is variably indebted to the American tradition of legal realism, the Critical Theory of the Frankfurt School, versions of neo-Marxist thought, French post-structuralism (especially the work of Michel Foucault), postmodernism, and deconstruction.

Critical Legal Studies scholars proclaim political ambitions that can generally be described as radical, alternative, and/or leftist. Many of the adherents of the perspective were influenced by their experiences of the anti-war, civil rights and other protest movements of the late 1960s. By the late 1970s and early 1980s, the intellectual efforts of critically minded legal scholars began to be more organized, emanating

---

[3] The major representatives of the Critical Legal Studies movement include Roberto Unger (1976, 1983, 1986), Duncan Kennedy (1983, 1997, 1998), and Richard Abel (see note 2), amongst others. Additionally influential empirical and theoretical analyses on Critical Legal Studies are provided by Galanter (1974), Gordon (1986), Kelman (1984), Tushnet (1991), and contributors in Fitzpatrick and Hunt (1987). For helpful overviews, see Bauman 1996; Gordon 1986; Hunt 1986; Miaille 1992; Milovanovic 1988.

in an institutionalization of the Critical Legal Studies perspective. A first Conference on Critical Legal Studies was organized in the United States in 1977, and related organizations, such as the Critical Legal Conference in the United Kingdom and "Critique du Droit" in France, were formed shortly thereafter.

The theoretical ideas of Critical Legal Studies comprise a number of distinguishable components. Most fundamentally, Critical Legal Studies is oriented at unmasking the actual workings of the law, typically in the courts and other arenas of legal decision-making. Critical of what the law does relative to its own principles, Critical Legal Studies adopts the stance of an immanent critique that is oriented at "trashing" the formalism and objectivism of the law. Against the ideology of liberal legalism, Critical Legal Studies argues that equality before the law is a myth. In its actual workings, the law reflects and furthers the economic, political, and other socio-structural inequalities that exist in society. Even those laws that are formally proclaimed to serve greater justice in reality serve to maintain social inequality. Given the structural nature of these inequalities, the changes that are needed to make the legal system more just have to surpass the technical efforts of legal reform and involve more fundamental efforts aimed at human emancipation.

The Critical Legal Studies perspective is empirically most focused on the role legal professionals play in sustaining the legal order despite law's internal contradictions, unfulfilled promises, and contribution to the creation of conflict and inequality. Critical Legal Studies scholars argue that indeterminacy is a key characteristic of the modern legal system. Legal reasoning and decision-making is anything but a neutral application of principles and is instead affected by dozens of biases on the part of legal professionals that depend on the personal ethical-political values they hold and the characteristics of the socio-structural context in which they were formed. Not only are judges and lawyers influenced in their conduct by their ideological and political commitments, the law masks this condition of value-bias by positing neutrality and justifying legal outcomes in terms of a formal application of statutes and precedents to specific cases.

The position of Critical Legal Studies scholars that a multitude of influences affect the outcome of legal decision-making reaffirms an intimate connection between law and morality. Given the indeterminacy of law, however, the normativity of law cannot be neatly demarcated but is designated as a patchwork quilt of different and contradictory values and ideas. Recapturing the legal-realist skepticism about the predictability of law, Critical Legal Studies scholars argue that the outcome of law is essentially unpredictable because it is influenced by many variables that are beyond formal legal reasoning. More so, even on the basis of existing legal standards of argumentation, very different conclusions can be reached, depending on the formative contexts in which arguments are made. Class, race, and gender divisions characterize the context of law. Focused on the inequalities of law along gender and racial lines, Critical Race Theory and feminist legal theory are off-shoots of Critical Legal Studies.[4] Adherents of Critical Race Theory principally question the neutrality of the law in terms of its color blindness and fairness towards all regardless of race, while feminist legal theory views law as an expression of a male-dominated society in which women are objectified and treated as inferior (see Chapter 10).

Critical Legal Studies adopts a perspective on law that is essentially political. The political nature of law does not refer to the relation between law and politics (through legislation), but more fundamentally implies that legal discourse, including the arguments made in the law and the decisions reached, cannot be structurally distinguished from political discourse. The claim to objectivity in law merely masks its political qualities. Critical Legal Studies does not only expose the political dynamics of the workings of the law, it is also activist in its orientation to bring about change to the legal system and to society as a whole. In order to transform law and give it the revolutionary purpose of dismantling the hierarchies of power and privilege, an empowered democracy has to be developed whereby political decisions become subject to debate by all who are involved rather than merely being proclaimed by legislators and legal professionals.

With its efforts to demystify the thought and behavior of the legal profession contrary to the ideal of legal autonomy, Critical Legal Studies has changed the landscape of legal scholarship to become more diverse in orientation. As a tradition in legal scholarship rather than in social science, Critical Legal Studies has had no great influence in the sociology of law. Sociologists of law have usually discussed

---

[4] See Delgado and Stefancic 2001 on Critical Race Theory and contributions in Dowd and Jacobs 2003 on feminist jurisprudence.

Critical Legal Studies as a perspective that formally shares certain characteristics with conflict-theoretical approaches in the sociology of law, which had developed well before the Critical Legal Studies movement hit the scene. In the secondary literature, Critical Legal Studies is sometimes presented as an approach in the sociology of law, even though no actual connections between the two perspectives can be established.[5] Because of its suspicions towards the value of social science, also, Critical Legal Studies has realized its achievements in legal scholarship without resource to relevant sociological work on law and inequality, despite the fact that such work is potentially insightful to the perspective of Critical Legal Studies as the following review will show.

Researching the legal profession: the case of gender inequality

The increasing diversity of the legal profession has not always been accompanied by increasing equality. On the contrary, the legal profession remains marked by various forms of inequality along racial, ethnic, religious, and gender lines. Catholic and Jewish lawyers are underrepresented in the prestigious partnerships of large law firms. Racial minorities are underrepresented in all levels of professional legal work. Since the reversal of segregation policies and the establishment of affirmative action programs, the number of minority students has increased over the years, but not as dramatically as has the number of female students. Women have begun to enter the legal profession at a very high rate, but confirming the findings on differential earnings in organizations from the institutionalist research of Bridges and Nelson (Chapter 7), sociological research has found that many forms of gender inequalities persist in the legal profession.

Illustrative of the power of sociological research on inequality in the legal profession are the studies by Fiona Kay and John Hagan on lawyers in Canada, specifically in the city of Toronto and the province of Ontario.[6] Among the most systematic research efforts investigating

---

[5] It is telling, for instance, that a recent article presented as an analysis of the paradigmatic overlap between Critical Legal Studies and the sociology of law offers only an overview of the Critical Legal Studies perspective (Priban 2002).

[6] See the book-length study, *Gender in Practice* (Hagan and Kay 1995), and related research articles (Hagan 1990; Hagan and Kay 2007; Hagan, Zatz,

women's positions in the legal profession, the research by Kay and Hagan shows that women who enter law face discrimination and are confronted with long-held assumptions about women's roles that lead them to not obtain equality relative to male legal professionals with respect to income, occupational opportunities, and mobility. In recent decades, women have made great advances in entering legal education and legal practice, but their position in the legal profession continues to be marked by many inequalities. Already having faced a sexualization of their presence in law schools, women have a harder time entering the legal workforce, especially in the more lucrative positions, and they report feelings and experiences of alienation, harassment, dissatisfaction, and discrimination once they have joined the profession. Female legal professionals not only receive lower incomes, they face a lower ceiling of job mobility because of the assumption that they will eventually abandon their careers to take up family responsibilities. Women also do not benefit as much as their male counterparts from having a degree from an elite law school.

As law firms have grown, Kay and Hagan show, the increased number of legal positions in law firms in bottom positions, not as partners, with relatively low income have disproportionately been taken up by women, who thus bore the brunt of the proletarianization of the legal profession. Women are underrepresented in private practice and in partnerships in law firms, positions in which they also move more slowly than men. In the law firms, moreover, women face higher expectations in terms of the hours they are expected to bill and the number of clients they are expected to bring in. At the same time, female lawyers tend to be given less legal work that is billable than male professionals and, unlike their male colleagues, they face negative consequences from parental leave. The inequalities women in law face relative to their male colleagues tend to persist even as their position and organizational setting improve. Furthermore, women leave private practice and law firms at a higher rate than men and, when they do, disproportionately tend to drop out of the profession altogether. Despite female professionals' limited success in the legal workforce, however, there are also indications that they are positively impacting

Arnold, and Kay 1991; Kay 1997, 2002; Kay and Brockman 2000; Kay and Hagan 1995, 1998, 1999).

law by working to introduce policy reforms aimed at creating a more respectful professional work environment.[7]

Conclusion

The role of the legal profession is at the heart of the integrative capacities of modern systems of law. In the sociology of law, the Weberian focus on the professionalization of legal work and the related Parsonian emphasis on the role of the professions with respect to law's integrative function produced a perspective of the legal profession that reaffirmed its centrality in the autonomy of law. Subsequent analyses in the sociology of the professions have challenged this perspective and offered more complicated pictures of professionalization. This in sociological thinking was not only the result of intellectual developments in sociology, particularly the move away from structural functionalism. It also harmonizes with empirical transformations of the legal profession, particularly the increasing diversity of the profession during the latter half of the twentieth century. The diversification of the profession of law also led to the development of the Critical Legal Studies movement that contributed to the development of perspectives within jurisprudence seeking to unmask the autonomy of law.

In its reception, the perspective of Critical Legal Studies has occasionally been condemned by other-minded legal scholars for its purported destructive qualities towards the unity of law and the nihilism and leftism it would have brought into the law schools. The sharp tone and defensive nature of this response, however, has largely proven to be unnecessary. For not only was the perspective of Critical Legal Studies developed by law professors working within the safe confines of the major professional law schools, the transformative intentions of Critical Legal Studies have not been realized, neither on a grand scale nor in the form of any locally confined guerilla attacks.

---

[7] Confirming the research findings of Kay and Hagan on the Canadian situation, sociological research in other nations where women have successfully entered legal education and legal practice also shows that female legal professionals do not enjoy a position of equality. See, for instance, the studies by Dixon and Seron 1995; Gorman 2005, 2006; Hull 1999; Hull and Nelson 2000; Laband and Lentz 1993; MacCorquodale and Jensen 1993; Pierce 2002; Roach Anleu 1990; Spurr 1990; Wallace 2006; and contributions in Schultz and Shaw 2003.

Without necessarily denying that practitioners of the Critical Legal Studies movement were animated by a committed interest in unrealized human opportunity, the movement has not, contrary to its intentions, been able to successfully challenge the authority of law and the role played therein by the legal profession. What the Critical Legal Studies movement has contributed to is a diversification of legal thought (especially in opposition to the law and economics perspective) as part of a transformation of law that marked the legal profession as a whole.

As a review of work on gender stratification in the legal profession has shown, sociological research on law and inequality transcends the boundaries of legal scholarship to offer an intellectually engaging, empirically founded, and scholarly meaningful investigation of the transformation of the legal profession. In its critical function to confront aspirations and realities in the diversification of the legal profession, empirically oriented sociological work fulfills a function more critical than any jurisprudential debunking exercise can accomplish. Moreover, sociological work on the limits of the legal profession can take advantage of sociological insights that are central in the sociology of law, particularly in the form of theories of professionalization. Further contributions in this area can therefore enrich the sociology of law in a manner that is both theoretically informed and substantively meaningful, while also contributing to unmask the study of the legal profession when it is less inspired by analytical aspirations and driven more by professional ambitions.

10 | Law and culture: the balance of values through norms

With the rise of capitalism and democracy, modern societies have not only differentiated relatively autonomous economic and political systems, they are further marked by a differentiation of a cultural system of values and an integrative system of norms. Values are conceptions about desirable ways of life, whereas norms are sanctionable standards of conduct. Values are oriented at guiding actions among individuals or within groups (through socialization), while norms are oriented at regulating interactions between individuals or across groups (in view of integration). Durkheim and Simmel were among the first sociologists to posit the coordination of values and norms as one of the most central problems to sociology. Parsons phrased this problem in terms of differentiation (between the fiduciary system and the societal community), but it took later developments in sociology to more fully recognize the implications of this differentiation and, accordingly, develop a variety of theoretical positions. The implications of these positions for the sociology of law, as being centrally occupied with societal norms, are considerable. Extending the theoretical discussion since Durkheim, this chapter will review some of the most important sociological perspectives of values and norms up to their most recent formulations, specifically in the work of Jürgen Habermas and its theoretical nemesis in postmodern perspectives and the approach of deconstruction.

From a thematic viewpoint, the discussion on the separation between values and norms will in this chapter be used to review work in the sociology of law surrounding matters that pertain to the interrelation between law and culture. Given the increasing diversity of values in contemporary societies, the complexity of modern culture and the contemporary self have increased the integrative burdens placed on law. The legal system has not always been able to respond adequately to this growing complexity and, as a result, important discrepancies have been observed in law's self-proclaimed ideals of fairness and equal treatment, on the one hand, and the reality of law in its handling of cultural diversity, on the other. Sociological research on racism, sexism, classism, and other forms of discrimination in and through the law most acutely reveals the modern dilemma of law in the relationship between values and norms, which under discriminatory legal conditions, appears as a conflict.

From the viewpoint of the sociology of law, special problems are also posed in terms of the peculiar form in which modern culture has evolved, particularly with respect to the increasing individualism of modern values. As individualist values have gotten an ever-stronger hold in modern societies, a wide range of private issues have emerged that, precisely because of their intimate nature, have become subject to regulation by law. Perhaps no issues are as private in modern societies as those that relate to life itself. The body of the contemporary self has consequently been subjected to legal regulations, as revealed from laws concerning birth, health, family, and death. Research on the legal aspects of matters related to health and the family has addressed important facets of these developments. The legal treatment of euthanasia, same-sex marriage, and abortion will be discussed as provocative case studies that show the continued need in modern societies to balance the diversification of values through norms.

Values and norms: from Durkheim to Habermas

In the context of modern societies, the role of law in balancing diverse values through norms is considerable and well recognized in the history of sociology.[1] The work of Durkheim offered a first systematic analysis of these issues in terms of a transformation from mechanical to organic societies, whereby the collective conscience changes from a cohesive set of strong beliefs to a modern individualist culture that is characterized by a plurality of value systems. Durkheim presented a relatively straightforward answer to the problem of normative integration, arguing that the substance and form of law adopts to the changing nature of the values system in such a way that law readjusts to maintain its integrative power. In pre-modern societies, there is no

---

[1] This section relies on some of the major writings of sociologists discussed in earlier chapters. Especially noteworthy are Durkheim (1893a, 1893b), Weber (1922a, 1922b), Parsons (1937, 1951), and Habermas (1983a, 1983b, 1992a, 1992b).

differentiation between values and norms and no separation between public and private issues. All matters of importance to the self and to society are public. With the transformation towards organic societies, however, law is adjusted in order to secure an integration of different cultural belief systems. Hence, law takes on a restitutive character that preserves the individualistic nature of the collective conscience.

Weber argued purposive rationalization to be the central characteristic of modernity. Yet, while emphasizing the form of rationalization, Weber also analyzed cultural shifts among the factors that enabled this process. In this respect the best example of Weber's cultural sociology is his study of the Protestant ethic's influence on the development of the capitalist mode of conduct. In matters of law, it was particularly the secularization of law that Weber held responsible for the disappearance of substantive irrationality and religious charisma from law. Better than Durkheim, Weber also understood the continued challenges posed to modern rationalized law in responding to variable cultural impulses, specifically in the form of a remaining tension between formal and substantive rationalization. Thus, Weber observed a technocratization of law on the basis of objective legal standards as well as sporadic returns to social law based on ethical postulates related to collectivist conceptions of justice.

Modernizing the classic tradition, Parsons took the problem of the relationship between values and norms head on. In his early work, he articulated this problem in terms of a theory of action as the connection between means and ends and suggested that interactions in society are coordinated because they are guided by common systems of ultimate ends into which the members of the society are socialized. In order to secure obedience to the values system, moral norms regulate or control action. This formulation betrays at least two key characteristics of Parsons' sociology. First, Parsons' approach is anti-positivistic in arguing that values have a special place in sociological theory (in the Weberian sense of acknowledging the importance of values from the viewpoint of the actor while maintaining value-freedom in sociology). Second, because of its functionalist orientation towards differentiation, Parsons' theory accords specified and related functions to the values (or fiduciary) and normative systems of society. The Parsonian model is at heart a cultural-idealist theory that posits that a society's values system shapes the societal community. Thus, as discussed in Chapter 5, law plays a central role as a system of normative integration, influenced by cultural values that form its subconstitutional stratum.

In Parsons' sociology, values and norms are conceptually differentiated, probably more sharply than in any other sociology up to that point. Yet, what Parsons gained in conceptual clarity is lost in the functionalist framework that conceives of the relation between values and norms in relatively unproblematic terms that emphasize social cohesion. Extending and correcting aspects of Parsons' sociology in the more critical direction of a conflict-theoretical perspective is Jürgen Habermas's conception of the interrelations between ethics, morality, and law. Habermas distinguishes between ethics (*Sittlichkeit*) and morality (*Moralität*) – a distinction that goes back to the philosophy of G.W.F. Hegel – to differentiate between the ethical values of the good, on the one hand, and the moral norms of the just, on the other. Ethics refers to the whole of values that, at an individual or group level, are held to be expressions of the "good life" or the manner in which one's life ought to be lived. Ethical evaluations are made in terms of the variable degrees of commitment among those who share a particular value. Morality refers to the whole of a society's norms that specify the manner in which a society ought to be organized. A discourse on morality is oriented at determining which normative order is more just in regulating the interactions among all members of society, irrespective of the ethical values they each adhere to.

Philosophically, Habermas argues against a moral skepticism to suggest that moral problems can be solved rationally. Habermas formulates such a rationalist approach in his discourse theory, which specifies that only those norms can be considered to be legitimate if their consequences can be accepted without force by all those concerned. This principle is an extension of Habermas's concept of the so-called ideal speech situation, which specifies that a rational discourse should be based on an absence of power differentials among the participants, sincerity in the expression of opinions, and equal rights of participation.

Sociologically, Habermas's discourse theory of morality and ethics finds expression in his theory of the democratic organization of law. To the extent that the legal system is democratically ordered, modern law can fulfill its primary task of mediating among a plurality of ethical value systems. Habermas judges the principle of discourse theory to be particularly important in culturally pluralistic societies, which have no single overarching moral authority on the basis of a unitary ethic. Modern societies are marked by a high degree of ethical diversity and are therefore in need of normative integration through law because of dissent and conflict among different value systems. The moral point of view of normative integration through law is called upon to transcend the diverse particularities of ethical lifeworlds. The integrative function of law becomes more acute as the degree of cultural diversity in a society increases to the extent that peaceful co-existence among society's members might be threatened without legal intervention. The need to integrate a diverse society while also pre-serving cultural differences thus appears as the most critical challenge of modern law. However, whereas Habermas's answer to this chal-lenge lies in a resolutely democratic organization of law, there are also recent currents in social theory which, against Habermas and other so-called modernist perspectives, have argued in favor of an accept-ance of the full diversity of ethical lifeworlds against any overarching and unitary intrusion from morality and law. In its most radical form, this position is articulated by postmodern theories and the perspective of deconstruction.

Postmodernism and deconstruction in theory

Postmodernism and deconstruction are two perspectives in social theory that have addressed the complexities of contemporary life in a very different way than the modernist sociological theories that stretch from Durkheim to Habermas.[2] Postmodernism refers to a broad and diverse theoretical movement that denies the validity of any overarching concept or unifying theoretical framework beyond a recognition of the complex diversity of cultural stories (narratives) and their variable meanings among the manifold groups, sub-groups, and individuals in modern societies. Postmodern perspectives respond to a new phase of social development that took place during the latter half of the twentieth century, whereby social and historical events

[2] The perspective of postmodernism is most distinctly associated with the work of Jean-François Lyotard (1979a translated as 1979b), while deconstruction was developed by Jacques Derrida (1990a, 1990b). On the influence of postmodernism and deconstruction in sociology, see the overviews and discussions by Denzin 1986; Lemert 1997; Mirchandani 2005; Murphy 1988; Ritzer 1997; Seidman 1991.

have become increasingly dynamic and interrelated in highly complex ways. Referred to as postmodernity, this epoch is argued to be distinctly different from prior social forms such as the class society of the industrial age.

The term postmodern dates back to as early as the late nineteenth century when the expression was used to refer to post-impressionist painting. The expression was also used in the world of art in the early half of the twentieth century (and has remained in vogue in this meaning until today), but it was in C. Wright Mills's work on *The Sociological Imagination* that the term was first used to refer to a new epoch in social development. Mills (1959: 166) wrote that the "modern age is being succeeded by a post-modern period," characterized by a questioning of the "inherent relation of reason and freedom." Mills argued that increased rationality could in the postmodern age no longer be assumed to lead to an increase in freedom. It was the task of sociology, therefore, to uncover and investigate the structural conditions of this new society in which freedom is abandoned in favor of the creation of a new human being, the "cheerful robot," who had come under the spell of the new society and its technological progress that offered a numbing comfort (Mills 1959: 172).

Mills's work did not directly influence the elaboration of postmodern social theory, but his position already anticipates some of the elements of contemporary postmodernism, as it was most sharply formulated by the French philosopher Jean-François Lyotard. In a short but influential book, *La Condition Postmoderne* (*The Postmodern Condition*), first published in 1979, Lyotard analyzes the conditions of knowledge in the present-day era of the information society. All knowledge, Lyotard argues, occurs in a narrative form that legitimates itself on the basis of some ultimate principle. The narrative of science, for instance, is legitimated on the basis of the Enlightenment's notion of a quest for universal truth. More specific forms of the scientific activity are guided by an additional narrative concerning its own standing, a meta-narrative, that posits a particular principle of legitimation. In the social sciences, for instance, such meta-narratives include the polar types of the technocratic orientation of functional differentiation in systems theory (Parsons) and the emancipatory perspective focused on conflict in critical theory (neo-Marxism).

In the present-day era, Lyotard argues, all meta-narratives have lost their credibility. Because of the increasing complexity of social life, each narrative can only be understood in terms of its own dynamics and principles, and no meta-narrative, no matter of what kind (scientific, literary), can lay claim to legitimate other narratives. The defining character of the postmodern age is the incredulity towards meta-narratives in light of an overabundance of micro-narratives. Recognizing this condition, postmodern social theory does not accept that any one concept or unifying theory can adequately capture the diversity of the human condition without distorting the diversity of the human experience and thereby imposing a form of conceptual violence. The multiplicity and fluid nature of the contemporary world, instead, has to be expressed by a series of multiple truths and representations if the terror of imposing one narrative on all other narratives is to be avoided. Instead of adopting a meta-narrative, postmodernism accepts only the validity of local micro-narratives and the multiple, discontinuous, and changing truths of diverse voices.

Deconstruction is a theoretical approach developed by the French philosopher Jacques Derrida. Deconstruction is the (f)act by which a text is shown to have multiple meanings. Even concepts that are in opposition to one another – male versus female, just versus unjust, legal versus illegal – deconstruction shows not to be clear-cut but fluid in meaning. Although Derrida undertakes such analyses throughout his work (as an act), he insists that deconstruction takes place in the text itself (as fact). Derrida applies most of his deconstruction activities to philosophical and literary texts, and it is mainly in the areas of literary studies and philosophy that his work has been influential. However, deconstruction is not restricted to the specific texts of philosophy and literature for, according to Derrida, all is text.

Although Derrida dissociated himself from the term postmodernism, deconstruction and postmodern perspectives share certain characteristics. Like postmodernism, deconstruction is aimed at undermining a stable frame of reference or legitimating meta-narrative that is claimed to underlie a text or narrative. In the case of deconstruction, the text itself is argued to undermine its own authority because its internal contradictions and multiple meanings eradicate the boundaries of the categories of opposition, which it seeks to assert. As such, deconstruction is a corollary to the postmodern idea that the unbelief towards a meta-narrative implies an endless multiplicity of meanings.

An interesting application of Derrida's approach for the sociology of law is his work on the mystical foundations of authority in which he identifies various aporias of law. An aporia is a puzzle, typically in philosophy, that presents an impasse, an insurmountable obstacle in an inquiry. In Derrida's deconstruction of the force of law, he reveals three such aporias. The aporia of singularity refers to the assumed but unavoidably violated principle of the generality of legal rules. Legal norms are supposed to be binding on everyone (generality), yet they are not so applied and instead appear variable in each concrete case (singularity). The aporia of undecidability refers to the fact that while the law guides judges, lawyers, and other legal professionals in their decision-making activities, there is no law that determines which particular law is to be applied in any given instance. The aporia of urgency, finally, refers to the fact that justice, by its own aspirations, must be immediate and cannot wait, yet the legal process takes time to unfold. In summary, while the law claims universal justice, each application or case of law demonstrates a particularity that reveals the arbitrary nature of law.

Postmodernism and deconstruction in law

With respect to the study of law, there have been several efforts, especially during the *fin de siècle* of the 1990s, to adopt principles of postmodernism and deconstruction. Although modernist theories continue to dominate contemporary sociological discourse on law, there are at least two noticeable influences from postmodernism and deconstruction. First, there has been a trend towards the adoption of the terms postmodern, postmodernism, and, to a lesser extent, deconstruction in rather vague meanings that have some unspecified relation to the rise of the post-industrial information age and the multicultural society. This is the fad and fashion of postmodernism and deconstruction. Second, there have been more deliberate and systematic efforts towards the development of a postmodern and/or deconstruction approach in the study of law. These efforts have especially influenced (socio-)legal scholarship dealing with inequalities and law and have less impacted related work in sociology. Taking to heart the declared incredulity towards meta-narratives, the practices of postmodernism and deconstruction defy disciplinary boundaries and have accordingly influenced scholarship on law in and across jurisprudence, socio-legal studies, and the sociology of law. More than is the case for other theoretical movements, therefore, a brief excursion is in order outside the disciplinary bounds of sociology to chart the influences of postmodernism and deconstruction on the study of law.

In jurisprudence, ideas from postmodernism and deconstruction have been adopted to approach law as a text or narrative. Prototypical is, in this respect, the perspective of Anthony Carty and Jane Mair (1990), who argue that the text of law is to be read as being self-referential, that is, it has no outside referent (other than other legal text).[3] Because of the increasing complexity of law, the structure of the text of law has changed dramatically. Where once law was a text of a vertical and autonomous source of power, deciding down upon legal subjects, postmodern law is fragmented and dissolved into multiple power sources to form a horizontal collage of multiple regulatory types. The once authoritative singular voice of law has thus given way to a diversity of multiple laws. Despite the multiplicity of a multitude of regulatory subsystems, however, legal texts still appeal to "vacuous universals in a language which is textually permeated with a violence which cannot be adjudicated by an external/vertical, objective standard" (Carty and Mair 1990: 396, italics omitted). The terror of the text is that there can be no escape to context but that, imprisoned in language, reference is inescapably made to universals (of rights, of justice), which are appealed to as if they are objective. By making such appeals in individual cases, for instance to acquire compliance to the terms of a contract in a dispute or to ascertain a right to the freedom of expression, legal subjects are under the illusion of establishing themselves as autonomous actors. Conversely, any questioning of the authority of the text is perceived as psychotic.

In sociology, one of the earliest constructive efforts to develop a deconstruction that also includes an application in the field of legal sociology is offered in a paper by Stephan Fuchs and Steven Ward (1994). The authors differentiate between radical and moderate deconstruction, whereby the latter contextualizes the meaning of statements and claims rather than accept from the former an attitude of extreme skepticism about all interpretation. On the basis of a moderate deconstruction, Fuchs and Ward apply deconstruction to sociological theory and law, especially court trials. In the case of sociological theory and

---

[3] For other discussions and applications of postmodernism in legal scholarship, see the contributions by Austin 2000; Feldman 1996; Grazin 2004; Veitch 1997.

other forms of scientific knowledge, they argue that deconstruction reveals that there are no firm principles to produce stable and lasting meaning. Instead, the statements of Western scientific knowledge, including those of sociology, are not purely objective but are culturally influenced. This cultural embeddedness implies that scientific claims can only be accepted as localized narratives. By means of example, the authors refer to the variable ways in which the works of the sociological classics have been received and interpreted at different moments throughout the development of sociology.

In the case of law, Fuchs and Ward argue that court trials function as deconstruction dramas. Legal materials, such as testimonies, evidence, case law, and written codes, are not merely given but need to be carved out of the chaos of all available materials and the noise of alternative interpretations. The strength of the facts presented in legal cases is not absolute but relative to the strength of competing accounts. In this competition between interpretations, four strategies are used to have one account triumph over another: (1) by reliance on rhetoric, authority is attributed to a statement because it abides by certain standards of presentation and style; (2) by showing the ideological persuasions of witnesses, their statements can be discredited; (3) by raising procedural objections, the form of an argument can be attacked to undermine its substance; and (4) by attacking a person's reputation, any statements made by that person can be invalidated. As these strategies are adopted in more or less convincing ways in court settings, the outcome of law is rendered unpredictable.

Illustrative of a postmodern perspective in the sociology of law is the work of Dragan Milovanovic (1992, 1994, 2002, 2003: 225–263). On the basis of various related social theories such as French post-structuralism and post-Freudian psychoanalysis, Milovanovic adopts a postmodern stance that conceives of the perceived accomplishments of contemporary societies as limited by the appearance of new forms of manipulation and control. Among the consequences of this recognition, foundational truths that were traditionally claimed to be objective and subject to scientific inquiry have become suspect. Doubt is cast on the modernist notion of the centrality and autonomy of the subject, appearing, for instance, as the rational actor in economics and the reasonable person in law. A postmodern perspective redirects attention to language (as it functions in text and narrative) to argue that there is no subject outside the structure of language, which

determines the subject and the manner in which the subject will understand others. Given the multiplicity of linguistic orders and meanings, any specific discourse frames language in a more directional
manner to give the multi-accentual nature of linguistic signs a uni-
accentual reading. In the case of legal education, for instance, students
are instructed in the precise meaning of such terms as intent, negligence,
and tort. Law students are taught how to use these juridical terms in
a manner that is appropriate to law.

From the postmodern outlook, Milovanovic has in collaboration
with Stuart Henry developed a so-called constitutive approach to law
(Henry and Milovanovic 1996, 1999). The constitutive perspective
transcends the view of law as being either autonomous or context-
ually dependent and instead favors a perspective of co-determination
among political, legal, economic, and cultural relations. The field of
law is seen as constituted by those who participate in law but also, at
once, as constituting the relations among them. The circularity of this
approach is intentional. The origin of the discursive field of law is less
important than are its dynamics and effects. The legal discourse on
crime, for instance, is framed in terms of an autonomously conceived
violator of legal codes. Yet, taking into account the insight that crime
cannot be analyzed in isolation from the wider structural and cultural
contexts in which it is produced, the constitutive approach opens up
alternative discursive formations. Specifically, a distinction is made
between crimes of reduction, which reduce a person to a certain position, and crimes of repression, which deny a person the ability to
achieve a particular position. Such a reformulation would open the
door to alternative responses to crime.

The Portuguese sociologist Boaventura de Sousa Santos (1987,
1995a, 1995b) has formulated one of the most original and systematic postmodern perspectives to the study of law. In line with French
postmodern social theory, Santos argues that the conventional paradigms of the sociological (and socio-legal) study of law are exhausted
and, moreover, that the theoretical alternatives that have been offered
are not satisfactory. Seeking to construct a viable alternative, Santos
develops a postmodern approach to law on the basis of what he calls a
symbolic cartography that is based on a perspective of law as a map.
Like a map, law distorts reality but not in an indeterminable manner.
Instead, maps represent and distort reality in three ways: (1) by
scaling the distance that exists in reality down to a scaling on the map;

(2) by projecting the shapes and nature of reality onto a surface with a center, and (3) by symbolizing selected features and details of reality by means of conventions.

The distortion principles of cartography are clarified by Santos in an analysis of modern law. First, in terms of scale, the legality of the nation-state is built on the assumption that law operates only on the scale of the jurisdiction of the state. However, contemporary law is sociologically more complex and involves at least three legal spaces: the local, the national, and the global. The multiple scales of legality thus range from the small-scale over the medium-scale to the large-scale. Events at each scale level may become legalized in interrelated ways. The suppression of a strike in a factory, for instance, may violate local labor rules, national labor law, as well as international legal codes on employment.

Second, with respect to projection, the legal system defines certain limits to its operation and organizes the legal space within those limits in terms of center and periphery. In highly industrialized societies, the limits of law are defined by its underlying logic in market capitalism. In the center, the market logic of law applies to issues that are closely related to the economics of capitalism, such as contract law. The market logic also gets transposed to the periphery, where its effects are more distorting of reality, such as in the case of welfare law.

Third and finally, reality is legally symbolized either as a succession of stages or in a multilayered manner. Santos argues that a succession-of-stages model, which, for example, might suggest a development from local to national and, eventually, to international law, is not as adequate in accounting for the present-day complexities of law as is the multilayered perspective. Echoing the theme of an insurmountable multiplicity of meanings in postmodern theorizing, Santos maintains that multiple layers of legality co-exist in society to create a condition of legal pluralism. However, unlike the traditional view of legal pluralism as it was developed in legal anthropology,[4] the postmodern approach emphasizes not a mere co-existence of various legal orders but a condition of inter-legality whereby various legal orders are in a state of superimposition, interpenetration, and an often conflictual state of interrelation among one another.

---

[4] The perspective of legal pluralism was introduced in the anthropology of law to contemplate the co-existence of different legal orders, especially in the context of colonized societies (see A. Griffiths 2002; Merry 1988; Moore 1973).

Legal inequalities: class, gender, and race and ethnicity

Postmodern and deconstruction perspectives argue for the recognition of diversity and multiplicity against a centered vision of society and social thought. As such, these perspectives open up a review of work in sociology of law on discrimination and inequality in and through law. However, the treatment of the theme of inequality in law, as this review will show, is not the exclusive province of postmodernism and deconstruction.

With respect to the class basis of inequalities in law, sociologists Carroll Seron and Frank Munger (1996) have reviewed the state of sociological theorizing and research to suggest that there has been a shift from (top-down) historical-structural and macro-sociological work to a more contemporary oriented focus that (from the bottom-up) interprets the legal experiences of individuals in various classes. Top-down theories, such as neo-Marxist conflict theory, define class in terms of people's positions with respect to the central economic and cultural institutions of society. The class structure depends on resources, such as education and income, and works to differentially distribute the effects of law. Research on the stratification of the legal profession fits in this perspective (see Chapter 9). By contrast, a newer wave of bottom-up theories of law and inequality has grown out of symbolic interactionism and other inductively grounded theories of society. These theories explain law and inequality as social processes that occur in concrete situations and contexts, giving greater weight to class identity and related experiences of inequality and exclusion. The relationship between law and inequality is understood from the interactions among individuals in particular settings, such as the courts, and their interpretations of class. The contributions on the narratives of legal consciousness by Ewick and Silbey (1998) fit in this framework (see Chapter 6).

From the perspective of a bottom-up approach, Seron and Munger argue in favor of a continued focus on class in studies on law and inequality in at least four areas of research. First, class plays a role in everyday life in mediating the impact of law. Poor people, for example, tend to have a low legal consciousness, i.e., they are unaware of how the law works and what their legal rights are. The social experiences in work and family life of these people may contribute to their lack of understanding of the law. Second, studies on class and the legal profession show that the rank and status of lawyers within the professions are dependent on the larger class structure of society. In this respect, it is telling that the elite world of top lawyers is dominated by the higher echelons of society and that the uneven distribution of lawyers' services reflects the power of wealthy and elite clients (see Chapter 9). Third, the class structure of society is also reflected in various aspects of the administration of law. Depending on class position, the law is differently applied and enforced. Harsher punishments involving extended prison stays are typically reserved for lower-class criminals (see Chapter 11). And, fourth, class provides a critical focus in seeking to understand the possibilities and limits of legal change.

In the areas of gender and racial and ethnic inequalities, postmodernist and deconstruction perspectives have more successfully infiltrated the sociological and socio-legal discourse, although traditional modernist perspectives are still prevalent as well. Extending the case of gender stratification in the legal profession discussed in Chapter 9, feminist legal theories in sociology and socio-legal studies have focused attention on the manner in which law reproduces and can be used to fight the gendered inequalities that exist in society at large.[5] Law thus functions as a preferred site where gendered inequalities can be addressed, while law also represents many of these inequalities. The fact that law has become a site for feminist struggles stems from the fact that many ways in which women were traditionally denied rights of expression and participation were based on law. Historically, the relative absence of women within the legal profession also contributed to the formation of a male-biased legal system. As legal reforms have gradually been implemented against gender discrimination, the limitations of the law as a tool of antidiscrimination have been shown in the continuation of inequalities along gender lines.

Feminist perspectives have responded to the continued challenges of gender inequalities despite legal reforms in at least two ways. First, some feminist scholars argue that women's inequalities will disappear once women are allowed to benefit from the arrangements of the existing social structure. Law should therefore promote the inclusion of women in the political arena, in the workforce, in education, and

---

[5] See the discussion on feminist legal theory by Fletcher 2002 and contributions in Dowd and Jacobs 2003.

in other important spheres of social life. This perspective of inclusion is a more traditional modernist response that reaffirms the value of a liberal and open democratic society. Second, other feminist scholars argue that society, including law, must recognize the significant differences that exist between men and women and value each in terms of their unique experiences and contributions. As it stands, important social and legal spheres are male-dominated, not only in terms of the overrepresentation of men, but in deeper historically constituted ways. Feminist legal reforms must therefore not merely expand women's rights in existing social and political arrangements, but ought to also lead to revise and challenge those arrangements to better reflect the diverse needs and desires of women. From this perspective, which harmonizes with insights from postmodernism, sameness between men and women can be neither the means nor end of equality through legal reform. Instead, equality by law should lead to a more profound change in the constitution of society, including law, so that women's differences from men and the differences among women are valued.

In terms of research studies on gender inequality and law, studies on spousal violence can serve as a useful illustration of the variety of feminist perspectives, the different conceptions of gender they manifest, and the related notions of law and legal reform they employ. Spousal violence has been approached from at least three theoretical perspectives.[6] First, theories of gender inequality argue that women and their contributions are in society valued as less worthy. Within this perspective fits research which finds that violence by men on women is typically instrumentally oriented in exerting control, while female violence against men is expressive and indicates a loss of control. In terms of the proper legal response, the law needs to be reformed to accommodate these different reasons of male and female spousal violence. Second, feminist theories of gender oppression argue that women's inequality is the result of a process of active oppression or patriarchy. This approach finds support in research that shows that the vast majority of victims of serious spousal violence are women. Legal reform should be oriented at implementing mandatory arrest

---

[6] This analysis is based on Jo Dixon's (1995) review of studies on spousal violence by Anne Campbell (1993), Ann Jones (1994), and Lawrence Sherman (1992). The classification of sociological gender theories applied to this literature is adopted from Lengermann and Niebrugge-Brantley (2000). For a non-feminist perspective on spousal violence, see Felson 2006.

provisions for the offender and instituting provisions for the female victims, such as shelters, to free themselves from abusive relationships. Third, sociological theories of gender difference conceive of women as having unique social positions and life experiences and, additionally, that even among women there are differences. This perspective can rely on studies that find that mandatory arrest policies tend to be more effective in cases of female victims who are married and/or have an employed partner, while conflict resolution methods are more effective in other cases. Legal reforms should thus take into account the differential deterrent effects of arrest and conflict resolution depending on the variable situations of the victims of spousal violence.

Research on law and inequality along racial and ethnic lines is surprisingly recent in origin. As is the case for the study of law from the perspectives of postmodernism and deconstruction, scholarship on gender and race and ethnicity tends to cross disciplinary boundaries in the human and social sciences. Even more than is the case with gender studies, the scholarship on law and racial and ethnic inequality is underdeveloped in the sociology of law, arguably only with the exception of relevant work in the area of social control and criminal justice (see Chapter 11). As discussed in Chapter 7, institutionalist perspectives have been especially well developed in research on the impact of civil-rights legislation and affirmative action policies, but this literature does not specifically focus on racial inequalities or treat race and racial discrimination as a central component of research, instead concentrating on the organizational filtering of the regulatory environment and a broad range of employment-related implications. In contrast to the sociology of law, jurisprudential work dealing with racial and ethnic legal inequalities has been better developed, especially in the popular jurisprudential field of Critical Race Theory.

As an off-shoot of the broader Critical Legal Studies movement, Critical Race Theory is a perspective in American jurisprudence that focuses on racial inequalities in and through law.[7] In view of the persistent patterns and ubiquitous nature of discrimination against racial and ethnic minorities in American society, even after the civil rights period of the 1960s, Critical Race Theorists critique liberal

---

[7] On Critical Race Theory, see the contributions in Crenshaw et al. 1995; Delgado and Stefancic 2000; Gates 1997. An analytical model to adopt principles of Critical Race Theory in social science is offered by Price (2004).

jurisprudence and legal reforms based thereon, such as affirmative action and so-called color-blind policies. Reforms based on the principles of liberal legal doctrine are argued to mask and, hence, further the interests and privilege of the white majority. Instead of adopting a traditional liberal outlook characteristic of the majoritarian mindset, Critical Race Theory reveals the different, unique, and suppressed and oppressed experiences of minority populations, expressed through the subversive strategies of narrating counter-stories, parables, and anecdotes from the minority points of view. These experiences are at once situated in their structural and cultural contexts, which are analyzed on the basis of insights gathered from the social and human sciences. Exemplifying a strong activist orientation, adherents of Critical Race Theory advocate a drastic reorganization of society and law, including a separation from the American mainstream in order to preserve minority diversity and separateness.

Unlike the broader Critical Legal Studies movement, Critical Race Theorists have been relatively successful in articulating principles and methods of scholarship that have influenced sociological and other social-science perspectives on law and racial and ethnic inequality. The reasons for the relative ease of receptivity of ideas from Critical Race Theory in social science are at least twofold. First, whereas sociology and other social sciences did not need to borrow ideas from Critical Legal Studies as they had themselves already developed a large body of conflict-theoretical perspectives, no such comparable richness in thought and research exists in the case of race and ethnicity. If mainstream sociology and social science would not accept at least some principles and ideas from Critical Race Theory, they might well be accused of perpetuating the inequalities they seek to address. Second, in emphasizing the unique experiences of racial and ethnic minorities in their confrontation with the alienating and oppressive dynamics of the dominant (majority) legal system, Critical Race Theory rhymes well with the skepticism towards the possibility of a unifying meta-narrative that has been advanced by postmodern and deconstruction perspectives.

A useful illustration of the application of insights from Critical Race Theory in a postmodern framework is the work of Bruce Arrigo on the legal reforms oriented at the protection of racial and ethnic minority populations (Arrigo, Milovanovic, and Schehr 2000; Arrigo and Williams 2000). Arrigo argues that a deconstruction of laws aimed at protecting minorities, such as in the form of affirmative action programs, reveals the form of such legislation as a gift. The majority ostensibly bestows the gift of socio-political empowerment upon underrepresented constituencies, but it does so only by reaffirming the hegemony and power of the gift-giving majority and its narcissism of giving. Thus, even with such legal programs in place, or, more precisely, because of them, the majority retains its power. A deconstruction of legal ideology, therefore, must lead to establishing equality in socio-political respects and embracing the multiplicity of races, ethnic groups, and genders across the whole of society. For justice and equality to be more adequately realized, legal reforms must be displaced and decentered and current legal and political conditions have to be altered profoundly. An affirmative postmodern framework should be built explicitly on the basis of a politics of difference, undecidability, and the transgression of conventional borders in order to embrace the confluence of multiple languages and experiences.

Turning to the modernist literature on law and racial and ethnic inequality, recent research by John Skrentny on affirmative action policies in the United States serves as an illuminating case study of the potential of sociological work on law and racial inequality.[8] Affirmative action has long been a hotly debated issue in US politics and culture, but it has until recently received little scholarly attention, especially in terms of its historical development. On the basis of an institutionalist perspective, Skrentny analyzes the origins and transformations of affirmation action policies and laws in terms of the role played by policy-making elites. The perceptions elites have of certain groups influence the likelihood that those groups will receive special protection in the form of affirmative action programs. Such perceptions include definitional aspects over what constitutes a particular group, moral issues regarding their perceived degree of suffering, and control aspects in view of the threat a group might pose in the absence of any special programs designed to protect their participation in

[8] Skrentny's work on affirmative action is presented in two books, *The Ironies of Affirmative Action* (Skrentny 1996) and *The Minority Rights Revolution* (Skrentny 2001), and related articles (Skrentny 2006; Frymer and Skrentny 2004). Other sociological work on law and racial and ethnic inequality from a modernist perspective has focused on a variety of issues, such as the legalities of slavery (Coates 2003), legal aspects of the civil rights movement (Barkan 1984), citizenship and immigration laws (Calavita 2005; Torpey 2000), and racial and ethnic discrimination in the legal profession (Pierce 2002, 2003).

society. Thus, African Americans, women, white ethnic groups and other immigrant communities have been received differently among policy elites. Further contributing to the development of affirmative action programs have been such factors as access to the elites and the degree of competition that exists among them. Access to elites is in turn affected by the degree of social movement activity that exists among groups that seek protection.

Interestingly, several ironies are revealed in the creation of affirmative action policies. Although affirmative action policies are aimed at securing equal opportunities and rights for African Americans, their creation was largely the result of efforts by white males. Though typically opposed from the right and advocated from the left, affirmative action benefited greatly during the days of the Republican administration of Richard Nixon in the first half of the 1970s. These efforts were likely made, Skrentny argues, in an attempt to neutralize African-American protest and prevent more radical policies instigated by the civil rights movement and the political left. Perhaps most ironic of all is the fact that affirmative action programs have had effects far beyond their original intent, which was predominantly centered on providing racial equality (in employment opportunities) for African Americans. Yet, many other groups, ranging from Latinos and Asian Americans to women and the disabled, have also benefited from the minority rights revolution.

Laws of body and self: the regulation of health and intimacy

Since Durkheim, sociologists have observed that cultural value systems in advanced societies are characterized by a growing diversity because of an ever-increasing individualism. The culture of the self has allowed the creation of private spaces of intimacy and the legalization of such spaces of self-expression as zones of non-interference. At the same time, however, modern legal systems have constituted the individual self by regulating the manner in which private acts, sometimes of a highly intimate character, are to be organized. For with the formation of self and individuality come important legal questions surrounding the relationship between private liberty and public responsibility. With laws regulating birth, marriage, divorce, and death, some of the most intimate aspects of life have become legally regulated. Especially relevant in this context is the regulation of various private matters related to health and life. Sociologists have developed research in these areas from the viewpoint of the interrelationships of law with medicine and family.[9] Case studies on euthanasia, same-sex marriage, and abortion may serve as indicative of the manner in which the sociology of law has addressed the regulation of body and self.

Euthanasia refers to the ending of a person's life, by medical means, on the basis of perceived intolerable circumstances of suffering under which the person lives. The deep moral debate over euthanasia is readily revealed in the terminology to describe the practice, which is variably referred to as physician-assisted dying, physician-assisted suicide, and mercy killing. John Griffiths and associates have examined social aspects of euthanasia in The Netherlands since the gradual legalization of the practice that began in the 1980s.[10] The Netherlands is presently among the few jurisdictions, besides Belgium and the US state of Oregon, where euthanasia is legal under certain circumstances. The legalization of euthanasia in The Netherlands did not happen overnight, but came about within specific socio-historical circumstances.

During the 1970s and early 1980s, Dutch attitudes towards euthanasia became more tolerant under the influence of increasing individualism, secularization, and social experimentation, creating a climate of *de facto* legalization. The initial acceptance of euthanasia through a tolerance regime was not initiated by legislation, but was the result of a complex process of interaction between the medical profession, the courts, the prosecutors, the government and the legislature, and authoritative reports on euthanasia. A report of the Dutch Medical

---

[9] Besides the research discussed in more detail in the remainder of this chapter, sociological work on the legal regulation of the private sphere includes studies on health and medicine (Frank 1983; Peeples, Harris, and Metzloff 2000), neonatal intensive care (Heimer 1999; Heimer and Staffen 1998), mental illness (Arrigo 2002; Hiday 1983), pregnancy and employment (Edwards 1996), marriage and divorce (Dingwall 1998; Ermakoff 1997; Zeigler 1996), and family and childhood (Dingwall and Eekelaar 1988; Richman 2002; Seltzer 1991; Sutton 1983).

[10] See the book, *Euthanasia and Law in the Netherlands* (Griffiths, Weyers, and Blood 1998), and related articles (Griffiths 1995, 1998, 1999; Weyers 2006). On the regulation of euthanasia in the United States and other nations, see Lavi 2005; Pakes 2005.

Association in 1984 defined certain requirements for euthanasia to be legitimately performed, including the voluntary nature of the patient's request, a well considered and lasting desire for the procedure, a suffering that is perceived as unacceptable to the patient, and consultation by a second doctor. Following the medical report, a bill was introduced in the Dutch parliament to bring about changes in the criminal code, resulting in the appointment of a Commission to investigate the matter further. The Commission issued a report in 1991 that did not lead to any legislative changes but that did further cultivate a climate of factual acceptance of euthanasia.

Hampering the development of an appropriate law on euthanasia, Griffiths and his colleagues argue, was a conflict in the meaning and use of certain key terms concerning euthanasia in the institutions of medicine and law. Concepts such as causality and intentionality that are central in legal matters of criminal responsibility do not harmonize with similar terms used in medical practice. Nonetheless, the legalization of euthanasia has recently been codified in Dutch law. The Termination of Life on Request and Assisted Suicide (Review Procedures) Act that went into effect in April 2002 specifies among the conditions of legality that the patient's suffering is judged unbearable and lacks any prospect of improvement, that the patient voluntarily and persistently requests the procedure, and that the procedure is performed in a medically appropriate fashion by or in the presence of a doctor.

Examining the impact of the legalization of euthanasia on the occurrence of the practice, Griffiths finds that there is no evidence to suggest that the number of cases of terminations of life without a patient's request would have increased in The Netherlands since the 1980s. The number of legal euthanasia cases, however, has increased, leading to conflicting interpretations on the part of advocates and opponents in the euthanasia debate. Griffiths (1998: 103) argues that the slippery-slope argument misunderstands the direction of legal development, because it assumes "a tendency toward relaxing legal control over medical behavior, whereas what is really going on is a quite massive *increase* of control." As an example of juridification, the legalization of euthanasia in The Netherlands has brought about a whole new set of norms regulating behavior that hitherto was unregulated. As such, medical practices dealing with death and, by implication life, have been legally domesticated.

Regarding the regulation of intimacy and family, research by Kathleen Hull has tackled the controversial issue of the legalization of same-sex marriages.[11] At present, same-sex marriages are legal in only a few countries (Belgium, The Netherlands, Spain, Canada, and South Africa) and in the US state of Massachusetts. Many other nations and some US states recognize same-sex couples legally only in the form of pseudo-marital civil unions. In the occasionally heated debate over same-sex marriage, various cultural and legal arguments and processes collide to shape the dynamics of the legal treatment of same-sex partnership. In the case of the United States, the issue erupted during the mid-1990s after a same-sex couple's challenge to their denial of a marriage license was upheld in court in the state of Hawaii. The state legislature of Hawaii then passed a bill that effectively outlawed same-sex marriage, leading to intensified public debate on the issue across the United States. In some states, same-sex marriage statutes were developed, but, with the exception of the state of Massachusetts, they were overturned by higher courts. At the federal level, there have been attempts to outlaw same-sex marriage by constitutional amendment. In 1996, US Congress passed the Federal Defense of Marriage Act by which a state could choose not to recognize a same-sex marriage even if it was recognized in another US state and whereby the federal government was not allowed to recognize same-sex marriages.

On the basis of interviews with members in same-sex relationships, Hull's research shows that same-sex partners have different attitudes about the meaning and desired effects of legalized same-sex marriage. Some same-sex partners favor the recognition of marriage because of the rights and practical benefits it would bring, while others view the legalization of same-sex marriages as an element towards the acceptance of homosexual relationships in society at large. The rights and benefits of legal marriage include practical provisions related to such important matters as health care and taxes. The broader impact of legalized same-sex marriages relates to the legitimacy of same-sex relationships, on an equal footing to other marriages, which could bring about a cultural and social normalization of homosexuality. Although most same-sex couples wish to have their relationship

---

[11] See Hull's book, *Same-Sex Marriage* (Hull 2006), and related articles (Hull 2001, 2003).

legally recognized and thereby embrace existing categories of legality, they differ in their practices to adopt alternative or cultural marriage practices, such as commitment rituals. Some couples use marriage-related terminology, such as wife, husband, or spouse, while others have enacted a public commitment ritual to formalize their partnership. These rituals act as quasi-legal regulations of marriage, affirming the seriousness of the commitment, ascertaining couple identity, and establishing similarities to legal marriages. Such rituals are rejected by same-sex couples who regard them as not meaningful in view of their non-legal status.

Rounding off this review, research on the legality of abortion strikes at the very heart of human intimacy and life. Sociological work on the legal regulation of abortion is surprisingly sparse. Most research by sociologists and other social scientists has focused on the moral abortion debate and the social movements that have crystallized around the (polar) opinions about abortion rather than investigated the legality of abortion in concrete socio-historical settings. In an analysis on the basis of a comparative test of the theories of Parsons, Luhmann, and Habermas, I have analyzed the dynamics and determinants of the constitutional regulation of abortion in the United States (Deflem 1998a).[12] In the US, abortion is regulated by state law. Yet, under the principle of judicial review, abortion statutes are subject to constitutional rulings by the US Supreme Court, the nation's highest federal court of appeal. The Supreme Court did not rule on the legality of abortion until 1973 at a time when abortion statutes across the United States had begun to be more diverse. Abortion had historically been criminalized since the mid-1800s, but during the 1960s and early 1970s several US states passed more and less liberal abortion laws while other statutes remained very restrictive.

In 1973, in the now famous decision of *Roe v. Wade*, the Supreme Court invalidated a 1857 Texas statute which prohibited abortions at any stage of pregnancy except to save the life of the mother. The Court decided that the decision to have an abortion was a matter of the pregnant woman's right to privacy. But it was also ruled that the privacy right is not absolute and that states have a right to protect

[12] Besides the findings reported in my article in *Social Forces* (Deflem 1998a), this review additionally relies on ongoing research on abortion law in the United States. For comparative perspectives, see Lee 1998; Fegan and Rebouche 2003; Linders 1998.

potential life. Based on medical data concerning fetal development, specifically the viability of the fetus to live independently outside the womb, a trimester framework was specified whereby abortion was legal during the first trimester, could be regulated during the second trimester in relation to matters of maternal health, and could be outlawed during the final three months of pregnancy "except where necessary in appropriate medical judgment for preservation of life or health of the mother" (*Roe v. Wade*, p. 705).

The *Roe* decision did not simply lead to liberalizing abortion law across the US states. Various states introduced a variety of restrictions to the legality of abortion, such as spousal and parental consent requirements that stipulated consent of the husband in the case of an abortion decision by a married women, consent of parents in the case of minors seeking an abortion, and detailed information about fetal development and abortion alternatives, such as adoption, on the part of abortion providers. In response, the Supreme Court was often called upon to rule on the constitutionality of such restrictions. In the decade following the *Roe* decision, the Court typically invalidated various state-imposed restrictions. But in 1989, in the case of *Webster v. Reproductive Health Services*, the Court ruled several restrictions, such as bans on the public funding of abortions and proscribed viability tests on fetuses of twenty weeks or more, to be constitutional. In 1992, the Court went a step further and, in the case of *Planned Parenthood of Southeastern Pennsylvania v. Casey*, decided to discard the trimester framework. States can now establish an interest in potential life by a determination of fetal viability that is not bound to a period during the pregnancy. Other restrictions on the legality of abortion were also ruled constitutional as long as they do not pose an undue burden on a woman's right to an abortion before the fetus has attained viability.

Since 1992, the fundamental regulation of abortion in the United States has not changed. One important issue that recently reached the Supreme Court was the matter of so-called partial-birth or late-term abortions. These abortions are performed through the surgical procedure of intact dilation and extraction whereby a fetus is removed from the womb after an incision is made at the base of the fetus's skull and a suction catheter is inserted causing the skull to collapse and allowing the fetus to pass through the birth canal. Federal bans against the procedure passed in the US House and Senate in the mid-1990s, but they were vetoed by then-President Bill Clinton. In 2003, the Partial-Birth Abortion Ban Act, which outlaws the dilation and extraction procedure except to save the life of the woman, was signed into law by President George W. Bush. Various US states passed similar bans as well. The United States Supreme Court first addressed the constitutionality of the procedure in the 2000 ruling of *Stenberg v. Carhart*, when the Court struck down (by a vote of 5 to 4) a Nebraska statute because the effect of the ban did not specify a point during pregnancy when the procedure would be banned and also did not contain an exception to save the woman's life. In 2007, however, in the case of *Gonzales v. Carhart* (2007), the Court decided (in another 5 to 4 ruling) that the federal Partial-Birth Abortion Ban Act was constitutional. The Court held the federal law to be constitutional because it was judged to be narrower than the Nebraska law, even though there is an exception only for cases posing a risk to the pregnant woman's life but not, more broadly, her health. The narrow provision of the Act concerns that fact that it only outlaws a particular type of late-term abortion procedure, whereby an intact fetus is partially removed from the mother before it is killed.

Partial-birth or late-term abortions are a relatively rare occurrence. What explains the intensity of debate and related legal and political activity, however, are the cultural dynamics surrounding its morality. Therefore, also, it is not certain at the present time that a pacification of the abortion debate in the United States has set in. On the one hand, the Supreme Court has since 1992 not reconsidered the constitutionality of abortion. In one of the few recent cases involving the legality of abortion, in the 2006 ruling of *Ayotte v. Planned Parenthood* concerning the parental notification requirement of the state of New Hampshire abortion law, the Court remanded the case on formal grounds. On the other hand, as the debate over partial-birth abortions shows, sentiments may erupt quickly and, as in the case of *Roe v. Wade*, the Supreme Court may likewise suddenly offer a ruling that impacts the abortion debate greatly.

Conclusion

The central sociological concern with integration in the light of the rise of individualism and diversity in modern culture has given rise to a variety of theoretical perspectives, ranging from functionalist and conflict-theoretical modernist approaches to postmodernist and deconstruction perspectives. In sociological studies of law and inequality, both modernist and postmodern perspectives have in recent years continued to proliferate, yet modernist theories have been able to better resist the invasion of postmodernism and deconstruction in work on inequalities based on class, which is arguably sociology's most traditional area of inequality. Moving progressively towards areas of inequality that historically have been less well recognized in sociology, specifically gender and, subsequently, race and ethnicity, postmodernism and deconstruction have been more successful in finding fertile grounds of application. With the increasing complexities of social life in cultural respects, also, analyses of class and inequality have generally declined in favor of work on inequality and law in terms of gender and race and ethnicity.

Even more than is the case in research on class and gender, the idea of the universality of law has led to a relative lack of attention towards legal differentiality along racial and ethnic lines, which is remarkable given that important historical instances of legal inequality inflicted on racial and ethnic minorities are well known. Among the all too obvious examples are the colonial experiences of European nation-states building their dominion across the world, the legal institutionalization of slavery in the United States and elsewhere, the formal removal of citizenship from Jews and other "non-Aryans" in Nazi Germany, the wide variety of manifestations of the legalization of discriminatory policies based on racial and ethnic background, and, of special significance in the present era, the debates surrounding asylum policies, citizenship, and immigration. The relative but nonetheless striking neglect of race and ethnicity in the sociology of law might be attributed to the underrepresentation of minorities in sociological scholarship. However, in sharp contrast, legal scholarship, which is similarly characterized in terms of racial and ethnic composition, has been able to focus on racial and ethnic legal inequality through the contributions of Critical Race Theory. Despite its undeniable accomplishments, the sociology of law clearly has more work to do in matters of inequality, especially along racial and ethnic lines, if it is to contribute usefully to the academic debate on these matters.

The primary function of law is integration. Yet, testifying to the value of the distinction between intended functions and achieved consequences, many social inequalities persist despite explicit legal guarantees of equality for all. The increasing diversity of modern societies under conditions of individualist cultural values further amplifies the peculiar difficulties of modern law. Jürgen Habermas (1991: 91) sharply formulated this problem in suggesting that "the sphere of questions that can be answered rationally from the moral point of view shrinks in the course of development toward multiculturalism." Under conditions of increasing diversity, the primary function of law becomes both more necessary as well as more difficult to accomplish. The diversity and individualism that marks modern culture particularly poses problems in terms of the regulation of intimate aspects of life that relate to health, family, and self. The history of same-sex marriage regulations and abortion law in the United States and the continued concerns about the Dutch treatment of euthanasia, for example, show how law may sometimes exacerbate, rather than settle, disputes in both the legal and cultural arenas. The heated and intense nature of these debates fuels activities in the legal and political arenas. Cultural confrontations and social movement mobilization, in turn, often accelerate following important legal and policy decisions. In the light of the complex interplay between culture and law, the limits of law's integrative capacities are revealed, and, ironically, law is shown to accelerate cultural debate and conflict over important moral questions. Thus, as much as it was true in the days of Durkheim, modern law remains a crucial indicator of a society's capacity to maintain social integration and preserve the peaceful co-existence of a plurality of lifeworlds.

PART IV

Special problems of law

11 | *Social control: the enforcement of law*

Regardless of whether law is defined in a more or less restricted sense as referring to formally legislated rules or as also involving other normative orders, for law to be socially valid, it has to be accepted among a community of legal subjects (legitimacy) and it has to be enacted and administrated in a specified manner (legality). The relevance of legality was brought out most clearly by Max Weber in his definition of law. But even in the case of extra-legal systems of normativity, which Weber called custom and convention, some force of compliance must be present. A normative order, in other words, must always be accompanied by mechanisms and systems of control that secure obedience through norm enforcement. Such systems of control range from very informal responses and normative expectations, such as public disapproval or private shame, to highly formalized systems of enforcement of law by police institutions and systems of surveillance and punishment. Enforcement is a special and unavoidable problem of law.

In modern sociology, the enforcement of law has been addressed primarily in the context of the sociology of social control, which, in recent years, has mostly become associated with the sociology of crime and deviance rather than the sociology of law. As this chapter will reveal, however, the concept of social control was originally more expansive in meaning than its current usage in terms of crime and/or deviance, which from the sociological viewpoint has been more intimately connected to the sociology of law. The reasons for the relative expulsion of crime and deviance and the control thereof, including criminal justice and criminal law, from the sociology of law are mostly not theoretical but historical, relating to the origins of criminology as a technology of crime control in the criminal justice system. In consequence, the contemporary sociology of social control cannot without reservation be institutionally located in the sociology of law, although the sociology of law must conceptually include a sociology of social control as well. This chapter will deepen the sociological focus on law to center on the mechanisms of enforcement that accompany legal systems. Although a separate book would be needed to discuss the wide variety of theoretical and substantive contributions in the sociology of social control, this discussion will focus on those dimensions of social control that enjoy a particular connection to law and concentrate on those perspectives and studies that transcend the boundaries of the study of crime and deviance by treating social control as a topic worthy of investigation in its own right.

After a review of the transformation of the concept of social control in modern sociology, this chapter will introduce the work by Michel Foucault on discipline and governmentality as one of the most influential recent theoretical developments on punishment and power that has been fruitfully applied in sociological studies of social control and law. Disagreement exists on the relative merit and limitations of Foucault's work, but, considering its scope and influence, no sociology of social control can be taken seriously today if it does not at least situate itself with respect to Foucault. This theoretical entry will allow for a discussion of sociological studies on a variety of dimensions and mechanisms of social control in the areas of policing, surveillance technologies, sentencing, and punishment.

The concept of social control

Among the oldest concepts in sociology, social control has historically undergone an important theoretical transformation.[1] From the late nineteenth century onwards, social control was primarily used in American sociology to refer broadly to a society's capacity to regulate itself without resorting to force. This broad concept of social control was understood in a benign sense of self-governance that emphasized a society's continued need for social integration through socialization despite trends of increasing individualism. Social control is what characterizes integration in society to the extent that it does need coercion. This concept of social control, implying harmony and progressivism, was in vogue until World War II, especially in US sociology.

---

[1] For overviews and discussions of the concept of social control, see Cohen 1985; Coser 1982; Deflem 1994; Scull 1988.

The broadly understood consensual notion of social control finds its sharpest expression in the works of George Herbert Mead (1934) and Edward Alsworth Ross (1926). Based on a psychology of human conduct (see Chapter 6), Mead conceived of social control in voluntaristic terms as the ability of individuals to modify their behavior by taking into account others' expectations, thus harmonizing one's self-control and the social control exerted by others. As clarified in Chapter 5, Ross articulated the role played by society's institutions in fostering social control and identified law as one dimension of social control, next to other institutions such as education, public opinion, and religion. As a constant function in society, this conception of social control applies to all the members of society, not just to those who violate normative expectations.

An important theoretical shift in the sociology of social control came about in the period following World War II, when the model of a consensual society could no longer be easily accepted given the rise of fascism and Nazism, the atrocities of the war, and the build-up towards the Cold War and the nuclear arms race. The concept of social control was now employed to refer to the more repressive and coercive forms of control that are instituted, not by socialization into norms, but on the basis of power and force. From the viewpoint of this coercive conception, social control functions are attributed to social institutions that are typically conceived of in more benign functional terms. From this perspective, for instance, sociologists Francis Fox Piven and Richard Cloward argued in their landmark study, *Regulating the Poor* (Piven and Cloward 1971), that welfare represents an effort to exert control over certain classes of people, such as the poor and the unemployed, in order to pacify the economically deprived classes and prevent social rebellion. By extension, this perspective of social control can be applied to the physically and mentally ill, the young and the old, and, ultimately, the deviant.

From the 1950s onwards, social control has been conceived more distinctly as the mechanisms and institutions that define and respond to crime and/or deviance. Corresponding to the dominant theory groups in criminological sociology, social control is now conceptualized as a functional response to crime, the societal reaction to deviance, or the reproduction of a social order beyond a mere focus on crime. First, from the perspective of crime causation theories, such as Edwin Sutherland's (1973) theory of differential association and

Robert Sampson and John Laub's (1993) life-course perspective, social control is conceived as a dependent variable caused by crime, functioning, in response to crime, as a mechanism of redress. Crime takes center stage in such a perspective as criminal behavior needs to be detected and punished by the forces of social control in order to prevent the disintegration of society.

Second, from the viewpoint of labeling or societal reaction theories, popularized by Howard S. Becker (1963) and Edwin Schur (1971) and currently represented by Erich Goode (1996) and Ross Matsueda (1992), crime is viewed as a societal construction on the basis of a process of criminalization of deviant acts. Whereas the original act of deviance is motivated by the actor, its subsequent criminalization is a function of the society that defines and responds to deviance. Social control is seen as constitutive of crime through a process of labeling, which typically does not take into account the needs and motives of the deviant actor but instead imposes a system of control that serves societal goals.

Third and finally, from the viewpoint of conflict theory, the interactionist focus of labeling theory is transcended by a more structurally oriented perspective that situates processes of social control within the broader society in which they take place. Instead of analyzing the interactionist order of rule-violator and rule-enforcer, a critical sociology focuses on social control in terms of the historically grown socioeconomic conditions of society and its mechanisms and institutions that are mobilized to maintain order. Particularly noteworthy among the critical theories of social control is the so-called revisionist perspective.[2] The revisionist perspective argues that historical changes in social control that are formally justified as more rational and more humane relative to former measures of control are in fact more efficient and more penetrating than the methods of old. Relatedly, alternatives of traditional forms of social control, such as treatment and re-socialization programs, that are meant to substitute punitive measures, in actuality, function to complement existing forms of social control, bringing about an expansion (or widening of the net) of

---

[2] Most influential and systematically formulated among the revisionist perspectives is the work of Stanley Cohen (1979, 1985). Revisionist theories have been applied to prisons and punishment (Cohen 1977), psychiatric institutions (Scull 1979), and private and public policing (G. Marx 1988; Shearing and Stenning 1983).

control. Moreover, such alternative forms of social control are also argued to ensure that each and every violation of rules, however minute or trivial, will not go undetected, because of an ever-more detailed nature (or thinning of the mesh) of control. Revisionist theories of social control have theoretically benefited most from the work of Michel Foucault.

Discipline and governmentality

The French philosopher Michel Foucault (1926–1984) has influenced the contemporary sociology of social control, and the sociology of law more broadly, in a very decided way by his groundbreaking work on the transformation and nature of power and punishment.[3] The central concern that occupies Foucault in his work on power is the qualitative transformation of punishment over the course of history, specifically the disappearance of punishment as a public and violent spectacle centered on the infliction of pain on the body to the emergence of a surveillance of the soul, and particularly the development of the modern prison system. In opposition to a political economy of power, Foucault's work offers a micro-physics of power that centers on the strategies, tactics, techniques, and concrete functionings of power.

Between the middle of the eighteenth and nineteenth centuries, Foucault shows, public executions gradually disappeared and punishment became hidden, detailed, and concealed. The prototypical expression of punishment during the eighteenth century was the public spectacle of a slow and lengthy torture, but, about eighty years later, it is a timetable that regulates prison life in minute detail. Foucault argues that the historical disappearance of torture, far from being a humanization of punishment, represents a qualitative change in the goals and means of power. The violent and public nature of torture is explained on the basis of the centrality of the power of the sovereign, the monarch, in the justification of law and, hence, the punishment of its violation. At once a judicial and a political affair, torture displays

---

[3] This section is primarily based on Foucault's study of the history of the prison in *Discipline and Punish* (1975) and related writings on power and governmentality (Foucault 1978a, 1978b, 1980, 1981). For overviews and discussions, see Deflem 1997; Garland 1997; Hunt 1997; Hunt and Wickham 1994; Smith 2000; Tadros 1998; Turkel 1990; Wickham 2002, 2006; and contributions in Wickman and Pavlich 2001.

the asymmetry between the condemned body and that of the sovereign. Torture gradually disappeared in favor of a detailed and transparent surveillance of the soul in the wake of reform proposals, developed from the second half of the eighteenth century onwards, that recommended leniency in punishment, but only in the form of a more efficient technology of control that would allow for a discreet but calculable exercise of power over the soul. New forms of punishment had to be nonarbitrary with a specific type of response to each crime to be sustained or decreased in terms of its positive effects towards re-education and reintegration of the wrongdoer. The modern prison system fits with the reform proposals, not as places of detention, but as sites of penitence and correction.

The new form of power that emerged alongside the transformation from torture to the prison is what Foucault calls discipline. In its objective to produce docile bodies, discipline is revealed in a machinery of power in which the body is manipulated, shaped, trained, and made to obey. Disciplinary effects are accomplished through at least four techniques. First, individual bodies are distributed in space according to such principles as enclosure (behind the walls of the prison, the factory, and the hospital), partitioning of bodies into individual cells, and allocation of bodies to functional sites and in ranks. Second, activities are minutely controlled by means of timetables that specify and coordinate different types of action. Third, activities are carefully arranged over time into sequenced sub-activities. And fourth, through a composition of forces, individual bodies are located in terms of the larger whole that functions as a maximum-efficiency machine. From the viewpoint of means, discipline relies on three techniques of correct training: (1) through hierarchical observation, individuals become visible and transparent to allow for detailed control and an appropriate transformation of behavior; (2) by means of a normalizing judgment, the deviant is not punished with an infliction of pain but corrected with exercise; and (3) on the basis of examinations, discipline produces knowledge that can be productively used towards the transformation of the self.

Foucault argues that the supreme expression of discipline can be found in the principle of the Panopticon. A system of surveillance that makes all visible, the Panopticon is a model that was originally developed by Jeremy Bentham for the design of a prison that would very economically be able to supervise prisoners. The Panopticon consists of a round building with individual cells that are separated from one another by concrete walls and that have bars in the front so that each prisoner can be seen by an observer located in the center of the building. Each inmate is visible to the observer while the surveillance itself is unverifiable as the inmates can never see if or when someone is watching them. In the modern system, discipline thus finds its prime manifestation by institution of a system of correction to produce docile and useful bodies by means of isolation, work, and an adjustment of the punishment depending on its gradual achievements.

Among the theoretically relevant insights derived from Foucault is that discipline is not confined to the prison but that its mechanisms work throughout society. The system of the Panopticon becomes a generalized function of panopticism that produces a disciplinary society. Other manifestations of disciplinary power are the hospital, as a place of internment and diseases, the factory, for the concentration of work, and the asylum, where the beggars and the economically non-productive are kept. The human sciences, such as psychiatry, medicine, and criminology, develop accordingly to justify and sustain discipline. Dispersed throughout society, also, disciplinary power cannot be captured in terms of a dichotomy between those who have power and those who are subjugated to power. Instead, disciplinary power is a blind function, a non-discriminating machine in which everyone becomes visible.

Perhaps most important for the sociology of social control and law is Foucault's notion that disciplinary power is productive and useful. This concept clashes radically with a traditional notion of power that is prohibitive and negatively oriented at inflicting pain on the body. Discipline clashes with the vision of law as a prohibitive rule and of law enforcement as a reactive force imposed upon those who break the law. Disciplinary power instead attempts to positively influence the individual's soul into obedience. At the same time, Foucault argues, the disciplinary nature of modern society does not explain all forms of power, for there still are traces of torture and other forms of traditional power. Moreover, indicating an important limitation to the effects of disciplinary power, there is always resistance against discipline. Modern society is disciplinary but not disciplined.

In his less developed but highly influential work on governmentality (a neologism for governmental rationality), Foucault extends the positive qualities of power to argue that the conduct of the members of a society is not subjected to, but implicated in, the exercise of sovereign power. In other words, people's behavior is taken into account in a positive way so that governmental power can center on the population and its truth by presupposing individuals as living subjects in order to further the fertility of territories and the health and movements of the population. Governmentality dates back to currents of European political thought of the sixteenth century where the notion developed that power concerned everything that is and happens, all events, actions, behavior, and opinions, because the state's wealth and strength were perceived to be dependent on the conditions of the population. In nineteenth-century Europe, the notion of governmentality is rediscovered in terms of an efficient economy of power that is targeted, not at a jurisdictionally circumscribed nation-state and its citizens, but at the fertility of a territory and the health and movements of the population. With the object of governmental power concentrated in the subjects and objects that it manages, governmentality breaks with a legalistic conception of power. Instead of the law of monarch or state, the governmental norm comes to represent what is useful to and, conversely, what harms society.

In order to put the governmental form of power into practice, knowledge systems developed on the territory and population of society, including criminological knowledge that centered on the criminal's life and species. Criminology could rely on the development of criminal statistics to reveal the general truths of the population as expressed in regularities about who was more likely to engage in criminal activities under which circumstances. Finally, to complete a triple alliance in furtherance of governmentality, systems of police developed to enforce governmental norms on the basis of a broad program of order and security. As will be clarified in the next section, the concept of police from the perspective of governmental power is broader than the perspective of police as law enforcement that has historically emerged.

Police and policing

Among the many topics sociologists studying police have devoted special attention to are the historical transformation of policing and its multiple forms across the world, a variety of issues raised by the technologies adopted in police work, and the implications of the structure of police organization and the professionalization of the police role. Historically, police has not always referred to criminal law enforcement.[4] Harmonizing with the Foucauldian notion of governmentality, the police function was initially, since the sixteenth century, not understood in a restricted sense as criminal law enforcement, but was very broadly conceived in terms of a general (governmental) program oriented at the welfare, wellbeing, and happiness of individuals on the basis of a broad system of government that included all possible aspects of public life. Instead of merely responding to violations of law, this governmental system of police (as policy) proactively and positively contributed to advance order and welfare. In this sense, police concerned such diverse matters as education, health, murder, religion, fire, fields, forests, and trade, rather than only being an instrument of law enforcement. As nation-states grew, police institutions developed that, complementary to the externally directed force of the military, specialized in matters of internal security. Thus took place a gradual delineation of the police (as law enforcement) in terms of rules formally defined in matters of order maintenance and crime control.

Even with a generalized transformation of the police function in terms of law enforcement, variations continued to exist among the police systems of different nations. In some societies, especially in continental Europe, the police task was very broadly defined. In the German Empire of the late nineteenth century, for instance, the police function was comprehensively understood to concern such diverse matters as murder, smoking in public places, and traffic. In other, more liberal nations, police powers were more confined in terms of constitutional rights and restricted to violations of narrowly conceived criminal laws. Colonial regimes again followed entirely different paths, closely related to the economic and political objectives of the imposition of colonial rule.

---

[4] For general introductions and historical-comparative overviews of the police, see Bayley 1975; Bittner 1990; Deflem 2002; Manning 1977, 2003; Reiner 1985; Skolnick 1966. In the coming pages, the focus is restricted to the role and function of public police, rather than private policing (Johnston 1992) and enforcement practices in non-criminal matters, such as in the case of health and safety regulations (Hawkins 2003; Hutter 1988).

Accompanying the historical transformation of the police function, the form which police systems took across societies varied considerably, with implications lasting until today. Historically, continental European systems of policing were militaristic in character and highly centralized, whereas British and American law enforcement tended to be civilian and locally organized. The British system was supervised by the national government from the early nineteenth century onwards, but there nonetheless remained much local variation in terms of degree of professionalism and structure of the force. In the United States, a federal supervision and organization of police functions developed only very gradually and policing remained a predominantly local affair organized in towns. Contrary to the European model, state and federal US police agencies developed slowly and were not expanded in any meaningful way until the early twentieth century.

Closely related to the socio-historical conditions of policing, the strategies and technologies that are used by police are not stable across space and time. This variability in policing practices relates to such technical aspects as whether or not police agents are uniformed and armed as well as to the variable styles and strategies used in police work. Among the many police innovations sociologists have paid attention to are the rise of community policing (Fielding 2002, 2005; Manning 2002), the internationalization of policing (see Chapter 12), the role of police in democratic nation-building (Bayley 2005), and the development of special police strategies, such as covert techniques in undercover police work (G. Marx 1981, 1988). Using the case of undercover policing as an example, problematic and ironic qualities are revealed in the dynamics and effects of policing as a primary mechanism of social control.

Undercover policing is a concealed form of policing that involves deception and provocation. The strategy has been increasingly applied, especially in societies, such as the United States, where overt police conduct is tightly regulated by law. An increase in crimes of a more concealed nature, public calls and support for anti-crime programs, and the availability of sophisticated technical means of crime detection and surveillance have additionally contributed to the increasing popularity of undercover policing. Undercover police work is ironic in itself in being a form of police work that clashes with the common perception of the police as uniformed agents who prevent or respond to crime. In terms of its effects, moreover, undercover policing has been found to be used for various reasons unrelated to crime control, especially political surveillance, revealing that police work cannot be conceived solely in terms of the control of crime. Besides the unintended consequences of victimization of innocent bystanders and the psychological and social burdens posed on the agents, undercover policing can lead to agents targeting one another or becoming the target of unsuspecting citizens. Arguably most ironic are the situations whereby undercover agents have been found to have fabricated evidence and escalated criminal activities.

The case of undercover policing shows the relevance of sociological work that is focused on the dynamics and determinants of the peculiar problems that are associated with policing. Ironic consequences of police work and misconduct on the part of the police are particularly noteworthy because of the special status attributed to the police as the representatives of the legitimate use of force.[5] In the literature on policing, many of these problems are specified in terms of police discretion and the role played therein by police culture and the structure of police organization. Police discretion refers to the fact that the police are unable to enforce each and every violation of law because of limits in resources and in view of the implications of over-enforcement on the part of citizens. Police officers therefore have to make decisions about whether and when enforcement is in order. Beyond administrative considerations, however, police behavior has been found to be highly selective (as a problem of differential enforcement) on the basis of a number of factors that are both intrinsic and extrinsic to the work. The probability of arrest, for instance, increases not only with the severity of the crime and the strength of the available evidence, but also as a result of perceived disrespectful behavior towards the police and the distance between rule-violator and rule-enforcer (Black 1980).

Differential law enforcement and other problems associated with the police role can be contextualized in terms of characteristics of the

---

[5] Recent research on problematic dimensions of police behavior centers on racism in police work and differential enforcement (Norris, Fielding, Kemp, and Fielding 1992; Weitzer 2000; Weitzer and Tuch 2005), politically motivated police activities (Cunningham 2004; Earl, Soule, and McCarthy 2003), violence and an excessive use of force (Jacobs and O'Brien 1998; Skolnick and Fyfe 1993; Terrill, Paoline, and Manning 2003), police corruption (Sherman 1978), and the militarization of policing (Kraska and Kappeler 1997).

police culture and the structure of police organization. With respect to culture, the police can be analyzed in terms of a professionalization process that, like the legal profession, makes a claim to occupational autonomy and gains control of access to the profession and supervision of its organization and activities (Manning 1977; Reiner 1985). Corresponding to this image, police organizations tend to exhibit a strong identity of self as the moral protectors of society, the "thin blue line" that stands between order and chaos. Accompanying this self-image is a perception of the outside world in highly moralistic terms that reinforces the morality and necessity of police action, leading to categorizations of citizens on the basis of their perceived likelihood to cooperate with or resist the police in the execution of their duties. A complex police personality that tends to be authoritarian and aggressive but also fluctuates between idealism and cynicism is the socio-psychological correlate to this culture.

In terms of structure, it is important to observe the dominant form of police institutions as bureaucratic organizations (Deflem 2002). Consistent with the perspective of Max Weber, bureaucracies are conceived as organizations, charged with the implementation of policy, that are hierarchical in structure, have their activities based on general rules, employ standardized methods, and are impersonal in the execution of their duties. Thus, bureaucratized police organizations are hierarchically ordered in a rigid chain of command and have formalized and standardized procedures of operation. Revealing a technical impersonality in conduct, bureaucratic police agencies handle cases on the basis of general rules guiding the collection and processing of evidence without regard to the person and in sole view of the stated objectives of crime control and order maintenance. In the bureaucratic model, police work is routinized on the basis of standardized methods of investigation, often strongly influenced by scientific principles of police technique, such as technically advanced methods of criminal identification.

An excessive bureaucratization of the police has been identified among the determining factors that contribute to a lack of accountability in police work and differential law enforcement. From the normative viewpoint of police reform, concerns over police bureaucratization have led to attempts to apply principles from restorative justice and community policing in order to reestablish confidence between the police and the public. From an analytical perspective, police bureaucratization has been studied in terms of the resulting autonomy police agencies acquire in respect of their position relative to governments (formal autonomy) and the ability of police to independently determine the appropriate means and specify the objectives of their activities (operational autonomy). In this process of police bureaucratization, technological advances in the areas of communication, transportation, and criminal detection have been found to be especially significant in influencing the course of police work, including the internationalization of the police function (see Chapter 12).

Technologies of surveillance

The role of advanced systems of technology in the transformation of social control extends well beyond their use by the police as the formal agents of control. Paralleling Foucault's observations on the dispersal of the Panopticon into a generalized function in society, so too have the technologies of control diffused into society to become a normal part of modern social life. Theoretically, the sociology of surveillance extends from the work of Foucault to investigate the contemporary dimensions of new highly technological forms of social control that are proactively applied to everybody, surveying a nation of suspects, in a very detailed way.[6] Selectively borrowing from and moving beyond Foucault, modern surveillance is argued to have no center from which power radiates but instead blurs the distinctions between private and public life and cuts across social classes. Through advanced systems of surveillance, such as video cameras and closed-circuit television, and computerized data storage systems, each and all are caught in a deeply penetrating and broad system of control. Such systems are oriented at making people act in certain ways, even to the extent of having them participate in their own surveillance. Modern systems of surveillance have the power to cross boundaries of space and time and are in this sense universal, yet they have been especially applied in open democratic societies as an ironic consequence of the relative absence of overt repression and brute force. Surveillance is a threat to a free society that only a free society can produce.

[6] Especially useful among the empirical and theoretical contributions of the sociology of surveillance are the writings of Gary Marx (1986, 1988, 1995, 2003, 2005, 2007) and William Staples (2000, 2003). See also Gilliom 1994; Lyon 2003.

Theorizing the implications of high-tech surveillance, some scholars argue for a modernist interpretation in line with revisionist theories of social control. Gary Marx (1988, 1995), most notably, has suggested the image of a surveillance society to capture the rise of covert and intense systems of control that penetrate deeply into social relationships. Seeking to make every thought and action visible, control technologies, such as video cameras and information databases, are themselves largely invisible. The technologies of the new surveillance are primarily extractive of personal information. As the amount of information that is collected is potentially unlimited, society is becoming transparent and porous. Engineering strategies of control can remove potential targets of crime, such as through the use of credit cards to replace cash or insulate targets from potential intruders, such as through the remote-controlled central locking of doors. Potential offenders can be incapacitated by direct engineering of their body, as in the case of chemical castration, and, in more ways than ever, offenders can be excluded from society by means of panoptic strategies in the community, such as through electronic home monitoring. The increased use of engineering strategies in social control suggests the development of a maximum security society in which technology takes over as the locus of control and in which every action of every body is being watched, listened to, recorded, and stored, rendering the whole of the community suspicious and guilty until proven innocent.

An alternative, postmodern perspective of surveillance is defended by William Staples (2000, 2003). Referring to the increased use of high-tech control mechanisms, the case is made that contemporary strategies of social control go beyond formal systems sanctioned by governments to constitute a broad range of power rituals in which the entire community is involved. In the form of computerized databases and audio-visual technologies, modern surveillance is located everywhere and impersonally targeted at everybody. Electronic systems of detection placed on anklets in house arrest, for instance, turn the home into a prison without the spectacle that comes with public punishment. Advanced audio-visual technologies, such as videocams built into cell phones, are inexpensive and ubiquitous. Postmodern surveillance applies to whole series of technological spaces, including homes with electronic alarm systems, schools that have become fortified security buildings, workplaces where the collection of employee information is routinized, and places of consumption and entertainment where taste is monitored and controlled. Among the most influential recent changes has been the proliferation of the internet, which, apart from being a means to distribute and retrieve information, is also used to extract information and modify behavior, for instance through advertising and individualized modifications of web pages on the basis of collected information. Staples interprets these developments as postmodern because they indicate the disappearance of a center of control. Alongside the relative decline of the influence and importance of the nation-state and formal systems of law and law enforcement, social life as a whole has become increasingly decentralized into a multiplicity of lifeworlds, which no grand narrative can adequately capture. Surveillance is everyday.

From a viewpoint that also contemplates the normative implications of the rise of the new surveillance, privacy and civil liberties have moved center stage to sociological analyses.[7] Among the problematic implications of engineered strategies of surveillance are the inability to see the larger context of alternatives and long-range consequences and the displacement rather than treatment of undesirable activities. Beyond questions of validity and reliability, an extensive use of technologies of control, while relatively low in economic cost, may make societies rigid and unable to adjust as circumstances change. A socially transparent society may be more orderly, but will lack creativity and freedom. Privacy is central to many of the concerns raised by new surveillance technologies. From the viewpoint of the individual, privacy is important to protect because the ability to control information about the self is linked to the dignity of individuals and their self-respect and wellbeing. Anonymity can also be useful in encouraging honesty and risk-taking. From the viewpoint of society, confidentiality in social relations can improve communication flows in professional relations that rely on trust, such as between a doctor and a patient. Besides the right to withhold information, privacy also includes the right to share information with others, which can be an important resource in establishing social relations. More broadly, a socially recognized respect for privacy is indicative of the values a nation seeks to embody.

---

[7] Gary Marx (1996, 1999) has explicitly addressed issues of privacy and civil liberties that accompany the rise of the new surveillance.

The process of punishment

In an influential book on the workings of lower criminal courts, Malcolm Feeley (1979) introduced the provocative idea about the administration of criminal law that the process itself is the punishment. Applied to the wide range of components involved in the punishment of crime, the dynamics of social control can indeed be identified to extend from criminalization through legislation over sentencing to the imposition of a penalty. These components of the punishment process are empirically often interrelated in ways more complex than a simple linear movement. Criminalization research has uncovered, for instance, that legislative activities sometimes follow the actions of control agents rather than offer the foundation for their enforcement activities. In this sense, it is important to note that lawmaking, law speaking in the courts, and the administration of penalties are to be distinguished only for analytical purposes.

In terms of the phase of criminalization through lawmaking, sociological attention has gone to the determinants and processes of legislative actions on a wide variety of criminal acts.[8] Originally introduced by labeling theorists, criminalization has typically been researched in the context of modes of conduct over which doubts are raised, based on a normative understanding, as to the appropriateness of their treatment in the criminal justice systems, such as in the case of the criminalization of abortion and homosexuality (Clarke 1987; Schur 1965), alcohol (Gusfield 1963), gambling and prostitution (Galliher and Cross 1983), mugging (Waddington 1986), "wilding" (Welch, Price, and Yankey 2004), and other forms of deviance approached from the moral panics perspective (see Chapter 8). Conflict theorists have extended this research to offer socio-historical and economic contextualizations of criminalization that offer more sweeping criticisms of the criminal justice system and of (capitalist) society as a whole. Cases of specific instances of criminalization are situated in the broader contexts of domination of lower classes and minority populations (e.g., Chambliss 1964; Ferrell 1993; Hall et al. 1978; Scraton 2004; Scheerer 1978).

In recent years, two important developments have taken place in the criminalization literature (Jenness 2004). First, on a theoretical

---

[8] Overviews of sociological work on legislative activities in the area of crime are provided by Jenness (2004) and Hagan (1980).

level, attempts have been made to transcend the traditional view of criminalization that is situated around the opposition of consensus and conflict models. More complex theoretical models have been suggested that identify a variety of factors in the origins of specific instances of criminalization. These factors range from the activities of individual moral entrepreneurs over social movement activities to a variety of broader structural conditions. Models of institutionalization and modernization are forwarded to offer a comprehensive view of how these various factors interplay. Research on hate crime legislation in the United States, for instance, has shown that linkages across states have influenced a diffusion of such legislation, a process that would be overlooked by a narrow focus on singular cases (Grattet, Jenness, and Curry 1998; Jenness 1999; King 2007). Diffusion processes in legislation have also been observed across nations (see Chapter 12). Second, from an empirical viewpoint, criminalization research has proliferated on a very wide variety of cases. Moving from a preoccupation with victimless crimes, typically explored from the labeling viewpoint, recent research has unraveled criminalization in settings as diverse as the criminalization of hate (Jenness and Grattet 1996; Savelsberg and King 2005), stalking (Lowney and Best 1995), child abuse (Jenkins 1998), immigration (Lee 2005; Welch 2002), and cyber crime (Hollinger and Lanza-Kaduce 1988). In the breadth of its orientation, research on criminalization complements the insights of the surveillance literature on the dispersal of social control throughout society.

Moving to the criminalization stage of law speaking in the courts, interesting sociological work has been conducted in the area of sentencing, specifically on the influence of sentencing guidelines.[9] Research has found that sentencing decisions are not based solely on the "facts of the case," but are instead influenced by a number of factors, some of which are external to the legal system. The range of sentencing options available to the courts is limited by statutory requirements for each type of offense as well as by supplementary guidelines. In the

---

[9] Sociological research on the impact of sentencing guidelines has been conducted by Jeffrey Ulmer (1997, 2005; Ulmer and Kramer 1996, 1998), Rodney Engen and associates (Engen and Gainey 2000; Engen and Steen 2000; Engen et al. 2002; Steen, Engen, and Gainey 2005), Celesta Albonetti (1999), and Joachim Savelsberg (1992). See also the helpful discussion by Savelsberg 2006. On the history of US sentencing guidelines, see Reitz 1996.

case of the United States, sentencing guidelines have been developed at the state level since the 1980s and at the federal level since 1985 when US Congress created the Federal Sentencing Commission. These guidelines were explicitly aimed to reduce the disparities that were found in sentencing practices, such as the relative over-sentencing of minorities, but they also represented an attempt by the federal government to curtail judicial discretion. In this sense, federal sentencing guidelines can be seen as a political intrusion on the autonomy of law, similar to the mandatory minimum sentences that were legislated as part of the war on drugs and the so-called "three strikes and you're out" statute that is in effect in the state of California and that specifies a life sentence for anyone having committed three felonies.

Most striking in sociological research on the impact of federal sentencing guidelines is the finding that considerable variability continues to exist despite the explicit intention of the guidelines to reduce sentencing disparities. Confirming the overwhelming significance of race in the US criminal justice system, racial disparities in sentencing have been observed most frequently and have additionally been found to vary with other offender and offense characteristics. Defendants' socio-economic background and sex also affect sentencing outcomes. Defendants who are higher placed in the stratification system, such as those with more education, and those who are male tend to receive less serious sentences. Sentencing disparities further exist across jurisdictional settings, for instance between large urban courts and small rural courts. Accounting for these disparities, scholars have argued that judges enjoy windows of discretion to consider substantive factors, including such extra-legal criteria as a person's race and gender, rather than rely on formal criteria.

Finally, in terms of the final stage of punishment in the imposition of a penalty, important transformations have taken place in recent years. Even the simplest of statistical data on the reality of punishment and incarceration may indicate the spectacular nature of these developments. In the case of the United States, the rate of incarceration has increased exponentially since the latter two decades of the twentieth century.[10] In 2005, more than seven million people, representing one out of every thirty-two adults, were under some form of correctional

---

[10] The numbers reported in this section are drawn from statistics provided by the Bureau of Justice Statistics (www.ojp.usdoj.gov/bjs).

supervision, including probation, jail, prison, and parole. By comparison, in 1980, the total number of people under correctional supervision were fewer than 2 million, a number that had risen to over 4.3 million in 1990. State and federal prisons, in which people convicted of major offenses are kept, held 1,446,269 inmates at yearend 2005, up from 743,382 in 1990 and 319,598 in 1980.

The tremendous increase in incarceration in the United States cannot be explained by the population growth (from about 226 million in 1980 to 281 million in 2000) as shown from the rise in the incarceration rate. In 1980, 139 people per 100,000 residents in the population were imprisoned, a number that rose to 297 in 1990, and 491 in 2005. The rise in incarceration is also not due to an increase in the number of offenses. Statistics show that more than half of the imprisoned population in state prisons consists of people locked up for violent offenses, while the rate of violent crime has gone down since the late 1980s. Since the early 1990s, however, more violent and property crimes have been reported to the police and more people have been arrested for drug-related offenses. Among all offenses for which defendants are brought to trial, most are in court for drug offenses. In the courts, also, the number of people processed, convicted, and sentenced to prison terms has steadily gone up since the early 1980s.

The increase in incarceration has especially affected America's minority communities. Based on the most recent available statistics, the total number of African-American prisoners exceeds the total number of white prisoners, although African Americans make up only about 12 percent of the total population, 75 percent of which is white. In 2004, 40 percent of all inmates in state and federal prisons were African-American, 34 percent were white, and 19 percent were Hispanic. At yearend 2005, there were 3,145 African-American, 1,244 Hispanic, and 471 white male prisoners per 100,000 males of their respective ethnic group. Gender disparities are even more pronounced. At yearend 2004, for instance, 1,391,781 men as compared to 104,848 women were incarcerated in a state or federal prison.

The general increase in punitiveness and the racial disparities that exist are confirmed from the statistics on capital punishment. Since the US Supreme Court in 1976 ruled the death penalty to be constitutional and 38 states and the federal government reinstated capital statutes, the number of prisoners on death row has steadily increased.

At yearend 2005, a total of 3,254 inmates, of which 1,805 were white and 1,372 African-American, were under sentence of death. All but fifty-two were men. The youngest of these inmates was twenty and the oldest was ninety. The death penalty is very differentially enforced from one US state to another state. Of the fifty-three people who were executed in fourteen states in 2006, twenty-four were executed in Texas.

The United States is not alone among Western democracies in having witnessed a growth in incarceration, although the trend is nowhere near as dramatic as in the US and considerable variations exist among nations' incarceration rates. The United Kingdom, for instance, has experienced a more consistent and less exponential increase in its prison population. But other democracies have experienced minor growth. Many sociological studies focus on selected components of punishment and incarceration,[11] but other inquiries have begun to offer more comprehensive investigations that take into account the broader socio-historical contexts in which developments of punishment take place.[12] Worthy of special mention among the latter perspectives is the recent work of David Garland (2002) on the culture of crime control. Garland argues that the current period represents a remarkable reversal of the period of penal welfarism of the 1970s when treatment programs and alternative justice methods were developed. In recent years, the rehabilitative ideal has all but disappeared in favor of punitive and expressive justice. Fear of crime and the rights of the victim and the public at large dominate crime policies rather than concerns for offender treatment and reintegration. Along with the expansion of the prison system, also, criminological knowledge has again begun to adopt classical principles of guilt and a focus on the characteristics of individual offenders rather than socio-structural crime conditions.

Two historical forces have, according to Garland, contributed to the transformations of criminal policy. First, important social, economic, and cultural changes took place across Western societies.

---

[11] See, for instance, Lynch 2000; Simon 1993 on parole; Lofquist 1993 on probation; Visher and Travis 2003; Western 2002 on the experience and impact of prison life; Featherstone 2005; Useem and Goldstone 2002 on prison riots.
[12] See, for example, Beckett and Western 2001; Bridges and Crutchfield 1988; Garland 1985, 1991a, 2002; Pratt 1999; Simon 2000, 2001; Sutton 2000; Wacquant 2001.

Market capitalism has expanded ever more, but inequalities have continued to exist and unemployment is high. On a cultural level, the modern family structure has changed in ways that have eroded the family's role as a traditional form of control. Politically, the state has been facing a financial crisis by being overburdened with demands related to welfare and not being able to meet rising expectations. Second, specific political and policy changes took place in response to these developments, especially in the United States and the United Kingdom, where conservative governments were from the early 1980s onwards committed to undoing the existing social policies based on community needs. New policies were developed on the basis of principles of individual responsibility, which implied a shift to economic freedom coupled with an increase in societal controls. Within this new constellation of control, the state alone is no longer able to provide all necessary measures. Commercialized and community-based systems of control are therefore developed to form a mixture of private and public systems of control aimed at engineering the effects of crime rather than solving its root causes.

As a consequence of the stated developments, there is a general increase in punitiveness in contemporary crime control, with ever more policies involving harsh punishments that are politically appropriated in populist terms (e.g., three strikes, zero tolerance). The middle classes are less willing to support welfare programs that they see as undeserving to the disadvantaged people to whom they would be applied. Rehabilitation and reintegration are forgotten ideals of the past. Crime is a normal fact of life, and situational and technological controls can at best manage the risk, predict the occurrence, and reduce the harm of crime. An unresolved tension, however, is posed in this new culture of control as, on the one hand, economic cost–benefit models dominate crime policies, while, on the other hand, there are strong political and popular pressures to punish criminals and protect the public no matter what the cost.

Conclusion

Evolving from a broad notion in terms of social order, social control has in modern sociology come to be conceived as the whole of practices and institutions involved with the response to crime and/or deviance, including the definition thereof. Crime causation theories are stubbornly resolute in their conception of social control as a functional response to crime and thus remain absorbed in studies on the causes of crime as criminal behavior. More fruitful from the viewpoint of the sociology of law have been developments associated with constructionist and critical perspectives that have made social control a study worthy of independent reflective analysis. Particularly influential has been the work of Michel Foucault in instigating new debates on a variety of structures and processes of social control in contemporary societies. Sociological perspectives in the Foucauldian framework turn away from a legal understanding of law in legislation and legal administration to focus on the concrete practices and technologies of control. As such, revisionist perspectives of social control once again demonstrate the value in the sociology of law of moving beyond the formalities of law, or beyond – in Weber's words – the juristic conception of law, to show that there are many sociologically worthy components of law to be found beyond the formal realm of lawyer's law.

Sociological work on policing shows that there is more to the enforcement of law than mere law enforcement. Perhaps because of the strong analytical value and counter-intuitive powers of sociological work on policing, the move in the sociology of law towards the study of social control has nowhere been less easily accomplished than in the case of policing. The relative neglect of the sociological study of policing, however, is striking not only because formal institutions of law enforcement are an intimate component of law, but also and particularly because the link between law and its enforcement has sociologically been well recognized, at least on a conceptual level. Weber's definitions of law and the state serve as the obvious examples. Until today, however, it remains true that the sociology of law has not devoted sufficient work to uncovering the patterns and dynamics of the function and institution of police. At least one reason for this development is the retreat of work on policing away from sociology into the technical fields of criminal justice and police studies. Similar observations can be made about work on surveillance and punishment, which has likewise been appropriated by criminal justice and a technically conceived criminology. These movements of retreat from the sociology of law have not only fragmented but also instrumentalized knowledge about policing, surveillance, and punishment in favor of questions that serve the administration of criminal justice rather than its analysis.

Nonetheless, despite the marginalization of social control in the sociology of law, there has by now developed a comprehensive literature that collectively can lay claim to constituting a meaningful contribution to the discipline. In the area of policing, particularly noteworthy are the studies that have unraveled many of the important dimensions of the police functions from a comprehensive sociological viewpoint. The sociology of surveillance, likewise, has contemplated the increasing reliance on technology beyond a mere technical and pragmatic framework to include both theoretically informed empirical work as well as inquiries on the societal impact of surveillance technologies in terms of civil liberties and privacy rights. Sociological work on sentencing and punishment, similarly, has contributed to develop analytically meaningful frameworks that solidly position relevant developments and practices within a broad societal and socio-historical context. Such work has also, and increasingly, begun to include comparative work and a focus on international and global developments.

12 | *The globalization of law*

The concept of globalization has arguably been used more often than any other label to describe a central development of the current age. After the nineteenth-century preoccupation with industrialization and the twentieth-century focus on modernization and development, the discourse on globalization has taken on the contemporary role of describing in a singular term the master pattern of recent and ongoing societal developments. Formally understood to include structures and processes of increased interdependence across the boundaries of national and otherwise delineated borders, globalization has entered the lexicon of social science only recently, but it has been adopted and applied in theory and research with accelerated speed over the past two decades.[1]

Testifying to globalization's meteoric rise in sociology, a search for academic sources about globalization included in the electronic database of Sociological Abstracts, shows that only nineteen articles mentioning globalization in the title or abstract were published until 1985, nine of which appeared between 1980 and 1985. Since then, no less than 9,216 such articles have been published, of which 8,462 appeared since 1996, and 5,439 since 2001 (end date: May 2007). Although most social-science research surely remains of a national or otherwise local character, globalization has, like no other recent development, influenced our view and thinking about society in a variety of substantive research areas.

After a brief period of hesitation, globalization has also been embraced by sociologists of law, who themselves have increasingly become more readily aware of one another's academic efforts in

---

[1] For theoretical expositions and general overviews of globalization in sociology, see Albrow 1996; Lechner and Boli 2000; Sassen 1998; Scholte 2000; Sklair 1995.

various parts around the globe.[2] Relying again on a count of sources included in Sociological Abstracts, 413 articles have appeared with the terms globalization and law or legal in the abstract, only 15 of which were published before 1985, 38 before 1996, and 259 since 2001. To be sure, the growing attention in the sociology of law to globalization still pales in comparison to the study of global developments in other social domains, particularly the economy. Out of all 8,108 sources mentioned in Sociological Abstracts with the term globalization in the abstract, no less than 3,529 also mention economy or economic. The relative lack of attention and initially somewhat hesitant adoption of globalization in the sociology of law is not surprising and does not imply any intellectual shortsightedness. As compared to the study of the economy, especially the free market and its spread and impact across national boundaries, globalization is theoretically more challenging to the sociology of law because it is inherently puzzling that law is subject to globalization trends when modern legal systems are primarily dependent on legislation in the context of national states that claim sovereignty. The geographically framed understanding of law is most clearly captured in the notion of jurisdiction.

This chapter will review how globalization has been addressed by sociologists of law. Two interrelated questions are addressed in sociological work on the globalization of law. Research has focused on the legal consequences of globalization in non-legal areas, while the globalization of law and its impact on other social institutions have been studied as well. It is the globalization of law itself that offers the more distinct contribution from the specialty area of sociology of law, but such research will often also include, at least implicitly, reflections on the legal ramifications of the structures and processes of globalization outside the realm of law.

As with any movement in scholarly thought, globalization has now risen to such popularity that it has also been devalued in some writings to become a mere buzzword. Disregarding such contributions, this review will analyze the sociological treatment of globalization in the areas of the creation of legal norms and the administration of law, including the role played by the legal profession, and on matters of

---

[2] The globalization of the sociology of law, including its practices and participants, will be discussed in the Conclusion of this book.

social control, especially policing. As in previous chapters, rather than aspiring to present a complete picture of sociological work on the globalization of law, several exemplary works will be reviewed to bring out the significance of this discourse in the sociology of law. A brief conceptual exposition will clarify some of the key issues in this literature.

Theorizing law and globalization

Because of the jurisdictional framing of legal systems, sociologists and other scholars of law had until the advent of the globalization approach developed research traditions that transcended the boundaries of national and local manifestations of law only in the forms of comparative and international studies. Although also transcending the boundaries of national and local manifestations of law, comparative legal perspectives and the field of international law are not to be confused with globalization studies of law. Comparative studies of law analyze the differences and similarities that exist between the legal systems of different nations and other locales, whereas international law refers to the whole of law that is created by inter-governmental agreements among states in the form of bilateral and multilateral treaties. Comparative and international studies of law affirm the boundaries and jurisdictional restrictions associated with national legal systems, whereas a globalization perspective takes into account the extent to which legal developments transcend such boundaries through the linkages that exist across space. The globalization of law presents a special challenge to scholarship on law because the degree of interlinking between national or otherwise local and global or otherwise border-transcending structures and processes has steadily been increasing in recent years. What then does jurisdictional sovereignty mean in the global village?

The globalization of law poses a number of theoretical and empirical challenges.[3] At the most general level, globalization changes the level of analysis from relations among citizens and between citizens

---

[3] See the helpful discussions and reviews on the globalization of law by Boyle 2007; Dezalay 1990; Flood 2002; Garcia-Vellegas 2006; Gessner 1995; Halliday and Osinsky 2006; Nelken 2002; Rodriguez-Garavito 2007; Röhl and Magan 1996. See also contributions in Dezalay and Garth 2002b; Santos and Rodríguez-Garavito 2005.

and the state to the level of the interrelations among states on a horizontal plane, in terms of conflict or cooperation, as well as on a vertical plane as relations among states also affect citizens, especially when they cross nation-bound borders, such as in the case of immigration and tourism. Because globalization by definition transcends spatial boundaries, there is no clearly demarcated locale to the study of globalization. Globalization occurs everywhere or at least in multiple places at once, posing formidable problems to conventional sociological conceptions of research design and subject selection.

Because of the peculiar form globalization takes, studies on the global dimensions of law must not only contemplate the movement of law in the direction of globalization, but also investigate how these global processes and structures in turn impact local and national developments of law. Globalization studies methodologically therefore always imply a comparative approach in which the cases are selected, not on the basis of criteria chosen for theoretical reasons by the researcher, but on the basis of actual interlinkages that exist among them. The collection of international statistical and other relevant empirical information is a special methodological concern.

As suggested by Terence Halliday and Pavel Osinsky (2006), at least four theories can be identified in the globalization of law literature. First are two competing theories that focus on globalization primarily as an economic reality. In this camp belongs the famous sociological perspective of world systems theory that is associated with the work of Immanuel Wallerstein (2004). Primarily focused on the worldwide diffusion of the capitalist market from the core of world society to its periphery, this perspective attributes relatively little attention to law because, in line with a general Marxist orientation, it assumes that global law is not sufficiently institutionalized to play a significant role in the mechanisms that drive the world system. Instead, the focus is on economic developments that are controlled by multinational companies and states (for instance, the present spread of neoliberal capitalism under direction of the United States). Contrasting with this perspective is an approach of law and economic development that, in the wake of the fall of communism in Eastern Europe, emphasizes the role played by private actors in building a new global order by reliance on the law as an instrument of change, specifically in the form of deregulation. The logic behind this theory is that laws of economic liberation and stimulation produce economic growth across nations. The law and economic development perspective relies on a Weberian approach to bring out the central role played by law in shaping global economic processes. As an extension of sociology's long-standing tradition of work on the relation between law and economy, scholarship in this area has especially focused on the formation of new global governance regimes, typically involving a variety of public and private agencies that are set up in response to the regulatory deficit that is created because the global spread of the market far exceeds the range of the regulatory mechanisms that are in place at the level of national states. Research in the sociology of law from this perspective has focused on global developments in the regulation of business practices, such as bankruptcy reform (see below).

A second set of theories on globalization and law, which is likewise divided between a conflict-theoretical and a consensually oriented perspective, focuses on globalization primarily in cultural terms. First, postcolonial theories conceive of the globalization of law in terms of a hegemonic spread of the rule of law that reproduces a juxtaposition between the so-called civilized and uncivilized world. The universality and transferability of modern systems of (Western) law are argued to rest on claims of a global modernization discourse that continues to give premium to Western notions of law despite the creation of new demarcations lines such as between (the rich and civilized) North and (the poor and as yet uncivilized) South. Unlike its economic counterpart in world systems theory, postcolonial perspectives are less interested in the sources of global law and instead focus on the impact of the transfer of the logic of Western law into the periphery. Second, a contrasting cultural perspective is offered by world polity theorists who argue that the evolution of modern legal systems across the world is characterized by a strong convergence that indicates the formation of a world polity, which (in line with neo-institutionalist theory) functions as a reservoir of cognitive schemas. The schemas of the world polity include conceptions of sovereignty and universalistic principles that are transmitted into different national legal systems through the activities of international governmental and nongovernmental organizations oriented at enforcing compliance with global normative standards. Sociological work on the diffusion of laws banning female genital cutting provides an interesting case in the world polity approach (see below).

Global legality: from lawmaking to law speaking

Turning to sociological research on the globalization of law, empirical studies have been devoted to the entire range of legal processes, extending from the creation of global norms over their administration in the courts and through other means of resolution, including the activities of legal professionals, to the global dimensions of enforcement and social control. This overview concentrates on exemplary case studies in the sociology of law, specifically dealing with global regimes on female genital cutting, the diffusion of legal bankruptcy reforms, the dynamics of international lawyering, and the formation of international criminal courts.

Research on the creation of norms banning the practice of female genital cutting immediately brings out many of the special concerns associated with globalization research, for not only do legal systems across the world respond differently and with unequal impact to this cultural phenomenon, just naming the practice is itself already problematic. Also known as female circumcision and female genital mutilation, female genital cutting is a practice that is deeply embedded in long-standing cultural traditions. Since the late 1970s and with increasing vigor in the 1990s, a movement took place towards the formation of a global prohibition regime against female genital cutting. Sociologist Elizabeth Heger Boyle has unraveled the dynamics and outcomes of this movement on the basis of a neo-institutionalist (world polity) perspective of globalization.[4]

Female genital cutting is practiced in various parts of Africa and, to a lesser extent, in some parts of the Middle East and Asia as well as among some immigrant groups across the world. Dating back several thousands of years, the practice does not have a clear justification. It is not primarily a religious custom, although representatives of some religious groups speak out in favor of the tradition, but is mostly rooted in cultural conceptions of sexual roles and women's sexuality. In some societies, female genital cutting has become so much a part of the culture that failure to perform the procedure is seen as a sign of

---

[4] Boyle's research is primarily reported in her book, *Female Genital Cutting* (Boyle 2002), and in related articles (Boyle and Preves 2000; Boyle, McMorris, and Gómez 2002; Boyle, Songora, and Foss 2001). Her neo-institutionalist theoretical perspective is co-developed with John Meyer (Boyle and Meyer 2002). See also Boyle 1998, 2000 for related research on global legal reform in other areas of law.

bad parenting that is met with shock and disgust. Efforts to eradicate female genital cutting date back many years, but began to take on more organized and global proportions since the 1970s when international groups such as the World Health Organization began to speak out against the practice, mostly on the basis of medical considerations. The movement to prohibit female genital cutting has since been additionally motivated by concerns over gender equality, violence against women and children, and human rights.

From the 1980s onwards, the global campaign against female genital cutting began to be effective in influencing the passage of legislation outlawing the practice. Almost all nations today, both those where female genital cutting is rare and those where it is common, have laws in place that ban the custom. However, although there is a global isomorphism noticeable in the prohibition against female genital cutting, research has also uncovered that there are important local variations in how these norms have come about and what impact they have. The cases of Egypt and Tanzania clarify some of these contextualizations of global law.

Egypt is not a major player on the international political scene, but the country enjoys a solid standing among Arab nations, is relatively prosperous, and entertains good relations with the United States and other Western nations. The practice of female genital cutting is very common in Egypt, with as many as 97 percent of women having been circumcised. From the 1980s onwards, Egyptian authorities were initially reluctant to respond to the growing international pressure to outlaw the practice. In the mid-1990s, a widely publicized media report on the widespread nature of female genital cutting in Egypt led to a worldwide public condemnation, after which the Egyptian government promised to enact a new law against the practice. The Egyptian parliament, however, refused to pass an anti-female genital cutting law, and instead a health decree specified that the procedure could only be performed one day a week in public hospitals. Eventually, only after additional pressures were mounted against Egypt, appropriate legislation was passed. The Egyptian case displays the ability of a nation-state to resist the will of the international community, in no small part because of its economic standing and relative ability to exercise autonomy.

The Egyptian case contrasts sharply with the Tanzanian experience. Tanzania is a very poor country with a huge international debt. The country is religiously diverse and has known much related political strife. The practice of female genital cutting is in Tanzania restricted to certain ethnic groups, affecting about 19 percent of the female population. Because of its international dependence, Tanzania has not been able to resist the adoption of legal norms prohibiting female genital cutting. Tanzania is not only dependent on financial aid from foreign institutions, which make loans and aid conditional upon certain conditions being met, the United States has since 1996 also engaged in a coercive reform strategy by making its loans to foreign countries explicitly contingent on the adoption of laws banning female genital cutting. Tanzania did not have the international leverage nor the economic might to resist international pressure and fairly swiftly enacted and enforced laws against female genital cutting.

The case of female genital cutting reveals that the invocation of laws that formally are very similar across the world can be highly variable in terms of their origins and impact, depending on the relative weakness or strength of the structural position of nations on the international scene. Additionally relevant is the way in which international and national factors interact, specifically how the institutionalization of cultural sentiments towards a practice such as female genital cutting at the national level contradicts or harmonizes with the institutionalization of legal norms at the level of the world polity.

The interplay between global norm making, on the one hand, and national lawmaking, on the other, is also at the center of the globalization of law in other areas of research besides female genital cutting. Given that law in the present-day context remains primarily a function of nation-state legislation, yet that law is at once also increasingly subject to globalization trends, it is reasonable to hypothesize that the globalization of law involves essentially the linking of global and national developments in matters of lawmaking and law administration. This conception of globalization confirms a central theoretical idea formulated by globalization scholars such as Roland Robertson (1992, 1995) that globalization implies an increasing interrelatedness between processes and events across national borders, involving a complex process of interpenetration between universalism and particularism.

In a series of elaborate research projects on corporate bankruptcy law, sociologists Terence Halliday and Bruce Carruthers adopt a law and economic development approach to account for the global diffusion of legal bankruptcy reforms.[5] Theoretically, the authors argue for a recursivity in the globalization of law to suggest that global norm making and national lawmaking go through a series of cycles. This process involves alternating cycles of lawmaking and law implementation at the national level, continued cycles of norm making at the global level, and cycles of mutual but uneven inter-dependency at the intersection of national and global developments, depending on the power and distance of nation-states relative to relevant global institutions and actors.

Empirically focusing on the international development of bank-ruptcy laws, Halliday and Carruthers study the legal regimes that determine if and how a corporate entity that is insolvent can be liquidated or reorganized. As part of the legal environment of business, bankruptcy laws set important standards that affect the conduct of organizations and the activities of various professionals. Looking at the dimension of the professions, bankruptcy cases in the United States are handled by lawyers, whereas accountants are in charge in the United Kingdom. In the handling of bankruptcy cases, these pro-fessionals are confronted with the market professionals of the economic field, such as creditors and shareholders. It is thereby observed that economic expertise does not always translate into expertise in legal matters. Indicating a relative autonomy of law and economy, bank-ruptcy presents a field of confrontation between legal and economic professionals.

Many nations across the world have bankruptcy laws in place and have passed these laws in an increasingly more interdependent manner. In the United Kingdom and the United States, bankruptcy reforms were taken in 1986 and 1978, respectively. In recent years, many other nations of the world have adopted such measures, partly in response to a growing movement towards the creation of a global standard. This process of globalization is itself dynamic and involves many international organizations that compete with one another and/or form alliances. A trend towards a common global standard can

---

[5] Situated in the growing area of law and economy at the global level (e.g., Braithwaite and Drahos 2000; Pollack and Shaffer 2001), Halliday and Carruthers's research focuses on bankruptcy reform in the United States and the United Kingdom (Carruthers and Halliday 1998) and the creation of legal insolvency regimes in China, Indonesia, and Korea (Carruthers and Halliday 2006; Halliday and Carruthers 2007).

be observed that substantively involves a transition from bankruptcy laws that focus on liquidation to laws that facilitate both liquidation and reorganization of businesses. This global diffusion process of bankruptcy laws was brought about by a number of global actors and institutions, including organizations of rich nations such as the Group of Seven (G7, now G8), international financial institutions such as the International Monetary Fund and World Bank, professional associations of lawyers and bankruptcy practitioners, international governance organizations such as the United Nations, and powerful nation-states, especially the United States.

Global norms are meaningless if they do not instill themselves into concrete locales at the national and regional level. In this localization of global developments, nationally specific solutions are offered in terms of a negotiated process that is affected by structural and cultural conditions. In the case of bankruptcy, reforms at the national level are the result of a negotiation of local and global forces that depends on a nation-state's relative power *vis-à-vis* global actors and its relative distance from relevant global processes and institutions. Although such negotiation is always in play, even in cases where nation-states are relatively powerless and where leaders and experts are far removed from global development, nation-states that are powerful and close to the global arena can more successfully negotiate legal regimes in terms that satisfy nationally defined interests. As such, the case of global insolvency regimes affirms the global legal arena as a contested field in which various nations and organizations can stake their respective claims with varying degrees of success.

As the cases of female genital cutting and corporate bankruptcy reform show, global legal regimes and their national constituent parts rely on actions from a diverse set of institutions and professionals with backgrounds in politics, economy, social movements, and law. In matters of lawmaking at the international and national level, the work done by legal professionals is inevitably crucial. Considering the increased globalization of the contemporary world, lawyers (especially those working in the traditions of Anglo-Saxon systems of law) are increasingly educated to deal with law on an international level (Flood 2002). The elite law schools in the United Kingdom and in the United States today offer more courses that have an international orientation. As a result, the global world of law is flooded by lawyers who will bring with them, and infuse into the global legal arena, principles of American and British law. In this sense, the profession of law itself has globalized into a new supra-national arena that co-exists, in areas of law less subject to global pressures, with a continuation of a nationally bound legal profession (Dingwall 1999).

The role played by lawyers in the international legal field is especially well uncovered in the recent research of Yves Dezalay and Bryant Garth.[6] Analyzing the mechanisms of arbitration in international commercial disputes, Dezalay and Garth show that the globalization of the legal field is enabled by the activities of legal professionals as "merchants" of law. Extending from the concept of field developed by Pierre Bourdieu (1987; see Garcia-Vellegas 2006; Madsen and Dezalay 2002), the authors focus on the legal field of international commercial arbitration as a virtual space in which national actors are provided opportunities to take part in this lucrative legal market. Businesses that engage in international contractual relationships to regulate decisions concerning such matters as the transnational sale of goods, distribution deals, and joint ventures often resort to arbitration procedures in order to avoid being submitted to the jurisdiction of a foreign court and to be able to conduct their legal affairs in private. The arbitrators tend to be private individuals, usually three per case, who are predominantly drawn from a rather small, yet growing circle of highly paid lawyers. With the expansion of the global market and the enormous monetary stakes involved, the resolution of international business disputes through arbitration has itself become big international business.

Dezalay and Garth find important internal and external factors at work in the transformation of international commercial arbitration. Internally, two generations of international arbitrators have over recent decades been increasingly engaged in an institutional palace war. A senior generation of "grand old men," mostly drawn from European legal elites, created the world of business arbitration on the basis of traditional values related to virtue and duty. In recent decades, a new generation of technocrats, typically employed in the large US law firms, has appeared to compete with the founding fathers of international commercial arbitration. To these young and enterprising

---

[6] See Dezalay and Garth's two major books, *Dealing in Virtue* (Dezalay and Garth 1996) and *The Internationalization of Palace Wars* (Dezalay and Garth 2002a). See also Dezalay and Garth 1995.

arbitration professionals, the charismatic qualities associated with the old guard of Europe's finest legal minds can be a source of error and need to be replaced by the new technical skills in matters of procedure and substance that can be acquired in the elite law schools.

In terms of the external conditions under which international commercial arbitration takes place, important economic and political transformations are to be noted. Especially significant have been the disputes involved in the international oil trade and the confrontation of the Western and Arab worlds. Other international divides posit the North versus the South and the West versus the East. Strikingly, a US style of legal practice has become the dominant model in the world of international law. Similarly, the political and economic model of Western liberal national states has spread across the globe. In this environment it becomes possible for regulatory structures to be built on a regional and international scale to gradually oust private mechanisms of international dispute settlement. As the business of international commercial arbitration is itself subject to market forces, Dezalay and Garth argue, regulatory regimes at the state and supra-state level may become fierce competitors of private arbitration.

The case of international commercial arbitration shows that the activities of international lawyers are framed from within particular national settings, so that the globalization of law is revealed to imply an increasingly dynamic interplay between national and extra-national processes. This interplay includes both an exporting as well as an importing side. On the exporting side, the recent rise in international arbitration of technocrats employed by US law firms has helped shape a new world of private justice that transfers American ideas of law. On the importing site, local elites cooperate in the process of legal diffusion to maintain the positions they hold in their own local communities. Showing the capacity of legal globalization to impact localities differentially, the export of legal expertise and ideals from the United States to other parts of the world has also shaped the political climate and economic situation in the importing countries. At the same time, local circumstances, especially the domestic power struggles, determine the chance and the direction of the importation of neoliberal economic principles and Western conceptions of law.

As is the case at the national level, the creation of legal norms at the international level does not equate with its administration in courts. In the global arena, this problem may be even more pronounced in the absence of adequate international bodies for formal adjudication. The case of the formation of international criminal tribunals therefore presents an interesting case for the study of the administration of international law. Research by John Hagan about the administration of international criminalization has done much to uncover the dynamics of the prosecutorial and court practices of the formation of international criminal tribunals.[7]

Historically, international criminal tribunals have received variable support in the international community. At the end of World War II, the precarious balance in international power relations that existed between the United States, the Soviet Union, and other powers facilitated the first-ever formation of an international criminal tribunal to deal with the crimes against humanity, war crimes, and genocide committed by the Nazi regime and the Japanese Empire. The Nuremberg and Tokyo war crimes tribunals were unprecedented but also short-lived realizations of the international will to administer international law and hold political regimes and their willing participants accountable under the banner of world law and justice. With the advent of the Cold War between the world's political super powers, an international consensus no longer existed for a permanent organization of an international criminal court. More recently, however, with the collapse of the communist regimes in Eastern Europe, there is a renewal of support for international adjudication, most clearly exemplified by the case of the International Criminal Tribunal for the Former Yugoslavia.

Located in the city of The Hague in The Netherlands, the International Criminal Tribunal for the Former Yugoslavia was created on the basis of a United Nations resolution in 1993 to prosecute crimes committed by individuals since the collapse of Yugoslavia and the eruption of ethnic conflicts and warfare among the various constituent republics of the former socialist state. To date, the Tribunal has indicted some 161 persons, ranging from regular soldiers and police officers to heads of government, including Slobodan Milosevic, the former President of Serbia (1989–1997) and the Federal Republic of Yugoslavia (1997–2000), who in 1999 became the first head of state

---

[7] See Hagan's (2003) book, *Justice in the Balkans*, and related articles (Hagan and Greer 2002; Hagan and Levi 2004; Hagan and Levi 2005; Hagan and Kutnjak 2006; Hagan, Schoenfeld, and Palloni 2006).

indicted for war crimes. Milosevic was extradited to the Tribunal a year after he had been forced to resign the presidency following a popular revolt. He died in prison in 2006 before his trial was completed.

The creation of the Yugoslavia Tribunal did not come about easily and faced many obstacles, not only because of the refusal of Serbia to surrender its sovereignty and cooperate with the international court. The international formation and activities of the court itself involved a power struggle over different models of international criminal administration and the creation of alliances among various international bodies, nongovernmental organizations, national governments, and the media. Hagan's research reveals that a main reason for the success of the Tribunal lay with the work of the professionals involved in maintaining the court's operations, especially Louise Arbour, the court's chief prosecutor from 1996 until 1999. Against the widely shared prospect that the Tribunal would never attain the status of a real working court, Arbour led her colleagues in advancing the work of the Tribunal and securing the arrest and prosecution of major war criminals, including, most notably, Milosevic. Arbour revealed a strong personal charisma that in a hospitable social setting could flourish and effectively help foster the development of the Tribunal. The actions of Arbour demonstrate the importance of institutional entrepreneurs in seeking to make law effective. The case of the Yugoslavia Tribunal also affirms the interdependence of global and national developments, specifically in terms of the need for global legal developments to be recognized as legitimate on the local level. In this respect, research has found that former Yugoslavians perceive the Tribunal to some extent as a foreign invasion and, therefore, feel that the war criminals prosecuted by the Tribunal should gradually be moved to local courts in the former-Yugoslavian republics. The developmental path of the globalization of criminal law is thus also observed to lead back to a localization thereof.

To what extent an international criminal court becomes a more permanent reality is difficult to predict. While a new global consensus may be emerging, especially surrounding the increasingly unavoidable discourse on human rights, the recent inability (or refusal) of the international community to intervene in conflicts involving genocide and war crimes, such as in Darfur, does not indicate a smooth path towards the formation of a global legal community. Striking, also, is the refusal of the United States to participate in the elaboration of the

International Criminal Court that was set up in 2002 as a permanent tribunal to prosecute individuals for genocide, crimes against humanity, and war crimes. Clearly, national sovereignty concerns are not a thing of the past. At the same time, the relatively successful operation of the International Criminal Tribunal for the Former Yugoslavia shows that advances in a global spread of the rule of law may be possible as part of a broader development towards the global diffusion of democratic norms.

Global control: the dynamics of world policing

As with other dimensions of law, the globalization of various aspects of social control has also been of increasing interest among social scientists. A word of caution is in order to delineate the field of the globalization of social control, which is often couched in terms of international policing or international law enforcement, because of the terminological confusion that may exist between the administration or enforcement of international (criminal) law, on the one hand, and the international or global dimensions of the control of crime and deviance, on the other hand. The former issue falls in the province of international law, the enforcement of which is a matter of administration (such as in the International Criminal Tribunals). However, the globalization of social control in matters of crime and deviance includes a multitude of global developments that are not related to violations of international norms but involve the control of the border-crossing dimensions of violations of national legal regimes, such as the control of international money laundering schemes, the policing of organized criminal activities, the control of the drug trade and the smuggling of goods and people, and the diffusion across the world of ideas and practices of policing and punishment (McDonald 1997; Reichel 2005). In what follows, my own work in the area of the internationalization of policing will illustrate the value of work on the globalization of social control from a sociological viewpoint rooted in a Weberian perspective of bureaucratization.[8]

---

[8] I have analyzed the historical antecedents of international police cooperation in my book, *Policing World Society* (Deflem 2002; see also Deflem 2000), and have subsequently investigated selected contemporary dimensions of international policing, especially in matters of terrorism (Deflem 2004, 2006a). This overview is partly based on Deflem 2007c.

As outlined in the previous chapter, police organizations in the modern world have increasingly taken on the form of bureaucracies. In formal and operational respects, the bureaucratization of policing has important consequences for the probability and form of international cooperation among police. Formally, police bureaucratization relates to the relative independence of police institutions from the governments of their respective national states. In operational respects, police bureaucratization implies that police institutions gain autonomy to determine the means as well as a specification of the objectives of their tasks. Over the course of history, these developments have influenced the globalization of policing in a variety of contexts.

The earliest forms of international policing mostly concerned activities directed against the political opponents of established autocratic regimes. Among the examples in the first half of the nineteenth century were unilaterally planned international police activities organized by the French, Hungarian-Austrian, and Russian governments, whereby agents would be secretly stationed abroad. An international organization of police was established in 1851, when the Police Union of German States was formed. Active until 1866, the Police Union included representatives from seven sovereign German-language nations to exchange information, through regularly held meetings and printed bulletins, in order to suppress political opponents of their respective conservative regimes. Indicating the limits of police cooperation for political purposes, the Police Union could not solicit support of police from other European states. The organization disbanded when war broke out between Prussia and Austria, the Union's two dominant members.

From the middle to the latter half of the nineteenth century, most international police activities were conducted unilaterally, typically by stationing agents abroad as attachés to embassies, or they were limited to *ad hoc* cooperation for a specific inquiry and restricted in scope of international participation to bilateral or limited multilateral cooperation. A gradual trend took place towards the formation of an international police organization that would enable cooperation on a wide multilateral scale. Under the influence of processes of bureaucratization, whereby police organizations began to conceive their activities on the basis of professional standards of crime control, the idea of international police cooperation was premised on the notion that police agencies no longer represented political regimes but instead were expert institutions specialized in the fight against crime as a social menace that affected all societies. Efforts by national governments to organize international efforts against political crimes, particularly anarchism, in the late nineteenth century consequently failed because of a lack of police support.

In the early twentieth century, various attempts were taken to create a permanent international police organization. Among the earliest efforts, the International Association of Chiefs of Police was created in Washington, DC in 1901. But, originating from an effort to increase the standards of law enforcement in the United States, the Association was a professional group that had little international support. In Europe, the first effort in the twentieth century to establish an international police organization also failed. In April 1914, the First Congress of International Criminal Police in Monaco was explicitly oriented at criminal (not political) violations, yet the attendants at the Congress did not include any police officials and the discussions were exclusively framed in legal and political terms. World War I broke out soon after the meeting, but even after the cessation of hostilities had ended, this initiative was not resumed.

The end of World War I brought about two important attempts to set up an international police organization. In New York, the International Police Conference was established in 1922 and remained active until the 1930s. Despite its name, the organization was a predominantly American organization that mostly concerned itself with fostering professional police relations. Far more successful was the International Criminal Police Commission (ICPC), established in Vienna, Austria, in 1923, which still exists under the name of the International Criminal Police Organization or Interpol. The ICPC was set up by police officials to independently organize cooperation in matters of international crime. Explicitly excluding political violations, various institutions were set up to exchange information swiftly among the member agencies, including international communication systems, regularly held meetings, and a central headquarters through which information could be routed to all members. The German annexation of Austria in 1938 led to the Nazi takeover of the ICPC headquarters and its subsequent move to Berlin during World War II. Shortly after the war, in 1946, the international police organization was revived and the headquarters were moved to France, where they still resides. At present, Interpol consists of police agencies from 186 nations.

Considering the forms that the globalization of policing takes, a persistence of nationality can be observed in international police work in at least three respects. First, police institutions prefer to engage unilaterally in international activities without cooperation from police of other nations. Considering the investment that is needed to instigate such activities successfully, the police institutions of powerful nations are at a marked advantage in this respect. The Federal Bureau of Investigation and the Drug Enforcement Administration of the United States are prototypical examples. Each of these agencies has several hundred agents permanently stationed abroad in dozens of countries. Second, whenever possible, police cooperation will be restricted to a particular task and limited in terms of the number of participating institutions. Third, nationally defined objectives remain paramount even when police institutions participate in larger cooperative operations and organizations. Cooperation is only enacted when it is conceived of as having a purpose related to nationally or locally defined enforcement objectives.

Among the conditions that shape the globalization of policing are developments in crime as well as its control. In matters of crime, the increasing interdependence of societies has brought about increasing opportunities to engage in criminal conduct with international implications. As technologies of transportation have evolved, so have the opportunities for criminal activities to spread across national borders and evade jurisdictionally confined enforcement. Changes in criminal developments bring about important fluctuations in the globalization of policing. Whereas international police operations during the first half of the twentieth century mostly focused on fugitives from justice who had committed violent and property crimes, the emphasis later shifted towards the policing of drug crimes and the control of illegal immigration. The fight against drug trafficking was arguably the leading motivator in international policing efforts during the 1970s and 1980s. From the late twentieth century onwards and with extreme vigor since the events of September 11, 2001, international terrorism and technologically advanced crimes, such as cyber crimes and international money laundering schemes, have become the leading focus of the international policing activities that are initiated by the police of many nations as well as at the level of international police organizations, such as Interpol and the European Police Office (Europol).

Besides variations in criminal developments, the organization of policing is itself also subject to globalization pressures, especially because of developments in the realm of technology. Advances in technological systems of communication, transportation, and criminal identification, in particular, have directly influenced the globalization of policing. Border-crossing technologies such as radio, telegraph, and the internet, automobiles, and air traffic, and the internationally exchangeable data from fingerprint and DNA analyses have directly contributed to the globalization of policing. Furthermore, economic trends have influenced an ever-increasing globalization of the private policing industry, which has largely followed the logic of the capitalist market to offer security as a worldwide available commodity. The global spread of private policing has also led to new partnerships with public police forces, especially in the areas of technologically advanced and financial crimes, such as cyber crimes and money laundering.

The globalization of the police function has never been more pronounced than it is today. In view of the high degree of inter-penetration of societies and institutions across national boundaries, it is also more than likely that the globalization of policing will continue to gain in importance as the twenty-first century unfolds. Especially the ongoing preoccupation with international terrorism may continue to propel the globalization process in the area of policing, thereby also bringing about important reconfigurations between police institutions and their respective governments. While police organizations have presently attained an unprecedented high degree of professional expertise in matters of crime control, they are now also again subject to political pressures to harmonize their work with the objectives of governments that conceive of international crime and terrorism as concerns of national security. A critical dynamic of police globaliza-tion in the near future will be to estimate how attempts to politicize policing will play out against the bureaucratic resistance police institutions can offer.

Conclusion

As the discussions in this chapter have shown, global developments of law take place in a variety of institutions, with diverse mechanisms, in many arenas, and with multiple outcomes. Analytically, various polar opposites can be distinguished that empirical cases exemplify in varying degrees. Globalization can imply universalization and homo-genization versus particularization and differentiation in terms of the degree to which global developments create similarities or reinforce differences across social units. Integration and centralization versus fragmentation and decentralization specify the impact of globali-zation. Focusing on the globalization of law in terms of a process extending from the creation of legal norms to their administration, research on female genital cutting, the diffusion of insolvency regimes, practices of international lawyering, the activities of international criminal courts, and the dynamics of international policing reveals the substantive breadth and theoretical contrasts that exist in sociological work on the globalization of law.

What research on the globalization of law (as on other institutions) shows is that globalization cannot simply be captured as a one-dimensional process towards the development of a homogenized world. Instead, what globalization primarily entails is a reconfigur-ation of the interrelationships between national and international developments. For example, the development of global legal norms has not halted the elaboration nor softened the impact of local and national jurisdictional authority. Besides, the globalization of law should not only be conceived in terms of the creation of international legal codes or agreements reached on the basis of bilateral and multi-lateral treaties, but also includes the importation and exportation (deliberate or not, directed or not) of legal norms and practices across geographically dispersed social units. It is thus more appropriate to conceive of globalization as the increasing interpenetration of local/national and interlocal/international developments. The study of globalization of law, therefore, should not lead scholars to neglect local and national developments. The policing of crime, for instance, will always remain a primarily local concern, simply because the dimensions of most crimes do not extend beyond the boundaries of local communities. Even in the global age, the notion of jurisdictional authority remains meaningful.

A peculiar dimension in studies of globalization, in the sociology of law and elsewhere, is that many discussions relate to concerns that have a strong normative resonance. Therefore, also, some works on the globalization of law are framed in highly normative terms, whereby globalization is not only understood as something to be analyzed, but also something to be opposed, a line of thinking that harmonizes with the actions of certain social movements, such as human rights groups and the so-called anti-globalization movement. Although the sociology of law such as it is understood in this book conceives of globalization in distinctly analytical terms, some globalization scholars in the area of law have, because of law's inescapably close connection to normative matters (crystallized in the problem of the legitimacy of legality), also explicitly referred to a discourse on justice and rights, especially human rights (Klug 2005). The globalization of law as the formation of a one-world culture is then often unmasked as a power struggle whereby the imposition of a supposedly universal "one-size-fits-all" style of law is critiqued as being detrimental to the fulfillment of justice on a local scale (Silbey 1997).

Finally, it is to be noted that sociologists and other students of law have not only begun to recognize the relevance of globalization in their subject matter, scholars of globalization in other areas of research have likewise begun to recognize the relevance of law. Nonetheless, more work needs to be done in this respect. Inasmuch as a recognition of the relevance of law in globalization is also a function of the relative popularity and acceptance of the specialty field of the sociology of law, additional work on the globalization of law and explicit efforts to link this work with the globalization discourse in sociology and other social sciences will contribute to fostering such synergetic contributions.

Conclusion: Visions of the sociology of law

It has been the primary intention of this book to review and discuss theoretical and substantive contributions in the sociology of law in order to present this disciplinary specialty as a unique and valuable academic endeavor. It has not been a goal of this book to offer an assessment of the discussed theoretical and substantive efforts in the sociological study of law beyond their merits as contributions to the field as a whole. To be sure, the present study has been informed by a theoretically driven orientation that guided the analytical framework used to review the history and systematics of the sociology of law. But the employed model allowed, and was explicitly conceived for, a plurality of perspectives to be brought out. In its treatment of themes in theory and research, this study has been necessarily selective, yet also focused on contributions that have been exemplary in representing and furthering the sociology of law.

It may be useful to conclude by identifying some central themes and issues that run through the sociology of law as it has unfolded over the course of its historical and intellectual development. Identifying these gains and pains of the sociology of law may also lead to guide our understanding of where the specialty area might be and should be going in the near future. A number of analytical concerns can be identified that frame the sociology of law within the broader field of the study of law, specifically concerning the sociological approach to and conception of law, the employed standards of scholarship in theory and research, the degree of unity and diversity among the sociology of law's contributions, and the possibility of interdisciplinarity in the study of law. In order to situate these analytical issues in a broad institutional context, separate attention first goes to the development of the sociology of law across national cultures. This book has primarily considered developments of Western sociology of law, especially as it has extended from its predominantly European roots and inasmuch as it is practiced in the United States and other parts of

271

the English-speaking world. Although the sociology of law in many nations is built on European foundations, various national developments in the specialty area are nonetheless distinct.

Cultures of the sociology of law

Reviewing the development and state of the sociology of law across the world, at least two central themes can be observed in the different national histories of the specialty area.[1] First, the sociology of law in various nations benefited from the activities of certain charismatic scholars that functioned as "moral entrepreneurs" to institutionalize the sociological specialty. In this respect, it will cause no surprise to learn that the sociology of law is developed strongly in Germany, the country of Max Weber and other important classic scholars, such as Simmel, Tönnies, Ehrlich, and Geiger. The normal course of development of German sociology was disrupted with the rise of Nazism. But after World War II, the sociology of law in Germany could continue its intellectually fruitful path, leading to nurture of the works of such giants of contemporary world sociology as Niklas Luhmann and Jürgen Habermas and many contemporary sociologists of law.

A second important characteristic of the development of the sociology of law is that the specialty has typically not evolved independently from within sociology alone, but has also grown out of the legal sciences. As a result of this peculiar history, the sociology of law experiences, until this day, difficulties in affirming itself as an academic specialty. In Germany, for instance, scholars debate whether the sociology of law should contribute to legal policy (in line with Ehrlich) or whether it should primarily be an academic enterprise

---

[1] Exemplifying the globalization of academic work, there is a wealth of published accounts on the sociology of law in many nations, including Poland (Fuszara 1990; Kojder and Kwasniewski 1985; Kurczewski 2001; Podgórecki 1999), Germany (Machura 2001a, 2001b; Rasehorn 2001; Rueschemeyer 1970), Italy (Baronti and Pitch 1978; Ferrari and Ronfani 2001; Pitch 1983; Treves 1981), France (Arnaud 1981; Noreau and Arnaud 1998), Bulgaria (Naoumova 1990), Finland (Uusitalo 1989), Scandinavia (Blegvad 1966; Hyden 1986; Mathiesen 1990), The Netherlands (Hoekema 1985), Belgium (Van Houtte 1990), Brazil (Justo and Singer 2001), Korea (Yang 1989, 2001), Japan (Upham 1989), China (Wei-Dong 1989), the United Kingdom (Campbell and Wiles 1976; Cotterrell 1990; Travers 2001), and the United States (Baumgartner 2001). See also Rehbinder 1975; Treviño 2001; and contributions in Ferrari 1990; Treves and van Loon 1968; Van Houtte and van Loon 1993.

(extending from Weber). Similarly, in the United States, there are contemporary currents in jurisprudence that, drawing on a line of development from Holmes to Pound and Llewellyn, seek to absorb the sociology of law within legal scholarship. In turn, the American sociology of law endeavors to affirm and position itself, with all due resistance against the jurisprudential pull, as a disciplinary activity. The tension between law and the sociology of law is also reflected on an organizational level. The Law and Society Association, for instance, was founded in 1964 by a group of US sociologists, yet the Association has in the course of its history become the premier home for socio-legal and legal scholars and lost much of its distinctly sociological focus. It was not until 1992 that the consequences thereof were fully realized, when a Sociology of Law section was formed within the American Sociological Association.

In many nations, the dual influences of charismatic leadership and institutional organization are confirmed, as a brief overview of national cultures in the sociology of law will illustrate. The sociology of law in Poland flourished particularly well because of the efforts of Adam Podgórecki, a follower of Petrazycki. Podgórecki was also influential in institutionalizing the sociology of law nationally as well as internationally. In 1962, he established the Polish Section of the Sociology of Law and in the same year he co-founded with William Evan the Research Committee of Sociology of Law in the International Sociological Association. The first President of the Research Committee was Renato Treves of Italy, a country that also enjoys a rich tradition of sociology of law. The Italian legal philosopher Dionisio Anzilotti was the first in 1892 to explicitly use the term sociology of law. After the fascist period, normal sociological activities were revived and Italian sociology of law could demarcate itself rather well from law, to wit the establishment of the specialty journal, *Sociologia del diritto*, as early as 1974.

Other nations have had a similarly fortuitous development in their sociology of law because of the influence of exemplary sociologists. French sociology of law can rely on a developmental path that stretches from de Montesquieu and Durkheim over Gurvitch and Lévy-Bruhl to modern scholars, such as Jean Carbonnier and André-Jean Arnaud, next to some of France's contemporary giants of social thought, including Bourdieu and Derrida. Despite the overwhelming presence of Durkheim, French sociology of law is caught in between law and sociology, as expressed in the dual labels of the specialty as juridical sociology (*sociologie juridique*) and sociology of law (*sociologie du droit*).

Other countries have been less fortunate in their organization of the sociology of law as an academic activity. In Brazil, for instance, sociologically oriented studies of law are conducted in the field of law, where they stand, with great difficulty, alongside of studies of law conducted by sociologists. Likewise, in some European nations, such as Belgium and Finland, sociology of law is institutionally and, as a result, oftentimes also intellectually part of the study of law at law schools. In the United Kingdom, the sociology of law co-exists with socio-legal research, whereby the latter is understood not only as a multidisciplinary field but also as a policy oriented activity. British academic sociology of law is relatively marginal to sociology at large, leading to the ironic consequence that several of Britain's best sociologists of law are more at home in the world of the sociology of law in the United States, although there too the specialty's standing is not always clearly recognized among fellow disciplinarians. More broadly, sociologists of law from across the globe are often better acquainted with one another than with sociologists from other specialty areas in their own nationally organized disciplines.

The sociology of law of some nations is less well-known on a global scale despite a sometimes long-standing history. In Japan, for example, the Japanese Association of the Sociology of Law was formed as early as 1948. The marginalization of certain national cultures relates to wider cultural, political, and economic forces. Linguistic barriers alone will prevent some otherwise relevant work from being widely known. Moreover, nations that are peripheral to world affairs and/or underwent difficult transitions to open and democratic societies tend to be importers rather than exporters of sociological ideas. The relative marginality of some nations can ironically produce a sociology of law that is well grounded in many relevant contributions from across the world.

Boundaries of the sociology of law

The most defining characteristic of the sociology of law is the specific manner in which it approaches law in disciplinary terms. There would not be anything shocking about the notion that the sociology of law is always part of sociology, were it not for the fact that the study of law is intimately related to one of the peculiar characteristics of law itself. For law always involves the study thereof as well and is characterized by a generally successful effort to monopolize its own observation. This stubborn resistance of law to not readily allow for external observations from the social and behavioral sciences was already recognized by Max Weber and led him to differentiate internal, external, and moral approaches to the study of law. Were it not for certain special characteristics of law itself, such a demarcation would have been redundant.

Historically, moreover, the social sciences developed in institutional and intellectual respects from scholarly traditions that squarely placed matters of policy and normativity within the realm of study. In consequence, the necessary lessons that were to be learned from Weber's conceptualization were very slow in coming throughout the history of the study of law, in general, and the development of the sociology of law, in particular. In Europe, the sociological study of law had to not only free itself from certain juridical roots, it also had to demarcate a distinctly social rather than psychological reality of law as the appropriate field of study. In the United States, the sociology of law was ironically placed in confrontation with a development in jurisprudence that had borrowed insights from the discipline, yet had placed them within the context of legal scholarship and made them subservient to its objectives. It took independent developments from within the discipline at large, rather than from within the field of the sociologically informed study of law, to find a place for the sociology of law and, in doing so, recapture and further build on the relevant contributions of the sociological classics. Only from then on could sociologists of law make good on the Weberian promise to carve a niche for the sociology of law and articulate its program along disciplinary lines.

Among the most distinct contributions that the sociology of law has to offer is a conceptualization of law that differs from and transcends its juridical understanding. Beginning with Weber's definition in terms of enforcement and Durkheim's conception of law as an indicator of moral solidarity, sociologists do not confine law to the realm of rules formally enacted in the context of legislation. Instead, law is sociologically broadened to an institution that also includes an entire range of practices, actors, and agencies at various levels of analysis in

multiple arenas of law. The sociological definition of law, importantly, involves not a mere broadening of the appropriate field of
study, but implies an entire rethinking of law itself. In this respect, a
general transformation can be observed from a more traditional
perspective on law in terms of the primary function of integration
(law as social control) to critical conceptions of law in societies characterized as fundamentally unequal (law as power) and the more recent
positioning of law in a broad field of regulatory practices (law as
governance). Irrespective of the specific qualities of such conceptualizations, it is the confrontation of the ideal of law with the many
facets of its reality that counts among the sociology of law's most
distinct contributions. Expressed in such conceptual distinctions as
between intuitive law and officially positive law, juristic law and
living law, official and unofficial law, and law in the books and law in
action, what the sociology of law most typically seeks to reveal are
the discrepancies that exist between the stated objectives and self-
understanding of law and the reality of law in terms of its origins,
course, and impact at the social level.

The basic effort in the sociology of law to reveal the limits of law's
self-proclaimed ideals does not imply a return to the normative foundations of pre-sociological approaches in the study of law, nor does it
entail a surrender to the instrumental objectives of legal scholarship.
For what sets the sociology of law apart from a normative or jurisprudentially guided evaluation of law is that its various understand-
ings of the social reality of law are based on research findings that
are drawn from theoretically informed and methodologically guided
investigations. In this respect, the development of the sociology of law
into a distinct and diverse field, harboring a multitude of theoretical
perspectives and methodological orientations, testifies not only to the
intellectual maturity of the sociology of law as a disciplinary specialty,
it also provides the sociology of law with strong scholarly foundations
relative to other perspectives in the field of socio-legal studies as well
as with respect to other specialty areas in the discipline of sociology.
The unity and diversity of thought in the sociology of law thus betrays
the continued relevance of the sociological classics and the theoretical
pluralism their respective approaches have brought about, ranging
from conflict and consensus perspectives to macro-sociological and
micro-theoretical variations as well as objectivist and normatively
grounded orientations. The theoretical richness of the sociology of

law is matched on a substantive level in the proliferation of research in various areas of inquiry, ranging from questions concerning the relations between law, economy, politics, social integration, and culture, to matters of social control and law's global dimensions. Within these various specialty areas, also, the sociology of law has witnessed the development of many novel contemporary theoretical perspectives that extend from the roots in classical and modern thought.

The difficult relation between the sociology of law and the legal sciences, which is experienced in many national cultures, also relates to the place and role of sociology relative to other social-science contributions in the study of law and, relatedly, the quest of interdisciplinarity. The most important lesson that in this respect can be reached from this book is that the sociology of law offers something unique and valuable next to the other specialty fields in the discipline as much as it does among other social-science perspectives of law. But it is a similar matter of course that this ambition does not imply any statement against other, non-sociological approaches in the study of law, whether they come from within law or from other social and behavioral sciences. This book, therefore, can also not be understood to imply a position against interdisciplinarity. With Weber, legal scholarship can be differentiated from the whole of the social and behavioral sciences of law in terms of the sharp differences that exist between their respective objectives. However, sharing a perspective oriented towards the analysis of law, rather than seeking to maintain its efficiency, the social and behavioral sciences differ from one another only in terms of approach and the relevant dimension of law that is the focus of their attention. From this perspective, interdisciplinarity always implies a strengthening of the boundaries and foundations of disciplinarity. As such, I hope that this book can contribute to building a truly interdisciplinary approach to the analysis of law in its varied manifestations by having clarified, and thereby uncovered the value of, the disciplinary contours of the sociology of law.

Bibliography

Abbott, Andrew. 1988. *The System of the Professions: An Essay on the Division of Expert Labor*. Chicago: University of Chicago Press.

Abel, Richard L. 1986. "The Transformation of the American Legal Profession." *Law and Society Review* 20(1): 7–18.

Abel, Richard L. 1988. *The Legal Profession in England and Wales*. Oxford: Blackwell.

Abel, Richard L. 1989. *American Lawyers*. New York: Oxford University Press.

Abel, Richard L. 1995. "What We Talk about when We Talk about Law." Pp. 1–10 in *The Law and Society Reader*, ed. R. L. Abel. New York: New York University Press.

Abel, Richard L., and Philip S. C. Lewis. 1988–1989. *Lawyers in Society*. 3 vols. Berkeley, CA: University of California Press.

Albonetti, Celesta A. 1999. "The Avoidance of Punishment: A Legal-Bureaucratic Model of Suspended Sentences in Federal White-Collar Cases Prior to the Federal Sentencing Guidelines." *Social Forces* 78(1): 303–329.

Albrow, Martin. 1975. "Legal Positivism and Bourgeois Materialism: Max Weber's View of the Sociology of Law." *British Journal of Law and Society* 2(1): 14–31.

Albrow, Martin. 1996. *The Global Age: State and Society beyond Modernity*. Stanford, CA: Stanford University Press.

Alexander, Jeffrey C. 1983. *The Modern Reconstruction of Classical Thought: Talcott Parsons*. Theoretical Logic in Sociology, Volume Four. Berkeley, CA: University of California Press.

Alexander, Jeffrey C. 1987. "On the Centrality of the Classics." Pp. 11–57 in *Sociological Theory Today*, ed. A. Giddens and J. Turner. Stanford, CA: Stanford University Press.

Alschuler, Albert W. 2000. *Law without Values: The Life, Work, and Legacy of Justice Holmes*. Chicago: University of Chicago Press.

Andreski, S. L. 1981. "Understanding, Action and Law in Max Weber." Pp. 45–66 in *Sociological Approaches to Law*, ed. A. Podgórecki and C. J. Whelan. New York: St. Martin's Press.

Andrini, Simona. 2004. "Max Weber's Sociology of Law as a Turning Point of his Methodological Approach." *International Review of Sociology/ Revue Internationale de Sociologie* 14(2): 143–152.

Anspach, Donald F., and S. Henry Monsen. 1989. "Determinate Sentencing, Formal Rationality, and Khadi Justice in Maine: An Application of Weber's Typology." *Journal of Criminal Justice* 17: 471–485.

Arnaud, André-Jean. 1981. *Critique de la raison juridique: Où va la sociologie du droit?* Paris: Centre National de la Recherche Scientifique. Online: www.reds.msh-paris.fr/publications/collvir/crj-html/crj.htm.

Arrigo, Bruce A. 2002. *Punishing the Mentally Ill: A Critical Analysis of Law and Psychiatry.* State University of New York Press.

Arrigo, Bruce A., and Christopher R. Williams. 2000. "The (Im)Possibility of Democratic Justice and the 'Gift' of the Majority: On Derrida, Deconstruction, and the Search for Equality." *Journal of Contemporary Criminal Justice* 16(3): 321–343.

Arrigo, Bruce A., Dragan Milovanovic, and Robert C. Schehr. 2000. "The French Connection: Implications for Law, Crime, and Social Justice." *Humanity and Society* 24(2): 162–203.

Atkinson, J. Maxwell. 1981. "Ethnomethodological Approaches to Socio-Legal Studies." Pp. 201–223 in *Sociological Approaches to Law*, ed. A. Podgórecki and C. J. Whelan. New York: St. Martin's Press.

Atkinson, J. Maxwell, and Paul Drew. 1979. *Order in Court: The Organisation of Verbal Interaction in Judicial Settings.* London: Macmillan.

Aubert, Vilhelm. 1963. "Researches in the Sociology of Law." *American Behaviour Scientist* 7(4): 16–20.

Aubert, Vilhelm, ed. 1969. *Sociology of Law: Selected Readings.* Baltimore: Penguin Books.

Aubert, Vilhelm. 1983. *In Search of Law: Sociological Approaches to Law.* Totowa, NJ: Barnes & Noble Books.

Auerbach, Carl A. 1966. "Legal Tasks for the Sociologist." *Law and Society Review* 1(1): 91–104.

Austin, Arthur. 2000. "The Postmodern Infiltration of Legal Scholarship." Review Essay. *Michigan Law Review* 98(6): 1504–1528.

Ball, Harry V., George Eaton Simpson, and Kiyoshi Ikeda. 1962. "Law and Social Change: Sumner Reconsidered." *American Journal of Sociology* 67(5): 532–540.

Banakar, Reza. 2001. "Integrating Reciprocal Perspectives: On Gurvitch's Theory of Immediate Jural Experience." *Canadian Journal of Law and Society* 16: 67–91.

Banakar, Reza. 2002. "Sociological Jurisprudence." Pp. 33–44 in *An Introduction to Law and Social Theory*, ed. R. Banakar and M. Travers. Portland, OR: Hart Publishing.

Banakar, Reza. 2003. *Merging Law and Sociology: Beyond the Dichotomies in Socio-Legal Research*. Glienicke, Berlin: Galda & Wilch Verlag.

Banakar, Reza, and Max Travers. 2002. "Law and Sociology." Pp. 345–352 in *An Introduction to Law and Social Theory*, ed. R. Banakar and M. Travers. Portland, OR: Hart Publishing.

Bankowski, Zenon, and Geoff Mungham. 1980. *Essays in Law and Society*. Boston: Routledge & Kegan Paul.

Barkan, Steven. 1984. "Legal Control of the Southern Civil Rights Movement." *American Sociological Review* 49(4): 552–565.

Baronti, Giancarlo, and Tamar Pitch. 1978. "Sociology of Law and the Problematic of the Social Sciences in Italy." *Law and Society Review* 12(4): 665–684.

Barrett, Jerome T. 2004. *A History of Alternative Dispute Resolution: The Story of a Political, Cultural, and Social Movement*. San Francisco, CA: Jossey-Bass.

Baum, Karl B. 1967. *Leon Petrazycki und seine Schuler*. Berlin: Duncker & Humblot.

Bauman, Richard W. 1996. *Critical Legal Studies: A Guide to the Literature*. Boulder, CO: Westview Press.

Baumgartner, M. P. 2001. "The Sociology of Law in the United States." *The American Sociologist* 32(2): 99–113.

Baxi, Upendra. 1974. "Durkheim and Legal Evolution: Some Problems of Disproof." Comment. *Law and Society Review* 8(4): 645–652.

Bayley, David H. 1975. "The Police and Political Development in Europe." Pp. 328–379 in *The Formation of National States in Western Europe*, ed. C. Tilly. Princeton, NJ: Princeton University Press.

Bayley, David H. 2005. *Changing the Guard: Developing Democratic Police Abroad*. New York: Oxford University Press.

Beccaria, Cesare. (1764) 1986. *On Crimes and Punishments*. Indianapolis, IN: Hackett Publishing. Online: www.crimetheory.com/Archive/Beccaria/index.html.

Becker, Gary S. 1974. "Crime and Punishment: An Economic Approach." Pp. 1–54 in *Essays in the Economics of Crime and Punishment*, ed. G. Becker and W. M. Landes. New York: National Bureau of Economic Research.

Becker, Gary S. 1976. *The Economic Approach to Human Behavior*. Chicago: University of Chicago Press.

Becker, Gary S., and William M. Landes. 1974. *Essays in the Economics of Crime and Punishment*. New York: National Bureau of Economic Research.

Becker, Howard S. 1963. *Outsiders: Studies in the Sociology of Deviance*. New York: The Free Press of Glencoe.

Becker, Peter, and Richard F. Wetzell, eds. 2006. *Criminals and their Scientists: The History of Criminology in International Perspective.* New York: Cambridge University Press.

Beckett, Katherine, and Bruce Western. 2001. "Governing Social Marginality: Welfare, Incarceration, and the Transformation of State Policy." *Punishment and Society* 3(1): 43–59.

Behrens, Angela, Christopher Uggen, and Jeff Manza. 2003. "Ballot Manipulation and the 'Menace of Negro Domination': Racial Threat and Felon Disenfranchisement in the United States, 1850–2002." *American Journal of Sociology* 109: 559–605.

Beirne, Piers. 1975. "Marxism and the Sociology of Law: Theory or Practice?" *British Journal of Law and Society* 2(1): 78–81.

Beirne, Piers. 1979a. "Empiricism and the Critique of Marxism on Law and Crime." *Social Problems* 26(4): 373–385.

Beirne, Piers. 1979b. "Ideology and Rationality in Max Weber's Sociology of Law." Pp. 101–131 in *Research in Law and Sociology,* Vol. II, ed. S. Spitzer. Greenwich, CT: JAI Press.

Beirne, Piers. 1991. "Inventing Criminology: The 'Science of Man' in Cesare Beccaria's 'Dei delitti e delle pene' (1764)." *Criminology* 29(4): 777–820.

Beirne, Piers, and Richard Quinney, eds. 1982. *Marxism and Law.* New York: John Wiley.

Belley, Jean-Guy. 1986. "Georges Gurvitch et les professionnels de la pensée juridique." *Droit et Société* 4: 353–371.

Benney, Mark. 1983. "Gramsci on Law, Morality, and Power." *International Journal of the Sociology of Law* 11(2): 191–208.

Bentham, Jeremy. (1789) 1970. *An Introduction to the Principles of Morals and Legislation,* ed. J.H. Burns and H.L.A. Hart. London: Athlone Press.

Bentham, Jeremy. (1792) 1843. "Truth *versus* Ashhurst; Or, Law as it is, Contrasted with what it is Said to Be." Pp. 231–237 in *The Works of Jeremy Bentham,* Vol. V. Edinburgh: Tait; London: Simpkin, Marshall. Online: www.law.mq.edu.au/Units/law420/LAW203S/Ashhurst.htm.

Berends, Miek. 1992. "An Elusive Profession? Lawyers in Society." Review Essay. *Law and Society Review* 26(1): 161–188.

Berger, Peter L., and Thomas Luckmann. 1967. *The Social Construction of Reality.* Garden City, NY: Anchor.

Bittner, Egon. 1990. *Aspects of Police Work.* Boston: Northeastern University Press.

Black, Donald J. 1972a. "The Boundaries of Legal Sociology." *The Yale Law Journal* 81: 1086–1100.

Black, Donald J. 1972b. Review of *Law, Society, and Industrial Justice,* by Philip Selznick. *American Journal of Sociology* 78(3): 709–714.

Black, Donald. 1976. *The Behavior of Law*. New York: Academic Press.

Black, Donald. 1979. "Common Sense in the Sociology of Law." *American Sociological Review* 44(1): 18–27.

Black, Donald. 1980. *The Manners and Customs of the Police*. New York: Academic Press.

Black, Donald. 1989. *Sociological Justice*. New York: Oxford University Press.

Black, Donald. 1995. "The Epistemology of Pure Sociology." *Law and Social Inquiry* 20(3): 829–870.

Black, Donald. 1997. *The Social Structure of Right and Wrong*. New York: Academic Press.

Black, Donald. 2000. "Dreams of Pure Sociology." *Sociological Theory* 18 (3): 343–367.

Black, Donald. 2002. "The Geometry of Law: An Interview with Donald Black." *International Journal of the Sociology of Law* 30(2): 101–129.

Black, Donald. 2007. "Relativity, Legal." Pp. 1292–1294 in *Encyclopedia of Law and Society: American and Global Perspectives*, ed. D. S. Clark. Thousand Oaks, CA: Sage Publications.

Blegvad, Britt Mari Persson. 1966. "The Systematic Position of Sociology of Law in Current Scandinavian Research." Pp. 2–19 in *Contributions to the Sociology of Law*, ed. B. M. P. Blegvad. Copenhagen: Munksgaard.

Blumer, Herbert. 1969. *Symbolic Interactionism: Perspective and Method*. Englewood Cliffs, NJ: Prentice-Hall.

Boon, Andy. 2005. "Postmodern Professions? The Fragmentation of Legal Education and the Legal Profession." *Journal of Law and Society* 32 (3): 473–492.

Boucock, Cary. 2000. *In the Grip of Freedom: Law and Modernity in Max Weber*. Toronto: University of Toronto Press.

Bourdieu, Pierre. 1987. "The Force of the Law: Toward a Sociology of the Juridical Field." *Hastings Law Journal* 38(5): 805–853.

Boyle, Elizabeth H. 1998. "Political Frames and Legal Activity: The Case of Nuclear Power in Four Countries." *Law and Society Review* 32(1): 141–174.

Boyle, Elizabeth H. 2000. "Is Law the Rule? Using Political Frames to Explain Cross-National Variation in Legal Activity." *Social Forces* 79 (2): 385–418.

Boyle, Elizabeth H. 2002. *Female Genital Cutting: Cultural Conflict in the Global Community*. Baltimore, MD: Johns Hopkins University Press.

Boyle, Elizabeth H. 2007. "Globalization – Processes of Legislative." Pp. 661–665 in *Encyclopedia of Law and Society: American and Global Perspectives*, ed. D. S. Clark. Thousand Oaks, CA: Sage Publications.

Boyle, Elizabeth H., and John W. Meyer. 2002. "Modern Law as a Secularized and Global Model: Implications for the Sociology of Law." Pp. 65–95 in *Global Prescriptions: The Production, Exportation, and Importation of a New Legal Orthodoxy*, ed. Y. Dezalay and B. G. Garth. Ann Arbor, MI: University of Michigan Press.

Boyle, Elizabeth H., and Sharon E. Preves. 2000. "National Politics as International Process: The Case of Anti-Female-Genital-Cutting Laws." *Law and Society Review* 34(3): 703–737.

Boyle, Elizabeth H., Barbara McMorris, and Mayra Gómez. 2002. "Local Conformity to International Norms: The Case of Female Genital Cutting." *International Sociology* 17: 5–33.

Boyle, Elizabeth H., Fortunata Songora, and Gail Foss. 2001. "International Discourse and Local Politics: Anti-Female-Genital-Cutting Laws in Egypt, Tanzania, and the United States." *Social Problems* 48 (4): 524–544.

Braithwaite, John, and Peter Drahos. 2000. *Global Business Regulation*. Cambridge: Cambridge University Press.

Brand, Arie. 1982. "Against Romanticism: Max Weber and the Historical School of Law." *Australian Journal of Law and Society* 1: 87–100.

Brantingham, Paul J., and Jack M. Kress, eds. 1979. *Structure, Law, and Power: Essays in the Sociology of Law*. Thousand Oaks, CA: Sage Publications.

Braybrooke, E. K. 1961. "The Sociological Jurisprudence of Roscoe Pound." Pp. 57–109 in *Studies in the Sociology of Law*, ed. G. Sawer. Canberra: The Australian National University.

Bredemeier, Harry. 1962. "Law as an Integrative Mechanism." Pp. 73–90 in *Law and Sociology*, ed. W. M. Evan. New York: The Free Press.

Brickey, Stephen, and Elizabeth Comack, eds. 1986. *The Social Basis of Law: Critical Readings in the Sociology of Law*. Ontario, Canada: Garamond Press.

Bridges, George S., and Robert D. Crutchfield. 1988. "Law, Social Standing and Racial Disparities in Imprisonment." *Social Forces* 66 (3): 699–724.

Brinton, Mary C., and Victor Nee, eds. 1998. *The New Institutionalism in Sociology*. New York: Russell Sage Foundation.

Brittan, Arthur. 1981. "The Symbolic Dimension of Law and Social Control." Pp. 167–185 in *Sociological Approaches to Law*, ed. A. Podgórecki and C. J. Whelan. New York: St. Martin's Press.

Brooker, Penny. 1999. "The 'Juridification' of Alternative Dispute Resolution." *Anglo-American Law Review* 28(1): 1–36.

Burns, Stacy Lee, ed. 2005. *Ethnographies of Law and Social Control*. *Sociology of Crime, Law and Deviance*, Vol. 6. Amsterdam: Elsevier.

Burstein, Paul. 1990. "Intergroup Conflict, Law, and the Concept of Labor Market Discrimination." *Sociological Forum* 5(3): 459–476.

Burstein, Paul and Kathleen Monaghan. 1986. "Equal Employment Opportunity and the Mobilization of Law." *Law and Society Review* 20(3): 355–388.

Burton, Steven J. 2000. *The Path of the Law and its Influence: The Legacy of Oliver Wendell Holmes, Jr.* Cambridge: Cambridge University Press.

Cain, Maureen. 1974. "The Main Themes of Marx' and Engels' Sociology of Law." *British Journal of Law and Society* 1(2): 136–148.

Cain, Maureen. 1980. "The Limits of Idealism: Max Weber and the Sociology of Law." *Research in Law and Sociology* 3: 53–83.

Cain, Maureen, and Alan Hunt, eds. 1979. *Marx and Engels on Law*. New York: Academic Press.

Calavita, Kitty. 2005. *Immigrants at the Margins: Law, Race, and Exclusion in Southern Europe*. Cambridge: Cambridge University Press.

Calavita, Kitty, Josephy Dimento, Gilbert Geis, and Gabrio Forti. 1991. "Dam Disasters and Durkheim: An Analysis of the Theme of Repressive and Restitutive Law." *International Journal of the Sociology of Law* 19: 407–426.

Campbell, Anne. 1993. *Men, Women and Aggression*. New York: Basic Books.

Campbell, C. M., and Paul Wiles. 1976. "The Study of Law and Society in Britain." *Law and Society Review* 10(4): 547–578.

Campbell, David. 1986. "Truth Claims and Value-Freedom in the Treatment of Legitimacy: The Case of Weber." *Journal of Law and Society* 13(2): 207–224.

Carlen, Pat, ed. 1976. *The Sociology of Law*. Keele, UK: University of Keele.

Carlin, Jerome E. 1962. *Lawyers on their Own: The Solo Practitioner in an Urban Setting*. New Brunswick, NJ: Rutgers University Press.

Carruthers, Bruce G., and Terence C. Halliday. 1998. *Rescuing Business: The Making of Corporate Bankruptcy Law in England and the United States*. Oxford: Oxford University Press.

Carruthers, Bruce G., and Terence C. Halliday. 2006. "Negotiating Globalization: Global Scripts and Intermediation in the Construction of Asian Insolvency Regimes." *Law and Social Inquiry* 31(3): 521–583.

Cartwright, B. C., and R. D. Schwartz. 1973. "The Invocation of Legal Norms: An Empirical Investigation of Durkheim and Weber." *American Sociological Review* 38(3): 340–354.

Carty, Anthony, and Jane Mair. 1990. "Some Post-Modern Perspectives on Law and Society." *Journal of Law and Society* 17(4): 395–410.

Cefaï, Daniel, and Alain Mahé. 1998. "Échanges rituels de dons, obligation et contrat. Mauss, Davy, Maunier: trois perspectives de sociologie juridique." *L'Année sociologique* 48(1): 209–228.

Chambliss, William J. 1964. "A Sociological Analysis of the Law of Vagrancy." *Social Problems* 12(1): 67–77.

Chambliss, William J. 1973. "Elites and the Creation of Criminal Law." Pp. 430–444 in *Sociological Readings in the Conflict Perspective*, ed. W. J. Chambliss. Reading, MA: Addison-Wesley.

Chambliss, William J. 1999. *Power, Politics, and Crime*. Boulder, CO: Westview Press.

Chambliss, William J., and Robert B. Seidman. 1971. *Law, Order, and Power*. Reading, MA: Addison-Wesley.

Chazel, Francois. 1991. "Emile Durkheim et l'elaboration d'un 'programme de recherche' en sociologie du droit." Pp. 27–38 in *Normes juridiques et régulation sociale*, ed. F. Chazel and J. Commaille. Paris: Librairie Generale de Droit et de Jurisprudence.

Chilton, Ronald J. 1970. "Social Control through Welfare Legislation: The Impact of a State 'Suitable Home Law'." *Law and Society Review* 5(2): 205–224.

Cicourel, Aaron V. 1968. *The Social Organization of Juvenile Justice*. New York: Wiley.

Clarke, A. 1987. "Moral Protest, Status Defense and the Anti-Abortion Campaign." *British Journal of Sociology* 38(2): 235–253.

Clarke, Michael. 1976. "Durkheim's Sociology of Law." *British Journal of Law and Society* 3: 246–255.

Clifford-Vaughan, Michalina, and Margaret Scotford-Morton. 1967. "Legal Norms and Social Order: Petrazycki, Pareto, Durkheim." *British Journal of Sociology* 18: 269–277.

Coates, Rodney D. 2003. "Law and the Cultural Production of Race and Racialized Systems of Oppression." *American Behavioral Scientist* 47 (3): 329–351.

Cochez, Caroline. 2004. *Le Droit dans l'année sociologique (1896–1925): Contribution a l'etude de la place dur droit dans les premiers temps de l'ecole Durkheimienne*. Master's Thesis, Université de Lille, France. Online: edoctorale74.univ-lille2.fr/fileadmin/master_recherche/T_l_ chargement/memoires/justice/ cochezc04.pdf.

Cocks, R. C. J. 1988. *Sir Henry Maine: A Study in Victorian Jurisprudence*. Cambridge, UK: Cambridge University Press.

Cohen, Stanley. 1972. *Folk Devils and Moral Panics*. London: MacGibbon and Kee.

Cohen, Stanley. 1977. "Prisons and the Future of Control Systems: From Concentration to Dispersal." Pp. 217–228 in *Welfare in Action*, ed. M. Fitzgerald et al. London: Routledge & Kegan Paul.

Cohen, Stanley. 1979. "The Punitive City: Notes on the Dispersal of Social Control." *Contemporary Crises* 3(4): 339–363.

Cohen, Stanley. 1985. *Visions of Social Control*. Cambridge, UK: Polity Press.

Cole, Stephen, ed. 2001. *What's Wrong with Sociology?* New Brunswick, NJ: Transaction.

Coleman, James. 1990. *Foundations of Social Theory*. Cambridge, MA: Harvard University Press.

Collins, Hugh. 1982. *Marxism and Law*. Oxford: Clarendon Press.

Collins, Randall. 1975. *Conflict Sociology: Toward an Explanatory Science*. New York: Academic Press.

Collins, Randall. 1994. *Four Sociological Traditions*. New York: Oxford University Press.

Comack, Elizabeth. 2006. "Theoretical Approaches in the Sociology of Law: Theoretical Excursions." Pp. 18–67 in *Locating Law: Race/Class/ Gender/Sexuality Connections*, ed. E. Comack. 2nd edn. Black Point, NS, Canada: Fernwood Publishing.

Cook, K. S., and J. M. Whitmeyer. 1992. "Two Approaches to Social Structure: Exchange Theory and Network Analysis." *Annual Review of Sociology* 18: 109–127.

Coser, Lewis A. 1956. *The Functions of Social Conflict*. Glencoe, IL: The Free Press.

Coser, Lewis A. 1982. "The Notion of Control in Sociological Theory." Pp. 13–22 in *Social Control: Views from the Social Sciences*, ed. J. P. Gibbs. Beverly Hills, CA: Sage.

Cossio, Carlos S. 1952. "Jurisprudence and the Sociology of Law: I & II." *Columbia Law Review* 52(3): 356–381; 52(4): 479–501.

Cotterrell, Roger. 1975. "Direction and Development in Anglo-American Jurisprudence and Sociology of Law." *Anglo-American Law Review* 4: 386–410.

Cotterrell, Roger. 1977. "Durkheim on Legal Development and Social Solidarity." *British Journal of Law and Society* 4(2): 241–252.

Cotterrell, Roger. 1983. "The Sociological Concept of Law." *Journal of Law and Society* 10(2): 241–255.

Cotterrell, Roger. 1986. "Law and Sociology: Notes on the Constitution and Confrontations of Disciplines." *Journal of Law and Society* 13(1): 9–34.

Cotterrell, Roger. 1990. "Sociology of Law in Britain: Its Development and Present Prospects." Pp. 779–803 in *Developing Sociology of Law: A World-Wide Documentary Enquiry*, ed. V. Ferrari. Milan: Dott A. Giuffrè Editore.

Cotterrell, Roger. 1991. "The Durkheimian Tradition in the Sociology of Law." Review essay. *Law and Society Review* 25(4): 923–946.

Cotterrell, Roger. 1992. *The Sociology of Law: An Introduction*. 2nd edn. London: Butterworths.

Cotterrell, Roger. 1994. *Law and Society*. New York: New York University Press.

Cotterrell, Roger. 1999. *Emile Durkheim: Law in a Moral Domain*. Palo Alto, CA: Stanford University Press.

Cotterrell, Roger. 2005. "Durkheim's Loyal Jurist? The Sociolegal Theory of Paul Huvelin." *Ratio Juris* 18(4): 504–518.

Cotterrell, Roger, ed. 2006. *Law in Social Theory*. Burlington, VT: Ashgate.

Cowan, Thomas A. 1968. "Sociological Jurisprudence." Pp. 335–341 in *International Encyclopedia of the Social Sciences*, Vol. VIII, ed. D. L. Sills. New York: Crowell, Collier and Macmillan, Inc.

Crenshaw, Kimberlé, Neil Gotanda, Garry Peller, and Kendall Thomas, eds. 1995. *Critical Race Theory: The Key Writings that Formed the Movement*. New York: New Press.

Crone, Patricia. 1999. "Weber, Islamic Law, and the Rise of Capitalism." Pp. 247–272 in *Max Weber and Islam*, ed. T. E. Huff and W. Schluchter. New Brunswick, NJ: Transaction.

Cunningham, David. 2004. *There's Something Happening Here: The New Left, the Klan, and FBI Counterintelligence*. Berkeley, CA: University of California Press.

Currie, Elliott. 1971. "Sociology of Law: The Unasked Questions." Review Essay. *The Yale Law Journal* 81: 134–147.

Damm, Reinhard. 1976. *Systemtheorie und Recht: Zur Normentheorie Talcott Parsons*. Berlin: Duncker & Humblot.

Davies, Celia. 1983. "Professionals in Bureaucracies: The Conflict Thesis Revisited." Pp. 177–194 in *The Sociology of the Professions*, ed. R. Dingwall and P. Lewis. New York: St. Martin's Press.

Davis, F. James. 1957. "The Treatment of Law in American Sociology." *Sociology and Social Research* 42(2): 99–105.

Davis, F. James. 1962. "Law as a Type of Social Control." Pp. 39–63 in *Society and the Law*, by F. J. Davis et al. New York: The Free Press.

Davis, F. James, Henry H. Foster Jr., C. Ray Jeffrey and E. Eugene Davis. 1962. *Society and the Law*. New York: The Free Press.

Dawson, Myrna, and Sandy Welsh. 2005. "Predicting the Quantity of Law: Single versus Multiple Remedies in Sexual Harassment Cases." *Sociological Quarterly* 46(4): 699–718.

De Espinosa, Emilio L. 1980. "Social and Legal Order in Sociological Functionalism." *Contemporary Crises* 4: 43–76.

Deflem, Mathieu. 1994. "Social Control and the Theory of Communicative Action." *International Journal of the Sociology of Law* 22(4): 355–373.

Deflem, Mathieu. 1995. "Théorie du discours, droit pénal, et criminologie." *Déviance et société* 19(4): 325–338.

Deflem, Mathieu, ed. 1996. *Habermas, Modernity and Law*. London: Sage.

Deflem, Mathieu. 1997. "Surveillance and Criminal Statistics: Historical Foundations of Governmentality." Pp. 149–184 in *Studies in Law, Politics and Society*, Vol. XVII, ed. A. Sarat and S. Silbey. Greenwich, CT: JAI Press.

Deflem, Mathieu. 1998a. "The Boundaries of Abortion Law: Systems Theory from Parsons to Luhmann and Habermas." *Social Forces* 76 (3): 775–818.

Deflem, Mathieu. 1998b. "The Democratic Deficit Revisited: Considering the Politics of Criminal Justice." Pp. 111–117 in *Politique, Police et Justice au Bord du Futur*, ed. Y. Cartuyvels et al. Paris: L'Harmattan.

Deflem, Mathieu. 1999. "Ferdinand Tönnies on Crime and Society: An Unexplored Contribution to Criminological Sociology." *History of the Human Sciences* 12(3): 87–116.

Deflem, Mathieu. 2000. "Bureaucratization and Social Control: Historical Foundations of International Policing." *Law and Society Review* 34(3): 601–640.

Deflem, Mathieu. 2002. *Policing World Society: Historical Foundations of International Police Cooperation*. Oxford: Oxford University Press.

Deflem, Mathieu. 2004. "Social Control and the Policing of Terrorism: Foundations for a Sociology of Counter-Terrorism." *The American Sociologist* 35(2): 75–92.

Deflem, Mathieu. 2006a. "Global Rule of Law or Global Rule of Law Enforcement? International Police Cooperation and Counter-Terrorism." *The Annals of the American Academy of Political and Social Science* 603: 240–251.

Deflem, Mathieu. 2006b. "Jurisprudencia sociológica y sociología del derecho." *Opinión Jurídica* 5(10): 107–119.

Deflem, Mathieu. 2007a. "Legal Profession." Pp. 2583–2584 in *The Blackwell Encyclopedia of Sociology*, ed. G. Ritzer. Oxford: Blackwell Publishing.

Deflem, Mathieu. 2007b. "Sociological Theories of Law." Pp. 1410–1413 in *Encyclopedia of Law and Society: American and Global Perspectives*, ed. D. S. Clark. Thousand Oaks, CA: Sage Publications.

Deflem, Mathieu. 2007c. "Policing." Pp. 970–973 in *Encyclopedia of Globalization*, ed. J. A. Scholte and R. Robertson. New York: Routledge.

Delgado, Richard, and Jean Stefancic, eds. 2000. *Critical Race Theory: The Cutting Edge*. Philadelphia, PA: Temple University Press.

Delgado, Richard, and Jean Stefancic. 2001. *Critical Race Theory: An Introduction*. New York: New York University Press.

Denzin, Norman, K. 1975. "Interaction, Law and Morality: The Contribution of Leon Petrazycki." Pp. 83–105 in *Sociology and Jurisprudence of Leon Petrazycki*, ed. J. Gorecki. Urbana, IL: University of Illinois Press.

Denzin, Norman K. 1986. "Postmodern Social Theory." *Sociological Theory* 4(2): 194–204.

Derrida, Jacques. 1990a. *Limited Inc.* Evanston, IL: Northwestern University Press.

Derrida, Jacques. 1990b. "Force of Law: The Mystical Foundation of Authority." *Cardozo Law Review* 11: 919–1070.

Dezalay, Yves. 1990. "The Big Bang and the Law: The Internationalization and Restructuration of the Legal Field." *Theory, Culture and Society* 7: 279–293.

Dezalay, Yves, and Bryant G. Garth. 1995. "Merchants of Law as Moral Entrepreneurs: Constructing International Justice from the Competition for Transnational Business Disputes." *Law and Society Review* 29(1): 27–64.

Dezalay, Yves, and Bryant G. Garth. 1996. *Dealing in Virtue: International Commercial Arbitration and the Construction of a Transnational Legal Order.* Chicago: University of Chicago Press.

Dezalay, Yves, and Bryant G. Garth. 2002a. *The Internationalization of Palace Wars: Lawyers, Economists, and the Contest to Transform Latin American States.* Chicago: University of Chicago Press.

Dezalay, Yves, and Bryant G. Garth, eds. 2002b. *Global Prescriptions: The Production, Exportation, and Importation of a New Legal Orthodoxy.* Ann Arbor, MI: University of Michigan Press.

Didry, Claude. 2000. "La Réforme des groupements professionnels comme expression de la conception Durkheimienne de l'état." *Revue française de sociologie* 41(3): 513–538.

DiMaggio, Paul J., and Walter W. Powell. 1991. "Introduction." Pp. 1–38 in *The New Institutionalism in Organizational Analysis*, ed. W. W. Powell and P. J. DiMaggio. Chicago: University of Chicago Press.

Dingwall, Robert. 1998. "Empowerment or Enforcement? Some Questions about Power and Control in Divorce Mediation." Pp. 150–167 in *Divorce Mediation and the Legal Process: British Practice and International Experience*, ed. R. Dingwall and J. M. Eekelaar. Oxford: Oxford University Press.

Dingwall, Robert. 1999. "Professions and Social Order in a Global Society." *International Review of Sociology* 9(1): 31–140.

Dingwall, Robert. 2000. "Language, Law, and Power: Ethnomethodology, Conversation Analysis, and the Politics of Law and Society Studies." Review Essay. *Law and Social Inquiry* 25(3): 885–911.

Dingwall, Robert. 2002. "Ethnomethodology and Law." Pp. 227–244 in *An Introduction to Law and Social Theory*, ed. R. Banakar and M. Travers. Portland, OR: Hart Publishing.

Dingwall, Robert. 2007. "Law, Sociology of." Pp. 2560–2564 in *The Blackwell Encyclopedia of Sociology*, ed. G. Ritzer. Oxford: Blackwell Publishing.

Dingwall, Robert, and J. M. Eekelaar. 1988. "Families and the State: An Historical Perspective on the Public Regulation of Private Conduct." *Law and Policy* 10(4): 341–361.

Dingwall, Robert, and Philip Lewis, eds. 1983. *The Sociology of the Professions: Lawyers, Doctors, and Others*. New York: St. Martin's Press.

Dixon, Jo. 1995. "The Nexus of Sex, Spousal Violence, and the State." Review essay. *Law and Society Review* 29(2): 359–376.

Dixon, Jo, and Carroll Seron. 1995. "Stratification in the Legal Profession: Sex, Sector, and Salary." *Law and Society Review* 29(3): 381–412.

Dobbin, Frank, and Erin L. Kelly. 2007. "How to Stop Harassment: Professional Construction of Legal Compliance in Organizations." *American Journal of Sociology* 112(4): 1203–1243.

Dobbin, Frank, John R. Sutton, John W. Meyer and Richard Scott. 1993. "Equal Opportunity Law and the Construction of Internal Labor Markets." *American Journal of Sociology* 99(2): 396–427.

Donohue, John J. III. 1988. "Law and Economics: The Road Not Taken." *Law and Society Review* 22(5): 903–926.

Dowd, Nancy E., and Michelle S. Jacobs, eds. 2003. *Feminist Legal Theory: An Anti-Essentialist Reader*. New York: New York University Press.

Doyle, Daniel P., and David F. Luckenbill. 1991. "Mobilizing Law in Response to Collective Problems: A Test of Black's Theory of Law." *Law and Society Review* 25(1): 103–116.

Drew, Paul. 1992. "Contested Evidence in Courtroom Cross-Examination: The Case of a Trial for Rape." Pp. 470–520 in *Talk at Work: Interaction in Institutional Settings*, ed. P. Drew and J. Heritage. New York: Cambridge University Press.

Durkheim, Emile. (1893a) 1967. *De la division du travail social*. Paris: Les Presses Universitaires de France. 8th edn. Online: classiques.uqac.ca/classiques/Durkheim_emile/division_du_travail/division_travail.html.

Durkheim, Emile. (1893b) 1984. *The Division of Labor in Society*. New York: The Free Press.

Durkheim, Emile. (1895) 1982. *The Rules of Sociological Method*. New York: The Free Press.

Durkheim, Emile. (1897) 1951. *Suicide: A Study in Sociology*. New York: The Free Press.

Durkheim, Emile. (1900a) 1922. *Leçons de sociologie: Physique des mœurs et du droit*. Paris: Les Presses Universitaires de France. Online: classiques.uqac.ca/classiques/Durkheim_emile/lecons_de_sociologie/lecons_de_sociologie.html.

Durkheim, Emile. (1900b) 1992. *Professional Ethics and Civic Morals.* London: Routledge.

Durkheim, Emile. 1901a. "Deux lois de l'evolution pénale." *Année sociologique* 4: 65–95. Online: classiques.uqac.ca/classiques/Durkheim_ emile/annee_sociologique/an_socio_3/evolution_penale.html.

Durkheim, Emile. (1901b) 1983. "The Evolution of Punishment." Pp. 102–132 in *Durkheim and the Law*, ed. S. Lukes and A. Scull. New York: St. Martin's Press.

Durkheim, Emile. (1912) 1965. *The Elementary Forms of the Religious Life.* New York: The Free Press.

Dwyer, Peter. 2004. "Creeping Conditionality in the UK: From Welfare Rights to Conditional Entitlements?" *Canadian Journal of Sociology* 29(2): 265–287.

Earl, Jennifer, Darah A. Soule, and John D. McCarthy. 2003. "Protest under Fire? Explaining the Policing of Protest." *American Sociological Review* 68(4): 581–606.

Easton, Susan, ed. 2008. *Marx and Law.* Aldershot, UK: Ashgate.

Edelman, Lauren B. 1990. "Legal Environments and Organizational Governance: The Expansion of Due Process in the American Workplace." *American Journal of Sociology* 95(6): 1401–1440.

Edelman, Lauren B. 1992. "Legal Ambiguity and Symbolic Structures: Organizational Mediation of Civil Rights Law." *American Journal of Sociology* 97(6): 1531–1576.

Edelman, Lauren B. 1996. "Introduction to Symposium on the Law and the New Institutionalism." *Studies in Law, Politics, and Society* 15(1): 3–7.

Edelman, Lauren B. 2002. "Legality and the Endogeneity of Law." Pp. 187–202 in *Legality and Community: On the Intellectual Legacy of Philip Selznick*, ed. R. A. Kagan, M. Krygier, and K. Winston. Lanham, MD: Rowman and Littlefield.

Edelman, Lauren B. 2004a. "Rivers of Law and Contested Terrain: A Law and Society Approach to Economic Rationality." *Law and Society Review* 38(2): 181–197.

Edelman, Lauren B. 2004b. "The Legal Lives of Private Organizations." Pp. 231–252 in *The Blackwell Companion to Law and Society*, ed. A. Sarat. Malden, MA: Blackwell.

Edelman, Lauren B., and Mark C. Suchman. 1997. "The Legal Environments of Organizations." *Annual Review of Sociology* 23: 479–515.

Edelman, Lauren B., and Mark C. Suchman. 1999. "When the 'Haves' Hold Court: Speculations on the Organizational Internalization of Law." *Law and Society Review* 33(4): 941–991.

Edelman, Lauren B., and Robin Stryker. 2005. "A Sociological Approach to Law and the Economy." Pp. 527–551 in *The Handbook of Economic*

Sociology, ed. N. Smelser and R. Swedberg. Princeton, NJ: Princeton University Press.

Edelman, Lauren B., Howard S. Erlanger, and John Lande. 1993. "Internal Dispute Resolution: The Transformation of Civil Rights in the Workplace." *Law and Society Review* 27(3): 497–534.

Edelman, Lauren B., Christopher Uggen, and Howard S. Erlanger. 1999. "The Endogeneity of Legal Regulation: Grievance Procedures as Rational Myth." *American Journal of Sociology* 105(2): 406–454.

Edwards, Mark Evan. 1996. "Pregnancy Discrimination Litigation: Legal Erosion of Capitalist Ideology under Equal Employment Opportunity Law." *Social Forces* 75(1): 247–268.

Ehrlich, Eugen. (1913a) 1967. *Grundlegung der Soziologie des Rechts*. 3rd edn. Berlin: Duncker & Humblot.

Ehrlich, Eugen. (1913b) 1962. *Fundamental Principles of the Sociology of Law*. New York: Russell & Russell.

Ehrlich, Eugen. 1916. "Montesquieu and Sociological Jurisprudence." *Harvard Law Review* 29(6): 582–600.

Ehrlich, Eugen. 1922. "The Sociology of Law." *Harvard Law Review* 36 (2): 130–145.

Ellickson, Robert C. 1991. *Order without Law: How Neighbors Settle Disputes*. Cambridge, MA: Harvard University Press.

Ellickson, Robert C. 2001. "The Evolution of Social Norms: A Perspective from the Legal Academy." Pp. 35–75 in *Social Norms*, ed. M. Hechter and K. Opp. New York: Russell Sage Foundation.

Emerson, Richard M. 1976. "Social Exchange Theory." *Annual Review of Sociology* 2: 335–362.

Engen, Rodney L., and Randy R. Gainey. 2000. "Modeling the Effects of Legally Relevant and Extralegal Factors under Sentencing Guidelines: The Rules have Changed." *Criminology* 38(4): 1207–1230.

Engen, Rodney L., and Sara Steen. 2000. "The Power to Punish: Discretion and Sentencing Reform in the War on Drugs." *American Journal of Sociology* 105(5): 1357–1395.

Engen, Rodney L., Randy R. Gainey, Robert D. Crutchfield, and Joseph G. Weis. 2002. "Discretion and Disparity under Sentencing Guidelines: The Role of Departures and Structured Sentencing Alternatives." *Criminology* 41(1): 99–130.

Ermakoff, Ivan. 1997. "Prelates and Princes: Aristocratic Marriages, Canon Law Prohibitions, and Shifts in Norms and Patterns of Domination in the Central Middle Ages." *American Sociological Review* 62(3): 405–422.

Evan, William M. 1959. "Power, Bargaining, and Law: A Preliminary Analysis of Labor Arbitration Cases." *Social Problems* 7(1): 4–15.

Evan, William M. 1960. "Value Conflicts in the Law of Evidence." *The American Behavioral Scientist* 4(3): 23–26.

Evan, William M. 1961. "Organization Man and Due Process of Law." *American Sociological Review* 26(4): 540–547.

Evan, William M., ed. 1962a. *Law and Sociology: Exploratory Essays.* Glencoe, IL: Free Press.

Evan, William M. 1962b. "Due Process of Law in Military and Industrial Organizations." *Administrative Science Quarterly* 7(2): 187–207.

Evan, William M. 1965. "Law as an Instrument of Social Change." Pp. 285–293 in *Applied Sociology: Opportunities and Problems*, ed. A. W. Gouldner and S. M. Miller. New York: Free Press.

Evan, William M., ed. 1980. *The Sociology of Law: A Social-Structural Perspective.* New York: Free Press.

Evan, William M. 1990. *Social Structure and Law: Theoretical and Empirical Perspectives.* Thousand Oaks, CA: Sage Publications.

Evan, William M. 1991. "Law and Society." Pp. 1075–1086 in *Encyclopedia of Sociology*, ed. E. F. Borgatta and M. L. Borgatta. New York: Macmillan.

Evan, William M., and Ezra Levin. 1966. "Status-Set and Role-Set Conflicts of the Stockbroker: A Problem in the Sociology of Law." *Social Forces* 45(1): 73–83.

Ewick, Patricia. 2004. "Consciousness and Ideology." Pp. 80–94 in *The Blackwell Companion to Law and Society*, ed. A. Sarat. Malden, MA: Blackwell.

Ewick, Patricia, and Susan S. Silbey. 1995. "Subversive Stories and Hegemonic Tales: Toward a Sociology of Narrative." *Law and Society Review* 29(2): 197–226.

Ewick, Patricia, and Susan S. Silbey. 1998. *The Common Place of Law: Stories from Everyday Life.* Chicago: University of Chicago Press.

Ewick, Patricia, and Susan S. Silbey. 2003. "Subversive Stories and Hegemonic Tales: Toward a Sociology of Narrative." *American Journal of Sociology* 108(6): 1328–1372.

Ewing, Sally. 1987. "Formal Justice and the Spirit of Capitalism: Max Weber's Sociology of Law." *Law and Society Review* 21(3): 487–512.

Featherstone, Richard. 2005. *Narratives from the 1971 Attica Prison Riots: Toward a New Theory of Correctional Disturbances.* Lewiston, NY: The Edwin Mellen Press.

Feeley, Malcolm M. 1979. *The Process is the Punishment: Handling Cases in a Lower Criminal Court.* New York: Russell Sage Foundation.

Fegan, Eileen V., and Rachel Rebouche. 2003. "Northern Ireland's Abortion Law: The Morality of Silence and the Censure of Agency." *Feminist Legal Studies* 11(3): 221–254.

Feldman, Stephen M. 1991. "An Interpretation of Max Weber's Theory of Law: Metaphysics, Economics, and the Iron Cage of Constitutional Law." *Law and Social Inquiry* 16(2): 205–248.

Feldman, Stephen M. 1996 "The Politics of Postmodern Jurisprudence." *Michigan Law Review* 95(1): 166–202.

Felson, Richard B. 2006. "Is Violence against Women about Women or about Violence?" *Contexts* 5(2): 21–25.

Ferrari, Vincenzo, ed. 1990. *Developing a Sociology of Law: A World-Wide Documentary Enquiry*. Milan: Dott A. Giuffrè Editore.

Ferrari, Vincenzo. 1989. "Sociology of Law: A Theoretical Introduction." Pp. 7–35 in *Two Lectures on the Sociology of Law*, by V. Ferrari and P. Uusitalo. Helsinki, Finland: University of Helsinki.

Ferrari, Vincenzo and Paola Ronfani. 2001. "A Deeply Rooted Scientific Discipline: Origins and Development of Sociology of Law in Italy." *The American Sociologist* 32(2): 61–77.

Ferrell, Jeff. 1993. *Crimes of Style: Urban Graffiti and the Politics of Criminality*. New York: Garland.

Fielding, Nigel G. 2002. "Theorizing Community Policing." *British Journal of Criminology* 42(1): 147–163.

Fielding, Nigel G. 2005. "Concepts and Theory in Community Policing." *Howard Journal of Criminal Justice* 44(5): 460–472.

Fine, Robert. 2002. "Marxism and the Social Theory of Law." Pp. 101–117 in *An Introduction to Law and Social Theory*, ed. R. Banakar and M. Travers. Portland, OR: Hart Publishing.

Fitzpatrick, Peter, and Alan Hunt, eds. 1987. *Critical Legal Studies*. Oxford: Basil Blackwell.

Fletcher, Ruth. 2002. "Feminist Legal Theory." Pp. 135–154 in *An Introduction to Law and Social Theory*, ed. R. Banakar and M. Travers. Portland, OR: Hart Publishing.

Flood, John. 2002. "Globalisation and Law." Pp. 311–328 in *An Introduction to Law and Social Theory*, ed. R. Banakar and M. Travers. Portland, OR: Hart Publishing.

Foucault, Michel. (1975) 1977. *Discipline and Punish: The Birth of the Prison*. New York: Pantheon.

Foucault, Michel. (1978a) 1991. "Governmentality." Pp. 87–104 in *The Foucault Effect*, ed. G. Burchell, C. Gordon, and P. Miller. Chicago: University of Chicago Press.

Foucault, Michel. (1978b) 1989. "Sécurité, territoire, et populations." Pp. 99–106 in his *Résumé des cours, 1970–1982*. Paris: Julliard.

Foucault, Michel. 1980. *Power/Knowledge: Selected Interviews and Other Writings*, ed. C. Gordon. New York: Pantheon.

Foucault, Michel. 1981. "*Omnes et Singulatim*: Towards a Criticism of 'Political Reason'." Pp. 223–254 in *The Tanner Lectures on Human Values*, Vol. II, ed. S. M. McMurrin. Salt Lake City: University of Utah Press.

Frank, Nancy. 1983. "From Criminal to Civil Penalties in the History of Health and Safety Laws." *Social Problems* 30(5): 532–544.

Freeman, Michael, ed. 2006. *Law and Sociology*. Oxford: Oxford University Press.

Freidson, Eliot. 1984. "The Changing Nature of Professional Control." *Annual Review of Sociology* 10: 1–20.

Freidson, Eliot. 1986. *Professional Powers: A Study of the Institutionalization of Formal Knowledge*. Chicago: University of Chicago Press.

Freidson, Eliot. 2001. *Professionalism, the Third Logic: On the Practice of Knowledge*. Chicago: University of Chicago Press.

Friedman, Lawrence M. 1976. *Law and Society: An Introduction*. Englewood Cliffs, NJ: Prentice-Hall.

Friedrichs, David O. 2001. *Law in our Lives: An Introduction*. Los Angeles: Roxbury.

Frymer, Paul, and John D. Skrentny. 2004. "The Rise of Instrumental Affirmative Action: Law and the New Significance of Race in America." *Connecticut Law Review* 36: 677–723.

Fuchs, Stephan, and Steven Ward. 1994. "What is Deconstruction, and Where and When Does it Take Place? Making Facts in Science, Building Cases in Law." *American Sociological Review* 59(4): 481–500.

Fuller, Lon L. 1964. *The Morality of Law*. New Haven, CT: Yale University Press.

Fuller, Lon L. 1968. "Some Unexplored Social Dimensions of the Law." Pp. 57–70 in *The Path of the Law from 1967*, ed. A. E. Sutherland. Cambridge, MA: Harvard University Press.

Fuszara, Malgorzata. 1990. "Sociology of Law in Poland." *Zeitschrift für Rechtssoziologie* 11(1): 42–50.

Galanter, Marc. 1974. "Why the 'Haves' Come Out Ahead: Speculations on the Limits of Legal Change." *Law and Society Review* 9(1): 95–160.

Galanter, Marc. 2004. "The Vanishing Trial: An Examination of Trials and Related Matters in Federal and State Courts." *Journal of Empirical Legal Studies* 1(3): 459–570.

Galanter, Marc, and Thomas Palay. 1991. *Tournament of Lawyers: The Transformation of the Big Law Firm*. Chicago: University of Chicago Press.

Galligan, Dennis J. 2007. *Law in Modern Society*. Oxford: Oxford University Press.

Galliher, John F., and John R. Cross. 1983. *Morals Legislation without Morality: The Case of Nevada.* New Brunswick, NJ: Rutgers University Press.

Garcia-Vellegas, Mauricio. 2006. "Comparative Sociology of Law: Legal Fields, Legal Scholarships, and Social Sciences in Europe and the United States." *Law and Social Inquiry* 31(2): 343–382.

Garfinkel, Harold. 1967. *Studies in Ethnomethodology.* Englewood Cliffs, NJ: Prentice-Hall.

Garland, David. 1983. "Durkheim's Theory of Punishment: A Critique." Pp. 37–61 in *The Power to Punish: Contemporary Penality and Social Analysis*, ed. D. Garland and P. Young. London: Heinemann Educational Books.

Garland, David. 1985. *Punishment and Welfare: A History of Penal Strategies.* Brookfield, VT: Gower.

Garland, David. 1991a. "Sociological Perspectives on Punishment." *Crime and Justice* 14: 115–165.

Garland, David. 1991b. "Punishment and Culture: The Symbolic Dimensions of Criminal Justice." Pp. 191–222 in *Studies in Law, Politics and Society*, Vol. XI, ed. A. Sarat and S. Silbey. Greenwich, CT: JAI Press.

Garland, David. 1997. " 'Governmentality' and the Problem of Crime: Foucault, Criminology, Sociology." *Theoretical Criminology* 1(2): 173–214.

Garland, David. 2002. *The Culture of Control: Crime and Social Order in Contemporary Society.* Chicago: University of Chicago Press.

Garland, David. 2006. "Concepts of Culture in the Sociology of Punishment." *Theoretical Criminology* 10(4): 419–447.

Garth, Bryant, and Joyce Sterling. 1998. "From Legal Realism to Law and Society: Reshaping Law for the Last Stages of the Social Activist State." *Law and Society Review* 32(2): 409–472.

Gates, E. Nathaniel, ed. 1997. *The Judicial Isolation of the "Racially" Oppressed.* New York: Garland.

Geiger, Theodor. 1920. *Das uneheliche Kind und seine Mutter im Recht des neuen Staates: Ein Versuch auf der Basis kritischer Rechtsvergleichung.* Münich-Berlin-Leipzig: Schweitzer.

Geiger, Theodor. (1946) 1979. *Über Moral und Recht.* Berlin: Duncker & Humblot.

Geiger, Theodor. (1947) 1964. *Vorstudien zu einer Soziologie des Rechts.* Neuwied am Rhein: Luchterhand.

Geiger, Theodor. 1969. *On Social Order and Mass Society.* Chicago: University of Chicago Press.

Geis, Gilbert. 1959. "Sociology, Criminology, and Criminal Law." *Social Problems* 7(1): 40–47.

Gephart, Werner. 1993. *Gesellschaftstheorie und Recht: Das Recht im soziologischen Diskurs der Moderne.* Frankfurt: Suhrkamp.

Gessner, Volkmar. 1995. "Global Approaches in the Sociology of Law: Problems and Challenges." *Journal of Law and Society* 22(1): 85–96.

Gibbs, Jack P. 1966. "The Sociology of Law and Normative Phenomena." *American Sociological Review* 31(3): 315–325.

Gibbs, Jack P. 1968. "Definitions of Law and Empirical Questions." *Law and Society Review* 2(3): 429–446.

Gibbs, Jack P. 2003. "A Formal Restatement of Durkheim's 'Division of Labor' Theory." *Sociological Theory* 21(2): 103–127.

Gillin, John Lewis. 1929. "New Developments in the Departments of Sociology in Relation to Courses in the Law School." *Annals of the American Academy of Political and Social Science* 145: 125–129.

Gilliom, John. 1994. *Surveillance, Privacy, and the Law: Employee Drug Testing and the Politics of Social Control.* Ann Arbor, MI: University of Michigan Press.

Goldberg, Chad A. 2001. "Social Citizenship and a Reconstructed Tocqueville." *American Sociological Review* 66(2): 289–315.

Goode, Erich. 1996. *Social Deviance.* Boston: Allyn and Bacon.

Goode, Erich, and Nachman Ben-Yehuda. 1994. *Moral Panics: The Social Construction of Deviance.* Cambridge, MA: Blackwell.

Gordon, Robert W. 1986. "Critical Legal Studies." *Legal Studies Forum* 10 (3): 335–340.

Gordon, Robert W. 1992. *The Legacy of Oliver Wendell Holmes, Jr.* Stanford, CA: Stanford University Press.

Gorecki, Jan, ed. 1975a. *Sociology and Jurisprudence of Leon Petrazycki.* Urbana, IL: University of Illinois Press.

Gorecki, Jan. 1975b. "Leon Petrazycki." Pp. 1–15 in *Sociology and Jurisprudence of Leon Petrazycki*, ed. J. Gorecki. Urbana, IL: University of Illinois Press.

Gorman, Elizabeth H. 1999. "Moving away from 'Up or Out': Determinants of Permanent Employment in Law Firms." *Law and Society Review* 33 (3): 637–666.

Gorman, Elizabeth H. 2005. "Gender Stereotypes, Same-Gender Preferences, and Organizational Variation in the Hiring of Women: Evidence from Law Firms." *American Sociological Review* 70: 702–728.

Gorman, Elizabeth H. 2006. "Work Uncertainty and the Promotion of Professional Women: The Case of Law Firm Partnership." *Social Forces* 85(2): 865–888.

Gottfredson, Michael, and Michael J. Hindelang. 1979a. "A Study of the Behavior of Law." *American Sociological Review* 44(1): 3–18.

Gottfredson, Michael, and Michael J. Hindelang. 1979b. "Theory and Research in the Sociology of Law." *American Sociological Review* 44 (1): 27–37.

Gould, Mark. 1993. "Legitimation and Justification: The Logic of Moral and Contractual Solidarity in Weber and Durkheim." Pp. 205–225 in *Current Perspectives in Social Theory*, Vol. XIII, ed. B. Agger. Greenwich, CT: JAI Press.

Gouldner, Alvin W. 1970. *The Coming Crisis of Western Sociology*. New York: Basic Books.

Grace, Clive and Philip Wilkinson. 1978. *Sociological Inquiry and Legal Phenomena*. New York: St. Martin's Press.

Grana, Sheryl J., Jane C. Ollenburger and Mark Nicholas. 2002. *The Social Context of Law*. Upper Saddle River, NJ: Prentice Hall.

Grattet, Ryken, Valerie Jenness, and Theodore R. Curry. 1998. "The Homogenization and Differentiation of Hate Crime Law in the United States, 1978 to 1995: Innovation and Diffusion in the Criminalization of Bigotry." *American Sociological Review* 63(2): 286–307.

Grazin, Igor. 2004. "On Myth, Considered as a Method for Legal Thought." *Law and Critique* 15(2): 159–181.

Greatbatch, David, and Robert Dingwall. 1994. "Divorce Mediation: The Virtues of Formality?" Pp. 391–399 in *Oxford Readings in Socio-Legal Studies: Family Law*, ed. J. M. Eekelaar and M. Maclean. Oxford: Oxford University Press.

Greatbatch, David, and Robert Dingwall. 1997. "Argumentative Talk in Divorce Mediation Sessions." *American Sociological Review* 62(1): 151–170.

Greenberg, David F. 1983. "Donald Black's Sociology of Law: A Critique." *Law and Society Review* 17(2): 337–368.

Griffiths, Anne. 2002. "Legal Pluralism." Pp. 289–310 in *An Introduction to Law and Social Theory*, ed. R. Banakar and M. Travers. Portland, OR: Hart Publishing.

Griffiths, John. 1995. "Legal Pluralism and the Theory of Legislation, with Special Reference to the Regulation of Euthanasia." Pp. 201–234 in *Legal Polycentricity: Consequences of Pluralism in Law*, ed. H. Petersen and H. Zahle. Aldershot, UK: Dartmouth.

Griffiths, John. 1998. "The Slippery Slope: Are the Dutch Sliding Down or Are They Clambering Up?" Pp. 93–104 in *Asking to Die: Inside the Dutch Debate about Euthanasia*, ed. D. C. Thomasma, et al. Dordrecht, The Netherlands: Kluwer Academic.

Griffiths, John. 1999. "Legal Knowledge and the Social Working of Law: The Case of Euthanasia." Pp. 81–108 in *Semiotics and Legislation:*

Jurisprudential, Institutional and Sociological Perspectives, ed. H. van Schooten. Liverpool, UK: Deborah Charles Publications.

Griffiths, John. 2006. "The Idea of Sociology of Law and its Relation to Law and to Sociology." Pp. 49–68 in *Law and Sociology*, ed. M. Freeman. Oxford: Oxford University Press.

Griffiths, John, Heleen Weyers, and Alex Blood. 1998. *Euthanasia and Law in the Netherlands*. Amsterdam: Amsterdam University Press.

Grodnick, Stephen. 2005. "Rediscovering Radical Democracy in Habermas's *Between Facts and Norms*." *Constellations* 12(3): 392–408.

Guibentif, Pierre. 2002. "The Sociology of Law as a Sub-discipline of Sociology." *Portuguese Journal of Social Science* 1(3): 175–184.

Gurvitch, Georges. 1940. *Éléments de sociologie juridique*. Paris: Éditions Aubier Montaigne.

Gurvitch, Georges. 1941a. "Major Problems of the Sociology of Law." *Journal of Social Philosophy* 6(3): 197–215.

Gurvitch, Georges. 1941b. "The Problem of Social Law." *Ethics* 52(1): 17–40.

Gurvitch, Georges. 1942. *Sociology of Law*. New York: Philosophical Library.

Gusfield, Joseph R. 1963. *Symbolic Crusade: Status Politics and the American Temperance Movement*. Urbana, IL: University of Illinois Press.

Habermas, Jürgen. (1981a) 1988. *Theorie des kommunikativen Handelns*. 2 vols. Frankfurt: Suhrkamp.

Habermas, Jürgen. (1981b) 1984. *The Theory of Communicative Action Volume 1: Reason and the Rationalization of Society*. Boston, MA: Beacon Press.

Habermas, Jürgen. (1981c) 1987. *The Theory of Communicative Action Volume 2: System and Lifeworld: A Critique of Functionalist Reason*. Boston, MA: Beacon Press.

Habermas, Jürgen. 1983a. *Moralbewußtsein und kommunikatives Handeln*. Frankfurt: Suhrkamp.

Habermas, Jürgen. (1983b) 1992. *Moral Consciousness and Communicative Action*. Cambridge, MA: The MIT Press.

Habermas, Jürgen. 1988. "Law and Morality." Pp. 215–279 in *The Tanner Lectures on Human Values*, ed. S. M. McMurrin. Salt Lake City: University of Utah Press.

Habermas, Jürgen. 1990. "Remarks on the Discussion." *Theory, Culture and Society* 7: 127–32.

Habermas, Jürgen. (1991) 1993. *Justification and Application: Remarks on Discourse Ethics*. Cambridge, MA: The MIT Press.

Habermas, Jürgen. 1992a. *Faktizität und Geltung*. Frankfurt: Suhrkamp.

Habermas, Jürgen. (1992b) 1996. *Between Facts and Norms*. Cambridge, MA: The MIT Press.

Habermas, Jürgen. 1995. "On the Internal Relation between the Rule of Law and Democracy." *European Journal of Philosophy* 3: 12–20.

Hagan, John. 1980. "The Legislation of Crime and Delinquency: A Review of Theory, Method, and Research." *Law and Society Review* 14(3): 603–628.

Hagan, John. 1990. "The Gender Stratification of Income Inequality Among Lawyers." *Social Forces* 68(3): 835–855.

Hagan, John. 2003. *Justice in the Balkans: Prosecuting War Crimes in the Hague Tribunal*. Chicago: University of Chicago Press.

Hagan, John, and Scott Greer. 2002. "Making War Criminal." *Criminology* 40(2): 231–264.

Hagan, John, and Fiona M. Kay. 1995. *Gender in Practice: A Study of Lawyers' Lives*. New York: Oxford University Press.

Hagan, John, and Fiona M. Kay. 2007. "Even Lawyers Get the Blues: Gender, Depression, and Job Satisfaction in Legal Practice." *Law and Society Review* 41(1): 51–78.

Hagan, John, and Sanja Kutnjak Ivkovic. 2006. "War Crimes, Democracy, and the Rule of Law in Belgrade, the Former Yugoslavia, and Beyond." *The Annals of the American Academy of Political and Social Science* 605: 130–151.

Hagan, John and Jeffrey Leon. 1977. "Rediscovering Delinquency: Social History, Political Ideology and the Sociology of Law." *American Sociological Review* 42(4): 587–598.

Hagan, John, and Ron Levi. 2004. "Social Skill, the Milosevic Indictment, and the Rebirth of International Criminal Justice." *European Journal of Criminology* 1(4): 445–475.

Hagan, John, and Ron Levi. 2005. "Crimes of War and the Force of Law." *Social Forces* 83(4): 1499–1534.

Hagan, John, Heather Schoenfeld, and Alberto Palloni. 2006. "The Science of Human Rights, War Crimes, and Humanitarian Emergencies." *Annual Review of Sociology* 32: 329–349.

Hagan, John, Marjorie Zatz, Bruce Arnold, and Fiona M. Kay. 1991. "Cultural Capital, Gender, and the Structural Transformation of Legal Practice." *Law and Society Review* 25(2): 239–262.

Hall, Stuart, Charles Critcher, Tony Jefferson, John Clarke, and Robert Brian. 1978. *Policing the Crisis: Mugging, the State, and Law and Order*. London: Macmillan.

Halliday, Terence C. 1983. "Professions, Class and Capitalism." *European Journal of Sociology* 24(2): 321–346.

Halliday, Terence C. 1985. "Knowledge Mandates: Collective Influence by Scientific, Normative and Syncretic Professions." *British Journal of Sociology* 36: 421–47.

Halliday, Terence C. 1986. "Six Score Years and Ten: Demographic Transitions in the American Legal Profession, 1850–1980." *Law and Society Review* 20(1): 53–78.

Halliday, Terence C. 1987. *Beyond Monopoly: Lawyers, State Crises and Professional Empowerment.* Chicago: University of Chicago Press.

Halliday, Terence C., and Bruce G. Carruthers. 2007. "The Recursivity of Law: Global Norm-Making and National Law-Making in the Globalization of Corporate Insolvency Regimes." *American Journal of Sociology* 112(4): 1135–1202.

Halliday, Terence C., and Pavel Osinsky. 2006. "Globalization of Law." *Annual Review of Sociology* 32: 447–470.

Hawkins, Keith. 2003. *Law as Last Resort: Prosecution Decision-Making in a Regulatory Agency.* Oxford: Oxford University Press.

Hechter, Michael, and Satoshi Kanazawa. 1997. "Sociological Rational Choice Theory." *Annual Review of Sociology* 23: 191–214.

Hedström, Peter, and Richard Swedberg. 1996. "Rational Choice, Empirical Research, and the Sociological Tradition." *European Sociological Review* 12(2): 127–146.

Heidegren, Carl-Goran. 1997. "Transcendental Theory of Society, Anthropology and the Sociology of Law: Helmut Schelsky – An Almost Forgotten Sociologist." *Acta Sociologica* 40(3): 279–290.

Heimer, Carol A. 1999. "Competing Institutions: Law, Medicine, and Family in Neonatal Intensive Care." *Law and Society Review* 33(1): 17–66.

Heimer, Carol A. 2001. "Law: New Institutionalism." Pp. 8534–8538 in *International Encyclopedia of the Social and Behavioral Sciences*, ed. N. J. Smelser and P. B. Bates. Amsterdam: Elsevier.

Heimer, Carol A., and Lisa R. Staffen. 1998. *For the Sake of the Children: The Social Organization of Responsibility in the Hospital and the Home.* Chicago: University of Chicago Press.

Heinz, John P., and Edward O. Laumann. 1982. *Chicago Lawyers: The Social Structure of the Bar.* New York: Russell Sage Foundation.

Heinz, John P., Edward O. Laumann, Robert L. Nelson, and Ethan Michelson. 1998. "The Changing Character of Lawyers' Work: Chicago in 1975 and 1995." *Law and Society Review* 32(4): 751–75.

Heinz, John P., Robert L. Nelson, and Edward O. Laumann. 2001. "The Scale of Justice: Observations on the Transformation of Urban Law Practice." *Annual Review of Sociology* 27(1): 337–62.

Heinz, John P., Nelson, Robert L., Sandefur, Rebecca L., and Edward O. Laumann. 2005. *Urban Lawyers: The New Social Structure of the Bar*. Chicago: University of Chicago Press.

Hembroff, Larry A. 1987. "The Seriousness of Acts and Social Contexts: A Test of Black's Theory of the Behavior of Law." *American Journal of Sociology* 93(2): 322–347.

Henry, Stuart. 1983. *Private Justice: Towards Integrated Theorising in the Sociology of Law*. London: Routledge & Kegan Paul.

Henry, Stuart, and Dragan Milovanovic. 1996. *Constitutive Criminology: Beyond Postmodernism*. London: Sage.

Henry, Stuart, and Dragan Milovanovic, eds. 1999. *Constitutive Criminology at Work: Applications to Crime and Justice*. New York: State University of New York Press.

Hiday, Virginia A. 1983. "Sociology of Mental Health Law." *Sociology and Social Research* 67(2): 111–128.

Hirst, Paul Q. 1972. "Marx and Engels on Law, Crime, and Morality." *Economy and Society* 1(1): 28–56.

Hirst, Paul Q. 1986. *Law, Socialism, and Democracy*. London: Allen & Unwin.

Hoekema, Andre Jan. 1985. "Dutch Trends in the Sociology of Law in the Past Two Decades." *The Netherlands Journal of Sociology* 2(1): 32–49.

Hoffmann, Elizabeth A. 2003. "Legal Consciousness and Dispute Resolution: Different Disputing Behavior at Two Similar Taxicab Companies." *Law and Social Inquiry* 28(3): 691–716.

Hoffmann, Elizabeth A. 2005. "Dispute Resolution in a Worker Cooperative: Formal Procedures and Procedural Justice." *Law and Society Review* 39: 51–82.

Hoffmann, Elizabeth A. 2006. "Exit and Voice: Job Loyalty and Dispute Resolution Choices." *Social Forces* 84(4): 2313–2330.

Hollinger, Richard C., and Lonn Lanza-Kaduce. 1988. "The Process of Criminalization: The Case of Computer Crime Laws." *Criminology* 26 (1): 101–126.

Holmes, Oliver Wendell. (1881) 1923. *The Common Law*. Boston: Little, Brown, and Company.

Holmes, Oliver Wendell. 1897. "The Path of the Law." *Harvard Law Review* 110(5): 991–1009.

Holmes, Oliver Wendell. 1899. "Law in Science and Science in Law." *Harvard Law Review* 12(7): 443–463.

Holmes, Oliver Wendell. 1918. "Natural Law." *Harvard Law Review* 32 (1): 40–44.

Homans, George C. 1958. "Social Behavior as Exchange." *American Journal of Sociology* 63(6): 597–606.

Homans, George C. 1961. *Social Behavior: Its Elementary Forms*. New York: Harcourt, Brace & World.

Homans, George C. 1964. "Bringing Men Back in." *American Sociological Review* 29(6): 809–818.

Hoogvelt, Ankie. 1984. "Jurisprudence, Sociological." P. 180 in *The International Encyclopedia of Sociology*, ed. M. Mann. New York: The Continuum Publishing Company.

Hopkins, Andrew. 1975. "On the Sociology of Criminal Law." *Social Problems* 22(5): 608–619.

Horne, Christine. 2000. "Community and the State: The Relationship between Normative and Legal Controls." *European Sociological Review* 16: 225–243.

Horne, Christine. 2004. "Collective Benefits, Exchange Interests, and Norm Enforcement." *Social Forces* 82(3): 1037–1062.

Horne, Christine, and Michael J. Lovaglia. 2008. *Experiments in Criminology and Law: A Research Revolution*. Lanham, MD: Rowman & Littlefield.

Horowitz, Irving L. 1993. *The Decomposition of Sociology*. New York: Oxford University Press.

Horwitz, Allan V. 1983. "Resistance to Innovation in the Sociology of Law: A Response to Greenberg." *Law and Society Review* 17(2): 369–384.

Horwitz, Allan V. 2002. "A Continuities Symposium on Donald Black's 'The Behavior of Law'." *Contemporary Sociology* 31(6): 641–674.

Hull, Kathleen E. 1999. "The Paradox of the Contented Female Lawyer." *Law and Society Review* 33(3): 687–702.

Hull, Kathleen E. 2001. "The Political Limits of the Rights Frame: The Case of Same-Sex Marriage in Hawaii." *Sociological Perspectives* 44(2): 207–232.

Hull, Kathleen E. 2003. "The Cultural Power of Law and the Cultural Enactment of Legality: The Case of Same-Sex Marriage." *Law and Social Inquiry* 28(3): 629–657.

Hull, Kathleen E. 2006. *Same-Sex Marriage: The Cultural Politics of Love and Law*. Cambridge, UK: Cambridge University Press.

Hull, Kathleen E., and Robert L. Nelson. 2000. "Assimilation, Choice or Constraint? Testing Theories of Gender Difference in the Careers of Lawyers." *Social Forces* 79(1): 229–264.

Hull, N. E. H. 1997. *Roscoe Pound and Karl Llewellyn: Searching for an American Jurisprudence*. Chicago: University of Chicago Press.

Hunt, Alan J. 1976. "Perspectives in the Sociology of Law." Pp. 22–44 in *The Sociology of Law*, ed. P. Carlen. Keele, UK: University of Keele.

Hunt, Alan J. 1978. *The Sociological Movement in Law*. Philadelphia: Temple University Press.

Hunt, Alan J. 1979. "The Sociology of Law of Gurvitch and Timasheff: A Critique of Theories of Normative Integration." *Research in Law and Sociology* 2: 169–204.

Hunt, Alan J. 1980. "The Radical Critique of Law: An Assessment." *International Journal of the Sociology of Law* 8(1): 33–46.

Hunt, Alan J. 1981a. "Dichotomy and Contradiction in the Sociology of Law." *British Journal of Law and Society* 8(1): 47–77.

Hunt, Alan J. 1981b. "Marxism and the Analysis of Law." Pp. 91–109 in *Sociological Approaches to Law*, ed. A. Podgórecki and C. J. Whelan. New York: St. Martin's Press.

Hunt, Alan J. 1983. "Behavioral Sociology of Law: A Critique of Donald Black." *Journal of Law and Society* 10(1): 19–46.

Hunt, Alan J. 1985. "The Ideology of Law: Advances and Problems in Recent Applications of the Concept of Ideology to the Analysis of Law." *Law and Society Review* 19(1): 11–38.

Hunt, Alan J. 1986. "The Theory of Critical Legal Studies." *Oxford Journal of Legal Studies* 6(1): 1–45.

Hunt, Alan J. 1993. *Explorations in Law and Society: Toward a Constitutive Theory of Law*. New York: Routledge.

Hunt, Alan J. 1995. "The Role of Law in the Civilizing Process and the Reform of Popular Culture." *Canadian Journal of Law and Society* 10 (2): 5–29.

Hunt, Alan J. 1997. "Law, Politics and the Social Sciences." Pp. 103–123 in *Sociology after Postmodernism*, ed. D. Owen. London: Sage.

Hunt, Alan J. 2001. "Introduction to the Transaction Edition." Pp. XI–LIV in *Sociology of Law*, by Georges Gurvitch. New Brunswick, NJ: Transaction.

Hunt, Alan J. 2002. "The Problematisation of Law in Classical Social Theory." Pp. 13–31 in *An Introduction to Law and Social Theory*, ed. R. Banakar and M. Travers. Portland, OR: Hart Publishing.

Hunt, Alan J., and Gary Wickham. 1994. *Foucault and Law. Towards a Sociology of Law as Governance*. London: Pluto Press.

Hutter, Bridget M. 1988. *The Reasonable Arm of the Law? The Law Enforcement Procedures of Environmental Health Officers*. Oxford: Clarendon Press.

Hyden, Hakan. 1986. "Sociology of Law in Scandinavia." *Journal of Law and Society* 13(1): 131–143.

Ingersoll, David E. 1981. "American Legal Realism and Sociological Jurisprudence: The Methodological Roots of a Science of Law." *Journal of the History of the Behavioral Sciences* 17(4): 490–503.

Irons, Peter. 1986. "Humanistic Legal Studies." *Legal Studies Forum* 10(3): 331–334.

Irwin, Michael John. 1986. *A Sociological Evaluation of the Development of Sociology of Law*. New York, NY: Vantage Press.

Jacobs, David, and Robert M. O'Brien. 1998. "The Determinants of Deadly Force: A Structural Analysis of Police Violence." *American Journal of Sociology* 103(4): 837–862.

Jenkins, Philip. 1998. *Moral Panic: Changing Concepts of the Child Molester in Modern America*. New Haven, CT: Yale University Press.

Jenness, Valerie. 1999. "Managing Differences and Making Legislation: Social Movements and the Racialization, Sexualization, and Gendering of Federal Hate Crime Law in the U.S., 1985–1998." *Social Problems* 46(4): 548–571.

Jenness, Valerie. 2004. "Explaining Criminalization: From Demography and Status Politics to Globalization and Modernization." *Annual Review of Sociology* 30: 147–171.

Jenness, Valerie, and Ryken Grattet. 1996. "The Criminalization of Hate: A Comparison of Structural and Polity Influences on the Passage of 'Bias-Crime' Legislation in the United States." *Sociological Perspectives* 39 (1): 129–154.

Johnson, Harry M., ed. 1978. *Social System and Legal Process*. San Francisco: Jossey-Bass.

Johnston, Barry V. 1989. "Sorokin Lives! Centennial Observations." *Footnotes*, The ASA Newsletter, 17(1): 1, 5.

Johnston, Les. 1992. *The Rebirth of Private Policing*. New York: Routledge.

Jones, Ann. 1994. *Next Time, She'll Be Dead: Battering and How to Stop it*. Boston, MA: Beacon Press.

Justo, Marcelo Gomes, and Helena Singer. 2001. "Sociology of Law in Brazil: A Critical Approach." *The American Sociologist* 32(2): 10–25.

Kagan, Robert A., Martin Krygier, and Kenneth Winston, eds. 2002. *Legality and Community: On the Intellectual Legacy of Philip Selznick*. Lanham, MD: Rowman and Littlefield.

Kant, Immanuel. 1784. "Beantwortung der Frage: Was ist Aufklärung?" *Berlinische Monatsschrift* 4: 481–494.

Kay, Fiona M. 1997. "Flight from Law: A Competing Risks Model of Departures from Law Firms." *Law and Society Review* 31(2): 301–336.

Kay, Fiona M. 2002. "Crossroads to Innovation and Diversity: The Careers of Women Lawyers in Quebec." *McGill Law Journal* 47(4): 699–742.

Kay, Fiona M., and Joan Brockman. 2000. "Barriers to Gender Equality in the Canadian Legal Establishment." *Feminist Legal Studies* 8(2): 169–198.

Kay, Fiona M., and John Hagan. 1995. "The Persistent Glass Ceiling: Gendered Inequalities in the Earnings of Lawyers." *British Journal of Sociology* 46(2): 279–310.

Kay, Fiona M., and John Hagan. 1998. "Raising the Bar: The Gender Stratification of Law-Firm Capital." *American Sociological Review* 63 (5): 728–743.

Kay, Fiona M., and John Hagan. 1999. "Cultivating Clients in the Competition for Partnership: Gender and the Organizational Restructuring of Law Firms in the 1990s." *Law and Society Review* 33(3): 517–555.

Kay, Fiona, Cristi Masuch, and Paula Curry. 2006. "Growing Diversity and Emergent Change: Gender and Ethnicity in the Legal Profession." Pp. 203–236 in *Calling for Change: Women, Law and the Legal Profession*, ed. E. Sheehy and S. McIntyre. Ottawa, ON: University of Ottawa Press.

Kazimirchuk, Vladimir. 1980. "Sociology of Law: Subject-Matter, Structure and Functions." Pp. 55–63 in *Marxist Conception of Law*, ed. P. N. Fedoseyev, I. R. Grigulevich, and N. I. Maslova. Moscow: USSR Academy of Sciences.

Kelly, Erin and Frank Dobbin. 1999. "Civil Rights Law at Work: Sex Discrimination and the Rise of Maternity Leave Policies." *American Journal of Sociology* 105(2): 455–492.

Kelman, Mark. 1984. "Trashing." *Stanford Law Review* 36: 293–348.

Kelsen, Hans. 1912. "Zur Soziologie des Rechtes: Kritische Betrachtungen." *Archiv für Sozialwissenschaft und Sozialpolitik* 34: 601–614.

Kelsen, Hans. 1915. "Eine Grundlegung der Rechtssoziologie." *Archiv für Sozialwissenschaft und Sozialpolitik* 39: 839–879.

Kelsen, Hans. 1955. *The Communist Theory of Law*. New York: Praeger.

Kennedy, Duncan. 1983. *Legal Education and the Reproduction of Hierarchy: A Polemic against the System*. Cambridge, MA: Afar.

Kennedy, Duncan. 1997. *A Critique of Adjudication (Fin de Siècle)*. Cambridge, MA: Harvard University Press.

Kennedy, Duncan. 1998. "Law and Economics from the Perspective of Critical Legal Studies." Pp. 465–474 in *The New Palgrave Dictionary of Economics and the Law*, Vol. II, ed. P. Newman. New York: Stockton Press.

Kettler, David. 1984. "Sociological Classics and the Contemporary State of the Law." Review Essay. *Canadian Journal of Sociology/Cahiers Canadiens de Sociologie* 9(4): 447–458.

Kidder, Robert L. 1983. *Connecting Law and Society*. Englewood Cliffs, NJ: Prentice Hall.

King, Michael, and Anton Schutz. 1994. "The Ambitious Modesty of Niklas Luhmann." *Journal of Law and Society* 21(3): 261–287.

King, Michael, and Chris Thornhill. 2006. *Luhmann on Law and Politics: Critical Appraisals and Applications*. Portland, OR: Oxford.

King, Ryan D. 2007. "The Context of Minority Group Threat: Race, Institutions, and Complying with Hate Crime Law." *Law and Society Review* 41(1): 189–224.

Klug, Heinz. 2005. "Transnational Human Rights: Exploring the Persistence and Globalization of Human Rights." *Annual Review of Law and Social Science* 1: 85–103.

Kojder, Andrzej. 2006. "Leon Petrazycki's Socio-legal Ideas and their Contemporary Continuation." *Journal of Classical Sociology* 6: 333–358.

Kojder, Andrzej, and Jerzy Kwasniewski. 1985. "The Development of the Sociology of Law in Poland." *International Journal of the Sociology of Law* 13(3): 261–272.

Kraska, Peter B., and Victor E. Kappeler. 1997. "Militarizing American Police: The Rise and Normalization of Paramilitary Units." *Social Problems* 44(1): 1–18.

Kritzer, Herbert M. 1999. "The Professions are Dead, Long Live the Professions: Legal Practice in a Postprofessional World." *Law and Society Review* 33(3): 713–759.

Kronman, Anthony T. 1983. *Max Weber*. Stanford, CA: Stanford University Press.

Krygier, Martin. 2002. "Selznick's Subjects." Pp. 3–16 in *Legality and Community: On the Intellectual Legacy of Philip Selznick*, ed. R. A. Kagan, M. Krygier, and K. Winston. Lanham, MD: Rowman and Littlefield.

Kurczewski, Jacek. 2001. "Sociology of Law in Poland." *The American Sociologist* 32(2): 85–98.

Laband, David N., and Bernard F. Lentz. 1993. "Is there Sex Discrimination in the Legal Profession? Further Evidence on Tangible and Intangible Margins." *The Journal of Human Resources* 28(2): 230–258.

Lande, Jerzy. 1975. "The Sociology of Petyrazycki." Pp. 23–37 in *Sociology and Jurisprudence of Leon Petrazycki*, ed. J. Gorecki. Urbana, IL: University of Illinois Press.

Lande, John. 2002. "Using Dispute System Design Methods to Promote Good-Faith Participation in Court-Connected Mediation Programs." *UCLA Law Review* 50: 69–141.

Lande, John. 2005a. "Shifting the Focus from the Myth of 'the Vanishing Trial' to Complex Conflict Management Systems, or I Learned Almost Everything I Need to Know about Conflict Resolution from Marc Galanter." *Cardozo Journal of Conflict Resolution* 6: 191–212.

Lande, John. 2005b. "Procedures for Building Quality into Court Mediation Programs." *Alternatives to the High Cost of Litigation* 23: 17–24.

Lande, John. 2006. "How Much Justice Can We Afford? Defining the Courts' Roles and Deciding the Appropriate Number of Trials,

Settlement Signals, and Other Elements Needed to Administer Justice." *Journal of Dispute Resolution* (1): 213–252.

Langer, Rosanna. 1998. "The Juridification and Technicisation of Alternative Dispute Resolution Practices." *Canadian Journal of Law and Society* 13(1): 169–86.

Lanza-Kaduce, Lonn, Marvin D. Krohn, Marcia Radosevich, and Ronald L. Akers. 1979. "Law and Durkheimian Order: An Empirical Examination of the Convergence of Legal and Social Definitions of Law." Pp. 41–61 in *Structure, Law, and Power: Essays in the Sociology of Law*, ed. P. J. Brantingham and J. M. Kress. Beverly Hills, CA: Sage Publications.

Larsen, Nick, and Brian Burtch, eds. 1999. *Law in Society: Canadian Readings*. Toronto: Harcourt Brace.

Larson, Erik W. 2004. "Institutionalizing Legal Consciousness: Regulation and the Embedding of Market Participants in the Securities Industry in Ghana and Fiji." *Law and Society Review* 38(4): 737–767.

Larson, Magali Sarfatti. 1977. *The Rise of Professionalism: A Sociological Analysis*. Berkeley, CA: University of California Press.

Lascoumes, Pierre, ed. 1995. *Actualité de Max Weber pour la sociologie du droit*. Paris: LGDJ.

Lauderdale, Pat, and Gerald Larson. 1978. "Marxist and 'Organizational' Approaches to Delinquency and the Sociology of Law: Crucial Problems in "Testing" the Perspectives." *American Sociological Review* 43(6): 922–925.

Lavi, Shai J. 2005. *The Modern Art of Dying: A History of Euthanasia in the United States*. Princeton, NJ: Princeton University Press.

Lechner, Frank J., and John Boli. 2000. *The Globalization Reader*. Malden, MA: Blackwell.

Lee, Ellie. 1998. *Abortion Law and Politics Today*. New York: St. Martin's Press.

Lee, Maggy. 2005. "Human Trade and the Criminalization of Irregular Migration." *International Journal of the Sociology of Law* 33(1): 1–15.

Lemert, Charles. 1997. *Postmodernism is Not What You Think*. Malden, MA: Blackwell.

Lengermann, Patricia M., and Jill Niebrugge-Brantley. 2000. "Contemporary Feminist Theory." Pp. 307–355 in *Modern Sociological Theory*, by George Ritzer. 5th edn. Boston: McGraw Hill.

Lessan, Gloria T., and Joseph F. Sheley. 1992. "Does Law Behave? A Macrolevel Test of Black's Propositions on Change in Law." *Social Forces* 70(3): 655–678.

Levine, Donald N. 1995. *Visions of the Sociological Tradition*. Chicago: University of Chicago Press.

Lévy-Bruhl, Henri. 1967. *Sociologie du droit*. Paris: Presses Universitaires de France.

Likhovski, Assaf. 1999. "Protestantism and the Rationalization of English Law: A Variation on a Theme by Weber." *Law and Society Review* 33 (2): 365–391.

Linders, Annulla. 1998. "Abortion as a Social Problem: The Construction of 'Opposite' Solutions in Sweden and the United States." *Social Problems* 45(4): 488–509.

Lindsay, Samuel M. 1930. "Social and Labor Legislation." *American Journal of Sociology* 35(6): 967–981.

Lipset, Seymour M. 1994. "The Social Requisites of Democracy Revisited." *American Sociological Review* 59(1): 1–22.

Llewellyn, Karl N. 1930. "A Realistic Jurisprudence: The Next Step." *Columbia Law Review* 30(4): 431–465.

Llewellyn, Karl N. 1931. "Some Realism about Realism: Responding to Dean Pound." *Harvard Law Review* 44(8): 1222–1264.

Llewellyn, Karl N. 1949. "Law and the Social Sciences – Especially Sociology." *American Sociological Review* 14(4): 451–462.

Llewellyn, Karl N. 1962. *Jurisprudence: Realism in Theory and Practice*. Chicago: University of Chicago Press.

Llewellyn, Karl N., and E. Adamson Hoebel. 1941. *The Cheyenne Way: Conflict and Case Law in Primitive Jurisprudence*. Norman, OK: University of Oklahoma Press.

Lofquist, William S. 1993. "Legislating Organizational Probation: State Capacity, Business Power, and Corporate Crime Control." *Law and Society Review* 27(4): 741–784.

Los, Maria. 1981. "Law from a Phenomenological Perspective." Pp. 187–200 in *Sociological Approaches to Law*, ed. A. Podgórecki and C. J. Whelan. New York: St. Martin's Press.

Lowney, Kathleen, and Joel Best. 1995. "Stalking Strangers and Lovers: Changing Media Typifications of a New Crime Problem." Pp. 33–57 in *Images of Issues: Typifying Contemporary Social Problems*, ed. J. Best. 2nd edn. New York: Aldine de Gruyter.

Luhmann, Niklas. 1972a. *Rechtssoziologie*. Reinbek bei Hamburg: Rowohlt.

Luhmann, Niklas. (1972b) 1985. *A Sociological Theory of Law*. London: Routledge & Kegan Paul.

Luhmann, Niklas. 1986. "The Self-Reproduction of Law and its Limits." Pp. 111–127 in *Dilemmas of Law in the Welfare State*, ed. G. Teubner. Berlin: Walter de Gruyter.

Luhmann, Niklas. 1990. "The Future of Democracy." *Thesis Eleven* 26: 46–53.

Luhmann, Niklas. 1992. "Operational Closure and Structural Coupling: The Differentiation of the Legal System." *Cardozo Law Review* 13(5): 1419–41.

Luhmann, Niklas. 1993a. *Das Recht der Gesellschaft*. Frankfurt: Suhrkamp.

Luhmann, Niklas. (1993b) 2004. *Law as a Social System*. Oxford: Oxford University Press.

Luhmann, Niklas. 1994. "Politicians, Honesty and the Higher Amorality of Politics." *Theory, Culture and Society* 11: 25–36.

Luhmann, Niklas. 1997. *Die Gesellschaft der Gesellschaft*. Frankfurt am Main: Suhrkamp.

Lukes, Steven. 2006. "Liberal Democratic Torture." *British Journal of Political Science* 36(1): 1–16.

Lukes, Steven, and Andrew Scull. 1983. "Introduction." Pp. 1–32 in *Durkheim and the Law*, ed. S. Lukes and A. Scull. New York: St. Martin's Press.

Lyman, Stanford M. 2002. "Toward a Renewed Sociological Jurisprudence: From Roscoe Pound to Herbert Blumer and Beyond." *Symbolic Interaction* 25(2): 149–174.

Lyman, Stanford M. 2004. *Law and Society: Jurisprudence and Subculture in Conflict and Accommodation*. New York: Richard Altschuler & Associates.

Lynch, Michael E. 1982. "Closure and Disclosure in Pre-Trial Argument." *Human Studies* 5: 285–318.

Lynch, Michael E. 1998. "The Discursive Production of Uncertainty: The OJ Simpson 'Dream Team' and the Sociology of Knowledge Machine." *Social Studies of Science* 28(5–6): 829–868.

Lynch, Michael E., and Simon Cole. 2005. "Science and Technology Studies on Trial: Dilemmas of Expertise." *Social Studies of Science* 35(2): 269–311.

Lynch, Monica. 2000. "Rehabilitation as Rhetoric: The Ideal of Reformation in Contemporary Parole Discourse and Practices." *Punishment and Society* 2: 40–65.

Lyon, David. 2003. *Surveillance after September 11*. Cambridge: Polity Press.

Lyons, David. 1991. *In the Interest of the Governed: A Study in Bentham's Philosophy of Utility and Law*. Oxford: Clarendon Press.

Lyotard, Jean-François. 1979a. *La Condition postmoderne: Rapport sur le savoir*. Paris: Editions de Minuit.

Lyotard, Jean-François. (1979b) 1984. *The Postmodern Condition: A Report on Knowledge*. Minneapolis: University of Minnesota Press.

MacCorquodale, Patricia, and Gary Jensen. 1993. "Women in the Law: Partners or Tokens?" *Gender and Society* 7(4): 582–593.

MacDonald, Gayle M., ed. 2002a. *Social Context and Social Location in the Sociology of Law*. Orchard Park, NY: Broadview Press.

MacDonald, Gayle M. 2002b. "Theory and the Canon: How the Sociology of Law is Organized." Pp. 13–22 in *Social Context and Social Location in the Sociology of Law*, ed. G. M. MacDonald. Orchard Park, NY: Broadview Press.

Macdonald, Keith M. 1995. *The Sociology of the Professions*. London: Sage.

Machura, Stefan. 2001a. "Die Aufgabe(n) der Rechtssoziologie: Eine Antwort an Theo Rasehorn." *Zeitschrift für Rechtssoziologie* 22(2): 293–297.

Machura, Stefan. 2001b. "German Sociology of Law." *The American Sociologist* 32(2): 41–60.

Madsen, Mikal R., and Yves Dezalay. 2002. "The Power for the Legal Field: Pierre Bourdieu and the Law." Pp. 189–204 in *An Introduction to Law and Social Theory*, ed. R. Banakar and M. Travers. Portland, OR: Hart Publishing.

Maine, Henry Sumner. (1861) 1970. *Ancient Law: its Connection with the Early History of Society and its Relation to Modern Ideas*. Glouster, MA: Peter Smith.

Manning, Peter K. 1977. *Police Work: The Social Organization of Policing*. Cambridge, MA: The MIT Press.

Manning, Peter K. 2002. "Authority, Loyalty, and Community Policing." Pp. 123–152 in *Crime and Social Organization*, ed. E. Waring and D. Weisburd. New Brunswick, NJ: Transaction.

Manning, Peter K. 2003. *Policing Contingencies*. Chicago: University of Chicago Press.

Manza, Jeff, and Christopher Uggen. 2004. "Punishment and Democracy: The Disenfranchisement of Nonincarcerated Felons in the United States." *Perspectives on Politics* 2: 491–505.

Manza, Jeff, and Christopher Uggen. 2006. *Locked Out: Felon Disenfranchisement and American Democracy*. New York: Oxford University Press.

Manza, Jeff, Clem Brooks, and Christopher Uggen. 2004. "Public Attitudes toward Felon Disenfranchisement in the United States." *Public Opinion Quarterly* 68: 276–87.

Manzo, John F. 1997. "Ethnomethodology, Conversation Analysis, and the Sociology of Law." Pp. 1–24 in *Law in Action: Ethnomethodological and Conversation Analytic Approaches to Law*, ed. M. Travers and J. F. Manzo. Brookfield, VT: Ashgate.

Marsh, Robert M. 2000. "Weber's Misunderstanding of Traditional Chinese Law." *American Journal of Sociology* 106(2): 281–302.

Marshall, Anna-Maria. 2006. "Communities and Culture: Enriching Legal Consciousness and Legal Culture." *Law and Social Inquiry* 31(1): 229–249.

Marx, Gary T. 1981. "Ironies of Social Control: Authorities as Contributors to Deviance through Escalation, Nonenforcement and Covert Facilitation." *Social Problems* 28(3): 221–246.

Marx, Gary T. 1986. "The Iron Fist and the Velvet Glove: Totalitarian Potentials within Democratic Structures." Pp. 135–162 in *The Social Fabric: Dimensions and Issues*, ed. J. F. Short. Beverly Hills, CA: Sage.

Marx, Gary T. 1988. *Undercover: Police Surveillance in America*. Berkeley, CA: University of California Press.

Marx, Gary T. 1995. "The Engineering of Social Control: The Search for the Silver Bullet." Pp. 225–246 in *Crime and Inequality*, ed. J. Hagan and R. D. Peterson. Stanford, CA: Stanford University Press.

Marx, Gary T. 1996. "Privacy and Technology." *Telektronik* 1996(1). Available online: web.mit.edu/gtmarx/www/privantt.html.

Marx, Gary T. 1999. "Ethics for the New Surveillance." Pp. 39–67 in *Visions of Privacy: Policy Choices for the Digital Age*, ed. C. J. Bennett and R. Grant. Toronto, Canada: University of Toronto Press.

Marx, Gary T. 2003. "A Tack in the Shoe: Neutralizing and Resisting the New Surveillance." *Journal of Social Issues* 59(2): 369–390.

Marx, Gary T. 2005. "Soft Surveillance: Mandatory Voluntarism and the Collection of Personal Data." *Dissent* 52(4): 36–43.

Marx, Gary T. 2007. "Desperately Seeking Surveillance Studies: Players in Search of a Field." *Contemporary Sociology* 36(2): 125–130.

Marx, Karl. 1842. "Debates on the Law on Thefts of Wood." Supplement to the *Rheinische Zeitung*, October–November 1842. Online: www.marxists.org/archive/marx/works/1842/10/25.htm.

Marx, Karl. 1844. *Economic and Philosophical Manuscripts of 1844*. Online: www.marxists.org/archive/marx/works/1844/manuscripts/preface.htm.

Marx, Karl. 1846. *The German Ideology*. Online at www.marxists.org.

Marx, Karl. (1848) 1978. "Manifesto of the Communist Party." Pp. 469–500 in *The Marx-Engels Reader*, ed. R. C. Tucker. New York: W. W. Norton.

Marx, Karl. (1867) 1978. "Capital, Volume One." Pp. 294–438 in *The Marx-Engels Reader*, ed. R. C. Tucker. New York: W. W. Norton.

Marx, Karl. 1869. "Report of the General Council on the Right of Inheritance." Written on behalf of the International Workingmen's Association. Online: www.marxists.org/history/international/iwma/documents/1869/inheritance-report.htm.

Mathiesen, Thomas. 1990. "Sociology of Law in Norway." Pp. 605–629 in *Developing Sociology of Law: A World-Wide Documentary Enquiry*, ed. V. Ferrari. Milan: Dott A. Giuffré Editore.

Matsueda, Ross L. 1992. "Reflected Appraisals, Parental Labeling, and Delinquency: Specifying a Symbolic Interactionist Theory." *American Journal of Sociology* 97(6): 1577–1611.

Matsueda, Ross L. 2000. "Labeling Theory: Historical Roots, Implications, and Recent Developments." Pp. 223–241 in *Explaining Criminals and Crime: Essays in Contemporary Criminological Theory*, ed. R. Paternoster and R. Bachman. Los Angeles, CA: Roxbury Press.

Mayhew, Leon. 1968a. *Law and Equal Opportunity: A Study of the Massachusetts Commission against Discrimination*. Cambridge, MA: Harvard University Press.

Mayhew, Leon. 1968b. "The Sociology of Law." Pp. 171–183 in *American Sociology: Perspectives, Problems, Methods*, ed. T. Parsons. New York: Basic Books.

Mayhew, Leon. 1968c. "The Legal System." Pp. 59–66 in *International Encyclopedia of the Social Sciences, Volume 9*, ed. D. L. Sills. New York: The Macmillan Company & The Free Press.

Mayhew, Leon. 1971. "Stability and Change in Legal Systems." Pp. 187–210 in *Stability and Social Change*, ed. B. Barber and A. Inkeles. Boston, MA: Little, Brown and Company.

Maynard, Douglas W. 1982. "Defendant Attributes in Plea Bargaining: Notes on the Modeling of Sentencing Decisions." *Social Problems* 29 (4): 347–360.

Maynard, Douglas W. 1984a. *Inside Plea Bargaining: The Language of Negotiation*. New York: Plenum.

Maynard, Douglas W. 1984b. "The Structure of Discourse in Misdemeanor Plea Bargaining." *Law and Society Review* 18(12): 75–104.

Maynard, Douglas W. 1988. "Narratives and Narrative Structure in Plea Bargaining." *Law and Society Review* 22(3): 449–482.

Maynard, Douglas W., and Steven E. Clayman. 2003. "Ethnomethodology and Conversation Analysis." Pp. 173–202 in *Handbook of Symbolic Interactionism*, ed. L. T. Reynolds and N. J. Herman-Kinney. Walnut Creek, CA: AltaMira.

Maynard, Douglas W., and John F. Manzo. 1993. "On the Sociology of Justice: Theoretical Notes from an Actual Jury Deliberation." *Sociological Theory* 11(2): 171–193.

Mayntz, Renate. 1969. "Introduction: Theodor Geiger: The Man and his Work." Pp. 1–35 in *On Social Order and Mass Society*, by Theodor Geiger, ed. R. Mayntz. Chicago: University of Chicago Press.

McCammon, Holly J. 1990. "Legal Limits on Labor Militancy: U. S. Labor Law and the Right to Strike since the New Deal." *Social Problems* 37 (2): 206–229.

McCammon, Holly J. 1993. "From Repressive Intervention to Integrative Prevention: The U.S. State's Legal Management of Labor Militancy, 1881–1978." *Social Forces* 71(3): 569–601.

McCammon, Holly J. 1994. "Disorganizing and Reorganizing Conflict: Outcomes of the State's Legal Regulation of the Strike since the Wagner Act." *Social Forces* 72(4): 1011–1049.

McDonald, Lynn. 1976. *The Sociology of Law and Order*. Boulder, CO: Westview Press.

McDonald, Pauline. 1979. "The Legal Sociology of Georges Gurvitch." *British Journal of Law and Society* 6(1): 24–52.

McDonald, William F., ed. 1997. *Crime and Law Enforcement in the Global Village*. Cincinnati, OH: Anderson Publishing.

McIntyre, Lisa J. 1994. *Law in the Sociological Enterprise: A Reconstruction*. Boulder, CO: Westview Press.

McLean, Edward B. 1992. *Law and Civilization: The Legal Thought of Roscoe Pound*. Lanham, MD: University Press of America.

Mead, George H. 1934. *Mind, Self and Society from the Standpoint of a Social Behaviorist*, ed. C.W. Morris. Chicago: University of Chicago.

Mehrotra, Ajay K. 2001. "Law and the 'Other': Karl N. Llewellyn, Cultural Anthropology, and the Legacy of the Cheyenne Way." Review Essay. *Law and Social Inquiry* 26(3): 741–775.

Meisenhelder, Thomas. 1981. "Law as Symbolic Action: Kenneth Burke's Sociology of Law." *Symbolic Interaction* 4: 43–57.

Melossi, Dario. 1986. "Marxist Sociology of Law." *Legal Studies Forum* 10 (3): 341–346.

Merry, Sally Engle. 1988. "Legal Pluralism." *Law and Society Review* 22 (5): 869–896.

Merton, Robert K. 1934. "Durkheim's Division of Labor in Society." *American Journal of Sociology* 40(3): 319–328.

Merton, Robert K. 1976. *Sociological Ambivalence and Other Essays*. New York: The Free Press.

Mertz, Elizabeth, ed. 2008. *The Role of Social Science in Law*. Aldershot, UK: Ashgate.

Miaille, Michel. 1992. "La Critique du droit." *Droit et société* 20/21: 75–92.

Mills, C. Wright. 1956. *The Power Elite*. New York: Oxford University Press.

Mills, C. Wright. 1959. *The Sociological Imagination*. New York: Oxford University Press.

Milovanovic, Dragan. 1983. "Weber and Marx on Law: Demystifying Ideology and Law: Toward an Emancipatory Political Practice." *Contemporary Crises* 7: 353–370.

Milovanovic, Dragan. 1988. "Critical Legal Studies and the Assault on the Bastion." *Social Justice* 15(1): 161–72.

Milovanovic, Dragan. 1992. *Postmodern Law and Disorder: Psycho-analytic Semiotics, Chaos, and Juridic Exegeses.* Liverpool, UK: Deborah Charles Publications.

Milovanovic, Dragan. 1994. "The Postmodernist Turn: Lacan, Psycho-analytic Semiotics, and the Construction of Subjectivity in Law." *Emory International Law Review* 8: 67–98.

Milovanovic, Dragan. 2002. *Critical Criminology at the Edge: Postmodern Perspectives, Integration, and Applications.* Westport, CT: Praeger.

Milovanovic, Dragan. 2003. *An Introduction to the Sociology of Law.* 3rd edn. Monsey, NY: Criminal Justice Press.

Mirchandani, Rekha. 2005. "Postmodernism and Sociology: From the Epistemological to the Empirical." *Sociological Theory* 23(1): 86–115.

Montesquieu, Baron de. (1748) 1977. *The Spirit of Laws.* Berkeley, CA: University of California Press.

Mooney, Linda. 1986. "The Behavior of Law in a Private Legal System." *Social Forces* 64(3): 733–750.

Moore, Sally Falk. 1973. "Law and Social Change: The Semi-Autonomous Social Field as an Appropriate Subject of Study." *Law and Society Review* 7(4): 719–746.

Morlok, Marin, and Ralf Kölbel. 1998. "Stop-Schilder in der Rechtssozio-logie: Stillstand und kompetente Bewegung im Verkehrsalltag." *Zeitschrift für Rechtssoziologie* 19(2): 136–162.

Morlok, Martin, and Ralf Kölbel. 2000. "Zur Herstellung von Recht: Forschungsstand und rechtstheoretische Implikationen ethnometho-dologischer (Straf-)Rechtssoziologie." *Zeitschrift für Rechtssoziologie* 21(2): 387–417.

Motyka, Krzysztof. 2006. "Law and Sociology: The Petrazyckian Pers-pective." Pp. 119–140 in *Law and Sociology*, ed. M. Freeman. Oxford: Oxford University Press.

Murphy, John W. 1988. "Making Sense of Postmodern Sociology." *British Journal of Sociology* 39(4): 600–614.

Murray, Topsy, Robert Dingwall, and John Eekelaar. 1983. "Professionals in Bureaucracies: Solicitors in Private Practice and Local Government." Pp. 195–220 in *The Sociology of the Professions*, ed. R. Dingwall and P. Lewis. New York: St. Martin's Press.

Myers, Martha. 1980. "Predicting the Behavior of Law: A Test of Two Models." *Law and Society Review* 14(4): 835–857.

Nagin, Daniel S., and Raymond Paternoster. 1993. "Enduring Individual Differences and Rational Choice Theories of Crime." *Law and Society Review* 27(3): 467–496.

Naoumova, Stefka. 1990. "Die rechtssoziologischen Forschungen in Bulgarien." *Zeitschrift für Rechtssoziologie* 11(1): 102–119.

Nee, Victor. 1998. "Sources of the New Institutionalism." Pp. 1–16 in *The New Institutionalism in Sociology*, ed. M. C. Brinton and V. Nee. New York: Russell Sage Foundation.

Nelken, David. 2002. "Comparative Sociology of Law." Pp. 329–344 in *An Introduction to Law and Social Theory*, ed. R. Banakar and M. Travers. Portland, OR: Hart Publishing.

Nelson, Robert L. 1994. "The Futures of American Lawyers: A Demographic Profile of a Changing Profession in a Changing Society." *Case Western Reserve Law Review* 44: 345–406.

Nelson, Robert L., and William P. Bridges. 1999. *Legalizing Gender Inequality: Courts, Markets and Unequal Pay for Women in America*. New York: Cambridge University Press.

Nielsen, Laura Beth. 2000. "Situating Legal Consciousness: Experiences and Attitudes of Ordinary Citizens about Law and Street Harassment." *Law and Society Review* 34(4): 1055–1090.

Nonet, Philippe. 1969. *Administrative Justice: Advocacy and Change in a Government Agency*. New York: Russell Sage Foundation.

Nonet, Philippe. 1976. "For Jurisprudential Sociology." *Law and Society Review* 10(4): 525–545.

Nonet, Philippe, and Philip Selznick. 1978. *Law and Society in Transition: Toward Responsive Law*. New York: Octagon.

Noreau, Pierre, and André-Jean Arnaud. 1998. "The Sociology of Law in France: Trends and Paradigms." *Journal of Law and Society* 25(2): 257–283.

Norris, Clive, Nigel Fielding, Charles Kemp, and Jane Fielding. 1992. "Black and Blue: An Analysis of the Influence of Race on Being Stopped by the Police." *British Journal of Sociology* 43(2): 207–224.

O'Malley, Pat. 1983. *Law, Capitalism, and Democracy: A Sociology of Australian Legal Order*. Sydney: Allen & Unwin.

Pakes, Francis. 2005. "The Legalisation of Euthanasia and Assisted Suicide: A Tale of Two Scenarios." *International Journal of the Sociology of Law* 33(2): 71–84.

Parsons, Talcott. (1937) 1949. *The Structure of Social Action*. 2nd edn. Glencoe, IL: The Free Press.

Parsons, Talcott. 1951. *The Social System*. New York: The Free Press.

Parsons, Talcott. 1954. "A Sociologist Looks at the Legal Profession." Pp. 370–385 in his *Essays in Sociological Theory*. Rev. edn. New York: The Free Press.

Parsons, Talcott. (1959) 1982. "Jurisdiction." Pp. 179–86 in *Talcott Parsons on Institutions and Social Evolution*, ed. L. H. Mayhew. Chicago, University of Chicago Press.

Parsons, Talcott. 1962a. "The Law and Social Control." Pp. 56–72 in *Law and Sociology*, ed. W. M. Evan. New York: The Free Press of Glencoe.

Parsons, Talcott. 1962b. "Hurst's *Law and Social Process in U.S. History*." Review article. *Journal of the History of Ideas* 23: 558–65.

Parsons, Talcott. 1967. *Sociological Theory and Modern Society*. New York: The Free Press.

Parsons, Talcott. 1968. "Law and Sociology: A Promising Courtship?" Pp. 47–54 in *The Path of the Law from 1967*, ed. A. E. Sutherland. Cambridge, MA: Harvard University Press.

Parsons, Talcott. 1977a. *Social Systems and the Evolution of Action Theory*. New York: The Free Press.

Parsons, Talcott. 1977b. "Roberto Mangabeira Unger, *Law in Modern Society*." Review article. *Law and Society Review* 12: 145–49.

Parsons, Talcott. 1978. "Law as an Intellectual Stepchild." Pp. 11–58 in *Social System and Legal Process*, ed. H. M. Johnson. San Francisco: Jossey-Bass.

Parsons, Talcott. 2007. *American Society: A Theory of the Societal Community*, edited and with an introduction by Giuseppe Sciortino. Boulder, CO: Paradigm.

Partridge, P. H. 1961. "Ehrlich's Sociology of Law." Pp. 1–29 in *Studies in the Sociology of Law*, ed. G. Sawer. Canberra: Australian National University.

Pashukanis, Evgenii B. (1924) 1980. *Selected Writings on Marxism and Law*. New York: Academic Press. Online: home.law.uiuc.edu/∽%20 pmaggs/pashukanis.htm.

Pasquino, Pasquale. 1991. "Criminology: The Birth of a Special Knowledge." Pp. 235–250 in *The Foucault Effect*, ed. G. Burchell, C. Gordon, and P. Miller. Chicago: University of Chicago Press.

Passmore, J. 1961. "Axel Hägerström and his Disciples." Pp. 111–136 in *Studies in the Sociology of Law*, ed. G. Sawer. Canberra, Australia: The Australian National University.

Paternoster, Raymond, and Sally Simpson. 1996. "Sanction Threats and Appeals to Morality: Testing a Rational Choice Model of Corporate Crime." *Law and Society Review* 30(3): 549–584.

Pearce, Frank. 1989. *The Radical Durkheim*. London: Unwin Hyman.

Pedriana, Nicholas. 2006. "From Protective to Equal Treatment: Legal Framing Processes and Transformation of the Women's Movement in the 1960s." *American Journal of Sociology* 111(6): 1718–1761.

Pedriana, Nicholas and Robin Stryker. 1997. "Political Culture Wars 1960s Style: Equal Employment Opportunity-Affirmative Action Law and the Philadelphia Plan." *American Journal of Sociology* 103(3): 633–691.

Peeples, Ralph, Catherine T. Harris and Thomas B. Metzloff. 2000. "Settlement has Many Faces: Physicians, Attorneys and Medical Malpractice." *Journal of Health and Social Behavior* 41(3): 333–346.

Petrazycki, Leon. 1893/1895. *Die Lehre vom Einkommen*. 2 vols. Berlin: H.W. Müller.

Petrazycki, Leon. (1905–1907) 1955. *Law and Morality*. Cambridge, MA: Harvard University Press.

Petrazycki, Leon. 1933. *Methodologie der Theorien des Rechts und der Moral*. Paris: Librairie du Recueil Sirey.

Phillips, Paul. 1980. *Marx and Engels on Law and Laws*. Totowa, NJ: Barnes and Noble Books.

Pierce, Jennifer L. 2002. "A Raced and Gendered Organisational Logic in Law Firms." Pp. 155–171 in *An Introduction to Law and Social Theory*, ed. R. Banakar and M. Travers. Portland, OR: Hart Publishing.

Pierce, Jennifer L. 2003. "'Racing for Innocence': Whiteness, Corporate Culture, and the Backlash against Affirmative Action." *Qualitative Sociology* 26(1): 53–70.

Pitch, Tamar. 1983. "Sociology of Law in Italy." *Journal of Law and Society* 10(1): 119–134.

Piven, Frances F., and Richard A. Cloward. 1971. *Regulating the Poor: The Functions of Public Welfare*. New York: Pantheon Books.

Podgórecki, Adam. 1974. *Law and Society*. Boston: Routledge & Kegan Paul.

Podgórecki, Adam. 1982. "The Theory of the Sociology of Law: Problem." Pp. 85–98 in *The Impacts of Sociology of Law on Government Action*, ed. A. Baratta. Frankfurt: Verlag Peter Lang.

Podgórecki, Adam. 1999. "Sociology of Law." Pp. 817–820 in *The Philosophy of Law: An Encyclopedia*, vol. II, ed. C. B. Gray. New York: Garland Publishing, Inc.

Podgórecki, Adam, and Christopher J. Whelan, eds. 1981. *Sociological Approaches to Law*. New York: St. Martin's Press.

Pollack, Marc A., and Gregory C. Shaffer, eds. 2001. *Transatlantic Governance in the Global Economy*. Lanham, MD: Rowman & Littlefield.

Posner, Richard A. 1974. "The Behavior of Administrative Agencies." Pp. 215–261 in *Essays in the Economics of Crime and Punishment*, ed. G. Becker and W. M. Landes. New York: National Bureau of Economic Research.

Posner, Richard A. 1986. *Economic Analysis of Law*. 3rd edn. Boston: Little, Brown and Company.

Posner, Richard A. 1995. "The Sociology of the Sociology of Law: A View from Economics." *European Journal of Law and Economics* 2: 265–284.

Posner, Richard A. 1998. "Rational Choice, Behavioral Economics, and the Law." *Stanford Law Review* 50(5): 1551–1575.

Pound, Roscoe. (1907) 1968. "The Need of a Sociological Jurisprudence." Pp. 9–18 in *The Sociology of Law: Interdisciplinary Readings*, ed. R. J. Simon. San Francisco: Chandler Publishing.

Pound, Roscoe. 1910. "Law in Books and Law in Action." *American Law Review* 44: 12–36.

Pound, Roscoe. 1912. "The Scope and Purpose of Sociological Jurisprudence, III: Sociological Jurisprudence." *Harvard Law Review* 25(6): 489–516.

Pound, Roscoe. 1923. "Law and Morals." Parts I and II. *Journal of Social Forces* 1(4): 350–359; 1(5): 528–537.

Pound, Roscoe. 1926. *Law and Morals*. Chapel Hill, NC: The University of North Carolina Press.

Pound, Roscoe. 1927. "Sociology and Law." Pp. 319–328 in *The Social Sciences and their Interrelations*, ed. W. F. Ogburn and A. Goldenweiser. Boston: Houghton Mifflin Company.

Pound, Roscoe. 1928. "Social and Economic Problems of the Law." *Annals of the American Academy of Political and Social Science* 136: 1–9.

Pound, Roscoe. 1931. "The Call for a Realist Jurisprudence." *Harvard Law Review* 44(5): 697–711.

Pound, Roscoe. 1932. "Jurisprudence." Pp. 477–492 in *Encyclopedia of the Social Sciences*, vol. VIII, ed. E. R. A. Seligman and A. Johnson. New York: The Macmillan Company.

Pound, Roscoe. 1942. *Social Control through Law*. New Haven, CT: Yale University Press.

Pound, Roscoe. 1943. "Sociology of Law and Sociological Jurisprudence." *The University of Toronto Law Journal* 5(1): 1–20.

Pound, Roscoe. 1945. "Sociology of Law." Pp. 297–341 in *Twentieth Century Sociology*, ed. G. Gurvitch and W. E. Moore. New York: The Philosophical Library.

Pound, Roscoe. 1959. *Jurisprudence*. 5 vols. St. Paul, MN: West Publishing Co.

Powell, Walter W., and Paul J. DiMaggio, eds. 1991. *The New Institutionalism in Organizational Analysis*. Chicago: University of Chicago Press.

Pratt, John. 1999. "Norbert Elias and the Civilized Prison." *British Journal of Sociology* 50(2): 271–296.

Priban, Jiri. 2002. "Sharing the Paradigms? Critical Legal Studies and the Sociology of Law." Pp. 119–133 in *An Introduction to Law and Social Theory*, ed. R. Banakar and M. Travers. Portland, OR: Hart Publishing.

Price, Joshua M. 2004. "Critical Race Theory's Dream Narratives: A Method for an Anti-Racist Social Science?" *Studies in Law, Politics, and Society* 32: 39–77.

Quensel, Bernhard K. 1997. "Logik und Methode in der Rechtssoziologie Max Webers: Ein Beitrag zur Klärung der grundlegenden Begriffe und Perspektiven." *Zeitschrift für Rechtssoziologie* 18(2): 133–159.

Quinney, Richard. 1973. *Critique of Legal Order: Crime Control in Capitalist Society*. Boston: Little, Brown.

Quinney, Richard. 1978. "The Production of a Marxist Criminology." *Contemporary Crises* 2(3): 277–292.

Raes, Koen. 1986. "Legalisation, Communication and Strategy: A Critique of Habermas' Approach to Law." *Journal of Law and Society* 13(2): 183–206.

Rasehorn, Theo. 2001. "Die Sektion Rechtssoziologie ist kein Max-Planck-Institut!" *Zeitschrift für Rechtssoziologie* 22(2): 281–291.

Reasons, Charles E., and Robert M. Rich, eds. 1978. *The Sociology of Law: A Conflict Perspective*. Toronto: Butterworths Publishing.

Rebach, Howard M. 2001. "Mediation and Alternative Dispute Resolution." Pp. 197–224 in *Handbook of Clinical Sociology*, ed. H. M. Rebach and J. G. Bruhn. 2nd edn. New York: Kluwer Academic/Plenum Publishers.

Rehbinder, Manfred. 1963. "Max Weber's Rechtssoziologie: Eine Bestandsaufnahme." *Kölner Zeitschrift für Soziologie und Sozialpsychologie* Supplement: 470–488.

Rehbinder, Manfred. 1975. *Sociology of Law: A Trend Report and Bibliography*. The Hague: Mouton.

Rehbinder, Manfred. 2003. *Rechtssoziologie*. Munich: Verlag C. H. Beck.

Reichel, Philip, ed. 2005. *The Handbook of Transnational Crime and Justice*. Thousand Oaks, CA: Sage Publications.

Reiner, Robert. 1985. *The Politics of the Police*. New York: St. Martin's Press.

Reitz, Kevin R. 1996. "The Federal Role in Sentencing Law and Policy." *Annals of the American Academy of Political and Social Science* 543: 116–129.

Rich, Robert M. 1978. *The Sociology of Law: An Introduction to its Theorists and Theories*. Washington, DC: University Press of America.

Richardson, James T. 2006. "The Sociology of Religious Freedom: A Structural and Socio-Legal Analysis." *Sociology of Religion* 67(3): 271–294.

Richman, Kimberly. 2001. "In Times of Need: Abused Women's Sources of Support and Changes in Legal Consciousness." *Studies in Law, Politics, and Society* 22: 171–194.

Richman, Kimberly. 2002. "Lovers, Legal Strangers, and Parents: Negotiating Parental and Sexual Identity in Family Law." *Law and Society Review* 36(2): 285–324.

Riesman, David. 1951. "Toward an Anthropological Science of Law and the Legal Profession." *American Journal of Sociology* 57(2): 121–135.

Riesman, David. 1957. "Law and Sociology: Recruitment, Training and Colleagueship." *Stanford Law Review* 9: 643–673.

Ritzer, George. 1997. *Postmodern Social Theory.* New York: McGraw-Hill.

Roach Anleu, Sharyn, L. 1990. "Men and Women Lawyers in In-House Legal Departments: Recruitment and Career Patterns." *Gender and Society* 4(2): 207–219.

Roach Anleu, Sharyn, L. 2000. *Law and Social Change.* London: Sage.

Robertson, Roland. 1992. *Globalization: Social Theory and Global Culture.* London: Sage.

Robertson, Roland. 1995. "Glocalization: Time-Space and Homogeneity-Heterogeneity." Pp. 25–44 in *Global Modernities,* ed. M. Featherstone, S. Lash, and R. Robertson. London: Sage.

Rocher, Guy. 1989. "Le Droit et la sociologie du droit chez Talcott Parsons." *Sociologie et Societés* 21: 143–163.

Rodriguez-Garavito, César. 2007. "Globalization – Non-Governmental." Pp. 654–656 in *Encyclopedia of Law and Society: American and Global Perspectives,* ed. D. S. Clark. Thousand Oaks, CA: Sage Publications.

Roe v. Wade, 93 S.Ct. 705 (1973). Available online: www.law.cornell.edu/supct/html/historics/USSC_CR_0410_0113_ZS.html.

Rogers-Dillon, Robin H., and John D. Skrentny. 1999. "Administering Success: The Legitimacy Imperative and the Implementation of Welfare Reform." *Social Problems* 46(1): 13–29.

Röhl, Klaus F. 1987. *Rechtssoziologie: Ein Lehrbuch.* Cologne: Carl Heymans Verlag.

Röhl, Klaus F., and Stefan Magan. 1996. "Die Rolle des Rechts im Prozeb der Globalisierung." *Zeitschrift für Rechtssoziologie* 17(1): 1–57.

Rokumoto, Kahei, ed. 1994. *Sociological Theories of Law.* New York: New York University Press.

Rose, Arnold M. 1962. "Some Suggestions for Research in the Sociology of Law." *Social Problems* 9: 281–284.

Rose, Arnold M. 1968. "Law and the Causation of Social Problems." *Social Problems* 16(1): 33–43.

Rosenfeld, Michel, and Andrew Arato, eds. 1998. *Habermas on Law and Democracy: Critical Exchanges.* Berkeley, CA: University of California Press.

Ross, Edward A. 1896. "Social Control, II: Law and Public Opinion." *American Journal of Sociology* 1(6): 753–770.

Ross, Edward A. (1901) 1926. *Social Control: A Survey of the Foundations of Order.* New York: Macmillan.

Rostain, Tanina. 2000. "Educating Homo Economicus: Cautionary Notes on the New Behavioral Law and Economics Movement." *Law and Society Review* 34(4): 973–1006.

Rottleuthner, Hubert. 1989. "A Purified Sociology of Law: Niklas Luhmann on the Autonomy of the Legal System." *Law and Society Review* 23(5): 779–798.

Rottleuthner, Hubert. 1994. "Rechtssoziologie." Pp. 216–239 in *Spezielle soziologien*, ed. A. Kerber and A. Schmieder. Berlin: Rowohlt.

Rueschemeyer, Dietrich. 1970. "Sociology of Law in Germany." *Law and Society Review* 5(2): 225–238.

Rueschemeyer, Dietrich. 1973. *Lawyers and their Society: A Comparative Study of the Legal Profession in Germany and in the United States.* Cambridge, MA: Harvard University Press.

Rueschemeyer, Dietrich. 1983. "Professional Autonomy and the Social Control of Expertise." Pp. 38–58 in *The Sociology of the Professions*, ed. R. Dingwall and P. Lewis. New York: St. Martin's Press.

Sahni, Isher-Paul. 2006. "Vanished Mediators: On the Residual Status of Judges in Max Weber's 'Sociology of Law'." *Journal of Classical Sociology* 6(2): 177–194.

Sampson, Robert J., and John H. Laub. 1993. *Crime in the Making: Pathways and Turning Points through Life.* Cambridge, MA: Harvard University Press.

Sandefur, Rebecca L. 2001. "Work and Honor in the Law: Prestige and the Division of Lawyers' Labor." *American Sociological Review* 66(3): 382–403.

Sandefur, Rebecca L. 2007. "Lawyers' Pro Bono Service and American-Style Civil Legal Assistance." *Law and Society Review* 41(1): 79–112.

Santos, Boaventura de Sousa. 1987. "Law: A Map of Misreading. Toward a Postmodern Conception of Law." *Journal of Law and Society* 14(3): 279–302.

Santos, Boaventura de Sousa. 1995a. *Toward a New Common Sense: Law, Science, and Politics in the Paradigmatic Transition.* New York: Routledge.

Santos, Boaventura de Sousa. 1995b. "Three Metaphors for a New Conception of Law: The Frontier, the Baroque, and the South." *Law and Society Review* 29(4): 569–584.

Santos, Boaventura de Sousa, and César A. Rodríguez-Garavito, eds. 2005. *Law and Globalization from Below: Towards a Cosmopolitan Legality.* Cambridge: Cambridge University Press.

Sarat, Austin, ed. 2004. *Blackwell Companion to Law and Society.* Malden, MA: Blackwell Publishing.

Sassen, Saskia. 1998. *Globalization and its Discontents: Essays on the New Mobility of People and Money.* New York: The New Press.

Savelsberg, Joachim J. 1992. "Law that Does Not Fit Society: Sentencing Guidelines as a Neoclassical Reaction to the Dilemmas of

Substantivized Law." *American Journal of Sociology* 97(5): 1346–1381.

Savelsberg, Joachim J. 2002. "The Section as an Institutional Safe Haven for the Sociology of Law." *Amici*, The ASA Sociology of Law Section Newsletter, 9(2): 5–6.

Savelsberg, Joachim J. 2006. "Sociological Theory in the Study of Sentencing: Lighthouse for a Traveler between Continents." Pp. 183–202 in *Sociological Theory and Criminological Research: Views from Europe and the United States*, ed. M. Deflem. Amsterdam: Elsevier.

Savelsberg, Joachim J., and Ryan D. King. 2005. "Institutionalizing Collective Memories of Hate: Law and Law Enforcement in Germany and the United States." *American Journal of Sociology* 111(2): 579–616.

Savelsberg, Joachim J., and Robert J. Sampson. 2002. "Mutual Engagement: Criminology and Sociology." *Crime, Law, and Social Change* 37(2): 99–105.

Sawer, Geoffrey, ed. 1961. *Studies in the Sociology of Law*. Canberra, Australia: The Australian National University.

Scheerer, Sebastian. 1978. "The New Dutch and German Drug Laws: Social and Political Conditions for Criminalization and Decriminalization." *Law and Society Review* 12(4): 585–606.

Scheppele, Kim L. 1994. "Legal Theory and Social Theory." *Annual Review of Sociology* 20: 383–406.

Schiff, David. 1981. "N. S. Timasheff's Sociology of Law." *The Modern Law Review* 44(4): 400–421.

Schluchter, Wolfgang. 1981. *The Rise of Western Rationalism: Max Weber's Developmental History*. Berkeley, CA: University of California Press.

Schluchter, Wolfgang. 2003. "The Sociology of Law as an Empirical Theory of Validity." *European Sociological Review* 19(5): 537–549.

Scholte, Jan A. 2000. *Globalization: A Critical Introduction*. New York: Palgrave.

Schultz, Ulirke, and Gisela Shaw, eds. 2003. *Women in the World's Legal Professions*. Portland, OR: Hart.

Schur, Edwin M. 1965. *Crimes without Victims: Deviant Behavior and Public Policy: Abortion, Homosexuality, Drug Addiction*. Englewood Cliffs, NJ: Prentice-Hall.

Schur, Edwin M. 1968. *Law and Society: A Sociological View*. New York: Random House.

Schur, Edwin M. 1971. *Labeling Deviant Behavior: Its Sociological Implications*. New York: Harper & Row.

Schutz, Alfred. 1970. *On Phenomenology and Social Relations*, edited and with an introduction by Helmut R. Wagner. Chicago: University of Chicago Press.

Schuyt, C. J. M. 1971. *Rechtssociologie: Een Terreinverkenning*. Rotterdam: Universitaire Pers Rotterdam.

Schwartz, Richard D. 1965. "Reply." *American Journal of Sociology* 70: 625–627.

Schwartz, Richard D. 1974. "Legal Evolution and the Durkheim Hypothesis: A Reply to Professor Baxi." *Law and Society Review* 8 (4): 653–668.

Schwartz, Richard D. 1978. "Moral Order and Sociology of Law: Trends, Problems, and Prospects." *Annual Review of Sociology* 4: 577–601.

Schwartz, Richard D., ed. 2006. Issue on "Law, Society, and Democracy: Comparative Perspectives." *The Annals of the American Academy of Political and Social Science* 603.

Schwartz, Richard D., and James Miller. 1964. "Legal Evolution and Societal Complexity." *American Journal of Sociology* 70(2): 159–169.

Schwartz, Richard D., and Jerome H. Skolnick, eds. 1970. *Society and the Legal Order: Cases and Materials in the Sociology of Law*. New York: Basic Books.

Scraton, Phil. 2004. "Streets of Terror: Marginalization, Criminalization, and Authoritarian Renewal." *Social Justice* 31(1/2): 130–158.

Scull, Andrew T. 1979. *Museums of Madness: The Social Organization of Insanity in Nineteenth Century England*. London: Allen Lane.

Scull, Andrew T. 1988. "Deviance and Social Control." Pp. 667–693 in *Handbook of Sociology*, ed. N. Smelser. Newbury Park, CA: Sage.

Seidman, Steven. 1991. "The End of Sociological Theory: The Postmodern Hope." *Sociological Theory* 9(2): 131–146.

Seltzer, Judith A. 1991. "Legal Custody Arrangements and Children's Economic Welfare." *American Journal of Sociology* 96(4): 895–929.

Selznick, Philip. 1957. *Leadership in Administration: A Sociological Interpretation*. Evanston, IL: Harper & Row.

Selznick, Philip. 1959. "The Sociology of Law." Pp. 115–127 in *Sociology Today*, ed. R. Merton, L. Broom and L. S. Cottrell Jr. New York: Basic Books.

Selznick, Philip. 1961. "Sociology and Natural Law." *Natural Law Forum* 6: 84–108.

Selznick, Philip. 1968. "The Sociology of Law." Pp. 50–59 in *International Encyclopedia of the Social Sciences*, vol. IX, ed. D. L. Sills. New York: Crowell, Collier and Macmillan, Inc.

Selznick, Philip (with the assistance of Philippe Nonet and Howard M. Vollmer). 1969. *Law, Society, and Industrial Justice*. New York: Russell Sage Foundation.

Selznick, Philip. 1973. "Rejoinder to Donald J. Black." *American Journal of Sociology* 78(5): 1266–1269.

Selznick, Philip. 1992. *The Moral Commonwealth: Social Theory and the Promise of Community.* Berkeley, CA: University of California Press.

Selznick, Philip. 1996. "Institutionalism 'Old' and 'New'." *Administrative Science Quarterly* 41(2): 270–277.

Selznick, Philip. 1999. "Legal Cultures and the Rule of Law." Pp. 21–38 in *The Rule of Law after Communism,* ed. M. Krygier and A. Czarnota. Aldershot, UK: Ashgate.

Selznick, Philip. 2004. "Selznick Interviewed: Philip Selznick in Conversation with Roger Cotterrell." *Journal of Law and Society* 31(3): 291–317.

Seron, Carroll. 1996. *The Business of Practicing Law: The Work Lives of Solo and Small-Firm Attorneys.* Philadelphia: Temple University Press.

Seron, Carroll, ed. 2006. *The Law and Society Canon.* Aldershot, UK: Ashgate.

Seron, Carroll, and Frank Munger. 1996. "Law and Inequality: Race, Gender ... and, of Course, Class." *Annual Review of Sociology* 22: 187–212.

Shamir, Ronen. 1993a. "Formal and Substantive Rationality in American Law: A Weberian Perpsective." *Social and Legal Studies* 2: 45–72.

Shamir, Ronen. 1993b. "Professionalism and Monopoly of Expertise: Lawyers and Administrative Law, 1933–1937." *Law and Society Review* 27(2): 361–398.

Shamir, Ronen. 1995. *Managing Legal Uncertainty: Elite Lawyers in the New Deal.* Durham, NC: Duke University Press.

Shearing, Clifford D., and Philip C. Stenning. 1983. "Private Security: Implications for Social Control." *Social Problems* 30(5): 493–505.

Sheleff, Leon S. 1975. "From Restitutive Law to Repressive Law: Durkheim's The Division of Labor in Society Re-visited." *European Journal of Sociology* 16: 16–45.

Sherman, Lawrence W. 1978. *Scandal and Reform: Controlling Police Corruption.* Berkeley, CA: University of California Press.

Sherman, Lawrence W. 1992. *Policing Domestic Violence: Experiments and Dilemmas.* New York: The Free Press.

Silbey, Susan S. 1997. "'Let them Eat Cake': Globalization, Postmodern Colonialism, and the Possibilities of Justice." *Law and Society Review* 31(2): 207–236.

Silbey, Susan S. 2002. "Mutual Engagement: Criminology *and* the Sociology of Law." *Crime, Law and Social Change* 37(2): 163–175.

Silbey, Susan S. 2005. "After Legal Consciousness." *Annual Review of Law and Social Science* 1: 323–368.

Silbey, Susan S., ed. 2008 *Law and Science.* Vol. I: *Epistemological, Evidentiary, and Relational Engagements.* Vol. II: *Regulation of Property, Practices, and Products.* Aldershot, UK: Ashgate.

Simmel, Georg. 1908a. *Soziologie: Untersuchungen über die Formen der Vergesellschaftung*. Leipzig: Duncker & Humblot.

Simmel, Georg. (1908b) 1964. "On the Significance of Numbers for Social Life." Pp. 86–104 in *The Sociology of Georg Simmel*, ed. K. H. Wolff. New York: The Free Press.

Simmel, Georg. 1917. *Grundfragen der Soziologie (Individuum und Gesellschaft)*. Berlin; Leipzig: G. J. Göschen.

Simon, Jonathan. 1993. *Poor Discipline*. Chicago: University of Chicago Press.

Simon, Jonathan. 2000. "Megan's Law: Crime and Democracy in Late Modern America." *Law and Social Inquiry* 25(4): 1111–1150.

Simon, Jonathan. 2001. "Fear and Loathing in Late Modernity: Reflections on the Cultural Sources of Mass Imprisonment in the United States." *Punishment and Society* 3(1): 21–33.

Simon, Rita J., ed. 1968. *The Sociology of Law: Interdisciplinary Readings*. San Francisco: Chandler Publishing.

Simon, Rita J., and James P. Lynch. 1989. "The Sociology of Law: Where We Have Been and Where We Might Be Going." *Law and Society Review* 23(5): 825–848.

Skapska, Grazyna. 1987. "The Sociology of Law in Poland: Problems, Polemics, Social Commitment." *Journal of Law and Society* 14(3): 353–365.

Sklair, Leslie. 1995. *Sociology of the Global System*. Baltimore, MD: Johns Hopkins University Press.

Skolnick, Jerome H. 1965. "The Sociology of Law in America: Overview and Trends." *Social Problems* 13(1): 4–39.

Skolnick, Jerome H. 1966. *Justice without Trial: Law Enforcement in Democratic Society*. New York: John Wiley & Sons.

Skolnick, Jerome H., and James J. Fyfe. 1993. *Above the Law: Police and the Excessive Use of Force*. New York: The Free Press.

Skrentny, John D. 1994. "Pragmatism, Institutionalism, and the Construction of Employment Discrimination." *Sociological Forum* 9(3): 343–369.

Skrentny, John D. 1996. *The Ironies of Affirmative Action: Politics, Culture, and Justice in America*. Chicago: University of Chicago Press.

Skrentny, John D. 2001. *The Minority Rights Revolution*. Cambridge, MA: The Belknap Press of Harvard University Press.

Skrentny, John D. 2006. "Policy-Elite Perceptions and Social Movement Success: Understanding Variations in Group Inclusion in Affirmative Action." *American Journal of Sociology* 111(6): 1762–1815.

Smith, Carole. 2000. "The Sovereign State v. Foucault: Law and Disciplinary Power." *The Sociological Review* 48(2): 283–306.

Smith, Philip. 2003. "Narrating the Guillotine: Punishment Technology as Myth and Symbol." *Theory, Culture and Society* 20(5): 27–51.

Somers, Margaret R. 1993. "Citizenship and the Place of the Public Sphere: Law, Community, and Political Culture in the Transition to Democracy." *American Sociological Review* 58(5): 587–620.

Somers, Margaret R. 1995. "Narrating and Naturalizing Civil Society and Citizenship Theory: The Place of Political Culture and the Public Sphere." *Sociological Theory* 13(3): 229–274.

Somers, Margaret R., and Fred Block. 2005. "From Poverty to Perversity: Ideas, Markets and Institutions over 200 Years of Welfare Debate." *American Sociological Review* 70(2): 260–287.

Sorokin, Pitirim. 1928. *Contemporary Sociological Theories*. New York: Harper & Brothers.

Sorokin, Pitirim. (1937–1941) 1962. *Social and Cultural Dynamics*. 4 vols. New York: Bedminster Press.

Sorokin, Pitirim. 1947. "The Organized Group (Institution) and Law-Norms." Pp. 668–695 in *Interpretations of Modern Legal Philosophies: Essays in Honor of Roscoe Pound*, ed. P. Sayre. New York: Oxford University Press.

Sorokin, Pitirim. 1956. Review of Law and Morality, by Leon Petrazycki. *Harvard Law Review* 69(6): 1150–1157.

Sorokin, Pitirim. 1957. *Social and Cultural Dynamics: A Study of Change in Major Systems of Art, Truth, Ethics, Law, and Social Relationships*. Rev. and abrdgd, 1 vol., Sorokin. New Brunswick, NJ: Transaction.

Sorokin, Pitirim. 1963. "Reply to my Critics." Pp. 371–496 in *Pitirim A. Sorokin in Review*, ed. P. J. Allen. Durham, NC: Duke University Press.

Spencer, Herbert. (1853) 1992. "Over-Legislation." In his *The Man versus the State, with Six Essays on Government, Society, and Freedom*. Indianapolis, IN: Liberty Fund. Online: www.econlib.org/LIBRARY/ LFBooks/Spencer/spnMvS7.html#Essay: %20Over-Legislation.

Spencer, Herbert. (1873) 1961. *The Study of Sociology*. Ann Arbor, MI: University of Michigan Press.

Spencer, Herbert (1876/1882/1896) 1897. *The Principles of Sociology*. London: Williams and Norgate.

Spencer, Herbert. (1884) 1992. "The Sins of Legislators." In his *The Man versus the State, with Six Essays on Government, Society, and Freedom*. Indianapolis, IN: Liberty Fund. Online: www.econlib.org/LIBRARY/ LFBooks/Spencer/spnMvS3.html#The%20Sins%20of%20Legislators.

Spencer, Martin. 1970. "Weber on Legitimate Norms and Authority." *British Journal of Sociology* 21(2): 123–34.

Spitzer, Steven. 1975. "Punishment and Social Organization: A Study of Durkheim's Theory of Penal Evolution." *Law and Society Review* 9(4): 613–638.

Spitzer, Steven. 1983. "Marxist Perspectives in the Sociology of Law." *Annual Review of Sociology* 9: 103–124.

Spitzer, Steven. 1985. "The Embeddedness of Law: Reflections on Lukes and Scull's 'Durkheim and the Law'." Review Essay. *American Bar Foundation Research Journal* 9(4): 859–868.

Spurr, Stephen J. 1990. "Sex Discrimination in the Legal Profession: A Study of Promotion." *Industrial and Labor Relations Review* 43(4): 406–417.

Stangl, Wolfgang. 1992. "Die fortschreitende Verzauberung der Welt des Strafrechts: Kritisches zur Rationalisierungsthese Max Webers." *Zeitschrift für Rechtssoziologie* 13(1): 44–64.

Staples, William G. 2000. *Everyday Surveillance: Vigilance and Visibility in Postmodern Life*. Lanham, MD: Rowman & Littlefield.

Staples, William G. 2003. "Surveillance and Social Control in Postmodern Life." Pp. 191–211 in *Punishment and Social Control*, ed. T. Blomberg and S. Cohen. Hawthorne, NY: Aldine De Gruyter.

Steen, Sara, Rodney L. Engen, and Randy R. Gainey. 2005. "Images of Danger and Culpability: Racial Stereotyping, Case Processing, and Criminal Sentencing." *Criminology* 43(2): 435–468.

Sterling, Joyce S. and Wilbert E. Moore. 1987. "Weber's Analysis of Legal Rationalization: A Critique and Constructive Modification." *Sociological Forum* 2(1): 67–89.

Stinchcombe, Arthur L. 1997. "On the Virtues of the Old Institutionalism." *Annual Review of Sociology* 23: 1–18.

Stoljar, S. J. 1961. "Weber's Sociology of Law." Pp. 31–56 in *Studies in the Sociology of Law*, ed. G. Sawer. Canberra: The Australian National University.

Stone, Alan. 1985. "The Place of Law in the Marxian Structure-Superstructure Archetype." *Law and Society Review* 19(1): 39–68.

Stone, Julius. 1965. "Roscoe Pound and Sociological Jurisprudence." *Harvard Law Review* 78(8): 1578–1584.

Stryker, Robin. 1989. "Limits on Technocratization of the Law: The Elimination of the National Labor Relations Board's Division of Economic Research." *American Sociological Review* 54(3): 341–358.

Stryker, Robin. 2001. "Disparate Impact and the Quota Debates: Law, Labor Market Sociology and Equal Employment Policies." *Sociological Quarterly* 42(2): 13–46.

Stryker, Robin. 2003. "Mind the Gap: Law, Institutional Analysis and Socio-Economics." *Socio-Economic Review* 1: 335–367.

Suchman, Mark. 2006. "Empirical Legal Studies: Sociology of Law, or Something ELS Entirely?" *Amici*, the ASA Sociology of Law section newsletter, 13(1): 1–4.

Suchman, Mark and Lauren Edelman. 1996. "Legal-Rational Myths: Lessons for the New Institutionalism from the Law and Society Tradition." Review Essay. *Law and Social Inquiry* 21(4): 903–941.

Sumner, William Graham. 1906. *Folkways: A Study of the Sociological Importance of Usages, Manners, Customs, Mores and Morals*. Boston, MA: Ginn.

Sutherland, Edwin H. 1973. *On Analyzing Crime*, edited and with an introduction by Karl Schuessler. Chicago: University of Chicago Press.

Sutton, John R. 1983. "Social Structure, Institutions, and the Legal Status of Children in the United States." *American Journal of Sociology* 88(5): 915–947.

Sutton, John R. 2000. "Imprisonment and Social Classification in Five Common-Law Democracies, 1955–1985." *American Journal of Sociology* 106(2): 350–386.

Sutton, John R. 2001. *Law/Society: Origins, Interactions and Change*. Thousand Oaks, CA: Pine Forge Press.

Sutton, John R., and Frank Dobbin. 1996. "The Two Faces of Governance: Responses to Legal Uncertainty in U.S. Firms, 1955 to 1985." *American Sociological Review* 61(5): 794–811.

Sutton, John R., Frank Dobbin, John W. Meyer, and W. Richard Scott. 1994. "The Legalization of the Workplace." *American Journal of Sociology* 99(4): 994–971.

Swedberg, Richard. 2003. "The Case for an Economic Sociology of Law." *Theory and Society* 32(1): 1–37.

Swedberg, Richard. 2006. "Max Weber's Contribution to the Economic Sociology of Law." *Annual Review of Law and Social Science* 2: 61–81.

Swingewood, Alan. 1975. *Marx and Modern Social Theory*. New York: Wiley.

Syracuse Journal of International Law and Commerce. 2005. Issue on "The Syracuse Conference on a World Rule of Law: American Perspectives." *Syracuse Journal of International Law and Commerce* 33(1): 1–231.

Tadros, Victor. 1998. "Between Governance and Discipline: The Law and Michel Foucault." *Oxford Journal of Legal Studies* 18(1): 75–103.

Terrill, William, Eugene A. Paoline III, and Peter K. Manning. 2003. "Police Culture and Coercion." *Criminology* 41(4): 1003–1034.

Thomas, Dorothy Swaine. 1931. "Some Aspects of Socio-Legal Research at Yale." *American Journal of Sociology* 37(2): 213–221.

Thompson, Kenneth. 1998. *Moral Panics*. London: Routledge.

Timasheff, Nicholas S. 1937. "What is 'Sociology of Law'?" *American Journal of Sociology* 43(2): 225–235.

Timasheff, Nicolas S. 1938. "The Sociological Place of Law." *American Journal of Sociology* 44(2): 206–221.

Timasheff, Nicholas S. (1939) 1976. *An Introduction to the Sociology of Law*. Westport, CT: Greenwood Press.

Timasheff, Nicholas S. 1947. "Petrazhitsky's Philosophy of Law." Pp. 736–750 in *Interpretations of Modern Legal Philosophies: Essays in Honor of Roscoe Pound*, ed. P. Sayre. New York: Oxford University Press.

Timasheff, Nicolas S. 1955. "Introduction." Pp. xvii–xxxviii in *Law and Morality* by Leon Petrazycki. Cambridge, MA: Harvard University Press.

Timasheff, Nicolas S. 1957. "Growth and Scope of Sociology of Law." Pp. 424–449 in *Modern Sociological Theory,* ed. H. Becker and A. Boskoff. New York: Dryden Press.

Timasheff, Nicolas S. 1963. "Sorokin on Law, Revolution, War, and Social Calamities." Pp. 246–275 in *Pitirim A. Sorokin in Review*, ed. P. J. Allen. Durham, NC: Duke University Press.

Tiryakian, Edward A. 1964. "Durkheim's 'Two Laws of Penal Evolution'." *Journal for the Scientific Study of Religion* 3(2): 261–266.

Tocqueville, Alexis de. (1835/1840) 2000. *Democracy in America*, translated, edited, and with an introduction by Harvey C. Mansfield and Delba Winthrop. Chicago: University of Chicago Press.

Tomasic, Roman. 1985. *The Sociology of Law*. London: Sage Publications.

Tönnies, Ferdinand. 1887. *Gemeinschaft und Gesellschaft: Abhandlung des Communismus und des Socialismus als empirischer Culturformen*. Leipzig: Reisland.

Tönnies, Ferdinand. 1922. *Kritik der öffentlichen Meinung*. Berlin: Julius Springer.

Tönnies, Ferdinand. 1931. *Einführung in die Soziologie*. Stuttgart: F. Enke.

Tönnies, Ferdinand. (1935a) 1963. *Gemeinschaft und Gesellschaft: Grundbegriffen der reinen Soziologie*. 8th edn. Darmstadt: Wissenschaftliche BuchGesellschaft.

Tönnies, Ferdinand. (1935b) 1940. *Fundamental Concepts of Sociology (Gemeinschaft und Gesellschaft)*. New York: American Book Company.

Torpey, John. 2000. *The Invention of the Passport: Surveillance, Citizenship and the State*. Cambridge, UK: Cambridge University Press.

Travers, Max. 1993. "Putting Sociology back into the Sociology of Law." *Journal of Law and Society* 20(4): 438–451.

Travers, Max. 1997. *The Reality of Law: Work and Talk in a Firm of Criminal Lawyers*. Aldershot, UK: Ashgate.

Travers, Max. 2001. "Sociology of Law in Britain." *The American Sociologist* 32(2): 26–40.

Travers, Max. 2002. "Symbolic Interactionism and Law." Pp. 209–226 in *An Introduction to Law and Social Theory*, ed. R. Banakar and M. Travers. Portland, OR: Hart Publishing.

Travers, Max, and John F. Manzo, eds. 1997. *Law in Action: Ethnomethodological and Conversation Analytic Approaches to Law*. Brookfield, VT: Ashgate.

Treiber, Hubert. 1985. " 'Elective Affinities' between Weber's Sociology of Religion and Sociology of Law: On the Adequacy Relation between Explanatory Models with the Help of which Weber Reconstructs the Religious and Legal Rationalization Process." *Theory and Society* 14 (6): 809–861.

Treves, Renato. 1981. "Problèmes actuels de la sociologie du droit en Italie." *Sociologie du Travail* 23(1): 106–111.

Treves, Renato and J. F. Glastra van Loon. 1968. *Norms and Actions: National Reports on Sociology of Law*. The Hague: Martinus Nijhoff.

Treviño, A. Javier. 1994. "The Influence of Sociology on American Jurisprudence: From Oliver Wendell Holmes to Critical Legal Studies." *Mid-American Review of Sociology* 18(1/2): 23–46.

Treviño, A. Javier. 1996. *The Sociology of Law: Classical and Contemporary Perspectives*. New York: St. Martin's Press.

Treviño, A. Javier. 1998. "Toward a General Theoretical-Methodological Framework for the Sociology of Law: Another Look at the Eastern-European Pioneers." *Sociology of Crime, Law, and Deviance* 1: 155–202.

Treviño, A. Javier. 2001. "The Sociology of Law in Global Perspective." *The American Sociologist* 32(2): 5–9.

Treviño, A. Javier, ed. 2006. *Classic Writings in Law and Society: Contemporary Comments and Criticisms*. New Brunswick, NJ: Transaction.

Trubek, David M. 1972. "Max Weber on Law and the Rise of Capitalism." *Wisconsin Law Review* 3: 720–753.

Trubek, David M. 1985. "Reconstructing Max Weber's Sociology of Law." *Stanford Law Review* 37: 919–36.

Trubek, David M. 1986. "Max Weber's Tragic Modernism and the Study of Law in Society." Review essay. *Law and Society Review* 20(4): 573–598.

Turk, Austin T. 1969. *Criminality and Legal Order*. Chicago: Rand McNally.

Turk, Austin T. 1976a. "Law as a Weapon in Social Conflict." *Social Problems* 23(3): 276–291.

Turk, Austin T. 1976b. "Law, Conflict, and Order: From Theorizing toward Theories." *Canadian Review of Sociology and Anthropology* 13(3): 282–294.

Turkel, Gerald. 1979. "Testing Durkheim: Some Theoretical Considerations." *Law and Society Review* 13(3): 721–738.

Turkel, Gerald. 1981. "Rational Law and Boundary Maintenance: Legitimating the 1971 Lockheed Loan Guarantee." *Law and Society Review* 15(1): 41–77.

Turkel, Gerald. 1990. "Michel Foucault: Law, Power, and Knowledge." *Journal of Law and Society* 17(2): 170–193.

Turkel, Gerald. 1996. *Law and Society: Critical Approaches*. Boston: Allyn & Bacon.

Turner, Bryan S. 1974. *Weber and Islam: A Critical Study*. London: Routledge & Kegan Paul.

Turner, Stephen P., and Regis A. Factor. 1994. *Max Weber: The Lawyer as Social Thinker*. New York: Routledge.

Tushnet, Mark. 1991. "Critical Legal Studies: A Political History." *The Yale Law Journal* 100(5): 1515–1544.

Twining, William. 1985. *Karl Llewellyn and the Realist Movement*. Norman, OK: University of Oklahoma Press.

Twining, William. 2005. "Social Science and Diffusion of Law." *Journal of Law and Society* 32(2): 203–240.

Tyler, Tom R. 1990. *Why People Obey the Law*. New Haven, CT: Yale University Press.

Udy, Stanley H., Jr. 1965. "Dynamic Inferences from Static Data." *American Journal of Sociology* 70(5): 625–627.

Uggen, Christopher, and Jeff Manza. 2002. "Democratic Contraction? The Political Consequences of Felon Disenfranchisement in the United States." *American Sociological Review* 67: 777–803.

Uggen, Christopher, Angela Behrens, and Jeff Manza. 2005. "Criminal Disenfranchisement." *Annual Review of Law and Social Science* 1: 307–322.

Uggen, Christopher, Jeff Manza, and Melissa Thompson, 2006. "Citizenship, Democracy, and the Civic Reintegration of Criminal Offenders." *The Annals of the American Academy of Political and Social Science* 605: 281–310.

Ulen, Thomas S. 1994. "Rational Choice and the Economic Analysis of Law." Review essay. *Law and Social Inquiry* 19(2): 487–522.

Ulmer, Jeffery T. 1997. *Social Worlds of Sentencing: Court Communities under Sentencing Guidelines*. Albany, NY: State University of New York Press.

Ulmer, Jeffery T. 2005. "The Localized Uses of Federal Sentencing Guidelines in Four U.S. District Courts: Evidence of Processual Order." *Symbolic Interaction* 28(2): 255–279.

Ulmer, Jeffery T., and John H. Kramer. 1996. "Court Communities under Sentencing Guidelines: Dilemmas of Formal Rationality and Sentencing Disparity." *Criminology* 34(3): 306–332.

Ulmer, Jeffery T., and John H. Kramer. 1998. "The Use and Transformation of Formal Decision Making Criteria: Sentencing Guidelines, Organizational Contexts, and Case Processing Strategies." *Social Problems* 45 (2): 248–267.

Unger, Roberto M. 1976. *Law in Modern Society*. New York: The Free Press. Available online: www.law.harvard.edu/faculty/unger/english/lawinmo.php.

Unger, Roberto M. 1983. "The Critical Legal Studies Movement." *Harvard Law Review* 96(3): 561–675.

Unger, Roberto M. 1986. *The Critical Legal Studies Movement*. Cambridge, MA: Harvard University Press.

Upham, Frank K. 1989. "What's Happening in Japan, Sociolegalwise." *Law and Society Review* 23(5): 879–890.

Useem, Bert, and Jack A. Goldstone. 2002. "Forging Social Order and its Breakdown: Riot and Reform in U.S. Prisons." *American Sociological Review* 67(4): 499–525.

Uusitalo, Paavo. 1989. "Sociology of Law in Finland." Pp. 36–51 in *Two Lectures on the Sociology of Law*, by V. Ferrari and P. Uusitalo. Helsinki, Finland: University of Helsinki.

Vago, Steven. 2005. *Law and Society*. 8th edn. Englewood Cliffs, NJ: Prentice Hall.

Van Houtte, Jean. 1990. "Sociology of Law in Dutch-Speaking Belgium." Pp. 63–93 in *Developing Sociology of Law: A World-Wide Documentary Enquiry*, ed. V. Ferrari. Milan: Dott A. Giuffré Editore.

Van Houtte, Jean and Francis van Loon. 1993. *Sociology of Law, Social Problems and Legal Policy in Europe*. Leuven, Belgium: Acco.

Van Hoy, Jerry. 1995. "Selling and Processing Law: Legal Work at Franchise Law Firms." *Law and Society Review* 29(4): 703–730.

Van Hoy, Jerry. 1997. *Franchise Law Firms and the Transformation of Personal Legal Services*. Westport, CT: Quorum Books.

Vandekerckhove, Lieven. 1996. "De Vroege Rechtssociologie." *Tijdschrift voor Sociale Wetenschappen* 41(2): 147–166.

Vandenberghe, Frédéric. 2005. "Entre science et politique: La conjonction du positivisme et du décisionnisme dans la sociologie du droit de Max Weber." *Canadian Journal of Law and Society/Revue Canadienne droit et société* 20(1): 157–169.

Veitch, Scott. 1997. "Law and 'Other' Problems." *Law and Critique* 8(1): 97–109.

Vincent, Andrew. 1993. "Marx and Law." *Journal of Law and Society* 20 (4): 371–397.

Visher, Christy A., and Jeremy Travis. 2003. "Transitions from Prison to Community: Understanding Individual Pathways." *Annual Review of Sociology* 29: 89–113.

Vogt, W. Paul. 1983. "Obligation and Right: The Durkheimians and the Sociology of Law." Pp. 177–98 in *The Sociological Domain: The Durkheimians and the Founding of French Sociology*, ed. P. Besnard. Cambridge, UK: Cambridge University Press.

Vogt, W. Paul. 1993. "Durkheim's Sociology of Law: Morality and the Cult of the Individual." Pp. 71–94 in *Emile Durkheim: Sociologist and Moralist*, ed. S. P. Turner. London: Routledge.

Voigt, Rüdiger, ed. 1980. *Verrechtlichung: Analysen zu Funktion und Wirkung von Parlamentarisierung, Bürokratisierung und Justiziali-sierung sozialer, politischer und ökonomischer Prozesse*. Königstein, Germany: Athenäum.

Wacquant, Loïc. 2001. "Deadly Symbiosis: When Ghetto and Prison Meet and Mesh." *Punishment and Society* 3(1): 95–133.

Waddington, P. A. J. 1986. "Mugging as a Moral Panic: A Question of Proportion." *British Journal of Sociology* 37(2): 245–259.

Wallace, Jean 2006. "Can Women in Law Have It All? A Study of Motherhood, Career Satisfaction and Life Balance." *Research in the Sociology of Organizations* 24: 283–306.

Wallace, Michael, Beth A. Rubin and Brian T. Smith. 1988. "American Labor Law: Its Impact on Working-Class Militancy, 1901–1980." *Social Science History* 12(1): 1–29.

Wallerstein, Immanuel. 2004. *World Systems Analysis: An Introduction*. Durham, NC: Duke University Press.

Walton, Paul. 1976. "Max Weber's Sociology of Law: A Critique." Pp. 7–21 in *The Sociology of Law*, ed. P. Carlen. Keele, UK: University of Keele.

Weber, Max. (1907) 1977. *Critique of Stammler*. New York: The Free Press.

Weber, Max. (1920) 1976. *The Protestant Ethic and the Spirit of Capitalism*. New York: Charles Scribner's Sons.

Weber, Max. (1922a) 1980. *Wirtschaft und Gesellschaft: Grundriss der Verstehenden soziologie*. Tubingen, Germany: J.C.B Mohr.

Weber, Max. (1922b) 1978. *Economy and Society: An Outline of Interpretive Sociology*, ed. G. Roth and C. Wittich. Berkeley, CA: University of California Press.

Weber, Max. (1922c) 1954. *On Law in Economy and Society*, ed. M. Rheinstein. New York: Simon and Schuster.

Wei-Dong, Ji. 1989. "The Sociology of Law in China: Overview and Trends." *Law and Society Review* 23(5): 903–914.

Weinberg, Lee S., and Judith W. Weinberg. 1980. *Law and Society: An Interdisciplinary Introduction*. Lanham, MD: University Press of America.

Weitzer, Ronald. 2000. "Racialized Policing: Residents' Perceptions in Three Neighborhoods." *Law and Society Review* 34(1): 129–155.

Weitzer, Ronald, and Steven A. Tuch. 2005. "Racially Biased Policing: Determinants of Citizen Perceptions." *Social Forces* 83(3): 1009–1030.

Welch, Michael. 2000. "The Role of the Immigration and Naturalization Service in the Prison-Industrial Complex." *Social Justice* 27: 73–88.

Welch, Michael. 2002. *Detained: Immigration Laws and the Expanding I.N.S. Jail Complex*. Philadelphia, PA: Temple University Press.

Welch, Michael. 2003. "Ironies of Social Control and the Criminalization of Immigrants." *Crime, Law and Social Change* 39(4): 319–337.

Welch, Michael. 2004. "Quiet Constructions in the War on Terror: Subjecting Asylum Seekers to Unnecessary Detention." *Social Justice* 31: 113–129.

Welch, Michael. 2006. *Scapegoats of September 11th: Hate Crimes and State Crimes in the War on Terror*. New Brunswick, NJ: Rutgers University Press.

Welch, Michael, and Liza Schuster. 2005. "Detention of Asylum Seekers in the UK and USA: Deciphering Noisy and Quiet Constructions." *Punishment and Society* 7(4): 397–417.

Welch, Michael, Eric Price, and Nana Yankey. 2004. "Youth Violence and Race in the Media: The Emergence of 'Wilding' as an Invention of the Press." *Race, Gender & Class* 11(2): 36–58.

Western, Bruce. 2002. "The Impact of Incarceration on Wage Mobility and Inequality." *American Sociological Review* 67(4): 526–546.

Weyers, Heleen. 2006. "Explaining the Emergence of Euthanasia Law in the Netherlands: How the Sociology of Law Can Help the Sociology of Bioethics." *Sociology of Health and Illness* 28(6): 802–816.

White, G. Edward. 1972. "From Sociological Jurisprudence to Realism: Jurisprudence and Social Change in Early Twentieth-Century America." *Virginia Law Review* 58(6): 999–1028.

Wickham, Gary. 2002. "Foucault and Law." Pp. 249–265 in *An Introduction to Law and Social Theory*, ed. R. Banakar and M. Travers. Portland, OR: Hart Publishing.

Wickham, Gary. 2006. "Foucault, Law, and Power: A Reassessment." *Journal of Law and Society* 33(4): 596–614.

Wickman, Gary, and George Pavlich, eds. 2001. *Rethinking Law, Society and Governance: Foucault's Bequest*. Portland, OR: Hart Publishing.

Wigdor, David. 1974. *Roscoe Pound: Philosopher of Law*. Westport, CT: Greenwood Press.

Wilkinson, Philip J. 1981. "The Potential of Functionalism for the Sociological Analysis of Law." Pp. 67–90 in *Sociological Approaches to Law*, ed. A. Podgórecki and C. J. Whelan. New York: St. Martin's Press.

Wilson, James Q., and Richard J. Herrnstein. 1985. *Crime and Human Nature*. New York: Simon and Schuster.

Wimberley, Howard. 1973. "Legal Evolution: One Further Step." *American Journal of Sociology* 79(1): 78–83.

Wolff, Kurt H. 1964. *The Sociology of Georg Simmel*. New York: The Free Press.

Wong, Kam C. 1995. "Black's Theory on the Behavior of Law Revisited." *International Journal of the Sociology of Law* 23(3): 189–232.

Woodiwiss, Anthony. 1990. *Rights v. Conspiracy: A Sociological Essay on the History of Labour Law in the United States*. New York: Berg.

Yang, Kun. 1989. "Law and Society Studies in Korea: Beyond the Hahm Theses." *Law and Society Review* 23(5): 891–902.

Yang, Kun. 2001. "The Sociology of Law in Korea" *The American Sociologist* 32(2): 78–84.

Young, Gary. 1979. "Marx on Bourgeois Law." Pp. 133–167, in *Research in Law and Sociology,* Vol. II, ed. S. Spitzer. Greenwhich, CT: JAI Press.

Zeigler, Sara L. 1996. "Wifely Duties: Marriage, Labor, and the Common Law in Nineteenth-Century America." *Social Science History* 20(1): 63–96.

Zeitlin, Irving M. 1985. "Max Weber's Sociology of Law." *University of Toronto Law Journal* 35(2): 183–214.

Ziegert, Klaus A. 1977. "Adam Podgórecki's Sociology of Law: The Invisible Factors of the Functioning of Law Made Visible." Review essay. *Law and Society Review* 12(1): 151–180.

Ziegert, Klaus A. 1999. "Sociological Jurisprudence." Pp. 814–817 in *The Philosophy of Law: An Encyclopedia*, vol. II, ed. C. B. Gray. New York: Garland Publishing, Inc.

Ziegert, Klaus A. 2002. "The Thick Description of Law: An Introduction to Niklas Luhmann's Theory." Pp. 55–75 in *An Introduction to Law and Social Theory*, ed. R. Banakar and M. Travers. Portland, OR: Hart Publishing.

Index